Small Office Networking

Second Edition

TechRepublic®
Real World. Real Time. Real IT.

Small Office Networking, Second Edition

Published by TechRepublic
ISBN 1-932509-84-4
Printed March 2005

Disclaimer

CD-ROM License

Credits

Director, TechRepublic Press	Carmen Barrett
Executive Editor, Premium Products	Erik Eckel
Production Manager	Marilyn Bryan
Graphic Artist	Kimberly Wright
Senior Editor	John Sheesley
Copy Editor	Julie Tonini
Director, Premium Products	Shana Riggs
Promotions Manager	Megan Hancock
Manager, Customer Service	Elisa Suiter

TechRepublic
1630 Lyndon Farm Court
Louisville, KY 40223
Tel.: 1.800.217.4339
Online Customer Support:
http://productorders.techrepublic.com

B077

Foreword

The proliferation of home and small offices poses new challenges for today's technology administrators. Remote and branch offices demand that IT services be available to telecommuters, mobile workers, and even traveling employees.

The second edition of Small Office Networking, TechRepublic's book and companion CD toolkit, is built specifically for those setting up and maintaining small offices. It collects proven solutions for ensuring that home, branch, and remote networks stay connected. Covering everything from networking fundamentals to Windows security, Small Office Networking, Second Edition, provides practical, real-world advice and walks technology administrators through all aspects of small office networking. From selecting a broadband provider to securing wireless connections, the book reviews how to:

- Master TCP/IP
- Troubleshoot Windows errors and network outages
- Leverage Windows' native firewall
- Share an Internet connection among multiple systems
- Configure VPNs
- Secure network files and systems

The CD toolkit contains timesaving checklists for these tasks and more:

- Building CAT 5 cables and walljacks
- Solving network outages
- Selecting the best ISP for your needs
- Deploying networks properly

The CD includes a special guide describing 802.11g wireless networking. You'll also find preventive maintenance checklists for both desktop systems and servers.

Together, the book and CD compose a powerful package designed to help you work more efficiently. With Small Office Networking, Second Edition, you'll quickly eliminate common errors, fix nagging problems, and maintain trouble-free small offices.

If you have suggestions or comments regarding this TechRepublic book, please e-mail us at **trproducts@techrepublic.com**.

Small Office Networking

Second Edition

Permissions and File Sharing

Troubleshooting

Wireless Networking

Security and Business Continuity

Networking Basics

What kind of home or small office network is right for you?

So you want to build a home or small office network but don't know where to start. It can be a daunting proposition, and there certainly are tons of products out there to choose from. Our guide to home and small office networking should help you answer some basic questions, such as:

- Should you go wireless?
- Do you need a special server to hold all of your data?
- Is a home or small office network expensive?
- Can I keep shared files out of the hands of some network users?

In this initial overview, we'll give you a snapshot of small-scale networking, beginning with some basic terminology. We'll compare wireless networks to traditional cabled networks, and then the server-based networking model to peer-to-peer networking. By the end of this chapter you'll have a better understanding of networking and be ready to start making decisions about what setup is right for you.

Networking terminology

Computer networking has its own unique vocabulary. Although we'll avoid as many acronyms and buzzwords as possible in this brief overview, a firm grasp of the following terms will help you understand the basic networking concepts we'll discuss throughout this book.

- **Node**—Any device, such as a PC, that is connected to a computer network.
- **Protocol**—The method that computers use to communicate with each other. Humans use a particular language, such as English, and computers use a specific protocol, such as Transmission Control Protocol/Internet Protocol (TCP/IP).
- **Server**—A computer that shares a resource, such as files or a printer, with other nodes on the network. Traditionally, a server is a dedicated computer that provides resources, such as shared files.
- **Switch**—A network device that connects network nodes and allows them to communicate with each other.
- **Network Interface Card (NIC)**—A specially designed board that is put inside a device that allows the device to connect to the network.

The components of a computer network

Computer networks, regardless of their design or equipment, all share certain attributes. First, they all include computers and peripheral devices. Second, all networks must have a communication medium such as cables; wireless networks use a special radio frequency (RF) signal that's transmitted through the air. Third, all networks must have a method, or protocol, for the devices to communicate with each other. For the most part, you can count on computers today using TCP/IP. Finally, all networks must have a common device that connects all its computers and devices, collectively known as its nodes. For the purposes of our example, we'll use a switch, although some networks use other kinds of devices (such as routers or hubs).

Traditional cabled networks

Until recently, all networks relied on connections based on network cables and networking devices, such as switches. This type of network configuration is relatively cheap, very fast, and more secure than the wireless network schemes now on the market.

Tried-and-true network cabling can be fantastic, but there are a few drawbacks. Obviously, you must connect each computer to the network using a cable, which can be quite difficult, especially if you live in a multistory house and want all the rooms to have a networked computer. In addition, if you want to move a computer to a new location, you must run a cable to the spot.

Figure A shows you a simple diagram of a home network. Our example has three desktop computers and a laptop connected to a switch. The centrally located

Figure A

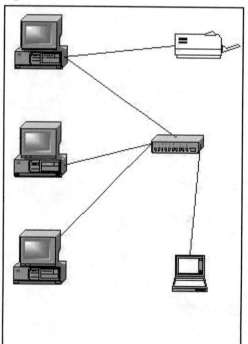

Figure B

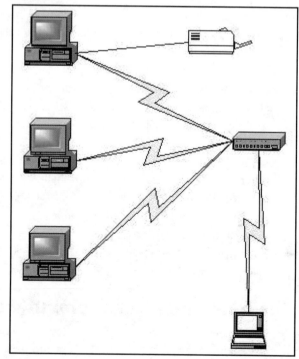

switch lets all the computers communicate with each other so that they can share files; the printer is connected locally to one of the networked computers. The computers could be located in the same room but could just as easily be located throughout the house.

Wireless networks

Wireless networks are the latest craze to hit the home networking market. This type of network offers much greater flexibility because you don't need to physically connect each device to the network. Computers communicate using specially built network adapters and a wireless access point, which is similar to a switch.

Freedom from cables comes with a price, however. Wireless networking devices are much more expensive than their physically connected cousins. You can find traditional network adapters for $20 or less, and an inexpensive wired switch for $50 or less; wireless network adapters cost around $100, and a wireless access point goes for at least $100. Even if you factor in the extra cost of cabling, wireless networks still cost more. In addition, wireless networks can be up to ten times slower than traditional networks, depending on the type of network adapters and switch you are using.

Wireless networks also are not as secure as wired networks. Wireless access points can broadcast their signal up to 800 feet, and the signal goes straight through walls. So if you live near someone who also has a wireless network, there's a good chance you'll be able to see each other's computers when you log on to your network. Although you'll still need a password to access the computers on another network, you're much more likely to have someone try to access your data with a wireless network.

However, before you write off wireless networks as being unsafe, please remember that there are definitely ways to prevent unauthorized access to your network. (These topics are covered later in this book.)

In **Figure B**, we've taken the same devices from our earlier example and designed a wireless network. The wireless access point should be centrally located in the house, while the computers can be virtually anyplace. In fact, you can take the laptop out onto the patio. As far as flexibility goes, you just can't beat wireless networking.

Server-based networking

In the past, virtually all computer networks were built around a centralized computer called a server. This computer held all the network's shared information; other network nodes connected to the server to use the data. The server-based networking model is still the popular choice in the business world because it's easy to manage and provides a great deal of security for information stored on the server.

However, server-based networking is relatively expensive, since at least one computer must be configured as a dedicated server. In addition, a network administrator typically needs specialized skills to manage a server, which often runs on an operating system specially designed for the purpose. For home use, this type of network design is definitely not necessary.

If you want to get some of the benefits of a server-based network, you can put a large hard disk in one of your networked computers and let that system hold most shared files. In this manner, you reap the benefit of having information located in one place without the expense and technical challenge of maintaining a server.

Peer-to-peer networking

The two network designs that we've illustrated in Figure A and Figure B are good examples of a peer-to-peer network. Peer-to-peer networking is easy to configure, inexpensive, and designed for home or small business use. In this type of a network, each computer shares information stored on it with the other computers, or peers, on the network. You can also share peripheral devices, such as printers and scanners.

The downside to peer-to-peer networking is that it's relatively insecure. Everyone on the network can access the files you've designated to be shared on an individual machine. Although this typically isn't a large concern for home users, it can be a problem if you store information such as tax documents on a shared drive. As you will learn in subsequent chapters, however, it's relatively easy to prevent others from seeing your sensitive information. Just remember that you must be careful about what you store on a shared drive.

The choice is up to you

As we've shown you in this brief overview, you have a variety of choices when designing your home network. If you want a fast, secure, and inexpensive home network, then a traditionally cabled network is the way to go. If running network cables throughout your house is unappealing or not even an option, then wireless may be your only choice.

You can also combine these network schemes by connecting a wireless access point to a wired switch. This approach can provide needed connection speed for computers you want to use for head-to-head gaming, while also giving you the flexibility to move around the house with your laptop.

When it comes to computer networking the only right choice is the one that works the best for you. ❖

What kind of Internet connection is right for your home network?

Is my modem slow, or is it my computer? What is a cable modem, and why do I need one? What is DSL? These are common questions for anyone who's considering an investment in a home network. In this chapter, we'll give you an overview of the three most popular methods of connecting your computer and home network to the Internet so that you'll be able to decide which type of connection is right for you.

A word about bandwidth measurements

Before we begin discussing the different types of Internet connections that are currently available, let's take a moment to learn how the speed of an Internet connection is measured. Once you understand this concept, you'll be able to tell if your connection is a Ford or a Ferrari.

Connection speeds are measured by the number of bits of data that can be transmitted in one second. Dial-up connections are typically measured in kilobits per second, or Kbps. Each character of data is made up of eight bits of information, and one kilobit equals one thousand bits. This means that in one second, a 56 Kbps modem is capable of transmitting roughly 56 thousand bits of information.

Broadband connections, such as DSL and cable, can reach speeds that are measured in megabits (Mbps), or millions of bits per second. So, if your connection is rated at 1 Mbps, it can transfer 1 million bits of information over your network every second.

Dial-up connections: old, unreliable, but still in use

Until fairly recently, the only way most home users could connect their computers to the Internet was with modems. Using this device, your computer dials the telephone number of your Internet Service Provider (ISP), establishes a connection with another modem, and provides you with an Internet connection.

By today's standards, a dial-up connection is considered quite slow and unreliable, especially if you want to download music files and photos or play Internet-based games. However, dial-up connections are still an excellent, inexpensive method of accessing the Internet if you travel frequently (you can find a simple phone line almost anywhere) or just send simple text e-mails to friends. In fact, now that dial-up is no longer a fashionable connection method, you should be able to find a reliable ISP that will charge you between $5 and $20 per month for a dial-up account, depending on how much time you spend online.

Whenever you connect to the Internet, you must think about how to protect your computer from unauthorized access or viruses. For the most part, hackers tend to ignore dial-up connections because they are relatively slow and are used only when you're connected to the Internet, which creates a limited window of opportunity for unauthorized access. To protect your system from viruses, you should install and keep up to date a virus scan package from a leading vendor such as Symantec or McAfee (we'll cover such packages a little later in this book).

Although it's possible to share a modem among computers, the configuration is complicated. Dial-up connections definitely have been replaced as the method of choice for serious Internet users.

If you plan on sharing your Internet access among computers on your home network, you should definitely get a broadband connection. There are currently only two high-speed models for home users to choose from: Digital Subscriber Line (DSL) and cable modems.

Digital Subscriber Line—a fast connection to the Internet

DSL is a broadband technology that uses your existing telephone lines and a DSL modem to connect your computer to the Internet at high speeds. This connection is "always on," meaning you no longer need to dial the ISP to make a connection. Simply launch your browser, and, voilà, you're online. In addition, you can use your telephone while you are online, allowing you to surf and talk on the phone at the same time.

Broadband connections are measured in two speeds: the download stream for data being sent to your computer and the upload stream for data being sent from your system. You can typically expect DSL download speeds to reach 1.5 Mbps and upload speeds to reach at least 128 Kbps.

As you would expect, this increase in speed will cost more than a dial-up connection. Most DSL providers charge between $45 and $55 per month for broadband connections. In addition, you'll likely have to pay an installation fee for a technician to install DSL service in your house (this fee varies depending on your provider).

DSL connections are quite reliable and are good to use when building a home network. Once all your computers are connected, they should be able to launch an Internet browser and view Web pages simultaneously, allowing everyone in the house to enjoy the Internet via one connection.

Security is an important issue with any broadband connection because your network is always connected to the Internet. That's a huge temptation to hackers. To avoid unauthorized use of your systems, you should purchase a software program called a firewall. This special software will prevent other users from accessing any computer on your home network. (We'll provide in-depth coverage of firewall software later in this book.)

One of the few major drawbacks to DSL is that it's not offered in all areas. If you are interested in using DSL, you should contact a service provider (such as your local telephone company) to determine if DSL is available in your area.

Combining high-speed Internet access with your cable television

The other option for home high-speed Internet access is the cable modem, which utilizes the same digital cable line that is being used for your cable television signal. Cable modem connections are usually more readily available than their DSL counterparts, and the installation is much easier. In fact, many providers offer a free self-installation kit that includes a line splitter and cable modem. The only prerequisite for using such self-installation kits is that you already have cable TV service installed.

Cable modems offer potentially higher speeds than DSL in roughly the same price range (the option to self-install can actually make cable broadband a little cheaper than DSL). The one catch is that your cable modem connection is shared with other subscribers who are located nearby, which can cause the connection speed to fluctuate when the broadband "pipe" is being used heavily. To help ease this burden, providers limit the number of homes that share a connection.

Despite sharing the connection, your speeds will still be quite high, easily reaching download speeds of 1.5 Mbps and upload speeds of 256 Kbps. In general, you'll usually have the fastest connection speeds using a cable modem.

Just as with DSL connections, cable modems are a good choice when you want to share your Internet connection among computers on your home network. Cable modem security concerns are the same as with DSL, because the connection is always on, so make sure that you have a firewall package installed to protect your computers from unauthorized access.

Sorting it all out

There's really no right or wrong choice when deciding whether to use a dial-up, DSL, or cable modem connection for your home network. All three types of connections let you use the Internet, but DSL and cable will do so more reliably and efficiently. You should base your decision on the amount of time that you spend on the Internet, the types of service that are available in your area, and the amount of money you want to spend. ❖

Lower costs give traditional business Internet options broad appeal

By Debra Littlejohn Shinder, MCSE

For large enterprise-level companies, choosing an Internet access method is relatively easy. Fire up the dedicated leased lines (and make mine a T-3, please), and shell out hundreds or thousands of dollars per month to the Telco and ISP—and don't forget the setup fees and cost of customer premise equipment (CPE).

Many small and medium size businesses also need reliable and reasonably fast Internet access, but they may not be able to afford T-carrier and other traditional commercial options. Cost and quality are often a trade-off, but awareness of the many options available makes it easier for you to select the most cost-effective and task-effective alternative. In this article, I will examine the different bandwidth factors you need to consider, and then I will discuss the traditional business Internet access options.

How much speed do you need?

Although it's generally true that *faster* is better, it's important to evaluate your company's real needs against the increased cost that, as a rule, comes with increased bandwidth, and to understand just how buzzwords such as *speed* and *performance* really correlate. To get the best solution for the least amount of money, you'll need to consider a number of factors.

EVALUATING BANDWIDTH ISSUES

Bandwidth, in this context, refers to the amount of data that can be transmitted over a link during a specified period of time. Network bandwidth is usually expressed in bits per second (bps), kilobits per second (Kbps), or megabits per second (Mbps).

Mbps isn't everything

In considering differences between two connections (or connectivity types), you'll want to consider at least three factors:

- Speed (expressed as Mbps for high speed connections)
- Reliability or uptime (the percentage of time that the link is "up" or functioning)
- Latency (the total amount of delay between the time a packet is sent and the time it arrives at its destination)

The least understood of these factors is latency. It is a product not only of the speed of the link on which the packet is transmitted, but also the time it takes network devices—such as routers—to examine the packet and forward it on its way. Latency often refers to the time it takes a connection to "get started," and is based on the round-trip travel of a message and response from a sender to a destination and back again. That is, you might have excellent download speed with a specific connection but have to wait a significant amount of time between the time you enter the command to download and the time the destination server responds and starts sending. That's called high latency. High latency can be caused by a large number of devices between the sender and destination, or it can be caused by a long distance that must be traveled by the packets (as with satellite connections, where the data must travel all the way up to geosynchronous orbit [22,300 miles above the equator] and back down again).

Traditional business options

The traditional choice for business connectivity—both in terms of connecting to the Internet and connecting the local networks of branch offices together—has been the dedicated leased line. This is a point-to-point physical connection (for example, between your company's network—actually, its router—and your ISP). Typically, this is a T-carrier (T-1 or T-3 line). Another type of *dedicated* link is frame relay, which is a one-to-many connection that uses virtual links between your network (and those of many other companies) and the Telco's frame relay network. Another Internet connectivity choice that was very popular for businesses several years ago and is still available (although its market has been cut into somewhat by the advent of broadband technologies) is integrated switched digital network (ISDN). These three traditional business options have one thing in common: rock solid reliability. Here is a look at the other advantages—and disadvantages—of each.

T-1: It's not just for millionaires anymore

A decade ago, T-1 was out of the reach of almost all individuals and most businesses. At several thousand dollars per month, it was a significant expense even for medium size companies. Today, it's possible to get a full 1.544 Mbps T-1 line in many locations in the U.S. for $500 per month or less. While still quite a bit more expensive than broadband (for similar speed), a dedicated leased line typically experiences far less downtime. There is a charge for the *local loop* from the Telco and a charge for service from an ISP. These charges are often combined on one bill. You'll need to rent or purchase a channel service unit/data service unit (CSU/DSU) and a router, as well.

T-1 runs over either copper wires or fiber optic. Each T-1 line carries 24 64-Kbps channels. It is also possible to purchase a "fractional T-1," or only some of the channels, for a lower total bandwidth. A full T-1 can support a hundred or more users performing low-bandwidth activities, such as Web browsing and e-mail.

TIP

T-1 can be used for voice lines as well as data (each of the 24 channels is used for one voice line).

The phone company generally installs T-1 service as two redundant lines so that if one goes down, service can be switched to the other. Response to problems of T-1 customers by both the Telco and ISPs is usually immediate. Your T-1 contract may come with a "guaranteed bandwidth" clause; in other words, with T-1, what you expect (1.544 Mbps) is what you get—unlike with many DSL and cable modem contracts, where you are promised bandwidth "up to" a particular level, but your speeds may fluctuate. This is often called a committed information rate (CIR). If your company's business depends on its Internet connectivity and requires high speed and guaranteed uptime (for example, if you host Web sites for others or run an e-commerce site for sales), T-1 may still be your best bet. This is especially true in a geographic area where low cost T-1 service is available.

Higher bandwidth leased lines (T-3 at 43.232 Mbps up to OC48 at 2.5 gigabits per second) cost thousands of dollars per month and are generally not financially feasible for most small businesses (nor do small businesses need the amount of bandwidth they provide). If your business is a heavy user of extremely high bandwidth applications, however, you can purchase more than one T-1 and aggregate the bandwidth.

Frame Relay: Low cost, moderate speed, high reliability

Frame relay uses two-way data paths called virtual circuits (either virtual switched circuits or virtual permanent circuits) between two locations, such as your company network and your ISP. For detailed technical data on how the technology works, see the **Basic Guide to Frame Relay Networking**. Frame relay works best with so-called "bursty" applications (where data is sent in bursts with time in between) rather than with those that need a steady stream.

Frame relay acts much like a dedicated line and gives you similar reliability and a CIR, but because the circuit is virtual (and thus the same frame relay switch can support more than one circuit), it costs less. You can usually purchase CIRs anywhere from 56 Kbps up to 1.544 Mbps. The CIR is your guaranteed minimum speed, but you will probably get higher "burst" speeds (for short amounts of time). Customer premise equipment requirements are the same as a T-1 (CSU/DSU and router).

ISDN: Going, going but not gone

ISDN comes in two varieties: basic rate ISDN (BRI) and primary rate ISDN (PRI). The first is a relatively low bandwidth solution, with two 64 Kbps data channels and a 16 Kbps control channel for total throughput of 128 Kbps (or you can use one channel for data and one for voice simultaneously). It is extremely reliable and bandwidth doesn't fluctuate. A BRI line from the Telco generally costs less than $100. ISDN ISP services come in two types: dial-up or dedicated (always on). Dial-up is comparable in price to dial-up analog modem pricing ($25 per month or less). Dedicated service varies widely in price, up to several hundred dollars per month, depending on the ISP.

> **TIP**
>
> Don't dismiss T-1 as "too expensive" for your small business without doing some checking. I've seen some amazing deals (in the range of $300 per month) in some areas. T-1 service prices can vary widely within a locality, too, so check with more than one ISP.

BRI service is an option to consider if you have only a few low bandwidth users (under 10) but need high uptime/reliability. An example would be a small business that uses the Internet primarily for e-mail and a little Web research, but which cannot afford to be without e-mail communication for hours or days. 128 Kbps is not fast enough to effectively run Web servers, unless the pages they host are text only and accessed by only a few outside users at a time. Multiple BRI lines can be aggregated, but this may not be as cost-effective as other alternatives.

PRI is a more expensive service that provides 23 data channels for a total data rate (using all channels) comparable to T-1 (plus one 64 Kbps data channel). The capacity can be reallocated at any time. That is, some channels can be used for voice when necessary then added back to the total data capacity when the voice calls are finished. The cost for PRI in many areas makes T-1 a more attractive alternative for Internet access. However, an advantage of ISDN over T-1 is that because it is *not* a point-to-point dedicated connection, it's easier to switch between ISPs.

Many options, lower costs

Small and medium size businesses have many more options for connecting to the Internet today than just a few years ago, and costs for most connectivity types continue to come down. In deciding which choice is the best option for your business, you should consider performance (speed), reliability, latency, and terms of service, as well as initial cost of equipment and monthly service charges. There is no one-size-fits-all solution that's right for everyone; each organization must consider the needs of its users, the technical expertise of its IT personnel, and the bottom line on its budget before making a decision. ❖

Broadband Internet options for budget-minded IT managers

By Debra Littlejohn Shinder, MCSE

The term *broadband* generally refers to the digital subscriber line (DSL) and Internet service provided by CATV companies (cable Internet). The first incarnations of both of these services were aimed at home users, but many companies now offer business-grade service as well (usually at a higher cost). While broadband is becoming more and more popular with consumers, such factors as downtime, fluctuating bandwidth, and capped upstream speeds often make consumer DSL and cable services unsuitable for running servers and other mission-critical tasks. Nonetheless, budget-minded IT managers are finding a place for business-class broadband services in their infrastructure.

In this article, I'll compare the advantages and disadvantages of broadband to help you decide which alternative will work for your business. I'll also consider less common broadband solutions, such as fixed wireless and satellite, SDSL, IDSL, and VDSL.

The bewildering varieties of DSL

DSL is a technology that allows high data transfer rates over regular copper phone wiring by using frequencies to send digital signals that can't be used for analog signals. Most consumer-grade DSL offerings are of a type called asymmetric DSL or ADSL. This refers to the fact that upstream and downstream bandwidth is not equal. Typical download speeds are 1.5 to 6 Mbps, while upstream is generally much slower—anywhere from 128 to 768 Kbps. Many providers offer several different packages with different bandwidth offerings, so you can tailor what you buy to fit your needs.

Business-grade ADSL

Business-grade ADSL usually costs more than consumer-grade service, but less than frame relay or T-1 for comparable connection speeds. The difference between a provider's consumer and business service usually isn't the amount of bandwidth (connection speed), but rather the level of service. Business customers are paying for amenities such as 24/7 tech support and installation management. For better reliability and performance, some providers connect business-grade customers to a tier-one IP backbone while home customers are connected to a tier-two backbone. With ADSL, the same line can be used simultaneously for phone calls and data transfer.

ADSL may be a cost-effective option if you have a small office that needs Internet services consisting mostly of downstream traffic. Because of the low upstream bandwidth, it's not the best choice if you want to run your own Web servers or other Internet-accessible servers.

Symmetric DSL

Symmetric DSL (SDSL) is usually offered as a business product. Upstream and downstream speeds are the same (up to about 3 Mbps). This makes it a better choice if you need to run servers, but it's more expensive and difficult to find SDSL providers in many geographic areas. Distance limitation is about 22,000 feet to the phone company central office (CO), and you don't get the ability to use the phone for voice as with ADSL.

Very high bit-rate DSL

Very high bit-rate DSL (VDSL) is an extremely fast service, up to 52 Mbps downstream and 16 Mbps upstream. The problem is that distance limitations are very narrow; you must be within about 4000 feet of a CO to get this service. VDSL uses fiber optic cabling, so it costs considerably more than lower speed DSL services—if you can find a provider at all. However, it is excellent for large amounts of users, very high bandwidth applications, and running multiple servers.

Other DSL types

The above are the most common types of DSL, but businesses may find other offerings available in their areas. These include:

- IDSL (DSL over ISDN lines): This is available in some areas where ADSL is not (up to about 35,000 feet from the CO), but IDSL doesn't give you much of a speed boost over regular ISDN (IDSL connects at 144 Kbps up and down).
- Rate adaptive DSL (RADSL): With this option, the modem can vary the speed based on the line quality/distance.
- Voice over DSL (VoDSL): Suited for telephony applications.

The negatives of DSL

Why hasn't DSL made the more expensive T-1 service obsolete? There are several disadvantages to DSL. The biggest is the distance limitation for service. Customers must be within about 18,000 feet of a CO to get ADSL, and other varieties have distance limits as well. Also, if you have "fiber to the curb" (fiber optic cabling), you won't be able to get ADSL. There are other types of DSL that run over fiber, but they're more expensive and not offered by as many providers. You can get T-1 service just about anywhere you can get voice phone service.

DSL is an option you should consider if your business is located in an area where the type of service you need is available. Service guarantees vary widely from one provider to the next, so you should review contracts carefully and compare both cost and terms of service to those of your other access options.

Cable companies get into the "business" business

Although still primarily marketed to home users, cable access is slowly evolving into a business solution, as well. As with DSL, business-grade packages cost more than those intended for residential customers and usually include 24/7 tech support. Business-grade cable Internet services can be faster (it is possible to get speeds upwards of 10 Mbps with cable, although most residential services provide between 500 Kbps and 1.5 Mbps), and upstream bandwidth may not be throttled as it is with residential service. Terms of service for consumer cable usually prohibit running servers (and providers limit upstream bandwidth to 128 to 256 Kbps to enforce this). Business packages will often allow you to run Web servers over your cable connection.

Cost for business-grade cable is generally comparable to that of business-grade DSL (although prices for both can vary widely depending on the geographic area and provider). You usually don't have multiple CATV providers to choose from within an area, as you may have with DSL, so the lack of competition sometimes drives prices up. An important consideration with cable Internet is to recognize that it is a shared technology. The more customers there are on an area of cable (in physical proximity), using it at the same time, the lower performance will be. There are also security considerations. It may be possible for other customers in your area to *see* your computers on their networks if you have a computer directly connected to the cable modem (rather than a router) and you have file and print sharing enabled on the computer's interface to the Internet. This is easily fixed by properly configuring the interface, but can be a problem in a small business that doesn't have trained IT personnel.

Cable may be worth checking into if you're in an area where DSL is not available, you need high speed access, you can't afford the high cost of T-1, and you don't need guaranteed bandwidth. If you're considering using cable Internet for your business, I recommend that you talk to other customers who've used the service and ask how well the service has performed for them.

Wire-free alternatives worth checking into

Newer technologies free you from the need for wiring, using the airwaves to send and receive network signals and transfer data. These include satellite and fixed (ground-based) wireless.

Satellite goes professional

Satellite Internet uses geosynchronous satellites, which stay in the same position in relation to the ground at all times. Thus, at your location, you can have an antenna (dish) that stays in a fixed position, which is used to send signals to the satellite and receive signals from it. The satellite provider's network is connected to the Internet backbone, and also is connected to a dish that transmits the signals to the satellite, which in turn transmits them to you. With most satellite systems, IP data is converted to digital video broadcast (DVB) by equipment at the sending location and goes to the satellite in that format, and is then converted back to IP at the recipient's end.

The biggest advantage of satellite is the fact that you can locate your office anywhere that has a view of the sky where the satellite is located. This means you can have Internet access out in the middle of a desert where there are no phone lines (assuming your provider offers two-way satellite access; as with early cable modem, some satellite services are one-way only).

There are a large number of companies providing satellite access. These tend to be focused on either residential customers (with speeds of around 400 Kbps, in many cases one-way) or large enterprise-level companies (with service costs of thousands of dollars per month). Some of the consumer-oriented companies such as Hughes Network (DirecPC) also offer business services.

Is the fix in for fixed wireless?

Fixed wireless technology uses ground-based broadcast towers to communicate between the service provider (called a wireless Internet service provider or WISP) and the customer. Fixed wireless is a viable option if your business is located in an area close to where the towers are located. Companies can provide wireless Internet and phone service using the same technology, and in some cases, the signals can be broadcast as far as 35 miles. The speed of the wireless connection depends on the provider's connection to the Internet backbone, the number of customers using that connection, and whether the provider throttles bandwidth. Cost varies, averaging $100-200/month to connect a small LAN.

A variation on the WISP is the "hotspot" wireless provider. These companies set up short-range wireless access points at airports, restaurants/coffee shops, hotels, and so on. You can connect your Wi-Fi (802.11) equipped laptop to the network and Internet at these locations by paying a fee for the session or by subscribing to a service that gives you unlimited usage of a particular provider's network. You can find a list of "hotspots" in various geographic areas by using the WiFinder Web site.

Bandwidth aggregation: Making the most of multiple connections

One way to get more speed at a relatively low cost is by aggregating the bandwidth from two or more connections. For example, if you need more than 1.5 Mbps downstream but don't need high upstream, you could purchase two DSL lines and combine them (using software such as Rainfinity's RainConnect) for a total downstream bandwidth of 3 Mbps. You can do the same with multiple T-1 lines, multiple cable connections, or even a combination of different types of lines. This has the added advantage of providing redundancy; if one line goes down, you still have one or more working lines for backup. ❖

Look for availability and reliability in a broadband provider

Steven Pittsley, CNE

I f you've decided to take our advice and upgrade to a broadband Internet connection, it's time to start doing your homework and answer some basic questions, such as:

- What service providers are in your area?
- Should you get DSL or a cable modem?
- How do you ensure that you'll get good service for a decent price?

We hope to shed some light on these issues as we compare DSL and cable modem services. And we'll give you some more important questions for vendors that will help you see if their services make the grade. But first, let's run through the key issues you should keep in mind as you evaluate ISPs.

Connection speed

When you start comparing connection types, one of the first topics to address is connection speed, or bandwidth. For best average connection speed, cable modems usually come out on top with download speeds that occasionally eclipse 1.5 Mbps and upload speeds between 128 Kbps to 384 Kbps. Please note that these speeds can fluctuate because you are sharing bandwidth with other users in your vicinity.

DSL, on the other hand, is a direct connection between your computer and the central office switch. This allows the connection speed to be fairly consistent, with download speeds reaching 1.5 Mbps and upload speeds of at least 128 Kbps. One thing that can slow down your DSL connection is the distance between your home and the central office switch. The farther away you are from the switch, the slower your connection will be.

Reliability

Another priority for you to consider is reliability. If a provider can give you excellent speed but its connection is frequently down, you'll be better off with a company that can provide more reliable service. Both cable and DSL providers usually have very reliable connections with very little downtime. However, it's always a good idea to ask other users what they think of their broadband providers. If you discover that a provider has unreliable service, you should look elsewhere.

Security

Security is a vital issue when connecting your computer to the Internet using a broadband connection. Because the connection is "always on," there's a heightened chance that unauthorized users can gain access to the files on your computer. You can prevent this by installing a software package called a firewall, which will keep unauthorized users from accessing the data on your computer. In addition to a firewall package, you should install a virus scan package and keep the virus definition files up to date. (We'll take a more in-depth look at firewalls and antivirus packages later in this book.)

Finally, if you believe that someone is trying to hack into your computer or you want to ensure that nobody can do so, you can simply physically disconnect the network cable on your computer from the broadband connection when you're not surfing the Web or sending e-mail. This is a drastic solution to the problem, but it will definitely prevent anyone from hacking into your computer or home network. Both DSL and cable modem connections face the same security concerns, so this should not sway you one way or the other.

Availability in your area

One issue that may make your broadband decision fairly easy is the availability of DSL or cable service. If you are in a large metropolitan area, you should be able to find plenty of DSL and cable companies. However, if you are in a suburban or small town locale, you may have only one broadband provider in the area. Cable service is generally more prevalent, but DSL providers are quickly closing the gap. Asking other computer enthusiasts in your area who they use for high-speed Internet access should provide a good idea of what providers are in your town. For starters, give your cable company a call and check out Web sites like **www.dslavailability.com** to see what services are available to you.

Cost

Both cable and DSL monthly fees are falling every day, and if you have several options in your area you should be able to find some very good deals. In general, the monthly fee for broadband service ranges from $45 to $55. The main variable to consider when shopping around is the installation price. Many providers include the cost to use their DSL or cable modem in the monthly price. Others, however, want you to purchase your own device; these vendors usually have lower monthly service costs.

Also keep an eye on the installation fees assessed when a technician installs your service. These fees can be quite steep, running $100 to $200. To help alleviate this expense, many companies provide self-installation kits for free. However, DSL installation usually requires some expertise with telephone wiring. If you already have cable television, the self-installation of a cable modem is usually pretty simple; if you don't have television service, a technician will have to perform the installation.

Which is better? The decision is really up to you. Both DSL and cable provide reliable high-speed Internet access at a similar price. As we stated earlier, cable modem service generally provides higher access speeds, but don't base your decision solely on this factor. You should also consider reliability, availability, and installation costs when deciding which broadband provider to use. Comparing several vendors should give you a clear picture of which company will give you the best value.

Questions you should ask potential vendors

Before talking to a broadband service provider, you should prepare a list of questions to ask. Here are several questions that will help you find the right service provider for your needs.

How many network outages have you had in my area in the last month? Instead of just asking if the provider's service is reliable, get quantifiable proof. You should expect a few outages because many factors can temporarily interrupt network service. By comparing the numbers from a few providers, it should be easy to determine which company has the more reliable service.

What is your average connection speed? Broadband providers will guarantee that you get certain minimum download and upload speeds. You can expect to get better speeds than these guaranteed numbers, but the provider should give you a good idea of what your typical connection speed will be.

What type of DSL/cable modem will I be required to use? This is important if you plan on sharing your connection with other computers on your home network. For instance, if the provider wants you to use a USB DSL/cable modem, you might be unable to connect it to a router that uses Ethernet connections. In addition, USB modems will be slower than their Ethernet counterparts.

How far away is the central office switch from my house? This question in particularly important for DSL services; the farther away you are from the switch, the slower your connection speed will be. You must be within two to three miles of a switch to get DSL service, so if your location is more than two miles away, you might see some degradation of your access speed.

How many e-mail accounts will I get and how do I access them? Nearly all service providers offer e-mail service, and many of them offer several e-mail boxes. If you need more than one account, be sure you know how many you will get. In addition, be sure that you understand how to access your e-mail account. Most often you'll use a program such as Outlook Express, but you should know the requirements before you sign up.

Do you offer free Web site hosting? Many service providers offer free Web site hosting to their customers. If you would like to have your own personal Web site, you should try to find a service provider who offers these services. (Typically, you'll need to pay for hosting services if you plan on having a lot of information or traffic at your site.)

Is there a contract, and how long is it? Any time you sign a contract, you should first know the specifics. Find out the length of the contract, the guaranteed connection speeds, the installation and monthly fees, and whether or not you can use the connection on your home network.

What is the installation cost? Providers are very good about advertising their low monthly fees, but installation costs are often buried in the fine print. Be sure that you know the cost of installation before you agree to have the service installed.

Do you have 24-hour, 7-day-a-week support? If you have connection problems at 3 A.M. and want to get technical support, you should know if someone will be manning the support line during that time. Very few providers fail to provide 24/7 support, but you should still ensure that your provider does.

Be demanding

Buyer beware—remember this cliché when shopping for an Internet service provider. You'll have many, many options to consider before selecting a provider, but by asking the questions we have outlined here, you should be able to compare several service providers and make a solid decision. Take your time to compare several plans, and you'll ensure that you'll find the right fit. ❖

Use the right networking components for your next cabling job

By Scott Lowe, MCSE

Does your organization contract out its cabling work, or is most of it done in house? In either case, you should know how to choose the cabling components and tools for any kind of installation. And, while most vendors are trustworthy, it's important to watch over their shoulders and make sure that the equipment they choose is up to standards and that the work they do is satisfactory. For that you need to know what to look for and how to choose the right equipment for your infrastructure. In this chapter, I'll take a look at some of the components you need to know about.

Key components

While it's often overlooked as a minor detail, choosing the right components can make a huge difference in your network. The decisions you make can mean the difference between a network that just gets the job done and one that works well today and is also ready for tomorrow.

I prefer to do a job once, possibly paying a little more up front, and not have to worry about it later when I need to upgrade a connection or add a new device to the network. The first rule is simple: the lowest bid is not always your best choice. Even though it's a cliché, it's often true: You get what you pay for.

The backbone of a network is built around these key components:

- The network cable
- The patch panel
- The network jack
- The gang box

Network cable is too complicated to completely cover it in this chapter. Instead, we'll dedicate the next chapter to selecting the proper cabling. For now, let's look at the remaining components in turn.

The patch panel

There isn't much to look for in patch panels, but it's important to check what there is. For example, check the rating. Is the panel rated for Category (Cat) 5, 5e, or the new Cat 6? In today's networks, you should consider patch panels and remote jacks that meet Cat 5e ratings at a minimum.

Cat 5e rated cabling and components undergo more rigorous testing than Cat 5 installations, such as tests for far end crosstalk (FEXT) and return loss. Another reason to use Cat 5e components, cabling, and installation is because Cat 5e supports gigabit Ethernet applications. With the original Cat 5 standards, the tests that are specific for a cabling plant to be deemed "gigabit Ethernet ready" are not performed.

While most people associate cable with different categories, all of the components in the overall system must meet the specifications for the entire system to rate a certain category. Your overall network is only as fast as your slowest component. So, if you purchase Cat 5e cable but you only install Cat 3-rated patch panels, your overall network will be limited to Cat 3 speeds—if it will work at all.

Angled jacks are also a good idea in many patch panel installations. You may have seen jacks angled toward the floor in some offices. These types of jacks place less stress on the patch cables that connect to them. As a consequence, they bring greater longevity to the system as a whole, as well as fewer cabling-related problems. Belkin makes a 12-, 24-, and 48-port patch panel system that includes angled connectors (**http://catalog.belkin.com/IWCatProductPage.process?Merchant_Id= &Section_Id=41&pcount=&Product_Id=19695&Section.Section_Path=/Root/ Networki...ndCables/PatchPanels/**).

The use of angled jacks in a patch panel is completely dependent on how you run cabling in your closets. If your patch cables angle downward toward the network equipment, angled patch panels may be useful. If your patch panels go off to the side of the rack and you use cable management to get to the network equipment, then angled patch panels won't be of much use to you.

The network jack

While it's important to choose appropriate components at the network center or equipment closets, it's just as important to choose jacks at the remote end that will help to maintain the quality of your infrastructure. The jacks you choose should conform to the standard you've chosen for your overall system.

If you're using Cat 5e equipment, then use a 5e wall jack as well (**www.cable4 pc.com/utp821.htm**). While some wall jack components are interchangeable with different faceplates, make sure of this before you buy a lot of both. The jack faceplate will cover the hole in the wall that you make to put up a gang box.

If you decide to run a number of different types of cables to the same jack location, such as telephone and/or video cables, most manufacturers also make RJ-11 or RJ-23 type telephone jack inserts as well as inserts with a cable TV "F" connector, which is the standard cable TV outlet type. If you're thinking way ahead, you may also be running fiber optic cabling at the same time. You'll be pleased to know that most manufacturers make matching connectors for fiber optic cables as well.

In addition to the patch panel, you can also get angled connectors for the remote wall jacks, where they're likely to be more useful. It's much more likely that the cables in offices will be moved around as people change offices, move furniture, and get new systems, so angled connectors can take some stress off patch cables that see a lot of use.

The gang box/wall connection

Fortunately, there isn't much to think about when selecting a gang box. A gang box is simply the housing behind the wall where your cabling will go and to which the faceplate will attach. A gang box looks like the housing behind the faceplate on your electrical outlets.

In my cabling jobs, I've found it's normally only feasible to install gang boxes when there's no drywall up yet. After drywall goes up, it becomes both expensive and difficult to put gang boxes in place. However, almost any electrical or cabling store will have a solution. This solution is basically a piece of metal that bends, or a piece of plastic with teeth. In either case, you simply need to cut a rectangular hole in the wall about the size of the piece of metal or plastic and insert the metal or plastic piece into the hole. With the metal units, you generally bend a piece of the metal around the back of the drywall to hold the unit in place. With a plastic unit, there are three pieces—the first piece is the housing, while the other two are small pieces that you place over the teeth that keep it connected to the wall. The entire purpose of these solutions is to give you something to screw a faceplate to. Without one of these, you'd have to screw directly into the drywall, and that can be problematic.

For the height of the box, it's useful to know the height of the electrical boxes that surround it. Even if the box is not a standard height off the ground, it will look much better when finished if it matches the height of the electrical boxes near it. To exactly match the height, you can use a tape measure or a tool such as the Siemon Wall Box Locator (**www.homecabling.com/hcnew/press_releases/ 01-11-01-mountit.asp**).

Don't forget permits and building codes!

In some areas, you need a permit to install network, cable TV, and telephone cabling and components. In most areas, a low voltage installation permit will suffice. If you don't get a permit and later have a problem or want to sell your house or building, you may have difficulty, so be careful and check this out before you begin. Always make sure your installations meet building codes. This is especially important for liability reasons.

Tools you'll need

Obviously, if you're planning to hire a contractor for all of your cabling work, you don't need any specialized tools. If, however, you decide to do the installation work yourself, or if you just want to be able to quickly and properly run a cable now and then, there are a few tools that can make the job much easier and more likely to succeed. Some of the tools you should have at your disposal are:

- **Hammer:** An essential tool for everything from replacing watch batteries and building houses to dealing with uncooperative coworkers, a hammer makes it easier to nail a gang box to a stud in network installation jobs where there is no drywall present yet.

- **Screwdriver:** Used to secure the patch panel to a rack and to secure faceplates to the wall. Also useful when you make a mistake and need to separate one of the RJ-45 snap-ins from the faceplate.

- **110 punch tool:** While most patch panels will come with a small plastic punch tool, I highly recommend buying a professional-grade unit. It is much sturdier, and it'll keep you from ruining your fingers when you slip. You can get a decent punch tool for around $50.

- **Cutters:** For trimming the ends of cables.

- **Network cable tester:** In order to know that your cable plant is going to work, you need to test the cables afterwards, and you'll need this tool to do it.

- **Cabling certification tool:** If you're a professional who installs network cabling for a living, it's critical to be able to certify that the cabling plants that you install are up to the job and to be able to prove that it is indeed category 5e and gigabit ready. If you're managing a very large cabling plant or are a cabling contractor, these are must-have devices.

THE 110 PUNCH TOOL

You may have seen some tools in the list that you're not immediately familiar with, such as the 110 punch tool. The reason for the name "110" is this—the patch panel that you use in networks uses a 110-type wiring interface. Individual network cables are placed at specific locations and then "punched" into the unit. "Punching" simply strips a small portion of the wire and pushes it deep into the patch panel grooves so that it makes contact with the metal and can transmit an electrical signal. Some punch tools also come with a 66-type punch head, which is commonly used in telephone/voice applications.

For network cable testers, my favorite cabling tester is the Microscanner Pro from Fluke. It's fairly inexpensive. Besides testing continuity to make sure that all of the cable pairs are intact and working, it verifies the length of the cable to make sure that you're within specifications. It also includes a wire-mapping adapter that can help you to verify that your cables are wired properly. This unit costs around $350, but it's worth it because it considerably reduces the time it takes to troubleshoot network problems and test your installations.

When it comes to cable certification tools, the Fluke OMNIScanner 2 is one of my personal favorites. It's capable of doing basic certification as well as producing reports that you can pass on to your clients. But be prepared to spend some money: These devices start in the low $5,000 range, and you can add options on top of it.

Don't get tied up in knots about cabling

While you may not actually be installing cable yourself, it's important to know how it's done so that you know what things will cost and can monitor contractors' work. If you do some of the work yourself, you definitely need to know how to do it right. Don't buy what's cheapest—buy what's best for your network and what best meets your needs. ❖

Know the facts about network cabling

By Scott Lowe, MCSE

When it comes to network design, one of the most important decisions you'll make is choosing and installing the right cable for your network. Even if you hire professional cabling contractors, it is important for you to know what they're doing and what to look for so that you can properly evaluate their work. In this chapter, I'll show how to choose the right cable and how to install it the right way the first time.

Fewer but better choices

If you're running the cable for a network today, your choices are much clearer than they were just a few years ago. Not so long ago, coaxial cable was still in widespread use. Unshielded twisted-pair cabling was primarily based on Category 3 standards, running at a maximum of 10 Mbps. Category 5 cable was still out of reach for most network administrators' budgets. Those with money to burn also had fiber to consider.

Standards were, at best, fuzzy. Several different standards were fighting it out for the supremacy of running 100 Mbps over unshielded twisted-pair. There was a lot of uncertainty about whether it was even possible to run data over copper at such speeds. Some critics claimed that 100 Mbps was only suitable for fiber.

Today, deciding on a particular type of cable isn't as much a matter of which cable will eventually become the standard as it is a matter of what you need to do right now and for the next few years. Most of today's network installations generally use some type of unshielded twisted-pair cabling, although some organizations are running fiber directly to their desktop machines.

AUTHOR'S NOTE: TWISTED-PAIR CABLING

I'll be focusing on twisted-pair cabling since that's the prevalent technology today. You still have the same choices of fiber, shielded twisted-pair, and coax cable that you had in the past. However, because unshielded twisted-pair is so inexpensive and has such a large market share, it's the first choice for most network administrators.

Many different kinds of unshielded twisted-pair (UTP) cabling are available, and you need to pick the one that will best serve your needs without breaking your budget. UTP cabling is generally rated by incremental "categories." For example, when someone is talking about Category 3 cabling, they mean a type of cabling commonly found in telephone and other voice applications or low-speed data transmission, and that has a transmission frequency of 16 MHz.

Different kinds of UTP cabling are available. Each type runs at a different speed and has different uses. The key types of UTP cable you'll encounter are:

- **Category 3:** Cat 3 was the earliest successful implementation of UTP. It's primarily used for voice and lower-speed data applications. It's rated for a maximum of 10 Mbps.
- **Category 4:** Cat 4 never achieved the popularity of Cat 3 or Cat 5. It's primarily used for voice and lower-speed data at a maximum of 16 Mbps.
- **Category 5:** As Fast Ethernet became a standard, Cat 5 became the basis for most high-speed data implementations. Cat 5 runs at a maximum of 100 Mbps.
- **Category 5e:** With the need for higher speeds, Gigabit Ethernet has become the new replacement for Fast Ethernet. To make it work, Cat 5e extends the life of Cat 5 cable. It can run at a maximum of 1,000 Mbps.
- **Category 6:** Cat 5e can run at gigabit speeds, but with 10-Gigabit Ethernet on the horizon, Cat 5e has stretched the Cat 5 standard to its limits. Cat 6 can currently run at 1,000 Mbps (1 Gbps). The Category 6 specification was released for publication very recently, however as designed, Category 6 cabling will be able to support speeds up to at least 10 Gbps.

For new installations, I highly recommend running a minimum of Category 5e cabling for both voice and data. In today's environment, there's no reason to use anything less. Cat 3 may be a little cheaper, but you'll lose this savings in the costs of replacement when you find out it can't go fast enough for you. Although you may get away with running regular Cat 5 cable, Cat 5e is only slightly more expensive. The incremental cost is well worth the speed advantage and future expandability you gain with Cat 5e.

Pay attention to the jacketing

UTP cabling is almost always sheathed in some type of plastic-like insulating material. Less expensive cabling uses PVC (polyvinyl chloride) as the jacket material. Not all environments can use this type of cabling, for both safety and legal reasons. When PVC burns, it gives off noxious dioxin fumes that are dangerous to those who breathe them. While a single burning PVC cable may not be deadly, firefighters who must enter burning buildings that have thousands of cables can be at risk.

Check your local laws—in many places, it's illegal to use PVC cables in any air-handling spaces, such as in the ceiling or below a raised floor. In these situations, you need to use a cable with a more expensive but much safer jacket called plenum. If your cables are just run into the wall and you're positive that they don't run in air handling spaces, you should be fine with standard Cat 5 cable. If you don't need it, don't incur the expense of plenum cable, which can be two to three times the cost of PVC.

Follow the rules

Second only to choosing the appropriate cable is making sure it's run throughout your organization in a manner consistent with standards that ensure the best possible performance. In fact, if you don't follow a few basic tenets, you could end up with an installation that's expensive but not functional. Here are a few basic rules you should follow when installing cable.

Watch the length of your cable runs

No cable run should be more than 100 meters (~327 feet) in length, including patch cables. The in wall/ceiling distance—also called the horizontal run distance—should be no longer than 90 meters. This allows for up to 10 meters for patch cables on either end of the connection.

Watch for interference

No cables should be run near devices that generate electromagnetic interference. This is one of the rules most often broken by amateur cabling installers. Devices that generate electromagnetic fields include heating/cooling units, printers, copiers, electrical wiring, video equipment, and much more. You should be very careful to keep UTP cabling at least 3 feet away from anything that can create an EM field. In addition, it's critical to keep UTP cabling as far away from fluorescent lighting as possible since cables are very susceptible to interference from fluorescent lights.

Handle with care

Take care not to damage cable when installing it. Don't exceed the bend radius of UTP cabling or it may not work as expected. It's generally accepted that cable that is bent within a radius of four times the width of the cable is not run properly. Be very careful not to flatten cable with a hammer or a staple. Hammer and staple indentations on UTP cabling can create problems like changing the signal's properties, resulting in a less efficient (or nonfunctional) network. If you're tying a bundle of cables together, use a zip tie that is secure but leaves a little wiggle room. If you tie the cables too tightly together, you run the same risks as when you flatten it. Finally, when pulling cable through the ceiling or conduit, be careful about how hard you pull at the cable. Don't exceed 25 pounds of pulling force in order to avoid stretching the cable, which can damage its electrical characteristics and render it out of compliance for high-speed data networks.

Use the right equipment

Wherever possible, make use of a ladder rack or a cabling tray with a solidly installed bottom. It will make your interconnections go much more smoothly.

Termination and testing of UTP: Category 5e

The next areas you need to focus on are properly terminating your cable and testing it to make sure that it's within specifications. I'm going to concentrate on the proper termination of Category 5e cabling because it is the latest officially standardized UTP cabling currently available and it supports gigabit Ethernet installations.

Like every other phase of cable installation, a set of standards governs the termination phase in order to ensure that the plant will support high-speed data.

One of the primary standards specifies exactly what should take place when the cable jacket is stripped back and the individual pairs untwisted to prepare them for termination. The twisting of Category 5e cabling is one of the characteristics that define the communication properties for the cabling and enable it to do its job. Removing too much twist from the cable results in an imperfect installation, and it can put the cable out of specification and possibly make it unable to support high-speed data transmission.

The current Category 5e specifications indicate that up to 13 mm of twist may be removed in order to support cable installation, and up to 40-60 mm of the jacket may be stripped away. This is the same at both ends of the horizontal run—i.e., at both the network closet patch panel and the wall jack—as well as for patch cables used with the system.

TESTING EQUIPMENT IS IMPORTANT

If you're a professional installing network cabling for a living, it's critical to be able to certify that the cabling plants you install are up to the job and to prove that it is indeed Category 5e and gigabit ready. The Fluke OMNIScanner 2 (**www.flukenetworks.com/us/Cabling/Copper+Cabling/ OMNIScanner/overview.htm**) is capable of doing this as well as producing reports that you can pass onto your clients. But be prepared to spend some money, as these devices start in the low $5,000 range, with options available. If you manage a very large cabling plant or are a cabling contractor, these are must-have devices.

Get to work

Installing cabling properly and for the long run is no walk in the park. Besides some very strict installation guidelines, you need to test each and every cable for specific parameters in order to make sure that your cable plant can support your requirements. Cabling isn't as complicated as it sounds, but if you're not careful, you can wind up wasting a lot of time and money. Follow these guidelines to do it right the first time. ❖

Prepare for Gigabit Ethernet networking

By Brien M. Posey, MCSE

I f you've been working with networks as long as I have, you probably remember the days when 10-Mbps Ethernet seemed fast. And when 100-Mbps "Fast" Ethernet debuted—Wow! Just when it seemed as if Ethernet couldn't get any faster, along came Gigabit Ethernet with speeds up to 1,000 Mbps (1 Gbps).

Even if you're not deploying Gigabit Ethernet right now, eventually you will. After all, just look at all of the Fast Ethernet equipment in your wiring closet. However, just because you're not deploying Gigabit Ethernet today doesn't mean you can't get your network ready to handle it. In this chapter, I'll show you what you need to do to prepare for Gigabit Ethernet.

What's so great about Gigabit Ethernet?

Although Gigabit Ethernet is growing in popularity, few people I know are actually running it yet. When I ask why, many explain that they'd been burned by ATM and weren't ready to go through that whole experience again. ATM was originally touted as *the* replacement for Ethernet. It was faster than Ethernet and didn't have some of Ethernet's initial problems, such as packet collisions.

However, ATM can be costly. It's also difficult to set up and doesn't work well in environments that require routing between many different subnets. In the end, ATM's performance can be disappointing.

This is what makes Gigabit Ethernet such a great technology. While Gigabit Ethernet is a high-speed medium, it's still Ethernet-based. This means that setting up a Gigabit Ethernet network isn't much different from setting up any other type of Ethernet network.

Best of all, since Gigabit Ethernet is a true Ethernet medium, it will interface with your existing Ethernet network. A Gigabit Ethernet switch can move packets between 10/100-Mbps and 1,000-Mbps networks without any type of packet translation. This not only leads to better efficiency than you'd get with ATM, but it also means less complexity and therefore less chance that something will go wrong.

How fast is it really?

Because Gigabit Ethernet supports transmission speeds of roughly 1,000 Mbps, many network gurus assume that installing a few Gigabit Ethernet NICs and attaching the cabling and a high-speed switch will make their networks perform at warp speeds. However, for several reasons the actual network speed will probably be a bit less.

Suppose for a moment that you were to install Gigabit Ethernet NICs in a server and a workstation, and then connect the two machines with a gigabit switch. Assuming there is no other traffic on the network, you'd probably expect traffic to flow between the two machines at 1,000 Mbps. Unfortunately, you'd be sadly disappointed. The truth is that, in most installations, Gigabit Ethernet implemented in the manner I've just described doesn't even come close to reaching gigabit speeds. In the example above, the best you could hope for is typically between 700 and 800 Mbps.

While 700 Mbps is a huge improvement over the 100-Mbps speed of Fast Ethernet, you're probably wondering why traffic is flowing at 200 to 300 Mbps below its potential. There are several factors that reduce Gigabit Ethernet's performance. One of the most common factors is the cabling.

Cabling considerations

One of the biggest considerations to take into account when implementing Gigabit Ethernet is cabling. When you first read the specs on Gigabit Ethernet, it sounds like an ideal technology, in part because it's compatible with the Category-5 (Cat-5) cable that you already have. However, just because you can use your existing Cat-5 cable for Gigabit Ethernet, it doesn't necessarily mean that you should.

Most big companies will probably be OK with existing copper Cat-5 cable. However, I've done network repair for many small organizations, and the cabling just wasn't up to par in more of them than I can count. For example, in one location, most of the PCs had 10/100 NICs, but the company was still using a 10-Mbps hub. I swapped the hub out for a 10/100 model, and all of the PCs with 100-Mbps cards began to fail. Upon closer examination I found that voice-grade phone cabling had been used instead of Cat-5 cable. When I told the facility's manager about the problem, he said that he had told the installers to use phone cable because it was cheaper than Cat-5 cable.

While this is an extreme example, other cable issues tend to be much more common. For example, although Cat-5 cable has eight wires, 10/100-Mbps Ethernet uses only four of them. I've seen quite a few organizations in which the cable installer saved time by only connecting the four wires that were actually used. In most cases like this, the other four wires are simply cut off. But I've also seen situations in which the additional wires were used to attach a second PC to the network or as wiring for a phone jack.

Even if your cable installer didn't use cheap cable or neglect to connect half of the wires in the cable, there are other Cat-5 issues that could cause problems when you use Gigabit Ethernet. For example, 10/100-Mbps Ethernet standards require that no cable run exceed 100 meters. However, Ethernet and Fast Ethernet tend to be very forgiving when cable lengths are exceeded, so many organizations tend to ignore the limit. Ignoring the 100-meter limit will come back to bite you when you implement Gigabit Ethernet.

Likewise, I've seen many Ethernet and Fast Ethernet networks in which Cat-5 cable segments are spliced together. While this isn't supposed to work, it does when spliced together well. However, splices tend to cause big problems for Gigabit Ethernet.

Before implementing Gigabit Ethernet, I strongly recommend making sure that your cabling is up to the job. I suggest running three different types of tests on your cabling. First, run a continuity test to verify that all eight wires are properly connected. Next, run a far-end crosstalk test. Finally, run a return signal loss test. If your cabling passes all three tests, the cable is adequate for Gigabit Ethernet use.

Speeding things up

As you can see, the condition and length of your Cat-5 cable can affect your network's performance in a big way. One way of getting around the problems caused by poor cable conditions or longer cable runs is to use fiber-optic cable instead of copper cable. Gigabit Ethernet is designed to work with either fiber or copper cable. However, merely switching to fiber-optic cable won't solve all your problems.

Fiber-optic cable is just as susceptible to problems as copper cable. While it's true that fiber is more secure than copper and supports higher data speeds and longer runs, fiber is also much more delicate than copper. Things like excessive epoxy on the cable ends, poorly made splices, too many splices, cable damage, and excessive cable bends can dramatically slow or even stop network traffic flowing through fiber. I personally prefer using fiber over copper in many environments, but even using good quality, properly installed fiber will only help you so much.

The reason is that most computers are incapable of producing packets at gigabit rates. Currently, most PCs produce packets at the CPU level and then pass those packets through the PCI bus to the NIC and across the network. While there are processors that can produce packets at gigabit speeds, it's important to remember that most of the time your processors are busy doing things other than producing packets. For example, in addition to producing packets, a server's processor is managing memory, running services, and maintaining the user interface.

Windows 2000 is more efficient than Windows NT and can produce packets faster, but this is still typically not enough to utilize a gigabit NIC's full potential. There are several new technologies that will help you get the most out of Gigabit Ethernet and may soon allow 10- or even 100-gigabit connections.

The PCI-X bus and other new technologies

One such technology is the PCI-X bus. The PCI-X bus is a new bus that's similar to the PCI bus but isn't as bandwidth-intensive when used in conjunction with PCI-X cards. This means that when a PCI-X bus and a PCI-X-based NIC are in use, packets can flow between the CPU and the NIC much more quickly than they could on a purely PCI machine.

While faster bus speeds will usually allow a gigabit connection to utilize its full potential, there are other new technologies at work. Some companies are developing NICs that have built-in microprocessors. The idea is having a CPU dedicated to the sole task of generating packets. Because this CPU is integrated into the card, it's guaranteed to be fast enough to produce packets at speeds for which the card is intended (1, 10, or 100 Gbps).

Still another experimental technology is bonding. Several NIC manufacturers have prototype NICs with multiple onboard fiber-optic ports. These NICs use several cables at once for parallel traffic flow, and they have an onboard microprocessor that does IP processing at the card level.

Currently, Gigabit Ethernet tends to be a bit pricey, and it probably won't deliver true gigabit performance across your network. I still believe that implementing Gigabit Ethernet is worthwhile in any organization with growing bandwidth needs. After all, a well-installed Gigabit Ethernet connection will perform at least seven times better than a standard Fast Ethernet connection.

The challenge when implementing Gigabit Ethernet is getting the most performance for the least cost. I recommend beginning the rollout by replacing your existing switches with switches that support 10/100/1000-Mbps connections and that support both fiber and copper.

Once you've replaced the switches, the next trick is to figure out where to begin implementing gigabit connections. I suggest using Gigabit Ethernet for all connections between switches. Remember that at any given time there's probably a lot of traffic flowing between your switches. Placing gigabit connections between the switches will prevent the switches from becoming a bottleneck.

Best of all, most switches aren't PCI-based and therefore can achieve true gigabit speeds. This means that, assuming your cabling is good, the traffic flowing between your switches can actually flow at 1,000 Mbps, regardless of the limits on other gigabit connections on your network.

The next thing I'd recommend is installing two gigabit NICs in each server. One of the gigabit NICs should be attached to one of your switches. Since workstations are also connected to the switches (but at lower speeds), this allows traffic to flow between the workstations and the servers. The reason for implementing this architecture is that it prevents a server's network interface from becoming a bottleneck.

For example, suppose that a workstation with a 100-Mbps NIC began a very network-intensive operation, such as copying a huge file off a server. If the server and the workstation both have 100-Mbps NICs, then it would be possible for the workstation to consume most of the server's available bandwidth. Of course, there are situations that would prevent this from happening, such as when traffic is already excessively high or when QoS is in use. But generally speaking, if the workstation consumes most of the server's bandwidth, there's little left for anything else. However, if the workstation has a 100-Mbps NIC and the server has a gigabit

NIC, then the workstation won't even come close to consuming all of the available bandwidth.

I'd recommend using the server's second NIC to connect to a dedicated switch that is linked only to servers (not workstations). Having a dedicated backbone between the servers makes it possible for server-related traffic, such as that generated by replication and other network functions, to flow through a dedicated network without placing any traffic on the main network.

I'd also suggest implementing specific gigabit connections with fiber-optic cable. Use fiber for any connection to a switch or server, and for any gigabit connection that requires a cable run exceeding 100 meters or that flows through an area in which radio interference, crosstalk, or attenuation might be a problem.

You should run your workstations at 100 Mbps for reasons that I explained earlier. As Gigabit Ethernet NICs become cheaper, you may later want to upgrade your desktop computers to gigabit speeds. If you do, however, I strongly advise that you run copper cable to the desktops. I've seen far too many cases of cable abuse over the years to recommend running a fiber-optic cable to someone's desk. Fiber-optic cable is too delicate to survive the abuse that users can subject a cable to.

Pump up the volume

Although relatively few people are using it compared to other forms of Ethernet, Gigabit Ethernet is quickly becoming more affordable, and eventually it will be as widely used as Fast Ethernet is today. Planning for Gigabit Ethernet today will save you money and effort when you eventually make the switch. Before you know it, you'll be running your network at gigabit speeds and wondering how it ever worked when it was slower. ❖

Protocols and Services   **2**

A crash course in TCP/IP

By Brien M. Posey, MSCE

A t first glance, TCP/IP (Transmission Control Protocol/Internet Protocol) may seem baffling. Many other protocols, such as NetBEUI and IPX/SPX, require no configuration. TCP/IP is different. Due to the seemingly endless number of options that you can configure within TCP/IP, many people become intimidated at first. In reality, however, TCP/IP isn't very difficult, but you have to gain some understanding of what you're configuring. So, I'm going to give you a crash course in TCP/IP. Although I won't be able to explore every feature in detail, I'll cover the important points.

The IP address

The most basic element of TCP/IP is the IP address. The IP address is a number that's unique to each computer. If you know a computer's IP address, you can communicate with that computer from anywhere in the world. Since TCP/IP is the protocol that the Internet uses and since Internet servers are located all over the world, TCP/IP must be routable. Thus, when you try to access an IP address, your computer must be able to tell whether or not that IP address is located on your local network. If the desired address is located on your local network, you won't have a problem reaching it. If it isn't on your local network, TCP/IP must know which network the IP address is located on in order to reach the address.

The network number represents the network that contains a given IP address. If you look through the various tabs of the TCP/IP properties sheet, you'll see that there's no field that allows you to specify the network number. Instead, the network number is part of the IP address.

An IP address is composed of a network number and a computer number. Your computer can distinguish those two numbers because of something called the subnet mask. The subnet mask is located in a field directly below the IP address on the TCP/IP properties sheet. A simple subnet mask would be something like 255.255.0.0. The numbers that make up the subnet mask indicate which portion of the IP address is the network number and which portion is the computer number. The four numbers of the subnet mask correspond directly to the four numbers in the IP address. For example, if you had a computer with an IP address of 147.100.100.25 and a subnet mask of 255.255.0.0, the first two numbers in the subnet mask (both are 255) indicate that the first two numbers of the IP address are the network number. The second two numbers (both are 0) indicate that the second two numbers of the IP address are the computer number. Therefore, in the IP address 147.100.100.25, the 147.100 portion denotes which network the computer is located on, and the 100.25 portion represents a particular computer on that network. Of course, subnet masks become much more complex than this example. For instance, you can subdivide an individual network.

The default gateway

Now that you know how TCP/IP determines whether a destination address is located on a local network or on a foreign network, you may wonder how it attaches to a foreign network, especially if that network is halfway around the world. Well, it completes this job by using routing tables. Routing tables, which are stored in your routers, tell the router where to connect in certain situations.

You should note that one of the TCP/IP configuration options is for a default gateway. The default gateway is the address where a TCP/IP packet is sent if TCP/IP can't locate the destination IP address on the local network. Usually, the default gateway points to the router that controls your building's link to the outside world (often through an Internet connection). Since this router has a table of other routers, it knows the address and location of these routers. The destination IP address helps the router determine to which router to pass the packet. Typically, a TCP/IP packet is passed through several routers before it arrives on the destination network and, finally, on the destination PC.

DHCP

If all of this information is making your head spin, there's one TCP/IP feature that will make your life easier: Dynamic Host Configuration Protocol (DHCP). DHCP allows you to set one or more servers on your network to act as a DHCP server. When a client computer that's set to use the DHCP option comes online, the DHCP server automatically configures TCP/IP on this computer. Of course, you still have to configure the DHCP server, but using DHCP saves you from all of the effort of configuring each client manually. It also keeps you from accidentally using a particular IP address more than once. DHCP is also useful if you have a limited number of IP addresses to work with; only the computers that are turned on at a given moment will use IP addresses.

WINS

On Windows-based networks, each computer has a name. The WINS option can be configured to contain the IP address of a Windows NT Server that's running a WINS service. The WINS service resolves computer names (NetBIOS names) to IP addresses. Thus, if you try to access a computer by its name, your computer will go directly to the WINS database and search for the name and IP address. It won't have to query every computer on the network to determine the right IP address. As you can imagine, using WINS really cuts down on network traffic.

DNS

DNS functions similarly to WINS, except that it manages domain names rather than computer names. A domain name is the type of name that you use on the Internet. For example, Microsoft.com is a domain name. When you point your browser to

www.microsoft.com, your computer will query a DNS server for the IP address that corresponds to the domain name. If the DNS server doesn't know the address, it asks another DNS server. This process continues until a DNS server somewhere along the line knows the address. Then, that server informs your computer—and all of the other DNS servers that are involved—of the domain name's IP address.

Conclusion

TCP/IP is more intimidating than other protocols because there are so many different options to configure. I've provided you with a brief explanation of how TCP/IP works. Now, you should have a better understanding of those options. ❖

Understanding Windows 2000 Automatic Private IP Addressing

By Steven Pittsley, CNE

Managing TCP/IP can be one of the biggest headaches a network administrator can have. Normally, if you want to assign IP addresses to client machines, you only have two choices—statically assign addresses or install DHCP on a server. No more!

Microsoft has included the Windows 2000 Automatic Private IP Addressing (APIPA) feature with Windows 2000. You'll find this to be helpful because it allows you to reap the benefits of automatic IP addressing without having to configure a DHCP server. However, APIPA can give network administrators a few headaches when it is enabled on your Windows 2000 Professional workstations. This article will provide you with an overview of this interesting new feature, showing you when it can be used to your advantage and when it should be disabled.

A quick review of DHCP

DHCP is a wonderful thing. When properly configured, DHCP reliably provides automatic IP addressing services on the network, relieving you of the burden that you face when manually assigning IP addresses to all of the devices that are on your network.

In case you've never worked with DHCP or aren't completely familiar with it, here's a quick look at the steps taken when a workstation tries to obtain an IP address from a DHCP server.

1. When the workstation starts, it searches for a DHCP server by broadcasting a DHCPDiscover message.

2. A DHCP server will respond with a DHCPOffer message. If a DHCP server doesn't respond with a DHCPOffer, the client's TCP/IP initialization fails. However, Windows 2000 Professional clients will continue to send DHCPDiscover messages in an attempt to lease a valid IP address.

3. When the client receives the DHCPOffer message, it will accept the offered address by replying to the DHCP server with a DHCPRequest message.

4. When the DHCP server receives the DHCPRequest, it will officially assign the IP address to the client and send a DHCPAck message, which will include information such as the default gateway and DNS server addresses.

5. The client uses the information in the DHCPAck message to complete its TCP/IP configuration.

Windows 2000 APIPA explained

To simplify IP addressing for novice users, Microsoft has added the APIPA feature in the DHCP request process described in the previous section. When APIPA is enabled and the workstation does not receive a DHCPOffer message from a DHCP server or is unable to renew the lease of an existing IP address, the Windows 2000 Professional DHCP client will assign itself an IP address.

Here's how it works. When a Windows 2000 Professional DHCP client fails to contact a DHCP server with the DHCPDiscover message, it will assign itself a class B IP address that falls within the range of 169.254.0.1 to 169.254.255.254, using the appropriate subnet mask of 255.255.0.0. After selecting an IP address, the client will check the network to verify that its self-assigned IP address is not already in use. If the address is not in use, the TCP/IP client will be configured using the self-assigned IP address. If the client determines that the IP address is in use, it will assign itself another address and perform the duplicate address check again. This check will be performed up to 10 times, after which it will fail and network services will not be started on the workstation.

Despite having a correctly configured TCP/IP stack that is using its self-assigned IP address, the Windows 2000 Professional client will continue searching for a DHCP server by broadcasting a DHCPDiscover message every five minutes. If a DHCP server is found, the normal address request process described above is followed and an appropriate DHCP-generated IP address is leased. The APIPA address will then be discarded.

Working with APIPA

To make APIPA easy to use for the nontechnical person, the APIPA service is enabled by default on a Windows 2000 Professional workstation. If your network has a single subnet with no routers and is not connected to the Internet, your IP addressing needs are taken care of. The clients will broadcast their DHCPDiscover messages, and when no DHCP server responds, APIPA will generate an IP address. Since all APIPA IP addresses use the 169.254 IP address range, all of the workstations on the network should be able to communicate with each other using these addresses. For the novice user, it doesn't get any easier.

When your Windows 2000 Professional workstations are connected to a multisegment network or to the Internet, the APIPA service should be disabled. To determine if

Figure A

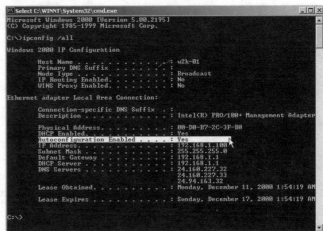

Typing IPCONFIG /ALL at the command prompt will show you if APIPA is enabled on that workstation.

APIPA is enabled on the workstation, type IPCONFIG /ALL at the command prompt. As shown in **Figure A**, the value of the Autoconfiguration Enabled field will be Yes.

There are two methods that you can use to disable APIPA on a Windows 2000 Professional workstation. First, you can manually assign an IP address to the workstation, which disables DHCP services. While this method does work, manually assigning IP addresses will soon become an administrative nightmare on all but the smallest of networks.

The more practical way to disable APIPA is by editing the registry settings on the workstation. Please note that editing the registry is dangerous and could result

Figure B

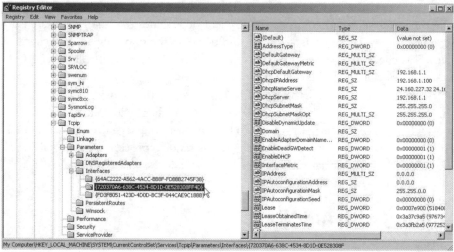

Edit the registry at the path shown above to disable APIPA.

Figure C

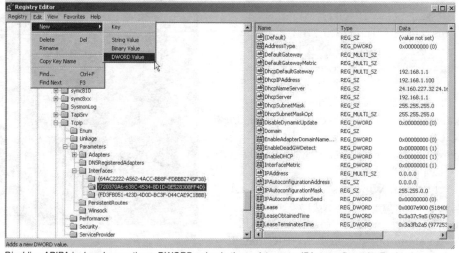

Disabling APIPA is done by creating a DWORD value in the registry entry IPAutoconfigurationEnabled.

in making your operating system unbootable. Always edit the registry with extreme caution. It's always advisable to back up your data first.

To begin disabling APIPA through the registry, run Regedit and drill down to the registry setting for the network adapter, as shown in **Figure B**. The path to the adapter is:

HKEY_LOCAL_MACHINE\SYSTEM\CurrentControlSet\Services\Tcpip\
  Parameters\Interfaces\<adapter>

To disable APIPA, you must add the registry entry IPAutoconfigurationEnabled. To do so, highlight the adapter and click the Edit menu. Choose New and then DWORD Value, as shown in **Figure C**.

Figure D

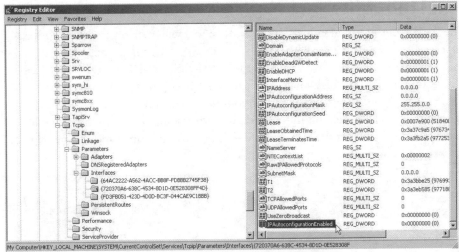

Once you add the value 0x0 and restart your workstation, APIPA will be disabled.

Figure E

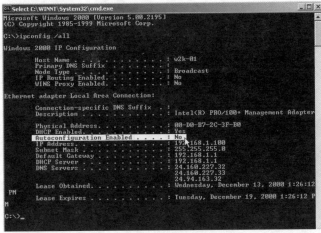

Use IPCONFIG /ALL again to verify that APIPA is disabled.

Add the registry entry as shown in **Figure D**, and ensure that the value is 0x0. When you have completed the entry, shut down and restart the workstation for the setting to take effect.

Once the workstation has restarted, you can use IPCONFIG /ALL from the command prompt to verify that Autoconfiguration Enabled is set to No, as shown in **Figure E**.

The registry entry that you just added will disable APIPA on just the one adapter. If your workstation has multiple network adapters installed, you can disable APIPA on all of them by adding the registry entry to:
HKEY_LOCAL_MACHINE\SYSTEM\CurrentControlSet\Services\Tcpip\
  Parameters\

Final thoughts

The APIPA service in Windows 2000 Professional will certainly make IP addressing easy for the novice user who has a small network. Unfortunately, those of us with larger networks are faced with a little extra work should we choose to disable this feature. If you use disk-imaging software such as Ghost, you'll only need to disable APIPA once for each image. If you must manually disable APIPA on each workstation, you'll have a bit more work, but after doing this a few times you'll see that, other than spelling the entry correctly, it doesn't add much more time to your workstation configuration. ❖

Understanding Internet connection sharing

By Debra Littlejohn Shinder, MCSE

The original purpose of networking computers together was to share hardware peripherals, like printers, and resources, such as data files and applications. Microsoft began to focus on setting up local area networks (LANs) and creating file and printer shares way back with Windows for Workgroups 3.11. It was not until the advent of Windows 98SE and Windows 2000, however, that a method was incorporated into the operating system to allow sharing of one very important resource: an Internet connection.

In this article, I'll discuss why connection sharing is needed, how an Internet connection can be shared among computers, and how translated connections work.

Why share an Internet connection?

As it became easier and more economically feasible for small and medium-size businesses and home users to go online in the 1990s, it also became obvious that a method was needed to allow multiple computers to access the Internet via one connection. In many offices and homes, the expense of separate phone lines, modems, and Internet service provider (ISP) accounts for each member of the firm or family was adding up fast. In the small business environment, allowing individual computer users to dial out via modems attached to their computers could present additional problems, including security risks.

Networking the computers and sharing one Internet connection over the LAN, just like sharing the connection to a printer, is the obvious solution. But it's not quite that simple; there are obstacles to overcome.

Overcoming obstacles to connection sharing

Communicating over the Internet uses the TCP/IP protocols, and one requirement of TCP/IP is that each computer on a network be assigned a unique IP address. This creates a problem if you want multiple computers to share an Internet connection. The typical dial-up account with an ISP (or cable modem or DSL connection) provides only one *public* IP address, which is dynamically assigned by the ISP to the modem when you establish the connection and is released when you hang up or are disconnected by the ISP server.

Public and private addressing

The IP addresses used to communicate on the Internet are *public* addresses. Ranges (blocks) of public addresses are assigned by the Internet Assigned Number Authority (IANA) to large organizations for use by computers on their networks and to ISPs for distribution to their customers. This ensures that there will be no duplication of addresses throughout the entire global Internet. Public addresses are also called registered addresses because they are registered with the IANA.

Several special blocks of addresses, called *private* or *reserved* addresses, are set aside by IANA and cannot be used on the public Internet. The Internet routers will not attempt to forward packets addressed to these private addresses.

The IP addresses allocated for private networks are specified in Request for Comments (RFC) 1597, which can be seen at **ftp://ftp.isi.edu/in-notes/rfc1597.txt**. These include the following three blocks of address space:

- 10.0.0.0 - 10.255.255.255
- 172.16.0.0 - 172.31.255.255
- 192.168.0.0 - 192.168.255.255

In addition to the private addresses, the address range 169.254.0.0 to 169.254.255.255 is reserved for the use of Microsoft's Automatic Private IP Addressing (APIPA), which allows computers that are configured as DHCP clients to assign themselves temporary IP addresses from the reserved range if they are unable to contact a DHCP server for address allocation.

The Internet Protocol (IP) uses the address to route data packets to the right computer. If several computers on a network share the same address, how will those packets get delivered to the correct machine? For example, if machine A sends an HTTP request over the Internet for a specified Web page, in order for the Web server responding to the request to send the page back to that machine's browser, it must know machine A's IP address (in addition to the port number, which is used to identify the application—in this case, the Web browser—making the request).

How, then, can different computers on a LAN communicate over the Internet using a single connection? There are two ways it can be done.

How does connection sharing work?

Multiple computers networked on a LAN can be connected to the Internet through one Internet connection by using a routed connection or a translated connection.

A *routed connection* requires either a dedicated routing device (such as a Cisco or other brand of router) or a Windows NT or 2000 server that has IP forwarding enabled to function as a software router. The key point to remember about routed connections is that, although they do allow you to connect to the Internet via a single modem and phone line (or other single physical connection point), they do not allow you to use a single public IP address. Every computer on the LAN that will communicate over the Internet must have its own unique IP address. Many ISPs charge extra to allocate multiple addresses.

A *translated connection,* on the other hand, does not require a separate hardware device, can be implemented without the expensive server operating system, and requires only one public registered IP address to connect all your LAN computers to the Internet.

Benefits of network address translation (NAT)

Network address translation (NAT) software has been around for a while. There are several third-party NAT solutions, such as Sygate (**www. sygate.com/products/ access_ov.htm**) and NAT32 (**www.nat32.com**), that were widely used to provide translated connections for computers running Windows 95 and NT 4.0.

With a translated connection, the computers on your LAN are assigned addresses from one of the private address ranges. The computer that is connected to the Internet (via modem, ISDN, DSL, or cable) is configured as the NAT host, which maps the Internet requests from the other computers (NAT clients) to a table that includes the client's private IP address and a port number. The NAT host then translates the address to the public IP address assigned to its external interface (such as a modem) and sends the packet out over the Internet. The table used to keep track of which computers on the LAN originate which requests is called the *address translation table*. This is how the host knows which internal computer should receive the response.

NAT IS NOT FOR EVERYTHING

Some applications and protocols do not work with NAT. This is because their packets don't contain the IP address in the IP header, or the TCP/UDP port is not in the TCP/UDP header. For example, IPSec cannot be used with address translation because the IP address is encapsulated inside the IPSec header. Some applications and services must be specially configured to work across the Internet.

With address translation, users on the LAN are able to send and receive data across the Internet using their Web browsers, e-mail clients, and other supported applications as if their computers were directly connected to the ISP. ❖

Setting up Internet connection sharing in Windows 2000 and 98SE

By Debra Littlejohn Shinder, MCSE

Though file and printer sharing has been around since Windows for Workgroups, it wasn't until the release of Windows 98SE and Windows 2000 that Microsoft gave us the ability to allow Internet connection sharing (ICS). In this article, I'll show you how to configure a shared Internet connection on a Windows 2000 Professional or Windows 98SE host computer. For background information, see "Understanding Internet connection sharing."

Microsoft's Internet connection sharing (ICS)

Windows 98SE, Me, and Windows 2000 all include network address translation (NAT) solutions so that you can connect your small network to the Internet without purchasing extra software. Microsoft calls this implementation of NAT Internet connection sharing (ICS). It is a lite version of NAT. (A more full-featured and configurable NAT is included in Windows 2000 Server.)

ICS can provide three basic services:

- Allocation of private IP addresses to the clients on the internal network
- Translation of private IP addresses to a single public address
- Name resolution

Because ICS provides address allocation and name resolution, it should *not* be used on a network that has a DHCP and/or DNS server. Doing so will cause a conflict between ICS and these services.

ICS is designed specifically for sharing an Internet connection on a small office/home office (SOHO) network that functions as a workgroup (peer-to-peer network). If you want to share an Internet connection on a Windows 2000 domain or a network with DHCP or DNS servers, you should use the NAT routing protocol—which is configured via the Routing and Remote Access (RRAS) console on a Windows 2000 server—instead of ICS.

Using ICS on Windows 2000 Professional and Windows 98SE

Although its functionality is the same on either operating system, enabling and configuring ICS is significantly different depending on whether you are using Windows 2000 or Windows 98SE. In this section, I'll show you how to set up ICS with both operating systems.

It is important to note that ICS is installed or enabled *only* on the computer that will share its connection to the Internet. The computer that will run ICS must have two connections: one to the internal network (LAN) and one to the Internet (a modem, ISDN or DSL terminal adapter, cable modem, etc.).

Installing and configuring ICS on Windows 98SE

In Windows 98SE, the first step is to install ICS. To do so, open the Add/Remove Programs applet in Control Panel. On the Windows Setup tab, select Internet Tools and click the Details button. In the dialog box presented, check Internet Connection Sharing, as shown in **Figure A**.

Click OK twice to exit the Windows Setup page, and you'll have ICS installed on your Windows 98SE computer. Note that you may be prompted to insert the Windows 98 CD installation disk. After the appropriate files are copied, the Internet Connection Sharing Wizard will start.

The wizard will walk you through the process of creating a Client Configuration disk, which is used to configure the other computers on your LAN that will connect to the Internet through ICS. (You can skip this step and configure the other computers manually if you prefer.)

You will be prompted to restart the computer, after which ICS will appear as an installed component in the computer's Network properties (accessed via the Network applet in Control Panel or by right-clicking the Network Neighborhood desktop icon and selecting Properties), as shown in **Figure B**.

Figure A

Install ICS in Windows 98SE via the Add/Remove Programs applet.

Figure B

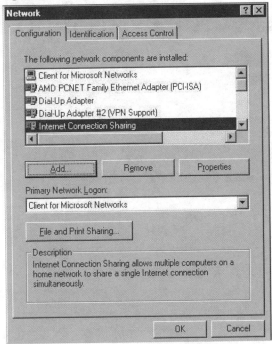

After you install ICS, it appears on the Configuration tab of the Network properties sheet.

Figure C

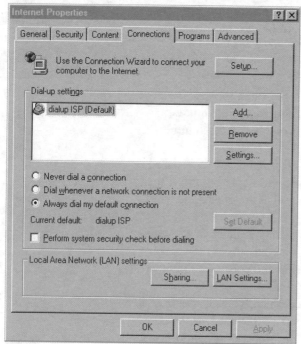

Click the Sharing button on the Connections tab of the Internet Properties sheet.

Figure D

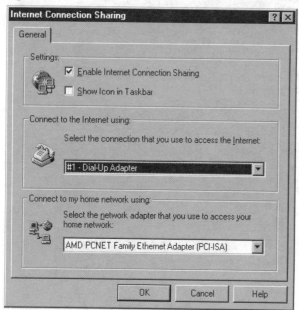

Enable and configure ICS with the Internet Connection Sharing properties sheet.

Now you can configure ICS properties. In Control Panel, open the Internet Options applet, select the Connections tab, as shown in **Figure C**, and then click the Sharing button.

On the General tab of the Internet Connection Sharing properties sheet (see **Figure D**), you can choose:

- To enable or disable ICS on this computer.
- To show or hide the ICS taskbar icon, which indicates how many computers are connected through ICS.
- The connection you use to access the Internet.
- The network adapter you use to connect to your LAN.

Once ICS is installed and configured on the host computer, you must configure the other computers on your LAN to connect through the ICS computer.

The ICS wizard sets the IP address for the ICS host computer's internal interface (the network card that connects to the LAN) to 192.168.0.1. There are two ways to set the IP addresses for the other computers on the LAN:

- **Use automatic addressing (preferred)**— In the TCP/IP properties of the network card for each client computer, select Obtain An IP Address Automatically. The ICS computer will act as a DHCP allocator and assign a different IP address on the 192.168.0.0 network to each computer.
- **Set IP addresses manually**—In the TCP/IP properties of the network card for each client computer, select Specify An IP Address and give each computer a different IP address on the 192.168.0.0 network (that is, 192.168.0.2, 192.168.0.3, etc.). Set the subnet mask for all computers to 255.255.255.0. Set the default gateway for all client computers to 192.168.0.1 (the IP address of the ICS host computer).

To set TCP/IP properties, select Network in Control Panel, select TCP/IP (<name of network adapter>) and then click the Properties button. The Properties sheet is shown in **Figure E**.

You can run the Client Configuration Disk created by the ICS wizard to configure the browser software on the client machines or skip to the section on configuring the browser's Internet options for Windows 2000 and follow the same steps.

Enabling ICS on Windows 2000 Professional

On Windows 2000 Professional, ICS functionality is built-in and does not have to be installed. Microsoft has simplified configuration of the host computer. To enable ICS on a connection that you want to share (for example, a dial-up connection to your ISP), open Start | Settings | Network And Dial-Up Connections. Right-click the connection to be shared and select Properties, as shown in **Figure F**.

This will open the Dial-Up Connection Properties sheet. Select the Sharing tab, as shown in **Figure G**.

If the connection being shared is a dial-up connection, you can enable on-demand dialing, which will cause the ICS host to dial up and connect to the ISP whenever an ICS client computer tries to access an external resource (for example, when the user enters a Web site URL that is outside the LAN or attempts to send or check Internet e-mail).

If you have network applications that you want to configure for the client computers, click Settings. You can add applications on the Applications tab. You will need to

Figure E

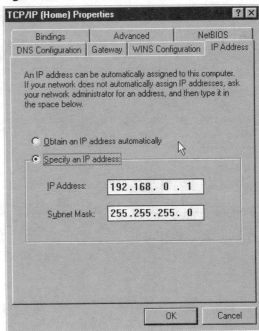

ICS can assign IP addresses automatically, or you can configure them manually.

Figure F

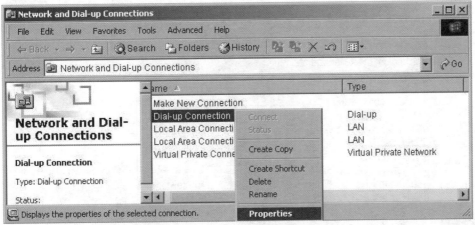

Right-click the connection you want to share and select Properties from the drop-down menu.

Figure G

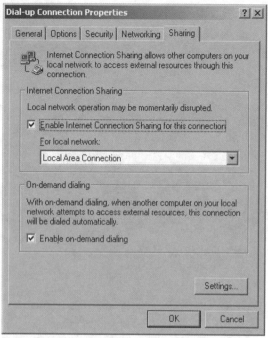

Enable ICS on the Sharing tab of the selected connection's properties sheet.

Figure H

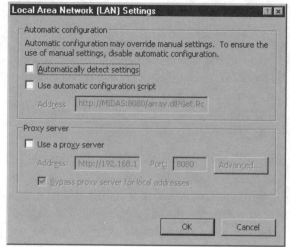

Clear all check boxes in the Microsoft Internet Explorer LAN Settings dialog box.

Figure I

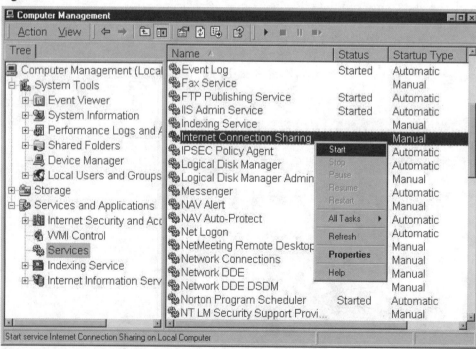

Ensure that the Internet Connection Sharing service is started using the Computer Management MMC.

know the TCP/UDP port numbers on your network to which the applications will connect. Likewise, you can configure services using the Services tab.

The clients that will access the Internet through the Windows 2000 ICS computer must be configured to obtain an IP address automatically (as described above). The ICS host computer's internal interface will be set to 192.168.0.1 and it will become a DHCP allocator, assigning IP addresses to the other computers on the LAN. The default gateway for each ICS client will be provided automatically. The ICS computer will also act as a DNS proxy to resolve fully qualified domain names (such as the URL entered in a Web browser) to Internet IP addresses.

Configuring your browser's Internet options

Ensure that the browser settings on the ICS clients (on Microsoft Internet Explorer, these setting are located in Tools | Internet Options | Connections | LAN Settings) are configured as follows (see **Figure H**):

- Do *not* set the browser to automatically detect settings (clear the check box).
- Do *not* set the browser to use automatic configuration script (clear the check box).
- Do *not* set the browser to use a proxy server (clear the check box).

The Internet connection should be set to Never Dial A Connection on the Connections tab.

Troubleshooting ICS problems

If you have set up ICS on the host computer, but users are unable to connect to the Internet from the client computers on the LAN, check the following:

- Ensure that TCP/IP is installed on the ICS clients and configured to obtain an IP address automatically. DNS should be set to obtain a DNS server automatically, and no default gateway should be specified. (The ICS host, acting as a DHCP allocator, will provide the clients with this information.)
- Ensure that the Internet options in the browser settings are configured as described in this article.
- Check that connection sharing is enabled on the correct adapter on the host computer. This must be the adapter that connects the host computer to the Internet.
- Ensure that the Internet Connection Sharing service is started.

Figure J

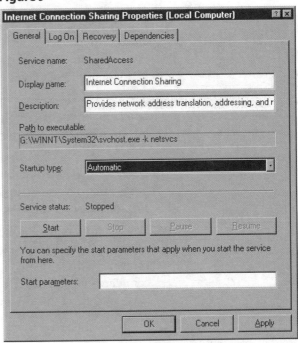

You can configure the service's properties to start automatically when Windows starts.

To check the status of the ICS service on a computer running Windows 2000 Professional, open the Computer Management console (right-click the My Computer desktop icon and select Manage), expand the Services And Applications node in the left console pane, and click Services. In the details pane, note the status of the Internet Connection Sharing service, as shown in **Figure I**.

If the service is not started, you can right-click it and select Start. You can change the start-up mode from Manual to Automatic by selecting Properties and configuring the properties sheet, as shown in **Figure J**.

More troubleshooting help

The following Q&As address some other common problems you may encounter in setting up a shared connection.

Q: After I enabled ICS on my computer, the computer lost connectivity to other TCP/IP computers on my LAN. What went wrong?

A: When you enable ICS on a host computer, its LAN card's IP address is automatically set to 192.168.0.1. If you were communicating with other computers on the local network using TCP/IP and static IP addresses on a network other than 192.168.x.x, you would no longer be able to communicate with them because your ICS computer would be on a different subnet. You need to set the TCP/IP properties of computers to obtain an IP address automatically. The ICS host will allocate IP addresses to them, and you will be able to communicate with them again.

Q: I enabled ICS on my Windows 2000 Professional computer and configured the ICS clients. I dialed up to the Internet and was able to browse the Web from the client computers. However, my ISP periodically disconnects my modem if it is idle for a time. When this happens, I can no longer access the Web from the ICS clients without going to the host computer and dialing the ISP.

A: You need to ensure that Enable On-Demand Dialing is checked on the Sharing tab of the Properties sheet for the Internet connection. This causes the ICS host to initiate a connection to the ISP whenever one of the ICS clients tries to access Internet resources.

Q: I want to share my Windows 2000 Professional computer's Internet connection, but I want to use a different private address range on my LAN instead of the 192.168.0.0 network. How can I do that?

A: You cannot modify the address range used by ICS, nor can you disable the DNS proxy or configure inbound mappings. If you need to do any of these things, you will need to use NAT (on a Windows 2000 Server) instead of ICS. NAT is configured via the RRAS console on the server computer and will work if you have a Windows 2000 domain controller, DNS server, or DHCP server on the network. ❖

Explaining that mysterious DNS

By Bryan Pfaffenberger

W hy not configure your own DNS server? It's easy—and what's more, you'll see a big payoff in the increased speed with which you can access the Web. Here's a conceptual introduction to the domain name service (DNS).

IP addresses

Viewed from the computer's perspective, the Internet is a vast field of numerical addresses—the so-called "dotted quad" addresses (such as 64.58.76.177) that you sometimes see when you're filling out information in network configuration dialog boxes. What you're seeing is an *IP address,* a 32-bit number that precisely identifies the location of a specific computer on the Internet. Generally, people don't like working with such numbers. For one thing, the numbers are hard to remember. What's more, the data you're looking for might move from one computer to the next. If you had to work with nothing but numerical IP addresses, using the Internet wouldn't be much fun. You'd have to keep track of lots of hard-to-remember IP addresses, and you'd have to keep your list updated so that you could locate the data you needed when its physical location changed. That's precisely why the Domain Name System was invented.

In brief

Briefly, the Domain Name System creates a human-friendly nomenclature for identifying Internet locations. In the example *www.techrepublic.com*, for instance, the first part—*www*—is the name of a specific network location within the techrepublic.com domain—and as you probably know, it's a "dot-com" domain because of the "com" appended to the name. A numerical IP address is still needed to access www.tech-republic.com, however. How does your Web browser obtain this address?

DNS explained

The *domain name service* (DNS) takes care of translating between human-friendly names (such as www.techrepublic.com) and those pesky numerical addresses. When you access the Internet, you fill out a networking dialog box that specifies the IP address of your service provider's DNS server, which lists the location of a given site in its massive, memory-based cache of linked domain names and IP addresses (or it knows how to ask another DNS server how to obtain the needed information). When you use your Web browser and click on an address such as *http://www.techrepublic.com*, your Web browser contacts the DNS server you've configured, submits the domain name information (www.techrepublic.com), and receives the IP address in reply. Your browser then uses the numerical IP address to access TechRepublic.

The DNS solves both of the major problems that existed before it was invented. First, it gives users a way of remembering specific Internet locations that's much better than using numerical IP addresses. Second, it enables Internet content providers to move data around without requiring every Internet user to memorize a new IP address. This is accomplished by means of domain name registration, a process in which an independent, third-party agency keeps track of the relationship between user-friendly domain names (such as www.techrepublic.com) and IP addresses (such as 64.58.76.177). Should TechRepublic decide to move its home page to a different location, it's easily done; the company contacts the registration agency and notifies the agency of the change. Meanwhile, certain authoritative DNS servers propagate the new address throughout the network so that, within a few hours, the whole Internet "knows" the new location.

If you're using Windows 2000, Linux, or UNIX, you can communicate with a DNS server without the aid of a Web browser. In Windows 2000, open a command window; in Linux or UNIX, launch a terminal window within X. Now type *nslookup www.techrepublic.com* and press [Enter]. The nslookup utility contacts the DNS server you've configured, obtains the IP addresses currently associated with this domain (as you'll see, there's more than one of them), and reports those addresses to you. Pretty cool, huh? (You need to be connected to the Internet in order for this command to do its trick.)

Now try accessing a new Web site—one that you haven't yet visited today—with your Web browser, and keep your eye on your browser's status line. You'll see that the process of accessing this site is indeed a two-step affair. In Internet Explorer, you'll first see the message Finding Site. In this phase, the browser is contacting the DNS server to obtain the site's IP address. When the browser locates the address, you'll see the message Web Site Found. At this point, the browser uses the numerical IP address to request the Web page you're after. You don't see the numerical IP address, but you do see the message Opening Page followed by Done. Try this a few more times, but always with sites you haven't yet accessed; if you redisplay a site you've already visited today, your browser will retrieve the page from its local cache, not the Internet, so the two-step process doesn't occur. But for the new sites, it's strictly one-two, one-two— and it's time consuming.

The time required to perform both of these steps (obtaining the numerical IP address from the DNS server and then requesting the page) starts to seem inordinately lengthy when you're accessing the Internet by any kind of dial-up connection. Why not cut one of these steps out completely? Technically, it's not that difficult to configure any reasonably capable, server-oriented operating system (such as Windows 2000 or Linux) to run a DNS server, and there's a huge payoff for doing so. Because you're running the server locally, your Web browser (as well as other Internet utilities) does not always have to go out to the network to retrieve the numerical IP address you need. The more you use your local DNS server, the more IP addresses it learns, until you get to a point that almost all of the sites you've accessed can be obtained by contacting the local server. The result is what appears to be significantly faster Internet access—and believe me, you'll love it. ❖

Using DNS Lookup with Windows

By Jim McIntyre

Whenever you browse the WWW or send an e-mail message, a domain name is used to send or receive information. Uniform Resource Locators (URLs), such as http://www.techrepublic.com, and e-mail addresses like jcmcintyre@yahoo.ca are easy for users to remember but are almost useless to computers. The Domain Name Service (DNS) is used to map the relationships between a human-readable hostname and the IP addresses associated with that hostname. DNS may also be used in reverse, mapping an IP address to a hostname. This chapter explains how two freeware DNS search tools available for use with Windows 9x, NT, and Windows 2000 may be used to provide DNS information. A full explanation of DNS is beyond the scope of this article, in which I'll assume that you have a basic knowledge of TCP/IP and DNS terminology.

Getting Sam Spade

I looked at a lot of DNS search tools while I was writing this article, and the one I prefer to work with is Sam Spade (**http://www.samspade.org/ssw/**). This utility has several good features:

- All tasks are multithreaded. Several queries may be run simultaneously.
- The output from searches is hotlinked. Simply click on an e-mail address, IP address, or hostname to run another query.
- Search results are easily logged.
- Sam Spade includes extensive online help.

Check out the home page for Sam Spade to find the latest version. Once you have downloaded it, simply double-click the icon to begin the installation procedure.

Configuring and running Sam Spade

Before you run Sam Spade, the program must be configured using the following procedure:

1. Within the application, navigate through Select | Edit | Options and click the Basics tab (see **Figure A**).

2. Enter the IP address of your DNS server, the maximum number of simultaneous connections (100 is plenty), and the IP address of your ISP's Web server.

Figure A

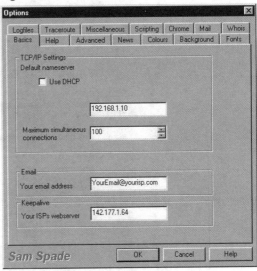

The Sam Spade configuration menu

3. When the correct information is entered, click on the Advanced tab. When the Advanced menu is active, activate the following three options by clicking on the check box:

- Enable Zone Transfers: Enables DNS Zone Transfers
- Enable Active Probing: Enables Port Scanning
- Enable Relay Checking: Enables Checking For An Insecure Mailserver

Once these entries are made, you're ready to run Sam Spade. Sam Spade includes several useful options for tracking down DNS-related information, including:

- **ping:** Used to see if a network host is alive and how long it takes IP packets to reach the host.

- **nslookup:** Finds the IP address associated with a hostname or the hostname associated with an IP address.

- **dig**: This tool is another form of nslookup. The dig utility will ask a DNS server for all information about a host by default.

- **traceroute:** Used to determine the route an IP packet takes from your system to a remote host.

- **finger:** Determines user information on a remote UNIX host.

- **SMTP VRFY**: Used to query an e-mail address to determine whether the address is valid and if the address is being forwarded.

- **whois:** Queries a whois server about who owns a domain name.

Figure B

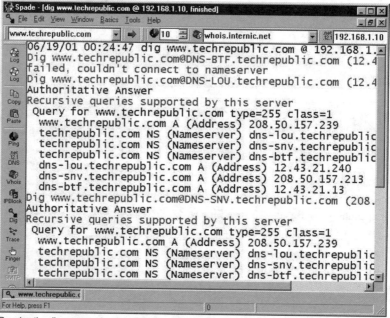

Running the dig command on www.techrepublic.com.

- **ip block whois**: Asks a whois server who owns a block of IP addresses.
- **Web browser**: The Sam Spade Web browser downloads the actual code used for a Web page, including the http headers and raw HTML. This feature is very useful for troubleshooting CGI scripts. In addition, because only the raw code is downloaded, features such as hidden form fields and white-on-white text can be exposed.

Once you have Sam Spade installed and configured, you're ready to start searching for DNS information. When Sam Spade is run, you will be presented with the window shown in **Figure B**. In this example, the result of running the dig command on www.techrepublic.com is shown. The utility allows users to select commands either from the icons on the left-hand edge of the window or from the Basics or Tools menus.

Figure C

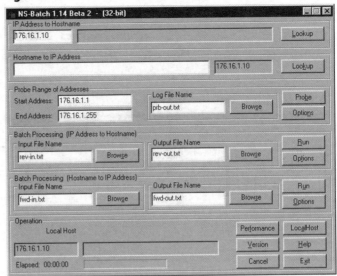

NS-Batch search screenties sheet.

You will probably find that Sam Spade is a welcome addition to your toolkit. Sam Spade is a utility worth considering if you need a powerful, flexible, and free DNS search tool for Windows.

NS-Batch for Windows

Another good freeware DNS search tool for Windows is NS-Batch (**www.jim-price.com/jim-soft.htm**). NS-Batch performs five basic, yet important, functions:
- Maps single hostname to IP address
- Maps single IP address to hostname
- Probes all IP addresses on a specified subnet and prints the probe results to a specified ASCII text file
- Uses an ASCII text file to input a list of hostnames to map to IP addresses
- Uses an ASCII text file to input a list of IP addresses to map to hostnames

The NS-Batch search screen is shown in **Figure C**.

NS-Batch lacks the flexibility of Sam Spade, but it is still very useful for administrators who need a tool capable of providing usable DNS-related information. The real strength of NS-Batch lies in its ability to accept search criteria from input files and then write or append search results to ASCII text files. Search results are displayed in the following order:
- The hexadecimal notation for the host IP address
- The host IP address in dot notation

- The hostname corresponding to the IP address
- The hostname in reverse notation
- The number of times (count) the IP address was found in the input file

Figure D shows the output generated when IP addresses from 192.168.1.1 to 192.168.1.20 are probed.

Figure D

```
test - Notepad
File  Edit  Search  Help
HexAddress,DecimalAddress,Hostname,RevOrderHostname,RevHostName,Status,Count
c0a80104,192.168.1.4,NotFound,NotFound,NotFound,,1
c0a80101,192.168.1.1,wolf01.wolf,wolf.wolf01,wolf01.wolf,FailedFwd,1
c0a80102,192.168.1.2,wolf02.wolf,wolf.wolf02,wolf02.wolf,FailedFwd,1
c0a80103,192.168.1.3,wolf03.wolf,wolf.wolf03,wolf03.wolf,FailedFwd,1
c0a80106,192.168.1.6,NotFound,NotFound,NotFound,,1
c0a80105,192.168.1.5,roundpipe.wolf,wolf.roundpipe,roundpipe.wolf,FailedNameLookup,1
c0a80107,192.168.1.7,NotFound,NotFound,NotFound,,1
c0a80108,192.168.1.8,NotFound,NotFound,NotFound,,1
c0a80109,192.168.1.9,NotFound,NotFound,NotFound,,1
c0a8010a,192.168.1.10,dns1.wolf,wolf.dns1,dns1.wolf,OK,1
c0a8010b,192.168.1.11,dhcp.wolf,wolf.dhcp,dhcp.wolf,OK,1
c0a8010c,192.168.1.12,ares.wolf,wolf.ares,ares.wolf,FailedFwd,1
c0a8010d,192.168.1.13,cst.wolf,wolf.cst,cst.wolf,OK,1
c0a8010e,192.168.1.14,cub.wolf,wolf.cub,cub.wolf,FailedNameLookup,1
```

NS-Batch search results

Once this information is available in ASCII text format, any word processor may be used to analyze the information. NS-Batch is very useful for administrators who want to perform DNS searches in Windows without having to deal with a complex interface.

Conclusion

The ability to perform DNS-related searches in Windows can easily be enhanced with the addition of some freeware tools. In this chapter, I covered some of the main features of two of these tools. Sam Spade is capable of performing DNS searches based on almost any criteria. NS-Batch is a much simpler tool, but it provides a very simple interface and makes search results available through ASCII text files. I encourage Windows users to try these and similar utilities. These tools provide a lot of information for experienced administrators and are great learning tools for less experienced users. ❖

How to migrate DNS information to Windows Server 2003

By William C. Schmied

Under Windows NT, DNS was a nice service to have on your server for resolving TCP/IP addresses, but it wasn't necessary. When Microsoft introduced Active Directory and Windows 2000, DNS became an essential service. If you've already deployed DNS on your network, you can save a lot of time and effort in your Windows Server 2003 deployment by migrating that information. Here's how.

Your options

There are two different ways you can migrate your DNS to Windows Server 2003—although one is definitely better than the other. Your available options are:

- Manually performing a zone transfer
- Manually copying the zone data files

It is recommended that you manually initiate a zone transfer to transfer the zone data from the old server to the new Windows Server 2003 DNS server, as it usually results in fewer errors. Should you decide to go ahead and manually copy the zone data files, you need to manually verify the integrity of the zones. As well, you cannot directly migrate to an Active Directory-integrated zone when you manually copy the zone data files—Active Directory-integrated zones do not use the standard zone data files that you would be able to copy from one location to another. If you are currently using standard zones and your long-range goal is to move to Active Directory-integrated zones, you will be able to do so after migrating the zone data using either available method.

Zone transfers

The easiest, and most preferred method, to migrate your DNS zone data is to manually imitate a zone transfer from the DNS server you are replacing to your new Windows Server 2003 DNS server. But what does this really entail? What must you do ahead of time?

You first should determine what type of DNS system you are migrating from. Is it a Windows NT 4.0 or UNIX BIND system that uses only standard DNS zone servers? Or is it a Windows 2000 Server-based system that is currently operating with an Active Directory-integrated zone? Migrating Active Directory-integrated zones is a simple task—just add the new server to the Name Servers tab of the zone properties and ensure that the new server is authorized to perform zone replication with the zone. Once DNS is operating properly on the new Windows Server 2003, you can then remove it from the Windows 2000 Server, if desired.

If you are migrating from a system that uses standard DNS zones, things get a little more complicated—but don't worry, it's still quite easy. The first thing to remember about zone transfers is how the standard DNS zone servers are arranged. Standard DNS zones operate in a single master arrangement where only one DNS server has the master writable copy of the DNS zone data. All other servers have read only copies. The two types of standard zone servers you may encounter are:

- **Standard primary server**: This server is the one that holds the one and only master writable copy of the zone data file. The zone data file is then replicated (via zone transfer) to all configured secondary zone servers using the standard zone data file text format. This server must make all the changes that must be made to the zone data file.

- **Standard secondary server**: This server holds a read-only copy of the zone data file in standard zone data file text format. Secondary zones can be created and used for many reasons, but the most common reason is to provide increased performance and redundancy for the DNS zone. Secondary zones are commonly seen in locations such as screen subnets (the DMZ) or in remote offices connected to the central office over a low-speed WAN link.

So, as you might suspect, in order to migrate your DNS zone data to a Windows Server 2003 computer, you will need to have a functioning standard primary server. You will also need to make the new Windows Server 2003 DNS server a standard secondary server in that zone by creating a new standard secondary zone on that server. Once this has been done, you will need to configure the standard primary server to allow zone transfers with the new Windows Server 2003 computer.

To create a new standard secondary zone, right-click on the Forward Lookup Zones node in your DNS console.

Be careful to select a secondary zone. Also be careful to specify the correct zone name (it must be spelled exactly the same as it is on the other DNS server) and the IP address of the DNS server hosting the zone file. When you are done, you will see your new zone in the Forward Lookup Zones node of the DNS console. To start the zone transfer, right-click on the new standard secondary zone and select Transfer From Master.

Once you have verified that the new standard secondary zone is functioning properly, you can decommission the existing primary zone server. You will now need to quickly change the secondary zone into a primary zone. For even better performance and security, you should consider making it Active Directory-integrated. Either way, you will need to right-click on the zone node and open the Properties dialog box. On the General tab, click the Change button in the Type area. This will open the dialog box that allows you to change the zone into a standard primary zone or an Active Directory-integrated zone, as desired. You will be prompted to confirm your decision.

If you change the zone into an Active Directory integrated zone, it will, by default, be configured to not use dynamic updates. From the General tab of the Zone Properties dialog box, you should change this setting as soon as you can to Secure Only to allow the greatest flexibility and security of your zone data.

Alternatively, you can perform the zone transfer method from the command line using the following command:

```
dnscmd ServerName /ZoneRefresh ZoneName
```

Again, you will need to have the standard primary zone server available and the secondary zone already created on the new Windows Server 2003 server before performing the zone transfer. You can, of course, create the standard secondary zone on your Windows Server 2003 DNS server from the command line as well by issuing this command:

```
dnscmd ServerName /ZoneAdd ZoneName /Secondary MasterIPaddress...
  [/file FileName
```

You can specify multiple IP addresses by separating them with a comma. The FileName value must be the exact file name of the standard primary zone, just the same as when you are creating the zone via the DNS console.

Manually copying zone data

Should you still want to manually copy your zone data, you can locate it in the following locations:

- Windows NT 4.0 Server: %systemroot%\system32\dns
- Windows 2000 Server: %systemroot%\system32\dns
- Windows Server 2003: %systemroot%\system32\dns

If you are copying a BIND DNS zone file, **Table A** provides you with the naming conventions used by BIND DNS and Windows Server 2003 DNS.

Thus, the forward lookup zone data file for the mcseworld.local zone would be named db.mcseworld.local on the BIND server and would need to be renamed to mcseworld.local.dns on the Windows Server 2003 computer. If the zone data was for the IP address range of 192.168.100.x, then the BIND server reverse lookup file would be db.192.168.100 and would need to be renamed to 100.168.192.in-addr.arpa.dns on the Windows Server 2003 computer.

Table A

Description	UNIX file name	Windows Server 2003 file name
Boot file	named.boot	Boot
Forward lookup zone file	db.*domain_name*	*domain_name.dns*
Reverse lookup zone file	db.*IP_network_forward_notation*	*IP_network*

Wrap up

That's about all there is to migrating your Windows NT 4.0 or Windows 2000 Server DNS zones to a new Windows Server 2003 computer. As long as you execute the process in the steps I've outlined here, you should encounter no problems. ❖

Tweak Win2K Server registry to improve TCP/IP performance

By Brien M. Posey, MCSE

Windows 2000 Server's TCP/IP Properties Sheet is a little deceptive in giving the impression that basic information, such as an IP address, subnet mask, default gateway, or DNS server, is all that's required to create connections. There's much more to TCP/IP than meets the eye; Windows simply requires a minimal amount of operator input and then establishes a TCP/IP connection based on that information and several preset options.

Unfortunately, an easy configuration doesn't always equal optimal performance. I'm going to show you various registry keys you can modify to increase TCP/IP performance on a Windows 2000 Server.

DANGER!

Modifying the registry is dangerous. Making an incorrect registry change can destroy Windows and/or your applications. Likewise, changing the TCP/IP registry keys can sometimes have an adverse effect on performance. Make a full system backup before you try any of the techniques described in this article. If you decide to tweak TCP/IP, you should make one change at a time (unless otherwise noted). Get a feel for the change that you've made before making any other changes. Some of the registry keys that I'll be showing you can have a rather dramatic effect when changed. To gain optimum results from the changes, you should make them to all of the servers and workstations on your network.

Adjusting the Maximum Transmission Unit size

Of all the registry tweaks that I've found for TCP/IP, perhaps the most useful is the ability to adjust the Maximum Transmission Unit (MTU) size. MTU size dictates the maximum packet size (in bytes) that the TCP/IP transport will attempt to transmit over the underlying network. Networks that use Internet Connection Sharing (ICS) or Point-to-Point Protocol over Ethernet (PPPoE) for their broadband connections must have an MTU size of 1,492 or lower to run efficiently.

An incorrect MTU size can make your network run slowly. Administrators tend to dismiss this problem as low bandwidth on the ISP's end, and that might be a source of the problem. But you'd be surprised at the difference an MTU adjustment can make.

The MTU is such a factor because, by default, Windows 2000 and Windows XP set the MTU size to 1,500. It's been my experience that if a network is running slowly, even the 1,492 value I mentioned earlier is too high. I usually have the best luck by setting the MTU to around 1,454.

You can check the MTU size for your environment by opening a command prompt on your administration workstation and typing

```
PING -F -I <MTUsize> <gateway>
```

where *MTUsize* is the size you want to experiment with and *gateway* is the gateway of your network. Start out by using an MTU size of 1,454. Doing so will make the command look something like this:

```
PING -F -I 1454 147.100.100.50
```

When you enter the command, the PING will either be successful or it will fail with a message stating that the data must be fragmented. If you receive the error message, decrease the MTU value and keep trying until you find a value that works. If the PING command works the first time, try incrementing the value by five or 10 until you see the error message. You can then narrow down to the appropriate value.

Once you've discovered an MTU size that works, the next trick is to embed the value into the registry. The key's actual location within the registry varies depending on the version of Windows you're using. If you're using Windows NT, the MTU key is located at:

```
HKEY_LOCAL_MACHINE\SYSTEM\CurrentControlSet\Services\Parameters\
  Tcpip
```

If you're using Windows 2000 or higher, the MTU key is located at:

```
HKEY_LOCAL_MACHINE\SYSTEM\CurrentControlSet\Services\Tcpip\
  Parameters\Interfaces\adapter ID
```

There's a good chance that the MTU key doesn't presently exist in your system and that you'll have to create it at the specified location. To do so, open the Registry Editor and create a new DWORD value called MTU. The minimum value for this key is 68, and the maximum value is the MTU for the underlying network.

Other MTU-related registry keys

Once you've set the MTU value for a PC or server, you may want to tweak some other MTU-related registry keys.

EnablePMTUDiscovery

Remote networks also have an MTU value, which is almost always different from that of the local network. Enabling this registry key tells TCP/IP to try to automatically detect the MTU for all networks along the path to a remote host. Once TCP/IP knows the MTU for all networks along a path, it can avoid using MTU values that that are too high, thus avoiding packet fragmentation and the performance problems that come with it.

The EnablePMTUDiscovery key doesn't exist in the registry unless you create it. However, this feature is enabled by default, so you would normally create this registry key only if you wanted to disable path MTU detection or experiment with turning path MTU detection on and off.

You would create the EnablePMTUDiscovery key at:

```
HKEY_LOCAL_MACHINE\SYSTEM\CurrentControlSet\Services\Tcpip\
  Parameters
```

If you decide to create the EnablePMTUDiscovery key, the key must be a DWORD key, which is assigned a Boolean value. Assigning the key a value of 1 enables path MTU discovery, while assigning the key a 0 disables it.

If you choose to disable path MTU discovery, TCP/IP uses a default MTU size of 576 bytes for all communications across remote networks. While 576 bytes certainly isn't an optimal packet size, at least you won't have to worry about packet fragmentation. I personally recommend leaving the path MTU discovery feature enabled unless you're having problems reaching remote hosts.

EnablePMTUBHDetect

If you're having remote communication trouble, the problem could be related to a black hole router. Black hole routers are configured not to return the Destination Host Unreachable messages that are used by path MTU discovery. Normally, when TCP/IP performs path MTU discovery, the process works by sending out a packet of data with the DF (Don't Fragment) bit set. If the PC sending out the packet receives a Destination Host Unreachable message, it means that the MTU for that particular network may be too high; in this case, TCP/IP will try to use a lower value.

If you want TCP/IP to detect black hole routers, you must create a registry key called EnablePMTUBHDetect beneath:

```
HKEY_LOCAL_MACHINE\SYSTEM\CurrentControlSet\Services\Tcpip\
  Parameters
```

The key must be a DWORD key with a Boolean value. Setting the key to 1 enables black hole detection, while setting the key to 0 disables black hole detection.

Black hole detection is disabled by default because enabling it increases the number of transmission retries when communicating with a host. This means that a lot of bandwidth can be consumed during the early phases of path MTU detection, and the initial connection to a host may be slower than normal.

The router packet queue

Windows NT, 2000, and XP can each function as routers between networks. By default, the routing function is disabled for security reasons. You can enable packet routing by navigating through the registry to:

```
HKEY_LOCAL_MACHINE\SYSTEM\CurrentControlSet\Services\Tcpip\
  Parameters
```

and setting the IPEnableRouter key to a Boolean value of 1.

If you choose to enable packet routing, there are several ways to optimize the routing process. The Windows implementation of TCP/IP has a built-in router cache and queue that are active only when the routing function has been enabled.

ForwardBufferMemory

Earlier, I showed you how to adjust your MTU value. If you've adjusted your MTU size, you may also want to adjust your forward buffer memory. The forward buffer memory controls how much RAM TCP/IP uses for storing packet data in the router packet queue.

Each packet queue data buffer is 256 bytes long. So, if you choose to set this registry key, the number you specify must be a multiple of 256. The default value is 74,240, which will accommodate 50 1,480-byte packets.

To set the number of packet queue data buffers, create a registry key called ForwardBufferMemory beneath:

```
HKEY_LOCAL_MACHINE\SYSTEM\CurrentControlSet\Services\Tcpip\
    Parameters
```

The key must be a DWORD value that's assigned the number of bytes of memory you want to allocate. The minimum value must never be smaller than your MTU size. Therefore, if your MTU size is 1,454, your minimum ForwardBufferMemory size would also be 1,454. The maximum size is 0xFFFFFFFF. However, I recommend keeping the value at a reasonable size.

For example, if your MTU is set to 1,454, I recommend setting ForwardBufferMemory to 50 to 100 times the MTU size. To keep the math easy, 100 times the MTU size of 1,454 would be 145,400. If you divide 145,400 by 256, you get 567.96875. Since 145,400 isn't evenly divisible by 256, take your answer and round it to the next highest whole number, 568. Now, multiply 568 by 256 to get 145,408. This would be the appropriate ForwardBufferMemory setting.

In case you're curious, just because each buffer is 256 bytes doesn't mean that your packets must also be 256 bytes long. When a packet length exceeds the buffer length, multiple buffers are used as needed to accommodate the packet. To save space, the packet's IP header is stored separately.

NumForwardPackets

Another registry key that may be of interest to you is the NumForwardPackets key located at:

```
HKEY_LOCAL_MACHINE\SYSTEM\CurrentControlSet\Services\Tcpip\
    Parameters
```

This registry key determines the number of IP packet headers that are designated for the router packet queue. It's a good idea to set this key to a fairly high value because when all allocated header space is used, TCP/IP will begin to randomly discard packets from the queue.

Like many of the other registry keys that we've looked at so far, the NumForwardPackets key doesn't exist by default. When creating this registry key, you should make the key a DWORD and assign it a number that will represent the maximum number of packet headers to store in the TCP/IP queue. If you choose not to create this registry key, Windows will use a default value of 50.

Setting an optimal value for the NumForwardPackets key can be tricky. The minimum size you should set this value to is the ForwardBufferMemory size divided by the largest IP data size.

The maximum NumForwardPackets value should be based on the ForwardBufferMemory value divided by the maximum IP packet size. Because the maximum IP data buffer size is 256, I recommend determining the maximum NumForwardPackets value by dividing the ForwardBufferMemory by 256. Earlier, I suggested setting the ForwardBufferMemory to 145,408. This means that the highest value you'd want to use would be 568, assuming you had an MTU size of 1,454 and were basing your ForwardBufferMemory size on 100 times the MTU size rounded to the next highest multiple of 256.

As you can see, there's a huge difference between Windows' default value of 50 and my maximum value of 568. I recommend going with the maximum value. Just remember to do the math and pick the true maximum value, rather than just using my numbers. There's no reason you can't use a number below the maximum value as long as you're above the minimum value. But if you go above the maximum value, you're wasting memory.

Keeping a packet alive

We've all seen connections time out when attempting to connect to a slow Web site or other slow resource. The connection times out because TCP/IP's TTL (Time To Live) counter expires.

When you transmit a packet, TCP/IP starts with a predetermined TTL value. The TTL counter is decremented by one every time a packet passes through a router or when one second ticks by. If the packet takes too long to get to its destination or to be acknowledged by the recipient, or if the route to the destination is too far away (too many hops), the packet will expire before being received.

If you have frequent problems with packets expiring too quickly, you can set the TTL to a higher value. The TTL is controlled by a registry key called DefaultTTL. If you want to use this key, you'll have to create it at:

```
HKEY_LOCAL_MACHINE\SYSTEM\CurrentControlSet\Services\Tcpip\
   Parameters
```

If you choose not to create the DefaultTTL key, Windows will use a default value based on the version of Windows you're using. Windows NT 3.51 and earlier versions have a default TTL value of 32, while Windows 2000 and higher have a default value of 128. If you create this key and set your own TTL value, the value you set should never be lower than the defaults, but it can be as high as 255.

Increasing performance over low-bandwidth connections TCP/IP was designed in the 1960s to function over long distances and low-bandwidth links. Although available bandwidth has increased dramatically since then, so has the amount of data being pushed through it. Even 40 years after TCP/IP's birth, low bandwidth is still an issue.

You can get the most out of your available bandwidth on a low-bandwidth link by minimizing the amount of overhead required by the TCP/IP protocol. One way to do this is to increase the window size. Increasing the window size increases the amount of data that can be transmitted before an acknowledgment is required from the recipient. Unfortunately, there's a downside to this approach. If a retransmission is required, a lot more data must be retransmitted. However, when everything is working properly, increasing the window size dramatically improves efficiency.

To increase the window size, create a DWORD registry key called TcpWindowSize at:

```
HKEY_LOCAL_MACHINE\SYSTEM\CurrentControlSet\Services\Tcpip\
    Parameters
```

The number you assign to the key reflects the number of bytes that a sender can transmit before requiring an acknowledgment. For maximum efficiency, the value you select should be a multiple of the TCP maximum segment size (MSS). The default for an Ethernet network is 8,760 (8,192 rounded up to an even multiple of the MSS).

Dig a little deeper

Although you can configure basic TCP/IP properties through Control Panel, there are lots of undocumented TCP/IP settings you can modify only through the registry. As you experiment with the various registry settings, be sure to document your original settings. Incorrectly setting any of the registry keys that I've discussed can bring TCP/IP to a grinding halt. ❖

How to configure and troubleshoot PPPoE connections in Windows XP

By Debra Littlejohn Shinder, MCSE

The demand for high-speed Internet access—faster than what can be attained with analog telephone lines and a traditional modem—has led to the popularity of broadband Internet service. Consumer broadband generally refers to two technologies: cable modem and digital subscriber line (DSL). Cable modem service is provided by CATV companies utilizing their installed infrastructure, over which cable TV signals are sent. DSL runs over copper telephone wires, and DSL Internet service is provided by the telcos themselves and by independent ISPs.

Using one of these two technologies, the service provider has a choice of several networking architectures that can be implemented. The architecture determines how the connection is made at the link level and how users are authenticated on the network.

Many broadband providers are choosing to use Point-to-Point Protocol over Ethernet (PPPoE). Although this has some advantages for the ISP, PPPoE has posed some problems for users in the past. The networking components of earlier Windows operating systems were based on the assumption that most users would connect to the Internet via an analog modem, using PPP over phone lines or the Serial Line Internet Protocol (SLIP). Windows XP has a built-in PPPoE client designed to make it easier for XP users to set up broadband connections. In this article, we discuss what PPPoE is and the reasons so many ISPs use it; how it works "under the hood"; how to configure Windows XP to make a PPPoE connection; and how to troubleshoot common PPPoE problems.

What is PPPoE and why do ISPs use it?

As its name implies, PPPoE is a variation of the Point-to-Point Protocol (PPP) used for dial-up connections using a serial line (as with an analog modem). PPP was designed as an improvement on the older SLIP, which was used for the same purpose but required manual configuration of a number of parameters and worked only with TCP/IP.

TCP/IP REQUIRED FOR INTERNET CONNECTION

PPP can be used with IPX, AppleTalk, and other network/transport protocols, as well as with TCP/IP. To connect to the Internet, however, TCP/IP is required.

PPP is a time-proven technology, one that ISPs are familiar with because they've used it for years on their dial-up analog connections. It provides some security, along with supporting the ability for the ISP to keep usage records on individual accounts through its password-authentication process.

When an ISP that has offered dial-up service begins offering service to broadband users, it is easier for the ISP to utilize PPPoE because it will work with the technology they already have in place. They will not have to spend time and money to change their existing systems.

PPPoE has a number of features that make it attractive to broadband ISPs: It can support multiuser sessions and multiple PCs (home and small office LANs), and it will work with DSL, cable, and wireless. PPPoE will work with Windows, Macintosh, and Linux systems.

Some users have complained about PPPoE because of the need to install third-party software (with non-XP systems), the incompatibilities some of the third-party programs have caused, and reported performance loss (slow overall Internet performance, slow PING times). It is also important to note that PPPoE makes a dedicated broadband connection behave like a dial-up connection, so that you may lose the "always on" aspect of DSL or cable. On the other hand, terminating the PPPoE session when you're finished using the Internet does provide a security advantage, since you're not continuously vulnerable to outside intruders.

How PPPoE works

PPPoE works similarly to a dial-up connection, but it uses the computer's network card in place of a modem. The ISP must be running a PPPoE server, and the user's computer must be running PPPoE client software (either the client built into Windows XP or third-party client software on operating systems that do not have the built-in PPPoE support).

PPPoE Discovery

Before a PPPoE communication session can be established, the PPPoE Discovery phase occurs. This is initiated when the user attempts to connect to the PPPoE server. The Discovery process is used by the client computer to "discover" the server, which is called an Access Concentrator. If there is more than one Access Concentrator on the network, the client will discover them all and select one during this process. A PPPoE session ID is established during this phase, and the client and server discover one another's Ethernet (MAC) addresses. Here is the step-by-step process:

- The client computer sends an Initiation packet to start the process. This is a broadcast message (goes to all computers on the network).
- The Access Concentrator(s) sends an Offer packet. If there is more than one Offer sent, the client will select one.

- The client sends a Session Request packet to the selected server. This is a unicast message (a "private" point-to-point communication between the two computers).
- The selected Access Concentrator sends a Confirmation packet to "seal the deal."
- The client and server move on to the PPP Session stage.

You will note that this process is similar to the negotiations that take place between a DHCP client and server.

PPP Session

The PPP connection between the client and the Access Concentrator is established after Discovery is complete and a communication session can take place. When PPPoE is used to send data, a PPP frame is created and encapsulated with a PPPoE header. This frame then becomes the payload of an Ethernet frame, which is sent over the Ethernet network. All the Ethernet packets are sent as unicast messages.

During the session, data is sent as with any PPP communication. Each packet must contain the session ID that was assigned during the Discovery phase.

To terminate a session, the client or server sends a Terminate-Request packet. The server may also send Echo-Request packets at regular intervals to ensure that the client has not abandoned the session. Once the session has been terminated, the client will have to start over and go through the Discovery phase (acquiring a new session ID) to begin communicating again.

MORE ON PPPoE PACKETS

For more detailed technical information about PPPoE packets and the Discovery and Session phases, see "RFC 2516: A Method for Transmitting PPP Over Ethernet" at **www.faqs.org/rfcs/rfc2516.html**.

Configuring the PPPoE client in Windows XP

Generally, broadband ISPs supply a PPPoE client program for their customers to use (for example, EnterNet or WinPoET). With Windows XP, there is no need to install third-party software to create PPPoE connections. The built-in PPPoE client can be used to connect to PPPoE servers that comply with industry standards.

Some versions of third-party PPPoE software will not run on XP; using the built-in client can be a permanent solution or an interim solution until updated versions of the third-party software are available.

Setting up the PPPoE connection

To configure the connection in XP, first open the Network Connections window by choosing Start | Control Panel | Network And Internet Connections. In the left pane, under Network Tasks (see **Figure A**), choose Create A New Connection.

This action invokes the New Connection Wizard. Select Next to start the wizard. On the following page, Connect To The Internet is selected by default. Ensure that it is selected, and chose Next. On the Getting Ready page, select the second option button, Set Up My Connection Manually, and choose Next. On the Internet Connection page, select the second option button, Connect Using A Broadband Connection That Requires A User Name And Password. Choose Next. On the Connection Name page, enter the name of your ISP, as shown in **Figure B**.

On the Connection Availability page, you'll be asked whether you want the new connection to be available to any user logged on to the computer, or only when your user account is logged on. Make the desired selection, and choose Next.

On the Internet Account Information page, shown in **Figure C**, you will be asked to type in the account name and password assigned by your broadband ISP.

Figure A

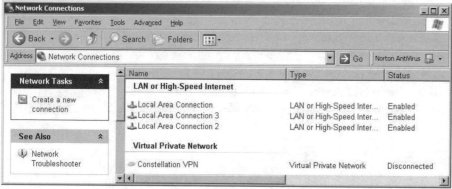

Use the Network Connections window to create a new PPPoE connection.

Figure B

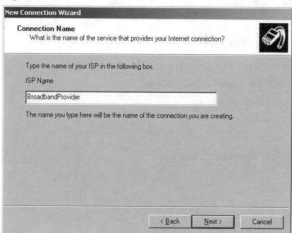

Enter the name of your broadband provider on the Connection Name page.

Figure C

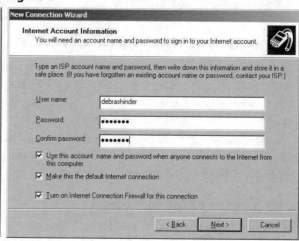

You must provide the username and password assigned by the ISP.

You will also have the options to:

- Specify that this account be used when any-one connects to the Internet from this com-puter (even if logged on to the computer with a different user account).

- Make this the default Internet connection (if you have multiple Internet connections configured).

- Turn on the Internet Connection Firewall for this connection (you should always use a fire-wall when connecting to the Internet, but you will uncheck this box if you are already using a third-party firewall product).

The last page of the wizard will summarize the selections you've made and give you the option to create a shortcut on your desktop to quickly access the connection, as shown in **Figure D**.

Click Finish to complete the wizard and create the connection. The new connection will now appear in the Network Connections window, along with any dial-up, LAN, or VPN connections you may have created previously, as shown in **Figure E**.

Using the PPPoE connection

Once you've configured your broadband connection, you can connect to the Internet by choosing the icon (on the desktop or in Network Connections) and selecting the Connect button, as shown in **Figure F**. Your username and password are saved; to change the saved password, click in the Password field.

Figure D

The wizard summarizes the choices you've made.

Figure E

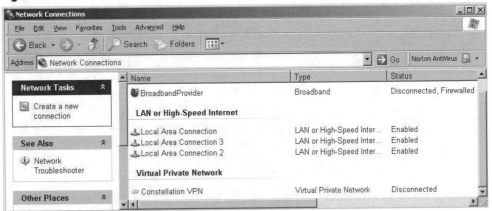

The broadband connection will appear in the Network Connections window.

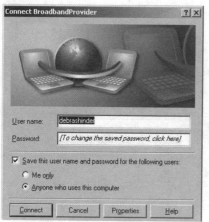

Choose the Connect button to use your broadband connection.

Troubleshooting PPPoE connections

Troubleshooting a PPPoE connection that does not work is similar to troubleshooting a dial-up connection. If you are unable to connect to the server at all, ensure that your cable or DSL provider is not experiencing an outage. Use standard TCP/IP connectivity tools (PING, IPCONFIG, TRACERT) to attempt to isolate the problem.

If you can connect to the server, but are then immediately disconnected, ensure that your username and password are correct. Check the broadband connection's properties (right-click the connection in Network Connections and select Properties).

On the Security tab, ensure that the security options are set to allow unsecured passwords. Choose the Advanced option and select Settings, and make sure that it is *not* set to require data encryption (which will disconnect you if the server does not support encryption). All protocol boxes should be checked under Allow These Protocols.

On the Networking tab, under Type Of Broadband Connection To Make, make sure that you've selected Point-to-Point Protocol over Ethernet (PPPoE) in the drop-down list and that Internet Protocol (TCP/IP) is checked. Highlight it and choose Properties. Ensure that the connection is set to obtain an IP address and a DNS server address automatically (unless the ISP has assigned you a static address and DNS server address to enter here manually).

Generally, the XP PPPoE client can discover the PPPoE service name automatically. However, with some providers, you may need to manually enter a service name. Do this on the General tab of the broadband connection's properties sheet.

An XP PPPoE bug

If you're using a PPPoE DSL connection to connect to the Internet and sharing your connection with Internet Connection Sharing (ICS), and the ICS clients aren't able to access some Web sites, this may be due to a known bug in the XP PPPoE client. Microsoft recommends that you try using the RASPPPoE client instead. You can download it at **http://user.cs.tu-berlin.de/ ~normanb/**. ❖

SOHO Applications

3

Configure a modem and dial-up connection for home network use

For many years computer enthusiasts have relied on modems and dial-up connections to get access to the Internet. Although dial-up is antiquated when compared to today's broadband standards, it is still widely used by those who don't need or can't get a high-speed connection. In this chapter, we'll discus how to install a modem and configure a dial-up connection in Windows 2000 and Windows XP. We'll also show you how to share your dial-up connection with the other computers on your network.

Installing a modem on your Windows 2000 computer

After following the instructions to physically connect the modem to your computer, you can begin installing the software driver for the device. (Of course, almost all systems manufactured in recent years come with a pre-installed modem.)

To begin the configuration procedure, you should click Start | Settings | Control Panel | Add/Remove Hardware. Click Next to bypass the welcome screen and then select the Add/Troubleshoot A Device option that's listed in the Choose A Hardware Task dialog box, shown in **Figure A**. Click Next to continue the installation.

Windows will interrogate the computer for new Plug and Play hardware. If it finds any new hardware, it will display the New Hardware Detection window, shown in **Figure B**. If the device shown in this window is correct, you should click Next to continue the installation.

The wizard will conclude with an informative screen and ask you to click the Finish button to complete installation of the new modem; that's all there is to this process. Because we're using Plug and Play devices, the installation is very straightforward.

Figure A

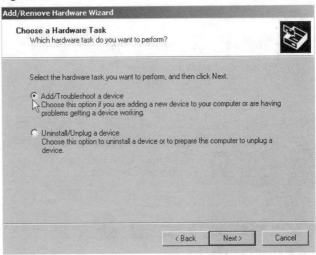

Choose to add a device in this dialog box.

Figure B

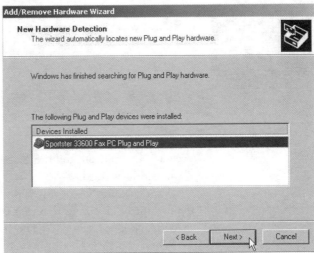

Windows will detect new hardware attached to your system.

Figure C

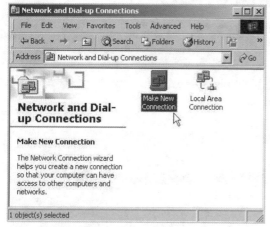

Double-click the Make New Connection icon.

Figure D

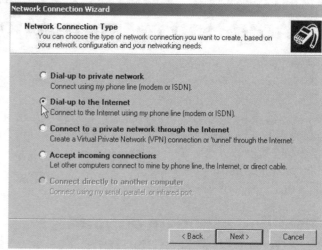

Choose to configure a dial-up connection to the Internet.

Figure E

We'll set up this dial-up connection manually.

Configuring your Windows 2000 dial-up connection

Once your modem has been installed, it's time to set up your dial-up connection. This process configures the communications software and allows your computer to establish and maintain a link with your Internet Service Provider (ISP). Generally, your ISP will give you detailed instructions regarding the setup of your dial-up connection, but we'll go through a basic configuration to give you an idea of what you will need to do.

To begin the dial-up configuration, click Start | Settings | Control Panel | Network And Dial-up Connections. This will open the window shown in **Figure C**. Double-clicking the Make New Connection icon will launch the Network Connection Wizard.

After clicking Next to bypass the welcome screen, you'll be asked to select the type of network connection that you want to configure. To configure a dial-up connection, choose Dial-up To The Internet, as illustrated in **Figure D**.

When you click Next, the Network Connection Wizard passes control to the Internet Connection Wizard. You'll use this wizard to configure a new or existing

Internet account. As you can see, you have three options. For the purposes of this example, we're going to select to set up the Internet account manually, as shown in **Figure E**. Click Next to continue.

The subsequent dialog box will ask how you want to connect to the Internet. In this case, select the option to connect through a phone line and a modem, as shown in **Figure F**, and click Next.

The wizard continues by asking you to supply the telephone number of your ISP, as shown in **Figure G**. After entering this information, click Next to continue.

You'll now be asked to provide the user name and password that you'll use to log on to your ISP, as shown in **Figure H**. (You'll get this information from the ISP, and you should have it in hand before beginning to configure your dial-up connection.)

After you enter your logon information and click Next, the Internet Connection Wizard asks you to provide a name for this connection. You can use whatever descriptive name you like.

The next dialog box asks if you would like to set up an Internet mail account, which will again depend on information you'll get from your ISP. For the purpose of this example, we declined to do so. The final screen of the Internet Connection Wizard notifies you that the new connection has successfully been configured. To complete the configuration, click the Finish button.

Once you have completed configuring your dial-up connection, it will appear in the Network And Dial-up Connections window, as show in **Figure I**.

Sharing your Windows 2000 dial-up connection

Sharing your newly created dial-up connection with other computers on your home network is actually very simple. First, open the Network And Dial-up Connection

Figure F

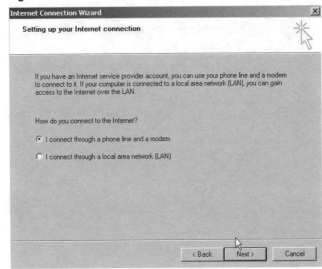

Choose to connect to the Internet via a phone line and modem.

Figure G

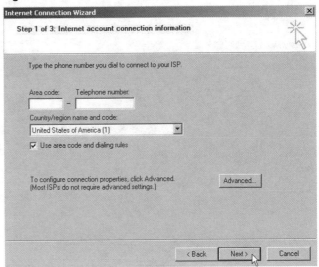

Tell the wizard the phone number of your ISP.

Figure H

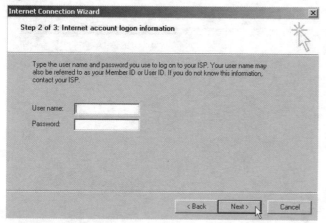

Input your ISP password information.

Figure I

Your new dial-up connection now appears in the Network And Dial-up Connections window.

Figure J

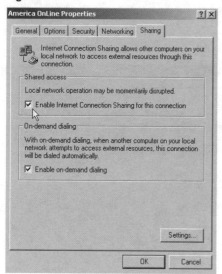

The Sharing tab options let other users access the dial-up connection.

Figure K

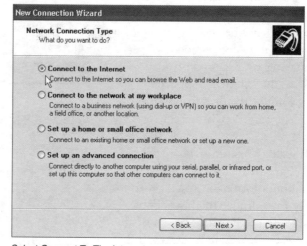

Select Connect To The Internet.

window, right-click on the dial-up connection, and select Properties. You should then click on the Sharing tab. To share your modem and dial-up connection, simply select the Enable Internet Connection Sharing For This Connection option, as shown in **Figure J**.

If you'd like the other computers on your network to be able to automatically connect to your ISP, select the Enable On-demand Dialing option. With this option set, other computers can simply launch their Internet browsers and the connection will be established automatically. Sharing an Internet connection in this manner makes using the connection much easier.

Modems and dial-up connections in Windows XP

Installing your modem and configuring the dial-up connection in Windows XP is no more difficult than it is with Windows 2000. However, the new Windows XP user interface makes performing these procedures a little bit different. In this section, we'll discuss how to install your modem and configure your dial-up connection using Windows XP.

After following the instructions to physically connect the modem to your computer, you should begin installing the software driver. With Plug and Play hardware, Windows XP will find the new device and install it for you with a minimum of fuss. Even the manual install that we'll walk through in our example is very straightforward. First, click Start | Control Panel | Add Hardware. This will launch the Add New Hardware wizard. You should click Next to bypass the welcome screen.

At this point the wizard will search for new Plug and Play devices that have been added to the computer. If any new devices are found, the computer will install the software. When Windows XP has finished installing the driver, you will see the wizard's completion screen. Click Finish to exit the wizard.

Configuring your Windows XP dial-up connection

Now that your modem and its driver software have been installed, it's time to begin configuring the dial-up connection that will allow you to connect to and communicate with your ISP. Once again, we're going to walk through a manual setup to give you an idea of what information is configured during this process.

To begin the configuration, click Start | Control Panel and double-click Network Connections. This will open the Network Connections window, where you'll click on Create A New Connection. This will launch the New Connection wizard. You should click Next to bypass the welcome screen.

At the Network Connection Type screen, select Connect To The Internet, as shown in **Figure K**, and click Next.

The resulting window is titled Getting Ready. As we stated earlier, since all ISPs have different instructions you will have to follow the ones that your ISP provides. The next few steps will provide you with an example of what configuring a dial-up connection entails. For the purpose of this example, select Set Up My Connection Manually, and click Next.

The wizard continues by asking you to select the type of Internet connection that you want to configure. You should select Connect Using A Dial-up Modem. Next, you'll be asked to enter a descriptive name for the new connection. The

Figure L

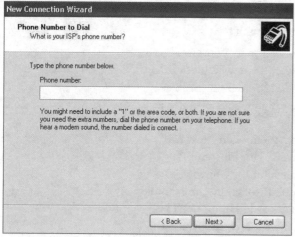

The wizard asks for your ISP's contact information.

Figure M

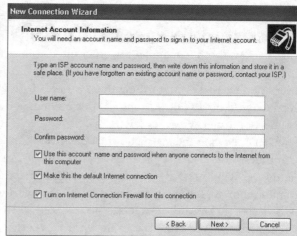

Input your user name and ISP password.

Figure N

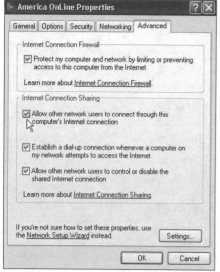

The Advanced tab displays the connection's sharing properties.

wizard continues by prompting you to enter the phone number for your ISP, as shown in **Figure L**.

Finally, you must enter the user name and password information that enables you to log in to your ISP account, as shown in **Figure M**.

After entering the logon information the dial-up configuration is complete; click Finish to end the wizard. When you return to the Network Connections window you'll see the new dial-up connection that you just configured.

Sharing your Windows XP dial-up connection

Sharing your dial-up connection in Windows XP is once again a fairly easy task, with the primary difference between XP and Windows 2000 being the steps that you must take to accomplish the task. To enable connection sharing in Windows XP, click Start | Control Panel and double-click Network Connections. To configure connection sharing, select your dial-up connection and click Change Settings Of This Connection, which is located in the left pane of the window.

When you see the properties of the dial-up connection, select the Advanced tab, and then select Allow

Other Network Users To Connect Through This Computer's Internet Connection, as shown in **Figure N**. The tab's other two options are selected by default and provide the capability for network users to dial the ISP when they connect to the Internet and to allow them to control or disable the shared Internet connection. Just as with Windows 2000, leaving these options selected makes sharing the connection easier for everyone.

Conclusion

As you can see, both Windows 2000 and Windows XP make it fairly easy for you to install your modem driver software, configure your dial-up connection, and share the connection with other computers on your network. Although individual ISPs will have different instructions for configuring the dial-up connection, all of them will require you to provide information similar to what we have shown you in this chapter. ❖

Add and configure network adapters

Configuring your network adapter is a fairly straightforward process that's no more complicated than installing any other peripheral device. In this chapter, we'll show you how to install and configure your network adapter in Windows 2000 and Windows XP.

Configuring a network adapter in Windows 2000

When you add a new device to your computer, Window's plug-and-play functionality usually recognizes the device and walks you through the installation. However, in this example, we'll show you how to manually install your network card drivers and configure your LAN connection in Windows 2000. This detailed look will help you become more familiar with the various issues involved in configuring your network connection.

After physically installing the network adapter (you'll need to reference your specific product manual for this process) you must load the software driver that allows the device to be used by your computer. To begin installing this software, go to the Start menu and open the Control Panel, then select System to open the System Properties dialog box. Click on the Hardware tab, and then click Device Manager, as shown in **Figure A**.

Figure A

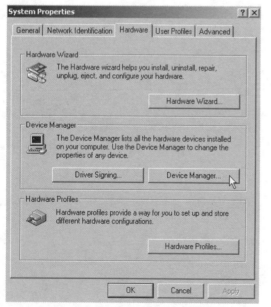

You'll install your NIC using the Device Manager.

Figure B

Device Manager reports a problem because our NIC has no driver installed.

Figure C

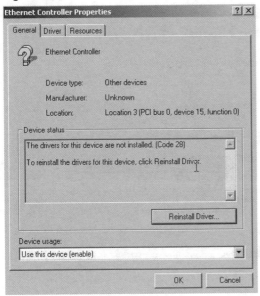

Use this interface to launch the install process.

Figure D

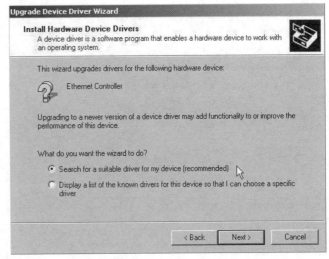

The wizard asks you to choose a method for finding the correct driver.

Figure E

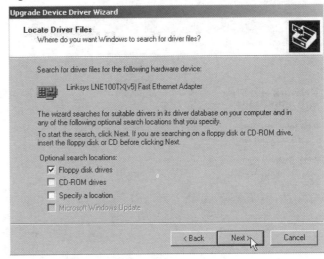

The Locate Driver Files screen appears next.

As you can see in the Device Manager window shown in **Figure B**, the Ethernet Controller (our NIC) is listed under Other Devices. The question mark next to the controller indicates that the device is having a configuration problem. This designation is caused because there are no drivers installed for the device.

To begin installing the software for the network adapter, double-click the device. This will display the Ethernet Controller Properties window, shown in **Figure C**.

There are a couple of different ways to install the new driver, but for this example we are going to use the Reinstall Driver button that you can see in Figure C. When you click this button, you'll launch the Upgrade Device Driver Wizard. You should click Next to bypass the welcome screen and display the Install Hardware Device Drivers screen, shown in **Figure D**.

We're going to use the default setting of searching for a suitable driver. After you click Next, the Locate Driver Files screen will appear, as shown in **Figure E**. You should select the appropriate locations where the driver files are stored and then

Figure F

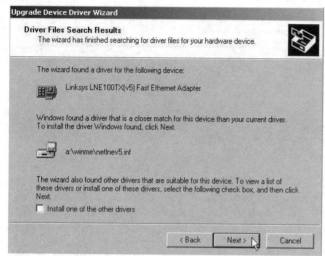

The wizard will report which driver it has found.

Figure G

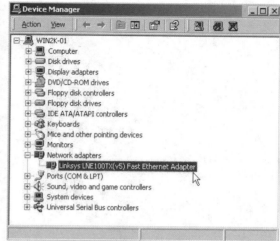

Device Manager now reports that the NIC is correctly installed.

Figure H

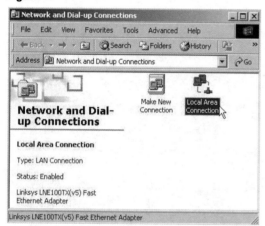

You'll use this dialog box to access your LAN settings.

click Next. For the purpose of this example, we're going to search for the driver files on the floppy disk drive only.

The wizard will begin its search for the driver files, and once it finds them it will present you with the Driver Files Search Results screen, shown in **Figure F**. If the correct driver is found, you should click Next to continue the installation. If no drivers are found, you can click the Back button to search in a different location. If additional drivers were found, as they were in our example, you can select the Install One Of The Other Drivers option and click Next. You will then be able to select a different driver to install.

After you click Next, the driver files will be installed and the wizard completion screen will appear. You should click the Finish button to end the wizard.

To verify that the driver has been installed, return to the Device Manager screen. The view should automatically be refreshed, and you should see the correctly installed device under the new heading of Network Adapters, as shown in **Figure G**.

Configuring the Windows 2000 LAN settings

To configure your LAN settings, right-click the desktop icon My Network Places and select Properties to open the Network And Dial-up Connections window, which will look similar to the one shown in **Figure H**.

Next, right-click on the Local Area Connection icon and select Properties. This will open the Local Area Connection Properties window, shown in **Figure I**.

This window provides you with a variety of options. You can configure your network adapter using the Configure button that's located near the top of the window; you can install and uninstall networking components; and you can use the Properties button to configure the components that are already installed.

To configure your network connection, you should highlight the Internet Protocol (TCP/IP) networking component and click the Properties button. This will open the Internet Protocol (TCP/IP) Properties dialog box, shown in **Figure J**. The settings that are shown in Figure J are the default settings that tell the computer to look for a DHCP server to obtain a TCP/IP address (this will likely be the case if you purchase a hardware router, which we'll discuss in a later chapter). If you want to manually assign a TCP/IP address, you would select the Use The Following IP Address option and then enter the TCP/IP address, subnet mask, and default gateway.

In our example, we've verified that the computer will use DHCP to obtain a TCP/IP address, and our network configuration is complete. After configuring network adapters on two or more of your network nodes, you should be able to share files and peripheral devices among the computers on your network.

Configuring a network adapter in Windows XP

Configuring your network adapter in Windows XP is basically the same process as for Windows 2000. However, the new Windows XP user interface has different

Figure I

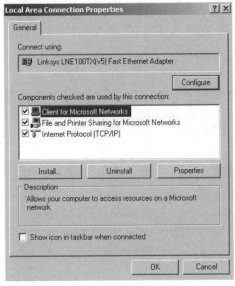

This window's options control your LAN settings.

Figure J

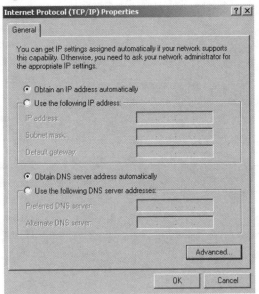

Your computer is set up to look for a DHCP server by default.

Figure K

XP's new interface slightly changes the route to the Device Manager.

Figure L

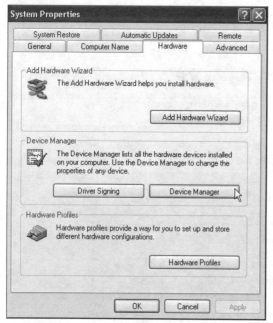

XP's Device Manager is very similar to the Windows 2000 version of the tool.

ways to reach the configuration screens. In this section, we'll show you one method of reaching configuration screens so that you'll be able to configure your network adapter in Windows XP.

In Windows 2000, you manually installed your network adapter using the Device Manager. You can do the same thing in Windows XP; however, to open Device Manager you select Start | Control Panel | System, as illustrated in **Figure K**.

Once the System Properties window is open, click on the Hardware tab and then select Device Manager, as shown in **Figure L**. You now should be able to follow the same steps that we showed you earlier to install the network adapter driver software.

After installing the network adapter driver, it's time to configure the Local Area Connection properties and ensure that it is configured to use DHCP, in our scenario of having a router for our network. Once again, the configuration is very much the same as with Windows 2000, but getting to the dialog box is slightly different. First, you must click on Start | Control Panel | Network Connections | Local Area Connection, as shown in **Figure M**.

This will open the Local Area Connection Status window, shown in **Figure N**. This window provides you with some basic information about your connection, which will come in handy when troubleshooting connectivity problems.

To configure your network connection, click Properties to open the Local Area Connection Properties dialog box. You can then highlight Internet Protocol (TCP/IP) and click the Properties button. You will then see the familiar Internet Protocol (TCP/IP) Properties dialog box, where you should select the option to Obtain An IP

Figure M

Follow this path to reach your local area connection's properties.

Figure N

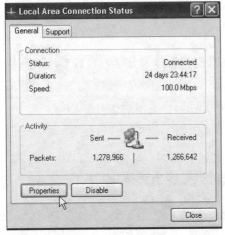

This information may come in handy later.

Address Automatically to activate DHCP with your router. (If you need to manually set addresses, follow the instructions we discussed earlier in this chapter.)

Wrap up

As you have seen, installing your network adapter and configuring your network connection is a fairly straightforward process in Windows 2000 and Windows XP. The new XP user interface requires you to reach the configuration screens a little bit differently, but the process of configuring the devices is basically the same in both operating systems. ❖

Add protocols, services, and network clients and bind them all to your NIC

The real work of creating your home network begins after you've successfully installed your network interface card (NIC), as we described in the previous chapter. To share files on a network and interconnect your systems, you'll need to make sure your system is running these three software components:

- a client
- a service
- a protocol

The process for adding these essential configuration options varies, depending on the version of Windows your system is running. In this chapter, we'll first run through the process in Windows 2000, and then we'll follow-up with a section on the same process in Windows XP. We'll include lots of figures to make sure you can follow along—don't worry, it's easier than it sounds.

Setting up protocols, services, and network clients in Windows 2000

If Windows 2000 was installed on your system with Typical Settings as the Networking Components option (this is common with most commercial

Figure A

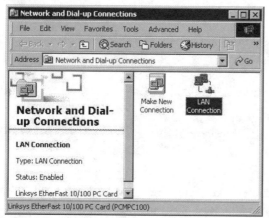

Select the connection you want to configure and double-click it.

Figure B

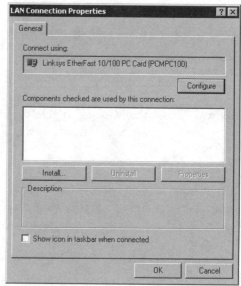

The LAN Connection Properties dialog box provides information about the installed components and NIC a connection uses.

pre-installs of the operating system), the following items should have been installed by default:

- **Client**—Client For Microsoft Networks
- **Service**—File And Print Sharing For Microsoft Networks
- **Protocol**—TCP/IP

However, instead of the Typical Settings option, the manufacturer or someone else may have specified customized settings, or someone may have had reason to delete these settings using Control Panel. If so, you'll have to reload them.

Adding the client

We'll start by running through the steps to install the client:

1. Click Start | Settings | Network And Dial-up Connections.

2. Select the Local Area Connection corresponding to the NIC for which you want to configure the network component settings. For this example, we selected LAN Connection, as shown in **Figure A**. Once you've selected the connection, double-click it.

3. Click Properties in the resulting LAN Connection Status dialog box.

4. Click Install in the resulting LAN Connection Properties dialog box, shown in **Figure B**.

5. Select Client in the resulting Select Network Component Type dialog box and then click Add. Two options appear by default when using Windows 2000 Professional: Client For Microsoft Networks and Client Service For NetWare. Since we're adding a machine to a Microsoft network (that's most often the case), we selected Client For Microsoft Networks and clicked OK.

6. After the client is installed, it will appear in the LAN Connection Properties dialog box. Check the box next to it to enable its use. Click Close, and the client network component installation is complete.

7. Close the open boxes by selecting OK, then Close.

Adding the service

You install services in Windows 2000 in the same manner as you install clients. However, in step number 5 as we described it above, select Service instead of Client from the Select Network Component Type dialog box.

You can choose from several services that are provided by default in Windows 2000:

- File And Print Sharing For Microsoft Networks
- QoS Packet Scheduler
- SAP Agent

Figure C

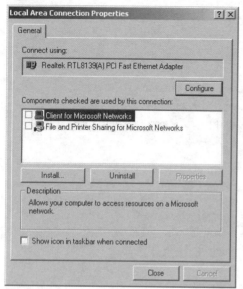

Check before installing a protocol to ensure it hasn't already been loaded.

Figure D

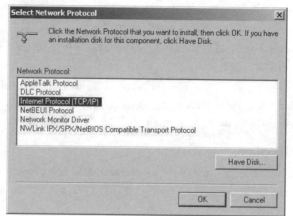

In the Select Network Protocol dialog box, specify the protocol you want to install.

Figure E

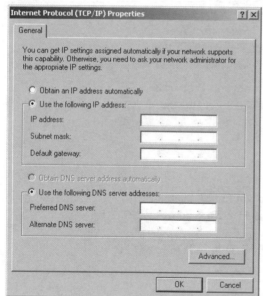

To specify an IP address, you'll have to provide the associated subnet mask, default gateway, and DNS server addresses.

For most home networks, you'll want to select File And Print Sharing For Microsoft Networks, since that's the service that permits the sharing of files, documents, spreadsheets, and other resources, such as printers, on a Microsoft network. Then simply click OK.

Just as with the client, you'll then have to check the box to enable the service and complete this installation step.

Adding the network protocol

When you need to install or reinstall TCP/IP or install another protocol, begin by selecting Start | Settings | Network And Dial-Up Connections. Right-click the connection you want to configure and select Properties.

Look for the protocol you want to use in the Components Checked Are Used By This Connection box, shown in **Figure C**. If the protocol isn't listed, you'll need to add it. It's possible, too, that the protocol has already been added but has been configured improperly.

Make sure the network client and service are installed (as we just did in the previous steps), then click Install. From the pop-up menu, double-click Protocol. Almost every computer, including those on your home network, relies on TCP/IP, so that's the protocol we'll install in this example.

From the Select Network Protocol dialog box, shown in **Figure D**, double-click Internet Protocol (TCP/IP) or select Internet Protocol (TCP/IP) and click OK. Both actions will select the TCP/IP option.

After installing the protocol, make sure the check boxes are selected for the network client, service, and protocol. The next step is to configure basic protocol settings.

If the system is to receive an IP address automatically from a Dynamic Host Configuration Protocol (DHCP) server, you can simply click Close and reboot. (This typically will be the case with a home network with a dial-up connection, which gets its address information from the DHCP server at your ISP. Broadband setup will vary widely, depending on your provider. We covered these issues in our earlier chapter on configuring broadband connections.) When rebooting, the system will send out a DHCP discover message. The DHCP server will snag that message off the network and fire back an IP address and subnet mask, an address for DNS services, and a default gateway (if the DHCP server is so configured).

If you want to specify a static IP address, click on TCP/IP and select Properties. In the General tab, select the Use The Following IP Address option, as shown in **Figure E**.

Once you've entered the IP address and its associated subnet mask, along with the addresses for the default gateway and DNS servers, click OK. When entering IP addresses, type periods to separate your dotted-decimal entries. Use the [Tab] key to move from box to box.

After you've provided the necessary addresses, you can specify any WINS servers you want to use by clicking the Advanced button. Click on the WINS tab, enter the WINS server address, then click OK.

In the WINS tab, you can also specify whether to enable LMHOSTS lookup and NetBIOS over TCP/IP. You can specify that the NetBIOS configuration be set based on a DHCP server setting. Click OK once you've set these values.

Click OK, click OK again, and click Close. Finally, close the Network And Dial-Up Connections box, and you should find your network connection working properly.

You can learn more about your network settings by running the IPCONFIG command. Do so by clicking Start | Run. Type *cmd* and click OK. Then, type *IPCONFIG /ALL*. The details of your network adapters will be displayed. You can use this information to further troubleshoot errors on your network. It will at least lend confidence that all network adapters are configured properly.

Setting up protocols, services, and network clients in Windows XP

Just like in Windows 2000, the necessary protocols, services, and network clients should be present under a typical Windows XP installation. Again, these items are:

OTHER AVAILABLE PROTOCOLS

Windows 2000 offers some other protocol options:
- AppleTalk
- DLC
- NetBEUI
- Network Monitor Driver
- NWLink IPX/SPX/ NetBIOS Compatible Transport

These protocols typically are useful for larger networks or those that will encompass multiple operating systems, so they are usually not particularly useful in a home network setting.

- **Client**—Client For Microsoft Networks
- **Service**—File And Print Sharing For Microsoft Networks
- **Protocol**—TCP/IP

Just in case you do need to add any or all of these items, here are the steps to follow.

Adding the client

Follow these steps to install the client:

1. Click Start | Settings | Control Panel.

2. Click Network And Internet Connections.

3. Click Network Connections.

4. Right-click on the Local Area Connection corresponding to the NIC for which you want to configure the network component settings and select Properties.

5. Click Install in the Local Area Connection Properties dialog box, shown in **Figure F**.

6. Select Client in the resulting Select Network Component Type dialog box and then click Add. Two options appear by default when using Windows XP Professional: Client For Microsoft Networks and Client Service For NetWare. Since we're adding a machine to a Microsoft network (the most common scenario), we will select Client For Microsoft Networks and click OK.

Figure F

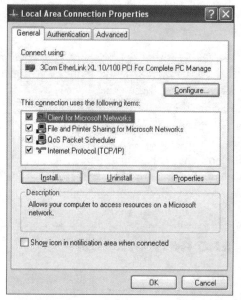

This dialog box displays properties for your connection.

Figure G

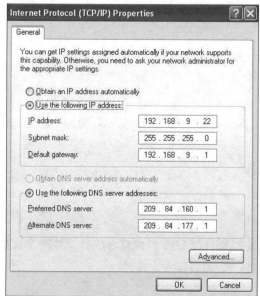

To specify an IP address, you'll have to provide the associated subnet mask, default gateway, and DNS server addresses.

7. After the client is installed, it will appear in the Local Area Connection Properties dialog box. Select the check box next to it to enable its use. Click Close, and the client network component installation is complete.

Adding the service

You install service components in Windows XP in the same manner that you install a client component. However, select Service instead of Client from the Select Network Component Type dialog box (step 6 above).

You can choose from several services that are provided by default in Windows XP:

- File And Print Sharing For Microsoft Networks
- QoS Packet Scheduler
- SAP Agent

Select File And Print Sharing For Microsoft Networks—which will let you share files, documents, spreadsheets, and other resources, such as printers, on a Windows network—and click OK. Select the check box to enable the service, and you've completed the service installation.

Adding the protocol

When you need to install or reinstall TCP/IP or install another protocol in Windows XP, begin by following these steps:

1. Click Start | Control Panel.

2. Click Network And Internet Connections.

3. Click Network Connections.

4. Right-click on the Local Area Connection corresponding to the NIC for which you want to configure the network protocols and select Properties.

If the protocol you want to install isn't listed, you'll need to add it. First, make sure that the network client and service are installed, as we discussed above. If these components are already available, click the Install button.

Next, from the pop-up menu, double-click Protocol (alternatively, you can click Protocol and click the Add button). Again, we'll stick with the ubiquitous TCP/IP protocol for our example. From the Select Network Protocol list box, select Internet Protocol (TCP/IP) and click OK. (If you already have TCP/IP installed, this selection will not be available.)

Windows XP offers other protocols, Network Monitor Driver and NWLink IPX/SPX/NetBIOS Compatible Transport Protocol. Three legacy protocols that were available in Windows 2000—AppleTalk, DLC, and NetBEUI—are no longer available by default in Windows XP.

After installing the TCP/IP protocol, make sure that the check boxes are selected for the network client, service, and protocol. The next step is to configure basic TCP/IP protocol settings.

If the system is to receive an IP address automatically from a DHCP server (which is most likely the case with a dial-up connection but not necessarily with broadband), you can simply close the Local Area Connection Properties dialog box and reboot your system. When rebooting, the system will send out a DHCP discover message. The DHCP server will snag that message off the network and fire back an IP address and subnet mask, as well as other network settings, such as IP addresses for DNS services, a default gateway, and myriad other options.

If you want to specify a static IP address, click on Internet Protocol (TCP/IP) and select Properties. In the General tab, select the Use The Following IP Address option, as shown in **Figure G**.

Once you've entered the IP address and its associated subnet mask, along with the addresses for the default gateway and DNS servers, click OK. When entering IP addresses, type periods to separate your dotted-decimal entries. Use the [Tab] key to move from box to box.

After you've provided the necessary addresses, you can click the Advanced button and specify any WINS servers you want to use. Click on the WINS tab, enter the WINS server address, and then click OK.

In the WINS tab, you can specify whether to enable LMHOSTS lookup and NetBIOS over TCP/IP. You can also specify that the NetBIOS configuration be set based on a DHCP server setting (if you're using DHCP). Click OK once you've set these values.

Click OK, click OK again, and click Close. Finally, close the Network And Dial-Up Connections box, and you should find your network connection working properly.

See, that wasn't so bad, was it? As in Windows 2000, you can learn more about your XP network settings by running the IPCONFIG command. Just click Start | Run, type *cmd*, and click OK. Then, type *IPCONFIG /ALL* to see the details of your network adapters. You can use this information to further troubleshoot errors on your network. It can give you a quick look at network protocol settings and provide confidence that all network adapters are configured properly. ❖

Create local user accounts for Windows 2K/XP peer-to-peer networking

By Greg Shultz

Sharing resources on Windows 9x/Me systems is as easy as opening Network Neighborhood and double-clicking the share name, and maybe typing a password if the resource is password protected. However, the process is a bit more complicated when setting up a peer-to-peer network that includes Windows 2000 or Windows XP systems because of the newer operating systems' increased focus on security.

To enable W2K Professional peer-to-peer networking, you'll need to manually add additional user accounts. Fortunately, the procedure is a little easier in Windows XP because of its Network Setup Wizard. Let's take a closer look at these two approaches.

Working with Windows 2000

If you're creating a peer-to-peer network composed of only Windows 2000 systems or a mixture of Windows 2000 and Windows 9x/Me machines, you'll need to manually add additional user accounts to the Windows 2000 systems. W2K Professional was designed to work in a domain-model network where all users are verified by a domain controller. When you set up W2K Professional systems on a peer-to-peer network, there's no domain controller, of course, but users still must be verified before they can access shared resources. So, you need to create local user accounts on your W2K Professional system for every computer that will need to access shared resources on that system.

Before you get started, you'll need to create list of the user account names and passwords on all systems on the peer-to-peer network. Once you have the list, you're ready to set up your accounts.

To begin, open Control Panel and double-click the Users And Passwords icon. When you see the Users And Passwords dialog box, shown in **Figure A**, click the Add button.

Figure A

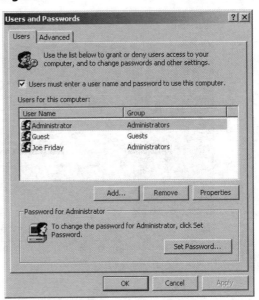

You need to set up user accounts on the Windows 2000 system for every user on the peer-to-peer network.

From this point, simply follow the directions in the Add New User Wizard to create an account with one of the usernames and passwords on your list. When you get to the last page in the Add New User Wizard, you'll need to specify the level of access for the new user account, as shown in **Figure B**. The access level you choose will depend on how much control you want the user to have; in most cases, a Standard user account will be sufficient.

When you click Finish, you'll return to the Users And Passwords dialog box, where you'll see the user account in the list, as shown in **Figure C**. Repeat these steps to set up the other user accounts. When you have finished, all users will be able to seamlessly connect to the Win2K Professional system and access shared resources.

Working with Windows XP

Microsoft realized that the demand for peer-to-peer networks is on the rise, so it made creating such network configurations as easy as possible with the Windows XP Network Setup Wizard. Basically, you launch the Network Setup Wizard on a Windows XP system and follow the onscreen instructions to configure a Windows XP system for peer-to-peer networking. When you get to the last step, you have the option to create a Network Setup Disk, which you can then use to configure Windows 9x/Me systems to participate along with Windows XP. Let's take a closer look at the procedure.

Figure B

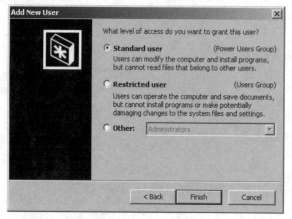

When you get to Add New User Wizard's last page, specify the access level for the user account.

Figure C

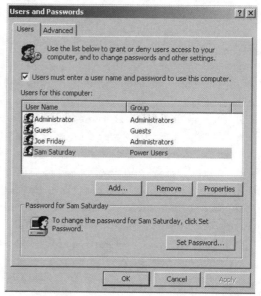

The new Sam Saturday user account allows this Windows 98 user to seamlessly access shared resources on the Win2K system.

Figure D

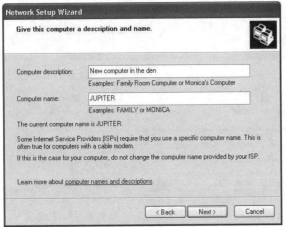

You'll need to assign the system a computer name.

Figure E

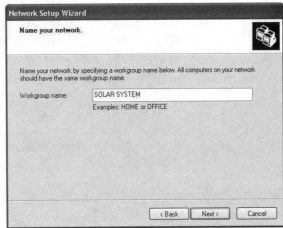

You must specify a workgroup name for the peer-to-peer network.

On your Windows XP system, open Control Panel and select the Network And Internet Connections category; then click the Network Connections icon. When you see the Network Connections window, select the Set Up A Home Or Small Office Network item on the Network Tasks Explorer Bar to launch the Network Setup Wizard.

The first two pages of the wizard contain helpful information that you should peruse. The page you'll see next depends on whether your peer-to-peer network already has an existing shared Internet connection. If it does, you'll see a page that prompts you to use the existing shared Internet connection. If it doesn't, you'll see a page asking you to choose an Internet connection method or to configure a network without an Internet link.

Figure F

As the last step of the process, you should create a Network Setup Disk.

Once you work through your Internet connection options, you'll see the Give This Computer A Description And Name page. At this point, you'll assign a computer name to your system, as shown in **Figure D**.

When you click Next, you'll be prompted to specify a workgroup name, as shown in **Figure E**. If you have an existing workgroup name, just type that same name here.

When you click Next, you'll see a summary screen that shows you the selections you've made so far. When you click Next, the wizard will apply your settings and configure your Windows XP system to participate in a peer-to-peer network. Once the configuration operation is complete, you'll see the You're Almost Done page, as shown in **Figure F**, and be prompted to create a Network Setup Disk.

Even though you may not need to use a Network Setup Disk, I suggest you go ahead and create one anyway, just to have it on hand.

At this point, your Windows XP system should be able to see and access shared resources on all other computers on the peer-to-peer network via My Network Places. Likewise, all the Windows 9x/Me systems on the peer-to-peer network should be able to see and access shared resources on the Windows XP system.

If that's not the case, you'll need to use the executable file on your Network Setup Disk to run the Network Setup Wizard and configure your Windows 9x/Me systems to participate in the peer-to-peer network. Remember that the Network Setup Wizard can run only on Windows 9x/Me systems. If your peer-to-peer network contains Windows 2000 systems, you'll need to follow the steps we covered earlier. ❖

XP Home vs. XP Pro networking: What's the difference?

By Jim Boyce

Whether you're getting ready to roll out Windows XP for your users or you just want to get up to speed with it on your own computer, which Windows XP flavor is right for you in terms of networking features? Do you go with the vanilla Home Edition version or spring for the chocolate, nuts, and marshmallow chunks in Professional? The answer isn't just about money, although with a $100 difference between the two, those extra munchies don't come cheap. I'll explain the main differences in networking features between the two versions of Microsoft's newest operating system to help you decide which one fits your appetite.

No domains at Home

One of the biggest differences for networking features between Windows XP Professional and Windows XP Home Edition is the lack of domain membership support in Home Edition. A Windows XP Professional computer can join a domain and function as a domain member. Domain membership extends the benefits of distributed security to the Windows XP desktop, enabling users to easily access domain resources. It also lets the user share resources with other users and authenticate those users against the domain rather than require individual accounts on the local computer.

By contrast, computers running XP Home Edition cannot be domain members, although they can access resources on a domain member in the same way workgroup members running other Windows platforms can access domain resources. They can connect to and use network file and printer shares, provided they have a valid account in the domain.

One of the biggest drawbacks to the lack of domain support in Home Edition is the corresponding lack of support for group policies. You can configure local policies on a Home Edition computer, but the computer naturally can't obtain group policies during domain logon because it can't be a domain member. This means you can't deploy the operating system with RIS, deploy applications with IntelliMirror, apply change control or restrictions, perform folder redirection, or accomplish any of the other feats of magic made possible by group policies.

Another advantage to using Windows XP Professional is that it defaults to using Kerberos for authentication. Kerberos offers the ability to reuse authentication credentials, providing single-sign-on capability. Although Home Edition provides password caching just like other Windows platforms (although it's more secure), it doesn't offer the same level of single-sign-on support provided by Windows XP Professional.

Table A

Feature	Windows XP Professional	Windows XP Home Edition
Domain Membership	Full domain membership and capabilities	Can't be domain members but can access resources on domain members with valid domain account
Group Policy (enables control, RIS, app. deployment, folder redirection, etc.)	Full support for group and local policies	No support for group or local policies
Authentication	Kerberos as default authentication method provides single sign-on capability	Does not provide single sign-on
IP Security	Fully support IPSec for computer-to-computer IP encryption	Does not support IPSec
Remote Control	Can act as Remote Desktop host and client; Terminal Server client	Client only to other Remote Desktop computer or Terminal Server, no host capability
Offline Files	Supports offline files	No offline files
Encryption	Includes Encrypting File System	No EFS
File Sharing	Simple File Sharing enabled by default, but can be disabled to configure NTFS permissions	SFS can't be disabled; must boot to Safe Mode to configure NTFS permissions
Web Services	IIS provides Web and FTP hosting for one site, SMTP virtual server; max. of 10 concurrent connections	No IIS; use third-party applications for Web services
Bridging Network Interfaces	Supported	Supported
Alternate TCP/IP Configuration	Supported	Supported
Wireless Networks and Wi-Fi Security	Supported	Supported

This chart offers a comparison of Windows XP Pro and XP Home.

IPSec

With an increased emphasis on network security, many companies are looking for ways to secure network traffic across the LAN as well as across the WAN. IP Security, or IPSec, provides that means. IPSec lets Windows XP Professional authenticate and encrypt all IP traffic to and from the computer.

IPSec functions at the endpoints of the connection—only the two computers engaged in the secure connection need to support IPSec. Intermediary routers or computers that route the traffic need not support IPSec. For that reason, IPSec is easy to implement in a variety of scenarios, whether the computers are connected across a LAN, WAN, or remote access connection.

IPSec encrypts the IP traffic before it leaves the local computer, securely encapsulating the data to make it secure from sniffing or other compromise. The receiving computer decrypts the data. The result is a completely secure connection over the most public of networks, such as the Internet. Although IPSec might seem more suited to encrypting traffic between routers, it is also an important security mechanism to secure traffic between individual computers. If you need to provide secure connections between client systems or between client and server, and a router-to-router solution isn't feasible, IPSec could be a major consideration for choosing Professional over Home Edition.

Remote Desktop

Those of us who have been in the IT community for very long are familiar with remote control applications like pcAnywhere and VNC. In fact, I use VNC and pcAnywhere on a daily basis for remote systems management. I also use them as an alternative to KVM switches for managing systems right in my own office. I like the response speed of pcAnywhere and the price of VNC (free) and its support for UNIX and Macintosh platforms.

Remote Desktop lets you connect to and use a remote computer running Windows XP Professional. Remote Desktop is a bit like a lightweight Terminal Services server, although as with most remote control applications, you can connect only one connection at a time to the remote computer. However, one connection to a client computer is generally all you really need. Remote Desktop works like other remote control applications: It's similar to sitting in front of the computer, except the performance is slower. The actual speed depends on the available bandwidth between the client and server.

You can use almost any Windows platform as a client to connect to and use a remote Windows XP Professional computer. Windows XP Home Edition includes a Remote Desktop Connection client, but not the server component. In addition, the Windows XP Professional CD includes Remote Desktop client software you can use on any platform.

You might not always have access to a client computer with the Remote Desktop Connection client installed, but that isn't a problem if you've planned ahead. The version of IIS included with Windows XP Professional includes a Remote Desktop Web Connection component—a combination of ActiveX controls and other components that lets remote users initiate a Remote Desktop connection to the computer from a Web browser. The session appears in the browser window rather than in a dedicated Remote Desktop Connection client window. The Remote Desktop Web Connection components don't have to be installed on the computer to be remotely managed. Instead, you can install the components on a Web server on the same network as the computers to be managed and connect through that one Web server to each of the Windows XP Professional computers on the network that has Remote Desktop enabled. This is a great feature that lets users access their systems from public Internet nodes.

Offline Files

The Offline Files feature in Windows XP originated in Windows 2000 and is carried over to Professional, but not the Home Edition. Offline Files creates a local cache of shared network files and folders, enabling you to continue to work on them even when the shared resource is unavailable—such as when the server is down or the client computer is disconnected from the network.

Offline Files is an excellent way to provide consistent and seamless access to network resources. The feature is nearly transparent to the user, which should mean relatively few support calls. However, you should also implement the Encrypting File System (EFS) if you need to ensure the best possible security.

EFS

EFS provides on-the-fly encryption/decryption of NTFS volumes, folders, and files. EFS is included in Windows XP Professional, but not the Home Edition. Encryption is handled by a secondary file system driver and is completely transparent to the user, who doesn't even need to know that a given folder on his or her computer is encrypted. The driver encrypts and decrypts the data on the fly, and encrypting a folder and its contents is as simple as setting a single attribute for the folder.

Simple File Sharing

Simple File Sharing (SFS) is one feature that confuses a lot of people who are new to Windows XP. SFS makes sharing pretty much a one-click operation and doesn't require that the user know anything about permissions. However, SFS causes all remote access to the computer to be authenticated against the local Guest account. While this provides easy sharing for users, it also offers little in the way of granular control over access to resources. You can't grant read-only access to one user or group and grant change permission to another because they are all authenticating against the same account. SFS is enabled by default for Windows XP Professional computers in a workgroup but is disabled for domain members.

With SFS enabled, the Security tab of a folder's property sheet is hidden, making it rather difficult to set ACLs on the folder. You can turn off SFS on a Windows XP Professional computer to make the computer act just like Windows 2000 in terms of sharing. Windows XP then lets you configure ACLs on the folder and apply restrictions on a per-user or per-group basis. However, Home Edition doesn't provide a way to turn off SFS. Instead, you have to boot the computer in Safe Mode to access a folder's Security tab. While this gives advanced users a way to control sharing, it's hardly a user-friendly approach to controlling file system access.

IIS

Windows XP Professional includes a stripped-down version of Internet Information Services (IIS), enabling a Windows XP Professional computer to host one Web and one FTP site on the computer. Home Edition doesn't include IIS.

The management interface is the same for IIS as that on Windows 2000. Like IIS on Windows 2000 Professional, Windows XP Professional is limited to 10 concurrent connections. This makes IIS a good choice for sharing printers that make use of the Internet Printing Protocol (IPP) and provides resources to other computers on the LAN when the traditional resource-sharing methods aren't ideal. It also lets users host and control their own personal Web sites. Plus, there is nothing to stop a Windows XP Professional computer from acting as a public Internet server in situations where the 10-connection limit isn't a factor. For example, you might use Windows XP Professional as an inexpensive staging server to test Web sites prior to publishing to the final target server.

IIS also includes the SMTP service to allow the computer to act as an SMTP server. The SMTP service accepts incoming connections as well as outgoing connections, but it is intended more as an SMTP relay service than a full-blown e-mail server. The service doesn't provide mailboxes but does support a drop folder for incoming messages not forwarded to another server. While you could write an application to pull messages from the drop folder, it isn't worth the effort considering the minimal cost of the many third-party e-mail servers that run on Windows XP. So the SMTP service is useful mainly as an outgoing e-mail server for messages generated by forms or scripts on the local computer. It's also useful for users who need to send outgoing messages for accounts hosted on remote servers that don't allow mail relay from the user's network.

What they have in common

Both Professional and Home Edition support some new features that simplify networking and add capabilities. For example, both let you bridge network interfaces, which can be handy in a home or small office network where you need to connect two disparate networks, such as a new wireless segment and an existing wired segment. Both also let you maintain an alternate TCP/IP configuration for a network interface. This is great for users who have one configuration for the notebook at the office and a different configuration for it at home.

New wireless technologies are supported by both versions for easy setup and configuration of wireless devices. Another commonality is the lack of NetBEUI. Although NetBEUI is included on the Windows XP CD, Setup no longer lists it as an available protocol. Instead, you have to click Have Disk and browse to the CD to install it.

So which one is right for my company?

What's the bottom line? If you need domain membership and group policy, improved security through IPSec or EFS, or granular protection of shared folders, Windows XP Professional is the solution. If not, you can take advantage of the other new features and streamlined interface provided by Home Edition. At a difference of $100 a seat, you might save a bundle on your next deployment. ❖

Understanding Windows XP Professional networking

By Brien M. Posey, MCSE

I've had several friends tell me they're making the upgrade from Windows 2000 Professional (Win2K Pro) to Windows XP Professional (XP Pro). The first couple of times someone told me this, it seemed a little strange because XP has been out for a few years. If you stop and think about it, though, upgrading today makes sense. Win2K Pro is about five years old. XP, on the other hand, is practically a brand-new operating system because of the long-awaited Service Pack 2. Since so many people are now making the switch to XP, it's time to take a close look at how networking differs between the two venerable operating systems.

Subtle differences

There are subtle differences between the way you access the various networking components in XP and the way you access those same components in Win2K Pro. However, even with the subtle differences, if you're proficient in Win2K Pro networking, you should have no trouble finding your way around in XP. Therefore, rather than telling you all about which icons have moved or which options have been renamed, I'll focus on the new networking features that might not be completely familiar to you. In the sections below, I'll provide an overview of each new networking-related feature.

The Windows XP firewall

If you wanted a personal firewall in Win2K Pro, you had to rely on third-party software. XP, however, offers its own personal firewall—perhaps the most drastic change in the way networking is handled. Originally, it was up to the end user or the system administrator to enable the XP firewall. But in Windows XP Service Pack 2, the firewall is enabled by default. This means that if you have any applications that receive data through nonstandard TCP or UDP ports, those applications may not work correctly under XP SP2 until the necessary ports are opened in the firewall.

To manipulate the firewall settings in XP, right-click the My Network Places icon and select the Properties command from the resulting shortcut menu. In the Network Connections window, right-click the connection that will manage the firewall settings, and select the Properties command from the shortcut menu. You'll now see the connection's properties sheet. At this point, select the properties sheet's Advanced tab, as shown in

Figure A

Figure B

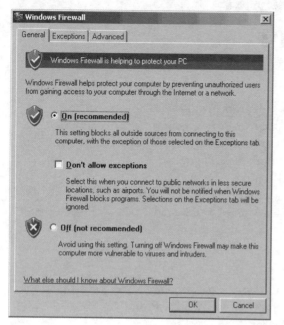

Figure C

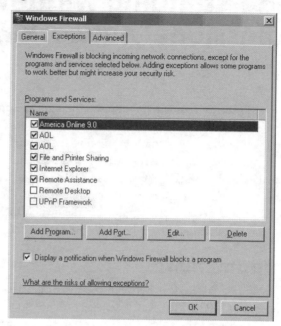

Figure D

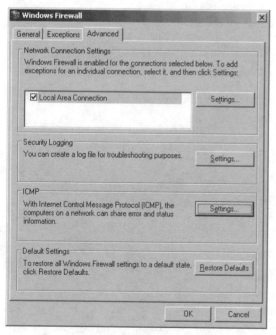

Figure A, and click the Settings button to reveal the Windows Firewall properties sheet.

As **Figure B** shows, the properties sheet's General tab allows you to enable or disable the firewall. The Exceptions tab, shown in **Figure C**, contains a list of ports that should be allowed to pass through the firewall. There are several Windows-related exceptions that are set up by default, but you can customize the list to fit your needs. There's also a check box on the General tab that you can use to prevent Windows from allowing any exceptions.

The Windows Firewall properties sheet also contains an Advanced tab, as shown in **Figure D**. You can use this tab to enable or disable the firewall for each network connection within your computer. You can also use this tab to specify a different set of ports that are allowed to pass through the firewall for each of your computer's network connections. Additionally, the Advanced tab allows you to create a firewall log that can be used for forensic purposes should a security breach occur.

Wireless networks

Another major networking change is in the way wireless networks are implemented. It's possible to establish a connection to a wireless network from a machine running Win2K Pro. Doing so is similar to connecting to any other type of network. You must configure your wireless NIC and then enter the necessary configuration information that will allow you to connect to the desired wireless network.

XP implements wireless networking differently. Win2K Pro was released roughly around the same time as Wi-Fi. Because Wi-Fi was such a new technology at the time, it was not in widespread use and Microsoft didn't have a clear picture of how Wi-Fi would eventually be used.

Today, however, Wi-Fi is everywhere. When Microsoft designed Windows XP, it acknowledged the fact that if you have a laptop and use it on the go, it's very unlikely that you'll remain connected to a single wireless network at all times. A single mobile user might connect to a dozen different wireless networks, if you count the networks at the corporate headquarters, satellite offices, and home. This doesn't even take into account networks at airports or hotels.

With Win2K Pro, each time a user connected to a different wireless network, the user would have to reconfigure the wireless NIC. Typically, this meant entering a different SSID, a WEP encryption key, and possibly a different IP address. XP, however, allows you to have multiple wireless configurations. XP actively seeks out any nearby wireless networks and notifies you of their availability. Whenever possible, XP will automatically configure your wireless NIC's settings to attach to whatever network you happen to be using at the moment.

Another nice thing about the way XP handles wireless networking is that you can set up a preferred network list. For example, suppose you have a wireless network, but so does your next door neighbor; you want to connect to your network and not his. Rather than having Windows lock onto whichever wireless network has the strongest signal at the moment, you can set up a preferred network list to tell Windows which network it should connect to.

Here's one more way that wireless networking has evolved: In Win2K Pro, if you wanted to use encryption over your wireless network, you were limited to whatever form of encryption the wireless NIC's driver allowed. Although this limitation still applies to XP, the operating system itself is 802.1x-aware, which is the authentication technology designed to solve the security problems inherent in WEP encryption.

Remote assistance and remote desktop

Two additional new networking technologies are remote assistance and remote desktop. These features are both designed to allow a machine that's running XP to be remotely controlled.

Remote desktop is based on the same technology as that used in the Terminal Services found in Win2K Server and Windows Server 2003. The remote desktop software allows an XP workstation to act as a remote access server / terminal server. Depending on how the machine is configured, users can connect to their workstation remotely by using either a dial-up or VPN connection. Users are then able to use a terminal service client to remotely control the machine in the same way they would if the machine were running a copy of PC Anywhere.

Remote desktop is primarily designed as a convenience feature that lets users access their PCs while away from the office. Remote assistance is a very similar feature, but it's designed to allow one user to assist another user who is having technical problems. For example, suppose a user was having trouble connecting to a particular network printer. Normally, the user would contact the help desk, which would either send someone over to solve the problem or try to talk the user through the operation over the phone. Both approaches are time-consuming. Fortunately, remote assistance allows the help desk staff to instantly help the user without actually having to travel to the user's location.

Remote assistance doesn't just allow the help desk staff to connect to someone's PC on a whim. Users who are having trouble must actually invite the help desk staff to remotely control their machine. To do so, they would select the Help option from the Start menu, followed by the Remote Assistance option. They could then send the invitation via e-mail or instant message, or they could create an invitation file, put it on a disk, and give it to someone. The recipient would then open the invitation, which would connect the recipient to the person who needed assistance.

Remote assistance caveats

Remote assistance comes with a few conditions. For instance, both the person who requests help and the person who is providing the help must be running XP. Also, there is currently no way of controlling who is being asked for help via remote assistance. Users could ask the help desk for assistance, but they could just as easily ask a coworker or friend who doesn't even work for the company. Furthermore, if a user asks for remote assistance, Windows will automatically open the necessary ports in the Windows Firewall. Fortunately, the corporate firewall will keep those outside the company from providing remote assistance to your users unless you specifically open the necessary ports. ❖

Easy networking for the SOHO with Windows XP

By Debra Littlejohn Shinder, MCSE

Many saw Windows 2000 as Microsoft's attempt to win the enterprise networking market. Now with Windows XP and all its enterprise-friendly features, the Small Office/Home Office (SOHO) network is back in the limelight. The Network Setup Wizard (called the Home Networking Wizard in the first betas) makes it easy to configure a small network and employ Internet Connection Sharing (ICS) to connect that network to the Internet. If you encounter problems along the way, the Home And Small Office Troubleshooter comes to the rescue. In this chapter, I'll take a look at the tools Microsoft has included in Windows XP Home and Professional editions to make SOHO networking a true no-brainer.

Welcome to easy SOHO networking

Windows XP's Help And Support Center (the new and improved Help file) has an entire section called Welcome To Home And Small Office Networking that walks you through the processes involved in setting up a small network, from buying hardware to sharing your Internet connection. A handy checklist ensures that you proceed in a step-by-step fashion (see **Figure A**).

Planning ahead

Before you begin to set up your small network, you'll want to determine the roles of each computer on the network, what resources will be shared, and which computers need Internet access. Other planning considerations include:

- Determining the topology and media type for your network: The topology is the shape or layout of the cabling; the media type refers to the type of cabling or wireless method used.

Figure A

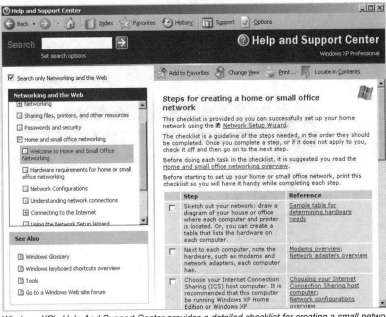

Windows XP's Help And Support Center provides a detailed checklist for creating a small network.

- Ensuring hardware compatibility: The network interface cards (NICs) in all the computers must have Windows XP drivers. (See the Hardware Compatibility List at **www.microsoft.com/hcl**.)

- Selecting a computer to be the ICS host: This is the computer that will connect directly to the Internet via modem, ISDN terminal adapter, DSL, or cable modem.

Off to see the wizards

Windows XP is full of wizards to guide you through the various setup processes. Like Windows 2000, XP includes a New Connection Wizard for setting up connections to the Internet, virtual private networks (VPNs), and LAN connections. New to XP is the Network Setup Wizard, which can be used to configure all the computers on your small network for peer-to-peer file and printer sharing, along with Internet connection sharing.

You can run the Network Setup Wizard (see **Figure B**) from the Windows XP CD-ROM on computers running the following operating systems:

- Windows 98 and Windows 98 SE
- Windows Me
- Windows XP Home or Professional Edition

When you insert the Windows XP installation CD, select Perform Additional Tasks from the splash screen. Then click Set Up Home Or Small Office Networking to start the wizard.

To run the wizard from inside Windows XP, click Start | Control Panel | Network Connections | Common Tasks | Network Setup Wizard. During the process, you can choose to create a floppy disk to run the Network Setup Wizard on the other computers on your network. On the other computers, you'll just run the Netsetup.exe command from the floppy.

Figure B

The Network Setup Wizard can be run on XP, Windows 98/98SE, and Me computers.

Figure C

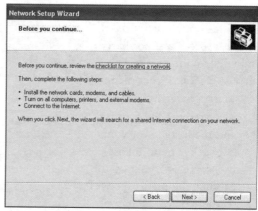

The wizard searches for a shared Internet connection on your network.

Figure D

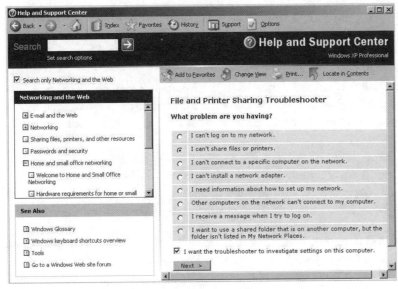

The troubleshooters use a series of questions to gather information about your problem.

When you run the wizard, it automatically searches for a shared Internet connection on your network, as shown in **Figure C**. Thus, you must connect the ICS host computer to the Internet and run the wizard on that computer before setting up the rest of the computers.

The wizard will even walk you through the process of enabling the Internet Connection Firewall and/or network bridging, both discussed later in this chapter.

Troubleshooters to the rescue

Microsoft has included a whole squadron of troubleshooters in Windows XP to address networking and connection problems, including:

- The Internet Connection Sharing (ICS) Troubleshooter
- The Modem Troubleshooter
- The File And Printer Sharing Troubleshooter
- The Drives And Network Adapters Troubleshooter

Troubleshooters for Outlook Express and Internet Explorer are also included, along with a Home And Small Office Networking Troubleshooter to specifically address problems common to the SOHO environment.

These troubleshooters are accessible through the Help And Support Center. They'll walk you through a series of questions designed to gather information about your networking problem and then suggest solutions or additional resources (as shown in **Figure D**).

SOHO security made easy

It's convenient and saves money to have all the computers on your home or office network share a single Internet connection using ICS. And it's great to be able to share your files, but it's not so great if you end up sharing them with strangers to whom you never intended to give access.

When your small network is connected to the Internet, it is possible for outsiders to gain access to the data on your computers' hard disks. Internal security may also be a concern in offices where certain files need to be kept confidential from some coworkers.

Microsoft anticipated this problem and included a new feature in Windows XP: the Internet Connection Firewall (ICF). Windows XP also offers new account management and password features to address internal security, in addition to carrying over Windows 2000's support for file encryption of data on the hard disk.

Built-in personal firewall

The ICF is set up automatically on the ICS host computer when you run the Network Setup Wizard.

To turn on the Internet Connection Firewall when creating a dial-up connection to an ISP in the New Connection Wizard, simply check the Turn On Internet Connection Firewall For This Connection check box, as shown in **Figure E**.

If you choose not to turn on the firewall when you create the connection, you can turn it on for this connection later by right-clicking the connection name in Network Connections (accessed via Start | Control Panel), selecting Properties, clicking the Advanced tab, and checking the check box under Internet Connection Firewall (see **Figure F**).

Once enabled, ICF monitors traffic that comes from the Internet to your private network or Internet-connected computer. It works by maintaining a table of the

Figure E

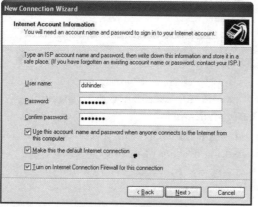

You can use the Internet Connection Firewall with any Internet connection.

Figure F

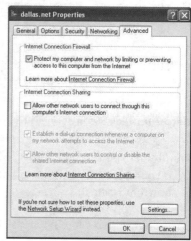

communications that were sent from the computer running ICF or the private network. When packets arrive from the Internet, they are checked against this table to determine whether the communication originated on your local computer or a computer on your private network. If not, the packets are discarded.

If you want to allow traffic across the firewall that did not originate from within (for example, HTTP traffic), you can configure a service definition to allow that traffic in. Do this by clicking the Settings button on the Advanced tab to display the Services sheet, which allows you to select the services you want to open up to outside (Internet) users, as shown in **Figure G**. By default, none of the services are selected.

Using the Security Logging tab, you can have the system create a file called pfirewall.log to record information about dropped packets and/or successful connections from the Internet. You can also determine whether to allow responses to Internet Control Message Protocol (ICMP) requests (such as ping echo requests) using the ICMP tab (see **Figure H**).

User account management

Another important aspect of protecting your small network involves user account management. The XP User Accounts applet, accessed via Control Panel, has a new look, as shown in **Figure I**.

A new feature in Windows XP is the ability to assign a picture to each user account. (This is available only for computers that are not members of a domain.) Also, in Windows XP Professional, the built-in Guest account is disabled by default. This protects the computer from logon by users who do not have a user account.

XP also provides a mechanism for switching between users without having to log off and log back on with the other account. With Fast User Switching, you can leave programs open and they will still be running when you switch back. This is another feature available only with peer-to-peer networks, not on computers that belong to domains.

Password protection

One way to ensure that unauthorized users can't log on with your account is to create a strong password, one that is difficult to guess

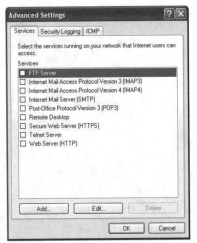

You can configure the firewall to allow outside users to access specific services.

Figure H

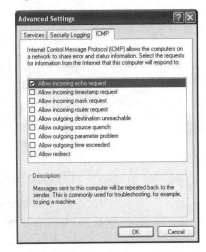

You can determine whether to allow responses to specific ICMP requests.

TIP

If you prefer the old look of Windows 2000, you need only modify the Appearance tab of your Display settings to select Windows Classic Style instead of Windows XP Style.

Figure I

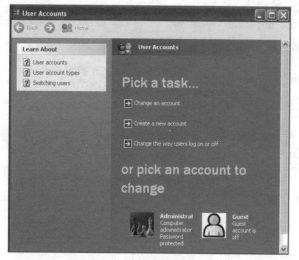

The User Accounts management applet has a new look in Windows XP.

Figure J

The Forgotten Password Wizard allows you to recover a forgotten password with a Password Reset disk.

or "crack" in a brute force attack. The problem with such passwords is that sometimes they're so strong that even the authorized user can't remember them.

Windows XP allows users to create a Password Reset Disk, which can be used to access an account for which the password has been forgotten, using the (what else?) Forgotten Password Wizard, as shown in **Figure J**.

Windows XP also allows you to use the Stored User Names And Passwords feature to manage passwords, such as those used to access password-protected Internet sites.

Growing without pains

SOHO networks, like many other things that start out small, have a tendency to grow. Although it is unlikely that your home or small office network will grow to the enterprise level (though it's also not completely impossible), there is a good chance that you will eventually add more computers, need more advanced capabilities, or otherwise reach a point where you'll want to take advantage of additional networking features built into Windows XP.

Microsoft has included support for a couple of features that might represent the "next step up" for your network:

- Network bridging
- Wireless networking

Let's take a brief look at each of these.

The network bridge

The network bridge lets you connect two local area network segments without routing. With Windows NT and 2000, you could enable IP forwarding and have the computer act as a router. With Windows XP, you can instead configure the computer to act as a bridge—a simpler connectivity configuration that does not require subnetting.

A network bridge can connect two different media types; for example, a thin coax network (10base2) can be connected to a UTP network (10baseT). Bridges also reduce broadcast traffic on the network. With Windows XP, you don't have to buy a hardware bridge; bridging is built into the operating system.

Going wireless

Windows XP offers much better support for wireless networking than its predecessors. This includes:

- 802.1x wireless
- Infrared wireless

The IEEE 802.11 and related specifications provide for implementation of wireless LANs, with provisions for authentication and encryption using spread spectrum radio transmission. Infrared connections use infrared light to transmit network signals and are often used for communications between computers and wireless peripherals such as keyboards and mice. Infrared communications are governed by the Infrared Data Association (IrDA) standards and protocols.

Conclusion

SOHO networking is booming as more and more small offices acquire multiple computers and recognize the advantages of sharing files, printers, disk space, and an Internet connection. As small offices become more sophisticated, they need more of the advanced networking capabilities previously found only in large networks, but in a simpler, easier-to-implement form.

Microsoft Windows XP was designed with the SOHO networker in mind. XP makes it easy to set up, maintain, troubleshoot, and secure a small network. Best of all, it includes support for more sophisticated capabilities that these networks will need to grow beyond the SOHO stage. ❖

TIP
If you have more than one network adapter installed on a computer and run the Network Setup Wizard on that computer, you will be asked whether you want to create a network bridge.

Connect LANs with Windows XP's Network Bridge

By Debra Littlejohn Shinder, MCSE

A new feature in Windows XP is the Network Bridge, which allows you to connect two LAN segments—even if they use different media types—without buying expensive hardware or third-party software. In this chapter, I'll look at the difference between bridging and routing and discuss how you can use a bridge as a low-cost alternative to routing. I'll also discuss how the network bridge works under the hood. After walking you through the process of configuring bridged connections, I'll explain how to troubleshoot problems with the network bridge.

Understanding network bridging

In the "real world," a bridge is a structure that spans the distance between two locations and provides a link or connection from one place to another. In networking terminology, a bridge serves a similar function in that it spans two local area networks and allows packets to get from one to the other.

How a bridge differs from a router

Bridges and routers are both network connectivity devices that connect network segments together. However, there are a number of differences between the two. First, traditional bridges work at the data link layer of the OSI model (layer 2), whereas routers operate at the higher network layer (layer 3). Both bridges and routers build and use address tables, but the bridge works with MAC (physical) addresses, and routers work with IP (logical) addresses.

Because these bridges work below the networking layer where routing takes place, nonroutable protocols such as NetBEUI can cross bridges. Routers are more sophisticated devices than bridges. A bridge generally provides a single path from one network segment to another; a router generally interconnects with other routers to reach many networks on a WAN and can provide several different paths to a destination. Bridges can be combined with routers to produce a *brouter* (rarely used today).

How a bridge differs from a repeater

A repeater is a connectivity device that operates at the physical layer (layer 1) of the OSI model and is used to extend the physical length of a network segment by repeating or regenerating the signals. A bridge also regenerates data when it forwards it across, but does so at the packet level rather than at the signal level. Repeaters can't connect segments that use different media access methods (for example, Ethernet and token ring), but some types of bridges, called translating bridges, can. Most important, repeaters pass everything across without examining addresses or distinguishing between addresses as bridges do.

The purpose of bridging

You can use a bridge to segment a network in order to reduce traffic congestion. The bridge "learns" which MAC addresses reside on which side of the bridge and builds an address table. The first time a message is sent to a particular address, the bridge sends (broadcasts) it to all computers on both sides. In this way, it discovers which side the address belongs to and adds the address to its table. Port numbers are used to represent the different segments. Then, when subsequent messages are sent to that address, the bridge knows to forward the packet to the appropriate segment if the destination address is on a different segment from the source, or, if the source and destination computer are on the same segment, not to forward the packet across the bridge. Consequently, unnecessary traffic doesn't cross the bridge.

Bridges can connect two network segments that use different media into a single subnet (for example, Ethernet and wireless), as long as they use the same network protocol (for example, TCP/IP). The bridge would also work to connect a group of computers networked together via Cat 5 cable with another group connected via thin coax.

You can use a bridge instead of buying a wireless access point. If you have a computer with a wireless NIC that needs to connect to the wired network, and one of the computers on the wired Ethernet network also has a wireless NIC, you can run the wireless adapters in ADHOC mode (no WAP required) and create the bridge on the computer that has both wired and wireless NICs.

How the XP Network Bridge works

Just as a router can be either a dedicated device or a software construct on a computer, so can a bridge. Microsoft has included bridging software in Windows XP (32-bit edition only) to make it easier for home and small business users, who don't need the sophistication of a router, to connect small LAN segments without spending extra money for a separate connectivity device. XP's Network Bridge is designed specifically for connecting LAN segments of mixed-media types. The bridge automates the process of forwarding data from one media type to another without requiring that you set up separate subnets for each media type and manually configure packet forwarding between the subnets.

The most common scenario consists of a small network that has both a cabled Ethernet LAN and an 802.11 wireless network that need to work together. Other possibilities include USB, IEEE 1394, or Home Phone Line Network Adapter (HPNA) networks. You need one computer that has network interfaces to both networks; this computer runs XP and has the bridge enabled. There can be only one bridge on an XP computer, but it can bridge multiple network connections as long as the computer has a network adapter installed for each.

TIP

XP's Network
Bridge works only
with Ethernet-com-
patible adapters.
Adapters on which
certain features—
such as the Internet
connection firewall
(ICF) and Internet
connection sharing
(ICS)—are enabled
cannot be part of a
bridge. If you want
to bridge those
connections, you
must first disable
ICF or ICS.

A peek under the hood of the Network Bridge

Windows XP's bridge uses a combination of traditional layer 2 bridging, also called transparent bridging and defined in IEEE 802.1D. The bridge puts the network adapters that belong to it in "promiscuous mode." This means that the adapter can intercept all packets that are transmitted—not just those addressed to it. The MAC address of every message is checked, and the bridge builds its database (address table) from the information.

Promiscuous mode requires that the adapters support that mode of operation. If they don't, the XP bridge uses layer 3 bridging. This bridging uses the address resolution protocol (ARP) to resolve MAC addresses to IP addresses, with the bridge acting as an ARP proxy. In this situation, the bridge maintains a layer 3 forwarding table that contains both IP and MAC addresses. Layer 3 bridging works only with the TCP/IP protocols, for the obvious reason that only TCP/IP uses IP addresses.

XP's bridge uses a common bridging algorithm called the spanning tree algorithm (STA). The STA is used to prevent bridging "loops" that can occur if there are multiple bridges on the network, a problem that arises when bridges receive duplicate copies of a message and update their address tables incorrectly in response. When a loop is formed, bridges forward traffic indefinitely. This causes unnecessary traffic that slows down network performance.

The STA creates a logical tree topology so that there will be only one path between any two segments. If a bridge fails, however, the algorithm allows the network to automatically reconfigure the topology for fault tolerance. The STA also ensures that the data will take the most efficient path.

Bridges communicate with each other about the network topology via STA packets, with each bridge identifying itself by its lowest-numbered MAC address (remember that a bridge has at least two network interfaces). The bridge with the lowest identification number is called the root bridge.

For more information about the STA, go to **http://support.baynetworks.com/library/tpubs/html/router/soft1000/bridge/2950A-19.html**.

Configuring bridged connections

XP makes it easy to configure bridged connections. If you have multiple network adapters installed (for example, an Ethernet 10BaseT card and an 802.11b wireless NIC), you can run the Network Setup Wizard, which will detect the multiple adapters and ask if you want to bridge the connections. To run the Network Setup

TIP

Note that it is possible for you to disable the STA by editing the registry. For instructions on how to do so, see "Manage Network Bridge Feature" (**www.winguides.com/registry/display.php/1245**). This article also contains instructions for disabling packet forwarding on the bridge.

Figure A

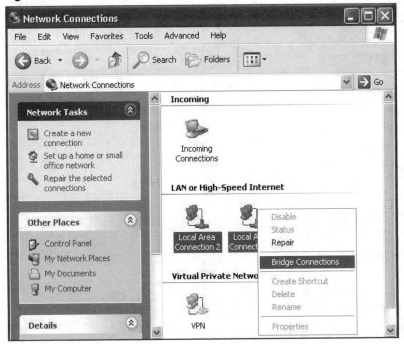

Select two connections you want to bridge, right-click, and choose Bridge Connections.

TIP
You might have multiple adapters installed because you have a NIC that connects to a broadband Internet connection device, such as a DSL or cable modem. These adapters cannot be bridged.

Wizard, select Control Panel | Network Connections and choose Set Up A Home Or Small Office Network in the left pane under Network Tasks. (Note that this option will not appear if your XP computer belongs to a domain.)

In fact, the default is to bridge connections, which causes bridges to be created inadvertently. If you don't want to create a bridge, you need to select Let Me Choose The Connections To My Network when you receive the message that "Your computer has multiple connections." Then clear the check boxes for all except one of the network adapters listed.

Creating the bridge

To create a bridge, you must have two eligible connections. Open the Network Connections applet from Control Panel and highlight the connections you want to bridge by using [Ctrl] and clicking to select each. Right-click and select Bridge Connections from the context menu, as shown in **Figure A**.

You will be asked to wait while Windows bridges the connections. This can take a few moments. Afterward, a new section titled Network Bridge will appear, with an icon representing the network bridge as well as the icons for the connections you have bridged, as shown in **Figure B**.

Figure B

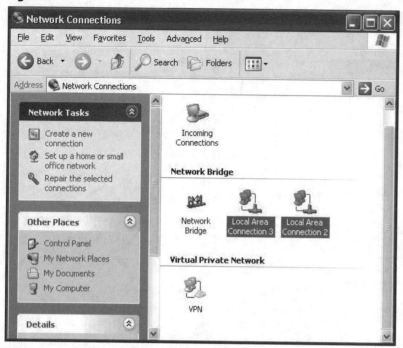

After you create the bridge, a new icon will appear in your Network Connections.

Figure C

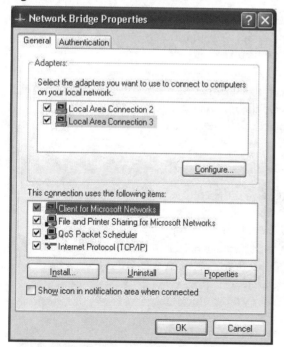

The properties for the bridged connections are now configured as part of the bridge.

Figure D

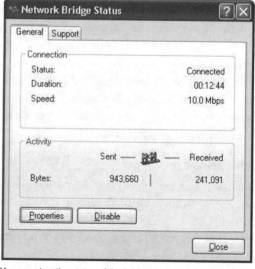

You can view the status of the bridge as you can with any network connection.

Now, when you double-click either of the original connection icons and click the Properties button, you'll no longer see the properties for the adapter. Instead, you'll see a message that says: "This adapter is part of the Network Bridge. To remove this adapter from the Network Bridge, or to modify bridge settings, right-click the Network Bridge, and then click Properties."

The properties sheet for the bridge will show the adapters that are part of the bridge and the network clients, services, and protocols used, as shown in **Figure C**.

Note that you can no longer add or remove items for the connections separately. Adding, removing, or changing the properties of any of the items used by the connection will apply to all adapters that belong to the bridge. You can view the connection status of the bridge, just as you can for any network connection, as shown in **Figure D**.

What have you accomplished by bridging the connections? Now the computers on both network segments can communicate with one another, and computers on one segment can connect to the Internet through a shared connection on the other segment.

Modifying, disabling, and removing the bridge

To disable the bridge, right-click its icon and choose Disable from the context menu. If you remove one or more of the network adapters that are part of the bridge, and there is only one adapter left, the bridge will keep using your system resources even though it is not serving any useful function, until you disable it. To remove a connection from the bridge, right-click the connection's icon (not the bridge icon) and select Remove From Bridge.

Troubleshooting bridge problems

If you are unable to create a network bridge, check the following:

- You must be logged on as a member of the administrator's group to create, modify, or remove the bridge.
- Be sure that ICF and ICS are not enabled on the connections you are trying to bridge.
- Group Policy settings must not prohibit the installation, configuration, and use of the network bridge. These settings are in the Computer Configuration\Administrative Templates\Network\Network Connections node of the local computer GPO. The settings are "location aware," which means they apply

only if you're connected to the same network from which the settings were obtained. When the settings are enabled, the network bridge service won't run, and the option to bridge connections won't appear in the context menu. For more information about how Group Policy affects Windows XP networking features, see Microsoft's online document "Using Group Policy Settings with Windows XP Home Networking Features" (**www.microsoft.com/windowsxp/ pro/techinfo/administration/homenetgp/default.asp**).

- The computer on which the bridge is created must stay on in order for the bridge to work. If that computer is turned off, the network segments will no longer be connected.

Summary

The network bridge, a handy new feature in Windows XP, can save you the cost of buying additional hardware devices and the hassle of configuring routing on your network when you need to connect two or more segments that use different types of network media. Bridging connections is easy—in fact, so easy that the Network Setup Wizard sometimes creates unwanted bridges. XP's Network Bridge software can use traditional layer 2 bridging or, if the network adapters don't support the promiscuous mode that is needed, it can use layer 3 bridging that relies on IP addresses and ARP. ❖

Connect anything with Universal Plug and Play in Windows XP

By Steven Pittsley, CNE

Imagine using My Network Places to browse for switches, routers, printers, digital cameras, and other peripheral devices. Now think about how convenient it would be if these devices were attached to the network and available for use without installing device drivers or performing a complicated setup routine. Does this sound too good to be true? It's not.

The first version of Universal Plug and Play (UPnP) was included in Windows Me, and although it was far from perfect, it was a solid first step. Windows XP includes a revision of UPnP and with it, you can install network printers, Internet gateways, and various electronic devices, such as digital cameras and video recorders. I'll cover here what an IT support professional should know about UPnP.

First things first: Secure your network

UPnP may make it easier to install and configure your network devices and peripherals, but it also has a couple of very serious security flaws that, if not patched, could give a malicious hacker the opportunity to gain control of your computer. If you haven't already installed the patch to correct this problem, read this section, download the new code, and immediately install it. After securing your machines, you may then read on.

Buffer overruns have become one of the tricks of the trade with which hackers perform their devious actions. In the case of UPnP, a hacker can send to the machine a malicious Notify message, which will imitate the UPnP service and give the hacker system-level privileges on the Windows XP machine. This will effectively give the hacker total control over the system.

Another popular hacker trick that can be exploited through the UPnP service is the denial of service (DoS) attack. Someone can manipulate this flaw and cause a DoS attack through two possible methods. The first occurs when a device's description is stored on a third-party server. In this scenario, a hacker could send a nefarious Notify request to a machine asking for its description. While this seems like a harmless task, it isn't regulated in the Windows XP UPnP service. If the server has the echo service running on a certain IP port, it's possible that the requesting system could be put into an endless cycle of downloading the description and clogging up the network with useless messages.

The second DoS attack method occurs if enough computers responded to the Notify request and flood the server with description requests. Again, the network would be brought to its knees by the overflow of useless messages.

The possibility of these types of attacks occurring relies on several circumstances being present, such as the UPnP service being installed. However, as more and more people begin to use UPnP, the chances of it occurring become greater. So, before you read any further, I recommend going to **www.microsoft.com/ downloads/release.asp?releaseid=34951&area=top&ordinal=7** to download the patch to fix this flaw.

Technical overview of Universal Plug and Play

Before I discuss some of the more technical aspects of UPnP, you should be familiar with some basic terms that are associated with this new technology:

- **Action:** A command that causes a service to perform a specific function
- **Service:** A function of a device that is controlled by the UPnP control point

What exactly is Universal Plug and Play?

In June of 1999, a group of computer industry organizations formed the Universal Plug and Play Forum. The goal of this group is to extend the simplicity that Plug and Play brought to device installation on network devices. From this group came what we now know as Universal Plug and Play (UPnP).

Before Windows 95, IT pros faced a daunting challenge when they decided to take the plunge and upgrade or add a peripheral device to a user's system. In those days, it took some understanding of how computers worked to install peripherals. Today, we barely need to think about these things because Plug and Play has made installing new hardware so easy. A novice can manage most installations.

Although UPnP is designed to make peripheral devices easier to install and use, it has very little in common with traditional Plug and Play. Both technologies make it easier for you to use peripheral devices, but that's where the similarity ends. The UPnP architecture is designed to let your users employ devices across a network, while traditional Plug and Play only allows them to install local peripherals.

UPnP is based on the premise of the peer-to-peer LAN and is designed for home, small business, and single-site networks. The UPnP architecture allows intelligent UPnP devices that are connected in a LAN to communicate with UPnP control points, such as a computer, that have been configured on the network. To do this, the devices use several different communication protocols and standards, including TCP/IP. Once the device has described itself and its capabilities, it will receive an IP address through DHCP, and network users will be able to use the device without going through a complicated setup process.

Because UPnP uses TCP/IP and other nonproprietary protocols, it is operating-system independent. This provides unparalleled flexibility. For instance, a user in a heterogeneous network will be able to discover and use peripheral devices that are attached to Windows workstations, Macintosh computers, or standalone devices such as switches and routers. This flexibility will give your users a wider variety of computing platforms to choose from and allow them to select the solution that best fits their needs.

- **Device:** A container holding one or more services that are available for use
- **Control Point:** UPnP client software responsible for sending and receiving actions and retrieving service and device descriptions
- **Subscription:** The relationship that is formed between the UPnP service and a control point
- **Event:** Messages that are sent from a device to a control point to provide continual information about the status of the device

Now that you understand some of the terminology that's associated with UPnP, let's look at how this technology works. UPnP is comprised of five components:

1. **Discovery:** When you connect a device or control point on the network, it advertises its presence using Simple Service Discovery Protocol (SSDP). The messages that are exchanged among devices and control points include information such as the device type, the kinds of services that are offered, a simple identifier, and a description URL that points to a location containing more detailed information about the device.

2. **Description:** Once a control point locates a device, it must obtain more detailed information about the device. During the Description process, the control point uses the URL description that was provided during Discovery. The URL points to an XML document that includes such things as the device make, model, serial number, and manufacturer name, as well as other URLs to vendor-specific Web sites.

3. **Control:** After the control point has received the detailed device description, the Control component begins to gather the information that it needs to use the device. The control point sends control messages to the control URL for the service. This message, which is transmitted using the Simple Object Access Protocol (SOAP), contains additional XML-based information that determines how the device will respond.

4. **Eventing:** Now that the control point has subscribed to the service, it requires occasional event messages that announce any changes in the device status. This process is called Eventing. During this process, the update messages sent are established using the General Event Notification Architecture (GENA). These messages are XML-based and are sent using HTTP.

5. **Presentation:** The final component of the UPnP networking architecture is Presentation. If the UPnP device provides a Presentation URL, it will be used for browser-based management of the device. The control point is used to determine the presentation URL from the XML-based description document, load the page into the browser, and allow you to manage the device.

Figure A

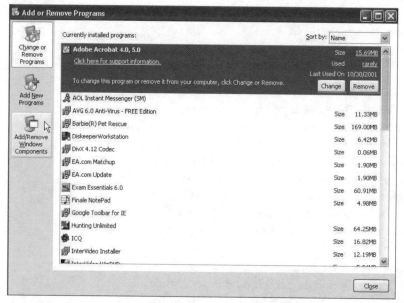

Figure B

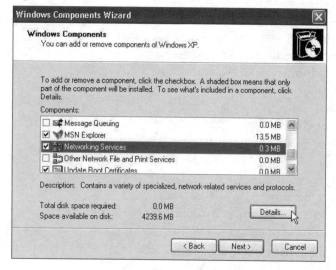

Activating and using UPnP

UPnP is, by default, not activated when
Windows XP is installed. This is good in
light of the security flaws discussed earlier.
Installing UPnP is an easy process that takes
just a few mouse clicks.

To begin the installation, select the Add
Or Remove Programs icon from Control
Panel. In the Add/Remove Programs dialog
box, click the Add/Remove Windows
Components button, as shown in **Figure A**.

The Windows Components Wizard dialog
box will be displayed, as shown in **Figure B**.
To reach the UPnP settings, select the
Networking Services option and then click
Details. To install UPnP, check the Universal
Plug And Play option, as shown in **Figure C**.

That's it. UPnP has now been installed on
your computer, and you're ready to use it.
To access UPnP devices on your network,
open My Network Places. They will be
displayed here, and you can use them by
double-clicking on the appropriate icon.

How Universal Plug and Play benefits the IT professional

At first glance, UPnP might appear to be yet another security flaw in Windows XP that needs patching and constant vigilance. But under the appropriate circumstances, UPnP can provide both users and IT professionals with substantial benefits. For example, UPnP technology can be used to manage UPnP-enabled network devices such as switches and routers. In addition, UPnP will make asset tracking and inventory much easier, without additional software to install and configure.

The increased functionality for users will definitely benefit the help desk and support staff. For example, when users need to use a different printer, they'll be able to locate the printer through My Network Places and print to it. There will be no more need to have the help desk staff configure the printer software because UPnP will handle those tasks. This will result in a more efficient use of the user's time and fewer issues for the help desk and support staff.

Figure C

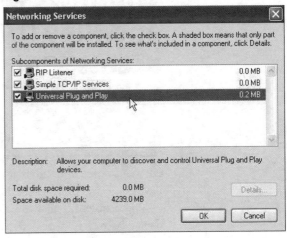

Conclusion

Even though Windows XP is the second Microsoft operating system to include UPnP, some bugs obviously need to be worked out. With all software, the early versions can be rough around the edges. UPnP is a wonderful idea to help make peripheral device installation and use as easy for the everyday user as it is for the sophisticated technician, which will simplify the IT pro's work. It's very early in the game, but the outlook appears promising, despite the security flaws found. For now, IT professionals will find UPnP useful for device management and for the increased flexibility that it provides. ❖

Windows XP and Universal Plug and Play (UPnP) smooth Internet access

By Dr. Thomas Shinder, MCSE

Have you ever faced this scenario? A user moves to a DSL or cable connection from a 56K modem and all the Internet games, chat tools, and voice and video applications stop working. ISP support staff frequently have to deal with this situation.

The problem is that the user didn't have a NAT (Network Address Translation) device between his or her machine and the Internet when he or she used the 56K dial-up connection. Now that the user is using a broadband router, he or she is forced to use NAT. NAT devices usually break applications using complex protocols that require dynamic port assignments on the external interface of the NAT device and those that require secondary inbound connections. The situation is often irreparable. The user may even get disgusted with the ISP and dump the broadband connection.

This whole scenario could have been avoided if the NAT device and the client applications supported Universal Plug and Play (UPnP) and NAT Traversal. The good news is that Windows XP includes APIs for client applications to take advantage of UPnP, and the Windows XP Internet Connection Services (ICS) and Internet Connection Firewall (ICF) are both UPnP-compliant.

What is Universal Plug and Play?

UPnP is a collection of networking protocols that allows UPnP network devices to automatically communicate with one another. TCP, UDP, IP, and HTTP are the core networking protocols driving UPnP. UPnP devices are DHCP clients that also support Automatic Private IP Addressing (APIPA) when a DHCP server isn't available.

UPnP is independent of network architecture. It works equally well on Ethernet, wireless, infrared, and any other network medium. Because UPnP is standards-based, it's operating-system-independent. UPnP standards are developed by the Universal Plug and Play Forum, which has almost 400 members representing virtually all the major hardware and software companies.

Key components of UPnP include:

- Automatic discovery of UPnP devices
- Automatic configuration of UPnP device protocols
- Automatic registration and deregistration of UPnP services
- Automatic network addressing

- Support for protocol bridging that allows UPnP devices to communicate with devices using other protocols such as X10

For example, suppose you want to connect a wireless network access point to your network. The wireless access point and the wireless clients both support UPnP. The wireless access point will obtain an IP address from a DHCP server. The wireless client will also obtain an address from a DHCP server. If there's no DHCP server online, both the access point and wireless client will self-assign addresses in the APIPA range (169.254.0.0/16).

The wireless access client will use UPnP protocols to discover the wireless access point. This is done using UDP multicast messages. The wireless access point listens on this multicast address. The wireless access point responds with UPnP device-specific information to inform the client of its capabilities and features.

The same technology can be used to enable a whole host of network devices and services. You can enable household devices such as radios, lights, VCRs, DVD players, televisions, heaters, air conditioners, and even clocks, to use UPnP. When these devices join the network, they announce themselves to a multicast address. Devices configured to respond to the multicast announcements get information about the presence and capabilities of these devices. Applications used to configure these devices can discover the devices automatically.

Network Address Translation challenges solved by UPnP

Traditional NAT servers replace the source address and port with the address and a random port number of the external interface of the NAT server. This works well for simple protocols such as HTTP and SMTP, but it can create problems for more complex protocols that require multiple response ports on the external interface of the NAT server. NAT servers also aren't aware of information stored in the data portion of the application layer header without the help of NAT editors and similar software fixes.

Windows XP's answer to these problems is NAT Traversal, which can automatically allow the UPnP-enabled NAT client application to communicate with a UPnP NAT device. NAT Traversal provides methods to allow the UPnP client to learn the public IP address of the NAT server and to negotiate dynamically assigned port mappings for UPnP NAT client applications.

NAT Traversal features can be built into any hardware device or software application. Applications that commonly cause troubles for NAT devices but work well when they're UPnP-enabled include the following:
- Multiplayer Internet games
- Audio and video communications
- Terminal Services clients and servers
- Peer-to-peer file sharing applications

When these applications are UPnP-enabled, access through the Windows XP ICS allows them to work seamlessly.

Case study: Windows XP Instant Messenger

The Windows XP Instant Messenger (Windows Messenger) application poses special problems for NAT devices. Network and firewall administrators often have to deal with the Instant Messenger's voice or video features not working. These problems are related to one or more of the following problems:

- Certain IM features require that a static port be used for all clients. This allows only a single client on the internal network to use that feature. Access for other clients is blocked.

- Some features require the NAT device to create port mappings that are accessible to an external client and have those map to a specific internal network client.

- When features embed the private address in the application-layer header, the Internet host receiving the private address cannot respond to the private network host.

Windows XP provides client support via the NAT Traversal APIs so that the Windows Messenger features will work with the Windows XP ICS and ICF. Some of the specific actions that UPnP support allows for include the following:

- The Windows XP Messenger can detect that it is behind an ICS gateway.

- The Windows XP Messenger can inform the ICS gateway which ports need to be dynamically opened to allow external clients to create new inbound secondary connections.

- The Windows XP Messenger is able to communicate to the ICS gateway which dynamic ports are required for audio, video, and data sharing (such as the Whiteboard feature).

- The ICS gateway is able to determine whether the peer Messenger client is also located on the internal network and will allow the two to communicate directly.

The ICS UPnP NAT Traversal features work nicely with the Windows XP Messenger because the UPnP client is able to communicate its requirements to the UPnP server. Without the aid of UPnP, making advanced features such as voice and video communications work through a NAT or combination NAT/firewall (such as ISA Server) is impossible. The fact is that you can't make voice and video work with ISA Server because there is no Application Layer Gateway (like the H.323 Gatekeeper Service) to support these protocols.

Conclusion

Windows XP supports UPnP so that network devices and services can communicate with one another automatically. UPnP uses TCP/IP protocols so that it can work seamlessly on existing networks. Windows XP ICS and ICF use UPnP NAT Traversal, which allows the UPnP-aware client application to negotiate required ports on the ICS NAT device. UPnP NAT Traversal solves many of the problems users have when trying to make applications that require complex protocols work with conventional NAT devices. We can expect to see in the future a number of household devices such as DVD players, VCRs, televisions, and stereos support UPnP so that they can be seamlessly integrated into an existing home network. ❖

Firing up Windows XP Internet Connection Firewall

By Steven Pittsley, CNE

With the advent of broadband, an increasing number of homes and small businesses are finding it easy to connect their LANs to the Internet. While this provides many outstanding benefits, it does increase the possibility of your network being attacked by unlawful users with malicious intentions. To help you thwart such an attack, Microsoft has integrated an Internet Connection Firewall (ICF) software package with its latest operating system, Windows XP. In this article, I'll show you how to enable and configure the ICF to effectively protect your home or small-business network from hackers looking to wreak havoc on an unsuspecting LAN.

Enabling the Windows XP ICF

Enabling the ICF is a straightforward process. First, access the Local Area Connection Properties in Windows XP: Right-click the My Network Places icon, select Properties, right-click the Local Area Connection icon, and then select Properties. In the Local Area Connection Properties dialog box, click on the Advanced tab. As shown in **Figure A**, enabling the ICF is as simple as selecting the option and clicking OK.

Figure A

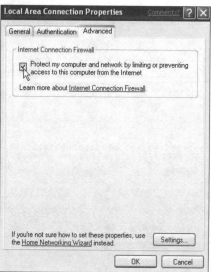

Figure B

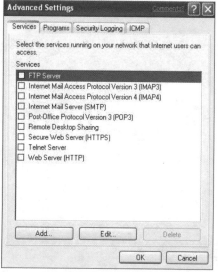

You'll use these four tabs to configure the ICF for your environment.

When the ICF is enabled, a red border will surround the Local Area Network icon. At this point, the software will be active, using the default configuration settings to protect your system from intruders.

Configuring the Windows XP ICF

After enabling the ICF, you'll need to configure it for your computing environment. Click on the Settings button located in the lower-right corner of the dialog box where you enabled the firewall (see Figure A) to gain access to the four tabs in the Advanced Settings dialog box: Services, Programs, Security Logging, and ICMP (see **Figure B**).

Services tab

The Services tab allows you to select the network services that users located outside of your network can use. For example, if you would like to host your own Web site, you can select the Web Server (HTTP) service, allowing users to access the site from the Internet. If you have an e-business with a secure site to collect payment information, you would also want to select the Secure Web Server (HTTPS) service.

In addition to the default services, you can add a service. Click the Add button to open the Service Settings dialog box, shown in **Figure C**. Enter a descriptive name for the service, the IP address of the computer that is hosting the service on your network, and the TCP or UDP port that this service uses.

Once you have decided which services to select, you must provide the IP address of the network computer that is hosting the service. Highlight the service, click the Edit button, and enter the IP address in the appropriate field. The Service Settings dialog box will look like the one shown in Figure C, except the description and default TCP or UDP port will be filled in and cannot be changed. If you're using a different port number, you'll have to add the service. To do so, click on the Add button on the Services tab. You'll be presented with a window similar to the one in Figure C, where you can enter the appropriate information.

Programs tab

The Programs tab, shown in **Figure D**, allows you to make a program available to users who are located outside of your network.

Figure C

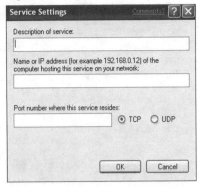

When you click OK, the new service will be displayed in the Services list.

Figure D

You might use this feature to allow access to programs that are hosted on your network.

Figure E

Figure F

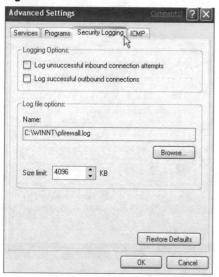

You can select the location to store the log file as well as specify a size limit for the log file.

Figure G

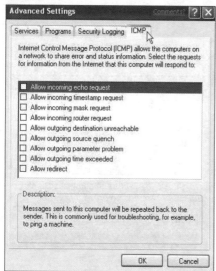

To add a program to the ICF, click the Add button on the Programs tab. The Program Settings dialog box will be presented, as shown in **Figure E**. You must enter a description of the program, the TCP or UDP server port number, and the TCP or UDP port range that the program will use. To modify an existing program configuration, you must highlight the appropriate program and click the Edit button on the Programs tab.

Security Logging tab

The Security Logging tab allows you to configure the firewall logging functions. As shown in **Figure F**, you can log the unsuccessful inbound connection attempts and the successful outbound connections.

ICMP tab

The ICMP tab, shown in **Figure G**, lets you configure how the computer will share information with other computers on the network or Internet using the Internet Control Message Protocol. The descriptions of each request option are as follows:

- **Allow Incoming Echo Request** allows the computer to respond to another machine that has sent a ping command.

- **Allow Incoming Timestamp Request** will reply to each message that the computer receives with a confirmation message that includes a timestamp.

- **Allow Incoming Mask Request** allows the computer to listen for and respond to requests for more information about its public network.

- **Allow Incoming Router Request** lets the computer share information about the routers that it recognizes.

- **Allow Outgoing Destination Unreachable** causes the computer to display a destination unreachable message when it doesn't receive information coming from the Internet.

- **Allow Outgoing Source Quench** will ask the sender to reduce the rate at which it is sending data when the computer can't keep up with the amount of data being received.

- **Allow Outgoing Parameter Problem** causes the computer to discard data with a bad header and display a bad header error message.

Windows XP Service Pack 2 update

Windows XP received a major Service Pack upgrade in August 2004, and with it came changes to how the Internet Connection Firewall (ICF) is configured. When you upgrade to Service Pack 2, ICF (now called Windows Firewall) is automatically turned on by default. This change may impact how your systems operate, especially if they use a port or application that the new Windows Firewall settings close. To configure Windows Firewall, simply right-click the My Network Places icon on the Start Menu and select Properties. Find the connection you need to configure, then right-click its icon. Select Properties to display the Connections Properties dialog box. Select the Advanced tab and click the Settings button to display the new Windows Firewall dialog box. This dialog box will allow you to turn off the firewall, make exceptions for certain programs, and configure advanced tasks.

- **Allow Outgoing Time Exceeded** allows the computer to reply with a time-out message when the computer discards a message due to a timeout.
- **Allow Redirect** lets the data that the computer sends be rerouted if the default route changes.

Conclusion

The Windows XP ICF is a solid product and, when configured correctly, it does a very good job of protecting your home or small-business network from external attacks. However, one major flaw in ICF is that it doesn't stop traffic to outbound Internet connections. This missing piece could allow a hacker to remotely control a network computer or use it as a zombie in a DDoS attack. To completely secure your network, you might look into using an additional firewall software package. One such product is ZoneAlarm Pro, which is made by Zone Labs and has a retail price of $39.95 for a single user license.

While this flaw would make me hesitant to use ICF as the only firewall protection for my small-business network, I'm sure that Microsoft will correct the omission through service packs or future releases of the product. Once it does this, ICF will be a very good choice of firewall software that the cost-conscious home user or small business will appreciate. ❖

WinXP Pro could be the best choice for remote workers

By Carol Bailey, MCSE+I

Many companies are now faced with the choice of whether to use Windows XP Professional on workstations and laptops or to standardize on Windows 2000 Professional. In the majority of cases, Windows 2000 is currently the preferred choice, for the following reasons:

- It requires less memory (which is particularly important if upgrading older machines).
- It reduces the total cost of ownership (TCO) by having the same platform for workstations and servers (if running Windows 2000 Server).
- Return on investment happens faster if users and IT staff have to learn only one platform.
- Many of the new features in XP are deemed "nice to have" rather than "must have" for businesses.

The XP exception

Of course, there are always exceptions. Possible reasons to deploy Windows XP Professional include cheaper licenses and a longer support cycle from Microsoft. In addition, if just one of those bells and whistles in the new XP feature set offers a significant business benefit, that could be reason enough to opt for XP. For example, users whose work regularly includes desktop publishing activities on TFT screens might find that XP's support for ClearType could tip the balance in choosing XP over Windows 2000.

And there's one small, often overlooked market where I think Windows XP Professional comes into its own and is a better choice than Windows 2000 (and previous Windows operating systems): remote workers, especially those who frequently work from home.

Many XP features suit the home worker particularly well. You're unlikely to hear or read about them because it's assumed that XP Professional will be deployed on corporate networks and XP Home Edition will be used at home. But home workers fall between these two markets. They require business features such as security and networking, yet most of the time, their computers function as stand-alone or workgroup machines, remote from corporate resources such as central servers and the help desk. Windows XP Professional offers a number of features that are not available in previous Windows versions, or in XP Home Edition. Strangely enough, it also offers many useful features that are not available when XP Professional is in a domain.

The home environment

It makes sense to consider this market when you're looking at platform choices. Home workers are increasing in numbers, and their technical environment can have a significant impact on their productivity and on your help desk. Resolving problems for home workers is usually more difficult for the help desk. It invariably takes longer and may require additional skills when the computer in question is remote and possibly a nonstandard build. The effect on the end user can be especially significant if alternative systems are not available when trying to recover from a problem.

Home workers are those who work away from the office but need occasional access to the corporate network, typically via a virtual private network (VPN). They can include mobile users as well as employees who often use their home computer(s) for work purposes in addition to having a computer at the office.

Home working is a good solution for many people because it decreases travel time and increases efficiency by minimizing typical office disruptions. Nowadays, a home computer with Internet connectivity is fast becoming the norm. Home workers can collaborate with coworkers in a number of ways, including e-mail, instant messaging, and teleconferencing, and they can access corporate resources with remote access (VPN or dial-up point-to-point).

On the downside, these home computers are particularly vulnerable to stability and security issues because they are outside the immediate realm of the corporate help desk, where standard builds are used, central servers safeguard data, and users have minimal rights. Home computers break free from this safety net because they lead a double life as home computers and work computers. This means that the user require full administrator rights so they can install software and devices and generally manage the system.

These home machines typically fulfill a home entertainment role and include access for multiple users (family members), gaming, and digital image and sound support. It's also not unusual for a household to have more than one computer, in which case, simple networking may also be set up. All of these things can present unique challenges—and some of the new features in XP can help to meet them.

Why XP over Windows 2000

I've assumed here that running a version of Windows older than Windows 2000 (such as Windows 9x, Windows Me, or Windows NT 4.0) is not desirable. So I'll be introducing Windows XP features that are different from Windows 2000 and that are particularly well suited to the home worker.

Some of these features, such as Remote Assistance and Remote Desktop, are well documented and form part of Microsoft's 70-270 exam objectives. But others may be less well known, particularly if they're not available in a domain environment. I've categorized them below into usability, security, and troubleshooting sections, although there is obviously some overlap. In my next article, I'll take a more detailed look at the advantages offered by these features.

Usability features
- Extensive support for wireless networks
- Network bridging
- Fast user switching
- Remote desktop
- Fax console
- Compressed (zipped) folders
- NetCrawler (for locating printers)
- File And Settings Transfer Wizard (or User Migration Tool)
- Locally shared folders
- Group taskbar buttons and configurable system tray ("notification area")
- Media Player 8
- Native support for DVDs and CD writing/rewriting
- Over 256 colors for Terminal Services clients

Security features
- Offline file encryption
- Internet connection firewall (ICF)
- Internet discovery and control
- Automatic updates

Troubleshooting features
- Remote assistance
- Password reset disk and password hints
- Driver roll-back
- System restore points
- Automated system recovery (ASR)
- Safe editing of Boot.ini
- Single registry editor
- Program Compatibility Wizard
- Faster execution of Chkdsk
- New options for Disk Cleanup
- Customized interface components

Why XP Professional over XP Home Edition?

When users are connected to the corporate network over a VPN, XP Professional offers a number of features that may be applicable for the home worker, especially if they need to connect to a domain:

- Active Directory Group Policy, including folder redirection and software installation/maintenance
- System policy support for NT4 domains
- Roaming user profiles
- Login scripts
- Logon that includes the Log On Using Dial-Up Connections option
- Offline files and folders
- Client service for NetWare

Security features

- Local policies (user rights, auditing, security options, desktop lockdown, etc.)
- EFS
- ACL Editor
- Full security sharing (Deselect Use Simple File Sharing (Recommended) under Folder Options | View, and you will have granular access to sharing options such as the user limit, permissions, caching, and ability to create a new share.)
- IPSec for secure transmission of data (e.g., with wireless connections, Internet connections, and VPN connections utilizing L2TP/IPSec)

Other miscellaneous enhancements

- Multiprocessor support (for number-crunching applications)
- IIS (to host Web and FTP sites, etc.)
- Running Remote Desktop to an office computer with Windows XP Professional. (If you're working at home and want to remotely access your work computer using Remote Desktop, you will need Windows XP Professional at home.)
- Multilanguage user interface. This requires the MUI-Pack, which is available only with volume licensing.

Product activation

But what about the pesky Windows product activation? If Windows XP is preinstalled from an OEM, or a copy is installed from the company's volume or select licensing agreement, it won't be an issue. Outside of that, most users will have to take the hit, with the knowledge that it should be a one-time event. When a network adapter is installed, up to five items can be changed in the computer without having to reactivate (three items, if there is no network adapter or if it is changed).

Reinstalling from scratch won't require reactivation if you are under the number of items, and you can reactivate up to four times in one year.

For most home workers, activation should present minimal inconvenience, and I think is a small price to pay for the other benefits you can gain.

Final analysis

Although the new feature set in Windows XP Professional seems to offer few business benefits for the corporate network, it definitely shines as the operating system of choice for home workers. Falling between the markets of the corporate environment and home user, remote workers need the best of both worlds to work effectively and securely from home.

Networking and security features not found in Windows XP Home Edition provide the computing environment required. And ease of use and troubleshooting safeguards not found in Windows 2000 equate to fewer technical problems—which ultimately translates into better productivity and a more profitable bottom line. ❖

Many features in Microsoft Windows XP Professional bring business value to remote workers

By Carol Bailey, MCSE+I

My previous article proposed that Windows XP Professional's ideal market was remote workers—especially those who spend significant time working from home—rather than corporate networks. I explained why WinXP Pro has distinct advantages over WinXP Home Edition, and I identified three main XP feature sets I think make XP pro stand out:

- Usability
- Security
- Troubleshooting

What follows is a brief description of each of these XP feature sets and the ways each applies specifically to home workers. Some of the features rely on options that are disabled in a domain environment, so a home computer running in a stand-alone or workgroup configuration can make full use of all of them.

Usability features

Extensive support for wireless networks

Windows XP supports IEEE 802.11 standard for wireless LANs, requiring minimal configuration. This is ideal for home wireless networks, where ease of use has a higher priority than throughput or security.

Network bridging

XP networking includes a bridge component for network adapters that transparently connects network segments so that the home network becomes a single IP subnet. This can be particularly handy when using Internet Connection Sharing. The option has little use for corporate networks, where more sophisticating routing and bridging hardware are used.

Fast user switching

The Fast User Switching feature employs the same technology as Terminal Services but on the desktop, so that multiple users can be logged on and keep their applications open without having to log off before somebody else can use the computer. This is disabled in a domain environment and can't be used with offline files. It does require more memory (2 MB per user, plus memory for running applications, with a minimum of 128 MB of RAM recommended).

Remote Desktop

Remote Desktop also utilizes Windows 2000 Terminal Services technology, but it does so to enable users to remotely access their Windows XP Professional machine. By default, administrators can automatically connect to the remote desktop, logging out any currently connected user and locking the computer while connected (for security purposes). Additional remote desktop users can be added, but they won't be able to log off a currently connected user—the connection will be refused. When connecting directly over the Internet (rather than over a VPN), remember that this feature uses RDP (TCP port 3389), which you may need to open on any intervening routers/firewalls.

Fax console

With an interface similar to most e-mail programs (Inbox, Outbox, Sent Items, etc.), the fax console is easy and intuitive to use. It includes a wizard to guide you through creating cover pages. In addition, it lets you prioritize faxes and delay sending, and you can import/export faxes to integrate with other fax programs. The Fax Monitor displays time and events related to sending and receiving faxes, including any transmission problems, and it helps determine connectivity status. This can save a remote worker from having to buy an additional fax machine.

Compressed (zipped) folders

This functionality is built around WinZip functionality, first seen in Windows Me and rarely mentioned in Windows XP documentation because it is assumed that NTFS compression makes this option superfluous. It works by marking a folder as compressed so that any files created or moved into that folder will become compressed and save disk space.

Home workers may find this useful when sending zipped files by e-mail or over the VPN, as well as when NTFS compression is not possible because the data needs to be accessible to older operating systems on the same machine—such as when multibooting with Win9x.

You can password-protect compressed folders (accessing them afterward will prompt for a password before uncompressing), but be forewarned: There is no password recovery option.

NetCrawler

By automatically searching and displaying shortcuts to network resources after crawling the Entire Network, this feature makes it easy to locate available network shares and printers. NetCrawler checks for new network resources at log on or when Printers And Faxes or My Network Places is opened or refreshed. It automatically deletes these shortcuts when they are older than 48 hours. This feature is disabled in a domain and when connected via VPN or to a Terminal Server.

File and Settings Transfer wizard (or User Migration Tool)

This feature is ideal if XP is replacing rather than upgrading a computer, allowing you to transfer your familiar and frequently used settings from another computer. It can also be used for transferring settings from another new boot option on a multiboot system. If you require more control/customization, make use of the more complex but more powerful User Migration Tool. Note: This works only with Win9x and Windows Me systems and not NT 4.0 or Windows 2000.

Locally shared folders

Locally shared folders aren't available in a domain environment. XP makes it easy for all users to access common files by providing a Shared Documents folder. Simply drag, paste, or move the files into this folder that you want to be accessible to all users that log on to the computer.

Group taskbar buttons and configurable System Tray (Notification Area)

A couple of small desktop changes—but definitely for the better. The Taskbar option Group Similar Taskbar Buttons keeps all taskbar buttons for the same program together and when the taskbar become crowded, automatically collapses multiple instances of the same program onto one button with chevrons.

Instead of putting up with a cluttered system tray after programs have been installed, you can hide inactive icons (the default) or selectively choose which icon should appear.

Media Player 8

Supports common digital media activities including CD/DVD playback, extended support for more audio cards and features, digital broadcast support and video mixing rendering, and media transfer to portable devices. This could be useful for remote workers that need to access cached audio and/or video clips of conferences, meetings, and/or company presentations.

Native support for CD burning

No need to install additional software for CD writing and rewriting. CDRW is ideal for a home worker's backups as a relatively cheap and reliable replacement for tape and ZIP drives.

Over 256 colors for Terminal Services Clients

This setting is buried in the group policies (Local Computer | Administrative Templates | Windows Components | Terminal Services | Limit Maximum Color Of Depth). Although the default is 256 colors as it is for Windows 2000, this setting allows you to set 24-bit as the highest option or Client Compatible, to automatically select the highest resolution the client can support. Note that higher resolutions will require more bandwidth.

Security features

Encrypt offline files

The offline files feature is ideal for home workers who work offline and then upload changes to the corporate network via the VPN. This feature in XP Professional now includes support for encrypting the offline files to ensure security. Although more commonly targeted at mobile users, the feature is also highly applicable for home workers who often share their computer with others.

Internet Connection Firewall (ICF)

XP now includes the Internet Connection Firewall (ICF), a stateful packet inspection firewall that monitors source and destination traffic to and from the computer, dropping any packets that do not originate from the computer. You can log dropped and allowed packets and open specified ports for incoming services (such as IIS and Remote Desktop). However, ICF does not monitor outgoing packets and assumes these are always legitimate, so it cannot monitor and prevent Trojan programs.

Some kind of firewall is essential these days when connecting over the Internet, so this native security feature is better than nothing—although you might want to supplement it with a more sophisticated desktop firewall.

ICF is not applicable in a domain and is most likely to be used in conjunction with Internet Connection Sharing (ICS), which also cannot be run in a domain because of conflicts with DHCP servers, routers, etc.

Internet Discovery & Control

This feature is another supplement to ICS that allows XP clients to monitor and manage the shared Internet connection.

Automatic updates

Automatic updates reduce the chance of home workers not installing critical security patches, because the process is automated by default. Behind the scenes, XP regularly connects to the Microsoft Web site and looks for needed patches. If it finds any, it automatically downloads them (still behind the scenes). Then, once the patches are downloaded, a screen pops up saying the latest patches are ready and asks the user if he or she is ready to install them.

How often have home workers neglected to install patches requested by administrators, thereby jeopardizing other computers on the corporate network when they dial in? This feature is of less use on corporate networks where administrators prefer full control over computer builds and want to minimize Internet traffic. It's ideally suited to the home worker and is fully configurable (via My Computer | Properties | Automatic Updates tab).

Troubleshooting features

Remote Assistance

Remote Assistance is based on Windows 2000 Terminal Services technology but takes it to a new level so that home workers can "hand over" their computer to the corporate help desk to look at and fix problems. Requests for help can be sent by file, e-mail, or Windows Messenger (the newer version of MSN Messenger that is built into XP). This can include collaboration between the user and the support pro, via text or voice messages and sending/receiving files.

Note that Windows Messenger will not work with ICS or NAT (which is employed on most corporate firewalls), but using Windows Messenger over a VPN connection works well.

Password reset disk and password hints

To safeguard against an inaccessible computer because of forgotten passwords, XP offers two features. The first is the creation of a password disk, which doesn't save the current password but allows you to reset it to a new value. The second is the ability to display a password hint on logon, similar to the feature provided on Web sites that require logon authentication. However, this password hint is visible to all users. Neither of these features is available in a domain.

Driver Roll Back

How often has a user installed a new driver that caused program errors or a computer crash? With XP, the user can fix this common problem by simply selecting the Roll Back option in Device Manager. This feature is ideal for home workers who have to install a range of new devices themselves, but it's less useful on corporate networks that have standard build images and that typically test new drivers before installing them on production machines.

Note that printer drivers can't be rolled back, and for other drivers, you can't roll back to drivers earlier than the last version. If you want to do either of these things, System Restore is the only option.

System Restore

Another powerful tool for troubleshooting, System Restore takes snapshots of the registry and certain critical system files so you can return your computer to a known working state. Although you can manually create a restore point (for example, before installing a new application/device), the system is clever enough to automatically create restore points at critical times such as when installing unsigned drivers, installing new versions via Automatic Updates, and restoring data from backup. It will also create a restore point every 24 hours (when idle) and optionally at preset intervals if configured in the registry. You can undo a system restore that doesn't resolve the problem.

Automated System Recovery (ASR)

NTBackup now includes the Automated System Recovery Wizard to create an image of your system partition (saved to tape or CD), together with a bootable floppy. When the computer refuses to boot normally, and/or other troubleshooting techniques such as Roll Back, System Restore, Last Known Good, and Safe Mode have failed, simply boot with the floppy disk to restore the saved image. This feature is ideal for home workers who need to quickly and easily get their computer back up and running when the corporate help desk is out of reach.

Safe editing of Boot.ini

Another small but useful troubleshooting aid for less technical users is the assistance given with editing the Boot.ini file, either with the command-line utility Bootcfg.exe or with the GUI System Configuration Utility. You can search for Windows installations and build a new file and add/remove switches without using a text editor to help ensure that home workers won't end up with a nonuseable Boot.ini (and therefore an unbootable computer).

Single registry editor

The full searching facilities and easier-to-use interface of Regedit have now been combined with the additional security options previously only found in Regedt32. This is a small but significant feature if you spend much time delving into the registry and it eliminates the confusion of having two registry editors.

Program Compatibility Wizard

This wizard allows you to try different settings to emulate older versions of the Windows operating system if you have software that will not run correctly on Windows XP. Although this is available for Windows 2000 with SP2, it's natively included with Windows XP.

Faster execution of Chkdsk

Chkdsk.exe in Windows XP supports new switches (/i and /c) that provide faster performance by skipping certain system files.

Disk Cleanup new options

This useful maintenance utility under Windows XP includes options for compressing old files and deleting old restore points to maximize disk space.

Customize interface components

All the fancy new graphic features in XP come at the cost of memory and ultimately performance. When this becomes an issue, XP allows you to fine-tune these features in My Computer | Properties | Advanced | Performance | Visual Effects. You can set a configuration for best appearance or best performance or customize exactly which interface components you want.

Final analysis

WinXP Pro's usability, security, and troubleshooting enhancements can provide added value to home workers. The details we've covered here should provide you with enough information to make a determination about whether your company could best be served by purchasing or recommending WinXP Pro for your home workers. ❖

WinXP Pro Remote Desktop lets you connect to your computer from any Windows computer

By Dr. Thomas Shinder, MCSE

Windows XP's Remote Desktop feature is great for SOHOs and small businesses. It acts as a mini Terminal Server, allowing a single terminal services connection to a Windows XP computer. Through Remote Desktop, you can connect to your computer from another computer on the same LAN or from any computer in the world, as long as that computer is running Windows. You need only install the Web Access Remote Connection, publish the Web Access Remote Connection to the Internet, and then publish the Remote Desktop connection to the Internet.

The beauty of this solution is that you don't need to install a Terminal Services client on the computer you use to remotely connect to your desktop. The Web Access Remote connection will automatically install the required software for you.

In this article I'll explain how to do the following:

- Configure the Windows XP Remote Desktop
- Install and configure the Windows XP Remote Desktop Web Connection
- Configure ISA Server publishing rules to publish the Remote Desktop connections to the Internet

Configuring the Windows XP Remote Desktop

When you install Windows XP, the Remote Desktop feature is installed by default, so you don't need to install anything further. However, you will need to enable it and assign user accounts for anyone who will need to remotely access the computer. You must be a member of the local machine's Administrator's group to configure your computer's Remote Desktop features.

To enable and configure the Windows XP Remote Desktop, follow these steps:

1. Click Start | Control Panel.
2. In Control Panel, click System.
3. Open the System Properties dialog box and then click on the Remote tab.
4. In the Remote Desktop frame (**Figure A**), place a checkmark in the Allow Users To Connect Remotely To This Computer check box to enable Remote Desktop Connections.
5. Click the Select Remote Users button.
6. The Remote Desktop Users dialog box (**Figure B**) will open, and in it you will see a list of users who are allowed to access the computer through a Remote

Desktop connection. If you need to add more users to the list, just click Add. If the computer is a member of a workgroup, you will only be able to add users who are contained in the local computer accounts database. However, if the machine is a member of a domain, you can add accounts from the domain's user accounts database. After adding users, click OK to close the dialog box.

7. Click Apply and then click OK in the System Properties dialog box.

At this point, the computer is ready to accept remote desktop connections from other computers. But the client computer must be running the Remote Desktop Connections. Also, because Terminal Services and the Remote Desktop Connection software are interchangeable, you can access the Remote Desktop with the Terminal Services client software. Next, you'll need to install and configure the Remote Desktop Web Connection.

Installing and configuring the Remote Desktop Web Connection

The client software to connect to the Remote Desktop is called Remote Desktop Connection. It's generally a revved-up version of the Terminal Services client software; however, the Remote Desktop Connection gives you more options.

It allows you to connect to your desktop with an Internet Explorer 4.0 or above Web browser. When you use the browser to connect to a Remote Desktop, a small ActiveX control is installed on the client machine. Then, the Remote Desktop Connection will appear within the Web browser.

The Remote Desktop Web Connection is actually a Web application that runs on Internet Information Server (IIS). The Web application installs the client ActiveX control and some .asp files used to log on to the Remote Desktop.

Figure A

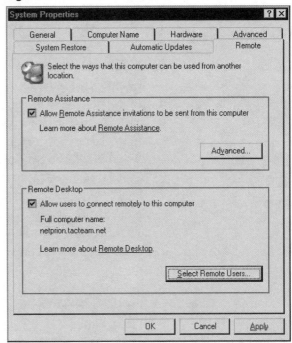

Figure B

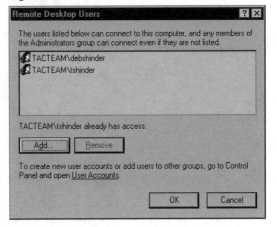

To install and configure the Remote Desktop Web Connection, follow these steps:

1. Click Start | Control Panel.
2. In Control Panel, click Add/Remove Programs.
3. In the Add/Remove Programs window, click the Add/Remove Windows Components button.
4. In the Windows Components Wizard dialog box, scroll through the list and click on Internet Information Services. Then, click the Details button.
5. In the resulting Internet Information Services (IIS) dialog box, click on the World Wide Web Service entry and then click the Details button.
6. In the resulting World Wide Web Service dialog box (**Figure C**), select the check boxes for Remote Desktop Web Connection and World Wide Web Service. Note that if you select the Remote Desktop Web Connection first, the World Wide Web Service will be automatically selected. Click OK.
7. Click OK in the Internet Information Services (IIS) dialog box.
8. Click Next in the Windows Components Wizard dialog box. You may be asked for the Windows XP Professional CD so be sure to have it ready. When the Completing The Windows Components Wizard page appears, click the Finish button.

After IIS is installed, you need to confirm that the virtual directory containing the Remote Desktop Web Connection software allows Anonymous authentication. To check on the security configuration for the Remote Desktop Web Connection virtual folder, follow these steps:

1. Click Start | Control Panel.
2. In Control Panel, click Administrative Tools.
3. Double-click on Internet Information Services.
4. In the left pane of the Internet Information Services console, expand your server name. Expand the Web Sites node and then expand the Default Web Site node. Right-click the Tsweb node and click Properties.
5. In the Tsweb Properties dialog box, click on the Directory Security tab. Click on the Edit button in the Anonymous Access And Authentication Control frame.
6. In the Authentication Methods dialog box (**Figure D**), confirm that the Anonymous Access check box is selected. The default user name is *IUSR_<server_name>* (where *server_name* is the actual URL or IP address of your server), and the Allow IIS To Control Password option is selected by default. Accept these settings and click OK.
7. Click OK in the Tsweb Properties dialog box. Close the IIS console.

At this point, the Remote Desktop Web Connection is fully functional for clients located on the same LAN. All you need to do is open a Web browser and type

Figure C

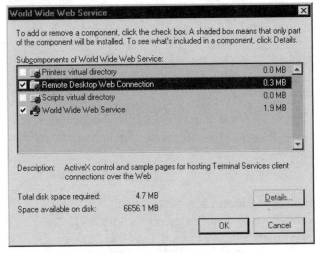

Figure D

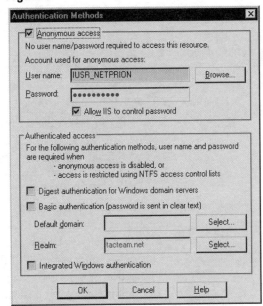

http://computer_name/tsweb. This will bring up the Remote Desktop Web Connection page (**Figure E**).

From this page, enter the name of your computer and select the screen resolution. You'll also have the option to enter your logon credentials on this page. After doing so, click Connect.

However, before you can access your Remote Desktop from the Internet, you will need to publish the Remote Desktop and the Remote Desktop Web Connection to the Internet.

Figure E

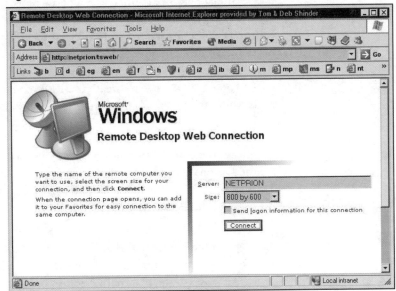

Publishing the Remote Desktop and Remote Desktop Connection to the Internet

When you use the Remote Desktop Web Connection to connect to a computer's Remote Desktop, you actually establish two connections. The first link is an HTTP connection made to TCP port 80, and the second link is an RDP connection made to TCP 3389. Only after the RDP connection is established do you actually have access to the Remote Desktop. Keep this in mind when you decide to publish the Remote Desktop Web Connection to the Internet.

There are several ways you can publish the Remote Desktop Web Connection to the Internet:

- Windows 2000 or Windows XP Internet Connection Services (ICS)
- Windows 2000 Routing and Remote Access (RRAS)
- ISA Server 2000

Because ISA Server provides the most secure method for publishing internal network services to the Internet, I'll explain how to publish the Remote Desktop Web Connection to the Internet using ISA Server.

DNS requirements

When you establish a connection to the external interface of the ISA Server, you want to be able to connect using fully qualified domain names (FQDN). If you manage your own DNS server, make sure you have two Host (A) records: one to support the HTTP connection and the other to support the RDP connection.

For example, if your domain name is Domain.com, you can create a Host (A) record for WWW for the HTTP connection and a Host (A) record for RDP for the Terminal Services connection. These records should resolve to the external IP addresses on the ISA Server that will be used for the Web Publishing Rule (used for the HTTP connection) and the Server Publishing Rule (used for the RDP connection). You then type *http://www.domain.com* in a Web browser to connect to the Remote Desktop Web Connection Web page. In the Server text box on the Web page, type *rdp.domain.com* to create the RDP connection to your Remote Desktop on the internal network.

Creating the Web Publishing Rule

You need to create a Destination Set to support your Web Publishing Rule. To create the Destination Set, follow these steps:

1. Open the ISA Management console, expand your server name, and then expand the Policy Elements node.
2. Right-click the Destination Sets node, point to New, and click Set.
3. Type in the name of the destination set. You might want to name it Remote Desktop Web Connection. In the Description text box, enter the FQDN that will resolve to the external IP address used by the Incoming Web Requests listener, and then click Add.
4. Click the Destination option button, and the resulting window will look like **Figure F**. Enter the FQDN that resolves to the external IP address used by the Incoming Web Requests listener. Click OK and then click OK again.

Next, you need to create the Web Publishing Rule.

1. Expand the Publishing node in the left pane of the ISA Management console.

Figure F

Add/Edit Destination   [?] [X]

○ <u>D</u>estination: [www.mydomain.com]   [<u>B</u>rowse...]

To include all computers in a domain, type ".domain.

○ IP <u>a</u>ddresses:

<u>F</u>rom: [   ]

<u>T</u>o (optional)   [   ]

To include a specific directory in the destination set, type the path
below.
To include all the files, use this format: /dir/*.
To select a specific file, use this format: /dir/filename.

Path:

[   ]

[OK]   [Cancel]

Figure G

New Web Publishing Rule Wizard   [X]

Rule Action
Specify how you want this rule to respond to requests from clients.

Response to client requests:

○ <u>D</u>iscard the request

◉ <u>R</u>edirect the request to this internal Web server (name or IP address):

[192.168.1.8]   [B<u>r</u>owse...]

☐ Send the original host header to the publishing server instead of the actual
   one (specified above).

Connect to this port when bridging request as H<u>T</u>TP: [80]

Connect to this port when bridging request as <u>S</u>SL: [443]

Connect to this port when bridging request as <u>F</u>TP: [21]

[< <u>B</u>ack]   [<u>N</u>ext >]   [Cancel]

2. Right-click the Web Publishing Rules node, point to New, and click Rule.

3. On the Welcome page, type Remote Desktop Web Connection in the Web Publishing Rule Name text box and click Next.

4. On the Destination Sets page, select the Destination Set you created to support the rule. Click Next.

5. On the Client Type page, select the Any Request option and click Next.

6. On the Rule Action page (**Figure G**), select the Redirect The Request To This Internal Web Server (Name Or IP Address) option. Enter the IP address of the computer configured to accept Remote Desktop Web Connections. Click Next.

7. On the Completing the New Web Publishing Rule Wizard page, review your settings and click Finish.

At this point the ISA Server will forward the HTTP requests to your Remote Desktop Web Connection computer. However, it won't be ready to actually connect to the Remote Desktop until you create the RDP Server Publishing Rule.

Creating the RDP Server Publishing Rule

You will need to first create an RDP Server Protocol Definition to support the Server Publishing Rule. Perform the following steps to create the RDP Server Protocol Definition:

1. Expand the Policy Elements node and right-click Protocol Definitions. Select New and then Definition.

2. On the Welcome page, type *RDP Server* in the Protocol Definition Name text box. Click Next.

Figure H

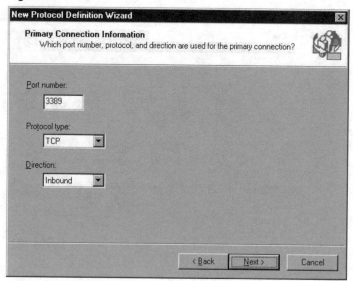

3. On the Primary Connection Information page (**Figure H**), type 3389 in the Port Number text box. Leave the Protocol type set to TCP. Change the Direction to Inbound. Click Next.

4. On the Secondary Connections page, accept the default selection, which is No, and click Next.

5. On the New Protocol Definition Wizard page, review your selections and click Finish.

After the Protocol Definition is created, you are ready to create the RDP Server Publishing Rule. To do so:

1. Right-click the Server Publishing Rules node in the left pane of the ISA Management console. Select New and then select Rule.

2. On the Welcome page, click RDP Remote Desktop in the Server Publishing Rule Name text box. Click Next.

3. On the Address Mapping page, enter the internal IP address of the server in the text box. Then, enter the external IP address on ISA Server and click Next.

Figure I

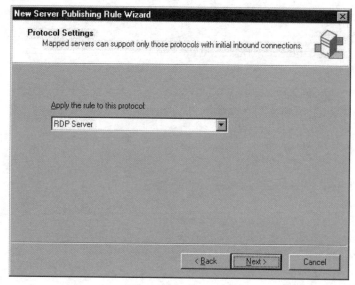

4. On the Protocol Settings page, select the RDP Server protocol (**Figure I**) and click Next.

5. On the Client Type page, select the Any Request option and click Next.

6. On the Complete The New Server Publishing Rule Wizard page, review your settings and click Finish.

Conclusion

The Windows XP Remote Desktop expands your SOHO network flexibility to reach to the world outside, giving you the ability to more easily work on the go. So if you need to connect to your desktop both from within your LAN and remotely when you're on the road, the Windows XP Remote Desktop is what you need. ❖

How to configure Windows XP client VPN connections

By TechRepublic Staff

VPNs have caught on quickly with small and medium-size businesses, primarily for three reasons:

- VPNs permit employees to connect to office resources from home or other locations using common hardware.
- VPNs provide secure connections.
- The cost to set up and maintain a VPN is low compared to other networking connection solutions.

In this chapter, we'll describe the process of setting up a VPN client connection within the Windows XP operating system.

If you're configuring laptops for remote VPN connections via DSL modem, LAN, or WAN connectivity, navigate through Start | Control Panel | Network And Internet Connections and click the Set Up Or Change Your Internet Connection link. Once the Internet Properties window opens (**Figure A**), click the Setup button, which will open the New Connection Wizard. In the wizard, you'll find four selections (instead of the five in Windows 2000 Professional). The connection type you'll select is Connect To The Network At My Workplace. Then, the next window will ask you to specify the type of connection you're creating. Select the Virtual Private Network Connection option and click Next. The next two screens will ask for the company name and the IP address of the VPN server. Once you've clicked through these screens, you'll be greeted with the final screen, which will ask if you'd like to add a shortcut to this

Figure A

You can configure a variety of settings for dial-up and VPN connections.

DIAL-UP

If you're connecting via dial-up, there are only two differences. In the New Connection Wizard, under the Network Connection screen, you'll select Dial-up Connection instead of Virtual Private Network connection, and you'll enter a phone number instead of an IP address.

Figure B

Supply your networking User Name and Password for authentication purposes.

connection to the desktop. If you want a VPN icon, click Yes; choose No if you don't. Click Finish.

If you need to change the telephone number or other settings associated with the VPN connection, you can do so easily through the Properties window (see Figure A).

Connecting to the VPN

To connect, double-click the shortcut—if you chose to create one—or select the connection by clicking Start | Connect To and selecting the name of the connection you created. Supply your User Name and Password for the network you wish to access (see **Figure B**) and you'll be ready to start enjoying the benefits of secure, remote access.

If you want to edit the settings for the connection, you can do so from the Properties window. You can modify Dialing and Redialing options, Security options, TCP/IP, and Advanced options, such as Firewalling and NAT. Several other options can be configured on the tabs in your connection's Properties window, including:

- Changing security settings of individual components.
- Selecting privacy settings for Internet zones.
- Configuring a proxy server.
- Determining which program Windows will associate with a specific service.

XP makes VPN a cinch

Windows XP includes a VPN functionality that is more robust and clearer than in previous versions of Windows. Given that more and more companies are turning to VPNs for security reasons, you need to understand how to configure this networking option. ❖

The Win9x VPN client connection guide

By Dr. Thomas Shinder, MCSE

VPN Servers go a long way toward saving money for companies with remote access clients. In the not-so-distant past, companies that wanted to give road warriors access to corporate internal network resources needed to install modem banks and multiple phone lines. The cost of installing multiple dial-up RAS servers was compounded by the long distance charges or costs incurred from 1-800 numbers. VPN servers remove this cost-rich hardware/telco layer and allow you to support dozens and even hundreds of remote access calls with a single VPN server and high-speed Internet connection.

Most of the articles I see on the Internet focus on how to set up and configure the VPN server. This makes sense, since most of the complicated work in setting up a VPN client/server solution is done at the VPN server. However, configuring VPN clients is not always a piece of cake. This is especially true when dealing with legacy VPN client operating systems, such as the Windows 9x line.

We'll look at how to configure your Win9x computers to be VPN clients that connect to Windows NT 4.0 VPN servers. You can use the same procedures to configure the Win9x clients to connect to Windows 2000 VPN servers. The only major difference between connecting to Windows NT 4.0 and Windows 2000 VPN servers is that the Windows NT 4.0 VPN servers do not support the L2TP/IPSec VPN protocol. However, this doesn't pose much of a problem for our Win9x VPN clients, because the only VPN protocol supported by Win9x operating systems is the Point-to-Point Tunneling Protocol (PPTP).

Windows 9x Dial-up Networking Service 1.4 (DUN 1.4)

Before getting into the nuts and bolts of configuring the Win9x VPN client, you need to familiarize yourself with the latest update to the Win9x Dial-Up Networking Service, DUN 1.4. There are several reasons why you'll want to download and install DUN 1.4, including:

- Support for 128-bit encryption.
- A Y2K fix for the VPN DHCP client component.
- Fixes that improve the stability of the PPTP connection.
- Support for internal ISDN adapters.
- Multilink support.
- Support for PPTP connections over a "LAN" or dedicated connection (such as DSL or cable).

NOTE

Windows Me does not require the DUN 1.4 Dial-up Networking update.

Check out Microsoft Knowledge Base article Q297774 (**http://support. microsoft.com/default.aspx?scid = kb;en-us;Q297774&SD = MSKB&**) for full details on DUN 1.4. There are several versions of DUN 1.4, one each designed for Windows 95, Windows 98, and Windows 98SE. Information about the updates and files for download can be found in Microsoft Knowledge Base article Q285189 (**http://support.microsoft.com/default.aspx?scid = kb;en-us; Q285189**). Be aware that you will need to restart the computer at the end of the DUN 1.4 installation.

Configuring the Windows 9x VPN client

The procedure for configuring the Windows 9x VPN clients is very similar, with only very minor differences between each version. Prior to configuring the PPTP VPN client connection on the Win9x client, make sure you have an Internet connection to the Internet VPN server. The Internet connection device can be an analog dial-up modem, ISDN terminal adapter, a DSL line, or a cable connection.

Let's use the Windows 95 client as an example of how to configure all the Win9x clients. Perform the following steps on your Windows 95 computer:

1. Click Start | Programs | Accessories. Point to Communications, and then click on Dial-up Networking.

2. The Dial-up Network Wizard Welcome dialog box will appear (**Figure A**). Click Next to continue.

3. On the next page, type in a name for the connection in the Type A Name For The Computer You Are Dialing text box. Click the down arrow in the Select A Device drop-down list box and select the Microsoft VPN Adapter option (**Figure B**). DUN 1.4 added this feature to your Windows 95 computer. Click Next.

4. On the Make New Connection page, type in the IP address or the Fully Qualified Domain Name (FQDN) of the VPN server that the Windows 95 computer will connect with (**Figure C**). If you use an FQDN, make sure that there is an entry in the public DNS that resolves to the IP address on your VPN server that is listening for incoming VPN connections. If you do not have a DNS entry for your VPN server, enter an IP address instead. Click Next.

5. On the last page of the wizard (**Figure D**), you'll be told that you've done everything right and that you've created a new connection. After clicking Finish, the connectoid will appear in your Dial-Up Networking folder.

6. Return to the Dial-Up Networking window. You should see the icon for the VPN connectoid you just created, and another connectoid for an ISP connection if you require a dial-up connection to access the Internet (**Figure E**).

Figure A

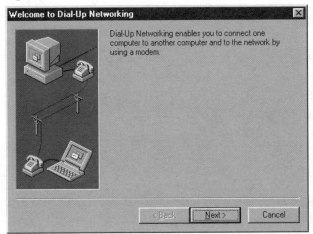

Figure B

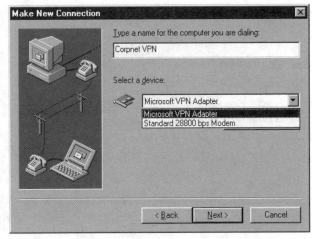

Figure C

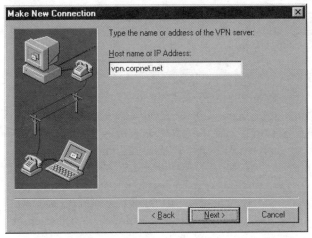

Figure D

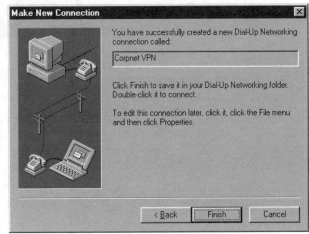

Further tweaking with VPN Properties

You might want to do some further tweaking of the VPN connection. Right-click the VPN connectoid and click Properties. On the General tab (**Figure F**), you can change the name or IP address of the VPN server. This is convenient because, if the name or address of the VPN server changes, you don't have to create a new connectoid. Just change an existing one.

You can make many customizations on the Server Types tab (**Figure G**). By default, the Log On To Network and Enable Software Compression options are enabled. For connections that support MS-CHAP,

Figure E

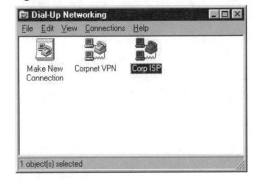

Figure F

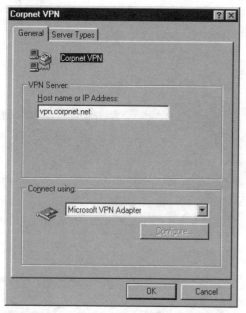

Figure G

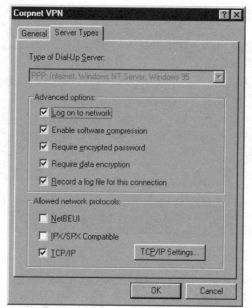

Set high encryption for the link.

Figure H

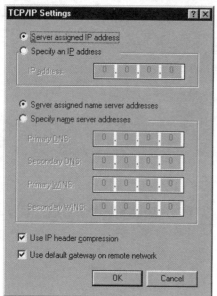

check the Require Encrypted Password box. If you want to use MS-CHAP version 2, the client will negotiate MS-CHAP version 2 with the VPN server first. If the server does not support MS-CHAP version 2, the client will drop down to support MS-CHAP version 1. Also, make sure that data encryption is enabled. If you want to optimize connection speed, uncheck protocols that you do not use. If you do not disable the protocols, the client will attempt to negotiate each one selected.

When you click on the TCP/IP Settings button at the bottom of the Server Types tab, you'll see what appears in **Figure H**. Most VPN servers will automatically assign IP addressing information to the VPN client. Therefore, you should leave the default settings Server Assigned IP Address and Server Assigned Name Server Addresses as they are. The Use IP Header Compression option should be set if the VPN server supports this option.

The most interesting option is the Use Default Gateway On Remote Network. When this option is selected, the VPN client uses the VPN interface as the gateway for all nonlocal network addresses. If the client dialed in to an

ISP first, the ISP assigned the computer a default gateway at the ISP to allow the client access to the Internet. However, when the Use Default Gateway On Remote Network option is enabled, the VPN client is assigned a new default gateway, which is the VPN server's VPN interface. The end result is that the VPN client cannot access the Internet once it connects to the corporate VPN.

If this option is disabled, the VPN client will be able to access both the internal corporate network and the Internet at the same time. This creates the possibility that the VPN client will be able to route packets from the Internet to the internal network. Allowing the VPN client to access the Internet through the ISP and also the corporate network through the VPN at the same time is poor security practice. This is akin to allowing users on the internal network to plug modems into their computers and thus bypass corporate Internet access policies.

The Windows 98/98SE VPN client

Configuring the Windows 98/98SE client works exactly the same as configuring the Windows 95 client. The interfaces are virtually identical after installing DUN 1.4. The only difference you'll see is found in the Connections menu in the Dial-up Networking window. In the Dial-up Networking window, click Connections and then click Settings.

Windows 98/98SE allows you to configure a redial value and a wait interval before redialing (**Figure I**). This option isn't available in the Windows 95 dial-up networking. You also have the option to be prompted before a dial-up connection is established. This is helpful when you use dial-up networking to map network drives via the VPN interface.

Click on the Security tab and you'll see what appears in **Figure J**. Both Disable Sending Of LAN Manager Passwords and Require Secure VPN Connections are enabled by default. LAN Manager password authentication is inherently insecure and should always be disabled. The secure VPN connection option will force 128-bit encryption. If the VPN server does not support 128-bit encryption, the connection attempt will fail. If this option is not enabled, the client will first negotiate 128-bit encryption. If the negotiation fails, it will fall back to 40-bit encryption.

Figure I

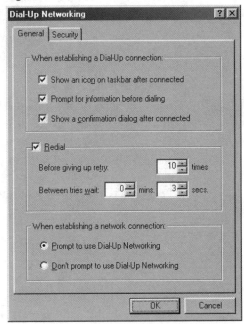

Figure J

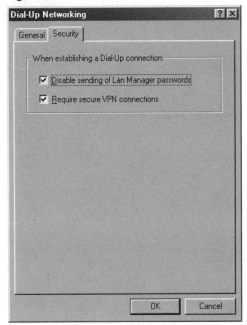

Some final thoughts on troubleshooting

There are a handful of troubleshooting issues you should be aware of before finalizing your VPN client/server solution. Many ISPs do not allow incoming GRE packets into their networks, or they require that the user pay extra for a "business account." If the VPN client cannot establish a VPN connection with the corporate VPN server, the user should contact his ISP to determine if GRE connections are allowed for the user's account.

Windows 9x clients will not be able to connect to VPN NLB server clusters if the NLB interface still has the actual IP address configured on the cluster servers. Only the virtual IP address can be listed on the external interfaces of the cluster members if you expect to connect down-level clients to a PPTP VPN NLB cluster. If the VPN client fails to connect to a PPTP NLB cluster, confirm that only the virtual IP address appears on the external interface of each of the cluster members.

If a WINS server is manually assigned to a NIC, the PPTP VPN client will not be able to obtain a WINS server address on the PPTP VPN interface. This is in spite of the fact that the WINS address is configured *only* on the NIC. Note that manually setting a DNS server address on the machine's NIC will not prevent the PPTP VPN client from obtaining a DNS server address from the VPN server.

You may run in to issues when users plug directly into the corporate network with an Ethernet card while at work, and then go home and try to connect to the same network through the PPTP VPN interface. The user may need to run the winipcfg utility from the Run menu to renew the IP address. If that does not work, the NIC may need to be removed before the VPN user can connect to the network remotely. ❖

Use Windows to set up a quick and easy router

By Brien M. Posey, MCSE

One of the lesser-known Windows server functions is that Windows can be configured to act as a basic router, similar to commercial routers such as those sold by Cisco Systems and other vendors. I'm going to explain the pros and cons of using a Windows server as a router. I'll then go on to show you how to configure both a Windows NT 4.0 system and a Windows 2000 system as a router. Finally, I'll show you how to manage the router from the Windows command line.

When to use Windows as a router

Before I actually show you how to configure Windows to act as a router, there are some issues that you need to be aware of. There are definitely benefits and drawbacks to using Windows as a router. The biggest benefits to using Windows as a router are cost and ease of configuration (especially if you're already familiar with Windows administration).

If you have a small office with a minimal IT budget, you can save money by adding routing functions to an existing Windows server rather than purchasing a hardware router. Of course, doing so does add some overhead to the server, so you must make sure that the server that you're using isn't running short on system resources, such as memory, disk space, or CPU time. You must also worry about security. By their very nature, hardware routers tend to be more secure than Windows routers. A big part of this is because the Windows operating system contains so many potential vulnerabilities that can be exploited.

The other situation where Windows can be a good solution is when you need a router for a temporary network that does not require high security. For example, an ad hoc network for a training seminar, a remote office that won't be functioning for more than a few months, or a small network that is in the process of being upgraded.

In this scenario, you can quickly set up a router with a Windows system and then return that system to use as a Windows server once its function as a router is no longer needed. That way, you don't have to invest in an expensive hardware router that you only need for a limited period of time.

Preparing the system

Now that I've gone over the pros and cons, it's time to look at setting up a Windows router. Whether you are using Windows NT or Windows 2000, you must begin by setting up your server's hardware. Since a router's primary purpose is to move traffic between two or more networks, your server will require at least two NICs, one for each network that it will attach to. (As you may know, a server with multiple NICs is referred to as "multihomed.")

Technically, even a Windows machine with a single NIC makes routing decisions and has a built-in routing table. However, if only a single NIC exists in the system, then there is only one exit point for a packet. This is why you must have two or more NICs in a system if you are going to use it as a true router.

As you have probably already figured out, you must also configure TCP/IP appropriately. If you will be using the server as a router, you'll want to assign a static IP address to each NIC in the server. You must make sure that you use an IP address range and subnet mask that's appropriate for the network that the NIC will attach to.

The default gateway address will differ depending on the way that your network is configured and on the Windows router's function. However, the default gateway address will either match the NIC's IP address or it will match the IP address of another router on the network if appropriate. Technically speaking, even if you assign each NIC a different default gateway, Windows will only use a single default gateway. If you look at the network card bindings, whichever NIC is bound first, that NIC's TCP/IP configuration will be used to determine the default gateway for the entire system. Using a single default gateway is Window's way of avoiding confusion.

Set up Windows NT 4.0 as a router

Now that I have explained how to get the server ready to become a router, let's take a look at how to configure Windows NT 4.0 as a router. If you're running Windows 2000, I'll show you the configuration procedure in the next section.

To enable routing on a Windows NT 4.0 Server, right-click the Network Neighborhood icon and then select the Properties command from the resulting shortcut menu. This will cause Windows to display the Network properties sheet. Now, select the Protocols tab and then select the instance of the TCP/IP protocol that's bound to the NIC of your choice and click the Properties button. This will display the TCP/IP Properties sheet. Select the Routing tab and then click the Enable IP Forwarding check box. Click OK to close the TCP/IP Properties sheet and then repeat the procedure for any other NICs in the system.

Now that you have enabled routing, packets will be able to flow between networks attached to the server. However, if you need for your Windows NT Server to exchange routing information with other routers on the network, you'll need to enable the RIP protocol. To do so, return to the Network properties sheet and select the Services tab. Click the Add button and then select RIP For Internet Protocol from the Select Network Services dialog box and click OK. Click OK one more time to close the Network Properties sheet. At this point, you may be prompted for your Windows NT installation CD and you may be asked to reboot the server as well.

Set up Windows 2000 as a router

The procedure for setting up Windows 2000 Server as a router is quite a bit different from setting up Windows NT 4.0, but, like NT, you must still begin by configuring your system's NICs. Once the NICs have been configured, enter the MMC command at the Run prompt to launch an empty Microsoft Management Console. At this point, select the Add / Remove Snap In command from the Console menu. This will display the Add / Remove Snap In properties sheet. Click the Add button found on the properties sheet's Standalone tab and you'll see a list of available snap-ins appear. Select the Routing and Remote Access option from the list and click the Add button followed by the Close and OK buttons. The Routing and Remote Access snap-in should now be available in the console.

At this point, navigate through the console tree: Console Root | Routing And Remote Access | Server Status. Right-click the Server Status option and select the Add Server command from the resulting shortcut menu. Select the This Computer option and click OK. When you do, you'll see your server appear (beneath the Server Status container) listed as being unconfigured. Right-click the listing for the server in the column to the left and select the Configure And Enable Routing And Remote Access command from the resulting shortcut menu.

When you do, Windows will launch the Routing And Remote Access Server Setup Wizard. Click Next to bypass the Welcome screen and you'll see a screen appear that lists some common configurations. Select the Network Router option and click Next. At this point, Windows will display the protocols that are loaded on your server and will ask you if you need to install additional protocols. If you've configured the server properly so far, TCP/IP should be on the list. Select the option that indicates that the protocol of choice is on the list, and click Next.

Windows will now ask you if you need to configure a demand dial connection to a remote network. Demand dial connections are great for redundancy, but, generally, if you are just configuring the server as a simple router, then you won't need to worry about demand dial routing. Therefore, select No and click Next. Windows will now show you a configuration summary screen. Click Finish and Windows will enable routing on the server and start the appropriate services. You'll now see various routing options appear beneath the server in the console tree.

In the next section, I'm going to show you how to configure routing from a command prompt. However, you might be interested in knowing that you can use the Routing And Remote Access console as a shortcut. If you select the Routing Interfaces container, the column on the right will display all of the NICs in the system. You'll also see internal and loop-back virtual devices. If, at a later time, you want to add a demand dial routing interface to the system, you can right-click the Routing Interface container and select the New Demand Dial Interface option from the shortcut menu. If you want to add an additional NIC, you must do so through the Network Properties sheet rather than through the Routing And Remote Access console.

Another option that you might be interested in is the IP Routing container. If you expand this container, you'll see that there is a General and a Static Routes container beneath it. If you select the General container, you'll see a summary of the system's routing interfaces and their corresponding IP addresses and the amount of traffic that has passed through each interface. If you right-click the General container, the resulting shortcut menu contains several options that you can use for displaying various TCP/IP and multicast information. You can even use this menu to add additional routing protocols.

If you select the Static Routes container, you'll see any static routes that have been configured on the system. You can create new static routes by right-clicking the Static Routes container and selecting the New Static Route option from the shortcut menu. This shortcut menu also has a Show IP Routing table option that you can use to display the server's entire routing table.

Basic routing commands

Now that I have shown you how to configure Windows to act as a router, you might be interested to learn how to configure the various routing options. The basic routing options are configured via Window's ROUTE command. Here is the basic syntax of this command:

```
ROUTE [-F] [-P] {command [destination][] }
```

The -F switch is optional. This switch tells Windows to clear the routing table of all gateway entries. If the -F switch is used in conjunction with other commands, then all gateway entries will be cleared prior to executing other instructions within the command.

The -P switch makes a specified route persistent. Normally, if a server is rebooted, then any routes that you specify via the ROUTE command are removed. The -P switch tells Windows to keep the route even if the system is rebooted.

The command portion of the ROUTE command's syntax is relatively simple. The command set consists of four options: PRINT, ADD, DELETE, and CHANGE. For example, if you'd like to display the routing table, you can use the ROUTE PRINT command. You can even use wild cards with this command. For example, if you only wanted to print routes pertaining to the 147.x.x.x subnet, you could use the command ROUTE PRINT 147*.

The ROUTE DELETE command works very similarly to the ROUTE PRINT command. Simply enter the ROUTE DELETE command followed by the destination or the gateway that you want to delete from the routing table. For example, if you wanted to remove the 147.0.0.0 gateway, you could enter the command ROUTE DELETE 147.0.0.0.

The ROUTE CHANGE and the ROUTE ADD commands have the same basic syntax. Typically, when using these commands, you would specify the destination, subnet mask, and gateway. You might also specify a metric and an interface. For example, if you wanted to add a destination using the bare minimal syntax, you could do so as follows:

```
ROUTE ADD 147.0.0.0 255.0.0.0 137.26.2.3
```

In this command, 147.0.0.0 is the new destination that you are adding, 255.0.0.0 would be the subnet mask for the destination, and 137.26.2.3 would be the gateway address. You can extend the command with the METRIC and IF parameters. Doing so would look something like this:

```
ROUTE ADD 147.0.0.0 255.0.0.0 137.26.2.3 METRIC 1 IF 1
```

The METRIC parameter is optional and specifies the metric or number of hops for the route. The IF parameter tells Windows which interface to use. In this particular case, Windows would use the NIC that's bound to Windows as interface 1. If you don't use the IF parameter, then Windows will automatically search for the best interface to use.

I have given you the basics behind using the ROUTE command. As you can see, there is nothing too difficult about using this command. If you need a little extra help with the command syntax though, just enter the ROUTE /? command at the command prompt. This will display the command's syntax and several usage examples.

Summary

As you can see, Windows can function quite well as a router. However, there are lots of issues to consider before configuring Windows to act as a router. In this chapter, I've discussed these issues and provided you with detailed instructions for configuring both Windows 2000 and Windows NT 4 as a router. ❖

Using Windows Server 2003 as a router on your network

By TechRepublic Staff

Windows Server 2003 has many powerful features, including a built-in router. Why would you want to use Windows Server 2003 for routing? Because you can? Okay, that's not really a good answer. But you've probably wondered why you'd use Windows Server 2003 as a router rather than using a dedicated router from Cisco, Bay Networks, or another manufacturer. In a lot of situations, a dedicated router makes more sense and is generally less expensive. There are situations, however, where it makes sense to use Windows Server 2003 for routing. Here's how you can configure Windows Server 2003 to act as a router on your network.

How Windows Server 2003 routing works

Windows Server 2003's RRAS service supports several capabilities, one of which is supporting dial-up clients through POTS, ISDN, and other connectivity options. You can use integrated Windows authentication or rely on a RADIUS server (which could be the RRAS server) to authenticate clients. PPTP and L2TP support enable the RRAS server to function as a VPN server, giving remote clients a means of establishing a secure, private network connection to the LAN through a public network such as the Internet. Typically, the VPN connections come in through a dedicated, 24/7 Internet connection.

For example, assume you have three network segments, which currently are not interconnected, and you're setting up a remote access server on one of those segments. At the same time, you want to provide dial-up capability to each segment by remote clients. In this situation, it makes sense to install a single RAS server and let it provide routing services to all segments. Windows Server 2003 can fulfill both roles with no problem. So, using Windows Server 2003 as a router makes sense when you're providing services to your LAN that require routing and no other routers are currently online to handle the traffic, or you don't want the additional expense and management of a dedicated router in addition to your server.

Another reason to use Windows Server 2003 for routing is to provide DHCP Relay services for DHCP clients that reside on network segments where there is no DHCP server. Windows Server 2003 includes a DHCP Relay agent that provides this functionality in conjunction with RRAS.

A third reason to use Windows Server 2003 RRAS for routing is ease of use. Although router manufacturers have come a long way toward improving the configuration and management interfaces for their routers, the GUI management tools in Windows Server 2003 make it very easy to configure and manage Windows Server 2003 routers.

A Windows Server 2003 RRAS server can function as a dedicated router, connecting other routers continuously, or it can function as a demand-dial router. In this latter scenario, the router dials and connects to a remote router only when traffic that requires routing to the remote network comes to the router. Demand-dial routing is often used to reduce connectivity costs. If you send traffic over a metered connection only once or twice a day, for example, why pay for a full-time connection? With demand-dial routing, the router dials the remote network when traffic needs to be routed, then disconnects automatically after a defined period of inactivity. This helps keep costs down by keeping the connection live only when needed.

Understanding IP routing

Without IP routing, the Internet and many private networks would stop functioning instantly. Routing is a crucial aspect of IP networking. Understanding how routing works is the place to start when you're thinking about setting up a Windows Server 2003 RRAS server to function as a router.

The primary function of a router, whether it is a dedicated box or a Windows Server 2003 router, is to route network packets between different network segments. When you open a browser to connect to a Web site, for example, your computer looks up the IP address of the remote site through DNS and then sends network packets to the remote site's IP address to request the site's content.

Your network router, identified by your workstation at its default gateway, receives the traffic, analyzes the destination IP address for the packets, and determines that the packets are destined for a network segment beyond your own. Based on its routing tables, the router sends the packet out on the appropriate interface to another router. The traffic gets routed through potentially several routers and eventually reaches the server where the site is hosted. Then, the process happens again in reverse for the traffic coming from the server to your computer.

Routers generally are connected to at least two subnets and, in effect, the router resides as a node in each of the subnets to which it is connected. This gives the router local connectivity to each of the subnets on which it resides and is the mechanism by which routing is possible. **Figure A** illustrates a router connected to three different subnets, which in turn are connected to other subnets and eventually the Internet. Each router is sometimes referred to as a "hop," and a packet's hop count is increased by one each time it passes through another router (more about this later).

Figure A

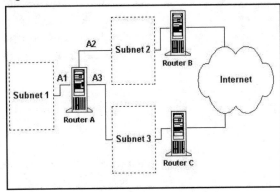

An example of a router connected to multiple subnets

As the figure illustrates, Router A connects subnet 1 to subnets 2 and 3, which are in turn connected to the Internet by other routers, B and C. Router A therefore is assigned three IP addresses, one in each subnet, making it a member of each subnet and directly accessible to the nodes in each connected subnet. When a client in subnet 1 sends traffic destined for subnet 3, the traffic is directed to the client's default gateway, which in this case is the IP address of the router at A1. The default gateway is defined in the client computer's TCP/IP properties.

The router analyzes the packets when they come in to determine the destination address. Discovering that the traffic is destined for subnet 3, the router directs the traffic out the interface A3, based on its internal knowledge that the destination node must reside on subnet 3.

But what happens when the traffic is destined for a subnet that resides beyond the router's locally connected segments, such as a remote Internet server? The router uses its routing table to determine which interface to use to route the traffic. The router's default route, which you configure, is the route used when traffic is destined for an address that resides beyond the router's local interfaces. The default route specifies the IP address of the router to which all traffic that isn't destined for a known interface (also determined by the routing table) should be routed. So, the router analyzes the packet, recognizes that the destination IP address doesn't match the subnets of defined routes in the routing table, and directs the packet to the default route. The router specified by the default route analyzes the packet and routes it based on its routing table.

Each route in a routing table falls into one of three categories:

- **Network route:** Provides a route to a specific network ID and all addresses within that network
- **Host route:** Provides a route to a specific host (A host route entry defines the host IP address as well as the network address.)
- **Default route:** Used to route traffic for which there is no corresponding network route or host route

The routing table contains routing entries against which the router checks the destination address of all packets to determine how to route each packet. Each entry in the routing table has specific general properties:

- **Network ID, host address, subnet mask:** These properties serve to identify the destination network ID or host address and the destination's subnet. If the router determines that the destination address stored in the packet's header matches these properties in a routing table entry, it forwards the packet to the forwarding address associated with the route (see next).
- **Forwarding address:** This is the address of the remote router to which the router forwards packets that match the network ID, host address, or subnet defined by the entry.

- **Interface:** This property specifies the local router port through which the traffic should be routed for packets that satisfy the criteria of the routing table entry.

- **Metric:** This value identifies the relative cost of the route, which is based on actual connection cost, available bandwidth, and other factors that you determine when you create a route. If more than one route exists for the same destination, the router uses the one with the lowest metric, if available.

Here's a summary of the whole process: A packet comes into the router. The router analyzes the destination address in the packet's header. The router then examines its routing table, attempting to match the packet's destination address against the network ID, host address, or subnet properties of each routing table entry. If a match is found, the router directs the packet to the forwarding address defined by the matching routing table entry, using the interface and metric to decide how to physically route the packet out of the router. If the packet's destination address doesn't match any of the routing table entries, the router sends the packet to the forwarding address defined by the router's default route. If no default route is defined, the packet is rejected and routing fails. The routing table is therefore the blueprint by which the router accomplishes its job.

How are routing entries added to the routing table? A router can learn its routes dynamically from other routers, or it can use statically defined routes, or static routes. With dynamic routes, routers communicate with one another to share learned routes, which enables routes to propagate to adjacent routers. Routing protocols are used to enable the routers to share this routing information. The two most common routing protocols are Routing Information Protocol (RIP) and Open Shortest Path First (OSPF), both of which are supported by Windows Server 2003.

The administrator who configures the router creates static routes manually. In a small network with few subnets, static routes are an effective means of routing all traffic. As the number of routers grows, however, dynamic routing becomes more desirable because of the reduced management overhead. You don't have to manage existing routes or create new ones when another segment is added to the network. Instead, the router learns its routing table from adjacent routers automatically when the router comes online.

Overview of RIP

Of the two routing protocols included with Windows Server 2003, RIP is easier to configure. RIP is limited to a maximum hop count of 15, making RIP useful for small- to medium-size installations. Any address more than 15 hops away is deemed unreachable by the router.

Each time a router boots, it re-creates its routing table. The routing table initially only contains the routing table entries for physically connected networks. A router using RIP periodically broadcasts announcements regarding routes, which enables adjacent routers to modify their routing tables. So, after a router comes online, it begins using RIP announcements to build its routing table. Also, RIP provides for triggered updates in addition to broadcast updates. These triggered updates occur when a router detects a network change, such as an interface going down. The router then broadcasts the change to adjacent routers, which modify their routing tables accordingly. When the interface comes back up, the router that recognizes the change broadcasts a triggered update to adjacent routers, which again modify their routing tables to accommodate the change.

Windows Server 2003 supports RIP version 1 and version 2. RIP v2 provides additional features over RIP v1, such as authentication for security and route filtering. RIP v2 also supports multicast broadcast of RIP announcements and several other features. RIP v1 routers are forward-compatible with RIP v2 routers, enabling them to coexist.

Overview of OSPF

OSPF was developed to address the needs of large networks, such as the Internet. Each OSPF router maintains a link-state database (LDB) that contains link-state advertisements (LSAs) from adjacent routers. The LSA contains information about a router, its connected networks, and configured costs. The cost is similar to a route metric discussed earlier, in that it defines the relative cost of using the route. OSPF uses an algorithm to calculate the shortest path for routing based on the information contained in its LDB, making it a very efficient means of routing. Adjacent routers recalculate and synchronize their LDBs as network changes occur, such as network interfaces going down or coming online.

OSPF is more complicated to configure than RIP. Its performance advantages are geared primarily toward very large networks, so if you're setting up a router for a small- or medium-size network, RIP is generally the better option. Where network size is a factor, however, OSPF is the better choice.

Unicast routing vs. multicast routing

Another important aspect to understand about routing is the difference between unicast routing and multicast routing. In unicast routing, a packet is sent from one node to only one other node, as illustrated in **Figure B**. This is the most common type of routing and the one you use every time you open a Web browser and browse an Internet site, retrieve your e-mail, move a file with ftp, and perform most other common IP-based network tasks.

In multicast routing, however, traffic is broadcast from one node to many nodes, as illustrated in **Figure C**. Multicasting is most commonly used for audio and video conferencing, enabling packets to be efficiently transmitted to multiple clients from a single host. Without multicasting, the packets would have to be transmitted multiple times to each client, generating a considerably larger amount of network traffic and imposing more overhead on the server. Plus, as you can imagine, conferencing would be difficult to set up without multicasting, as the conferencing server would need to be preconfigured with the list of all participants. With multicasting, the participants simply listen on a designated multicasting address, which can be allocated by a DHCP server to automate configuration.

Configuring a unicast router

As with other RRAS configurations, you can use the RRAS wizard to configure Windows Server 2003 as a router. Setup installs RRAS by default, so you only need to enable and configure the server according to your routing needs. To start the RRAS wizard, open the RRAS console from the Administrative Tools folder. Right-click the server and choose Configure And Enable Routing And Remote Access. In the wizard, select the option to configure a network router. The wizard prompts you for the following information:

- **Protocols:** Select the protocols to be supported for routing, such as TCP/IP and/or IPX. If the protocols are not installed, the wizard gives you the option of adding them. By default, all installed protocols are enabled for routing, but you can choose to disable some if you don't want the protocol to be routed.

- **Use demand-dial connections:** You can choose to enable demand-dial routing at this point or accomplish the task later.

In addition to configuring the router through the wizard, you also can enable routing manually. You need to choose this latter option if the server is already configured and enabled for RRAS (such as a VPN server) and you want to add routing to the server's list of roles.

To enable routing for a server that already has RRAS enabled, open the RRAS console from the Administrative Tools folder. Right-click the server and choose

Figure B

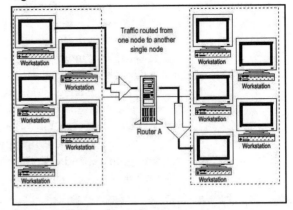

Unicast routing directs packets from one node to another.

Figure C

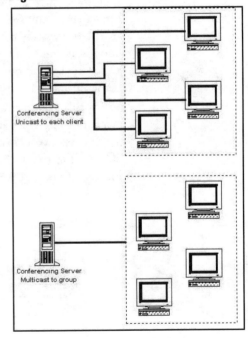

Examples of conferencing with and without multicasting

Properties. Select the Router check box and then select the type of routing you want to support, either LAN or LAN and demand-dial. Then click OK.

Next, configure the IP address for which RRAS performs routing on that interface. By default, Windows Server 2003 uses the first interface to process routing tasks on that interface, and on interfaces with only one address, no configuration is needed. If the interface has multiple addresses, however, you'll need to reconfigure RRAS if the default address is not the one you want to use. To configure the address, open the RRAS console, expand the server, and expand the IP Routing branch. Click General and, in the right pane, right-click the interface you want to modify and choose Properties. Use the Configuration page to set the IP address, subnet mask, and default gateway (if needed) for the interface. To set the metric for the interface, click Advanced.

Configuring a router with static routes

At this point, I assume you have the server enabled for routing and have configured the desired address on each interface. Now it's time to think about how you'll implement routing. As mentioned earlier, you can use static routes, RIP, or OSPF (if the router only routes traffic between two subnets, you don't need to worry about creating routes or using RIP or OSPF). Let's take a look at static routes, which are a good option if you're setting up your Windows Server 2003 RRAS router in a small network.

For this example, we'll use privately addressed network segments. **Figure D** shows our sample network structure. We'll work on configuring router B, which we'll assume has two network interfaces. As Figure D illustrates, router B resides on subnets 192.168.0.n and 192.168.1.n. The IP addresses of the router's interfaces are 192.168.0.20 (LAN 0) and 192.168.1.1 (LAN 1). In these examples, I've renamed the network interfaces from their default names of Local Area

Figure D

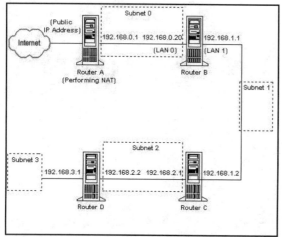

Sample network for configuring routing

Connection and Local Area Connection 2 to LAN 0 and LAN 1, respectively. It's a good idea on multihomed systems to rename the interfaces to help you keep track of what's what. To rename the interfaces, open the Network And Dial-Up Connections folder, right-click an interface, and choose Rename.

Let's add a static route at Router B to route traffic to the 192.168.2.0 subnet (subnet 2) through interface LAN 1. To add a static route, first open the RRAS console. Expand the IP Routing branch and click Static Routes. Either right-click in the right pane or right-click Static Routes and choose New Static Route. RRAS displays the Static Route dialog box in which you provide the following data:

- **Interface:** Choose the network interface that RRAS should use to route traffic that meets the static route criteria. In this example, you want to configure a static route for traffic destined for 192.168.2.0 to be routed through LAN 1, so select the LAN 1 interface.

- **Destination:** Rather than create a host route, you'll create a network route. Enter the network ID of the destination network, which in this example is 192.168.2.0. Remember that the router compares the destination IP address of incoming packets against this network address to determine if the route entry matches and if the route is appropriate for routing the packets. You can specify a network address, host address, or use 0.0.0.0 for this value (this latter option creates a default route). Use the low network address to specify a network address, as I did in this example, or specify the actual IP address of the host if creating a host route.

- **Network mask:** Specify the subnet mask of the destination network or host. In this example, enter 255.255.255.0, the subnet mask for our Class C private network.

- **Gateway:** Specify the IP address to which packets matching the route criteria are routed. In this example, you need to specify the IP address of Router C on the 192.168.1.0 subnet. As you can see from Figure D, the address to enter is 192.168.1.2.

- **Metric:** Enter the relative cost for the route by specifying a metric. If more than one route exists, the one with the lowest metric is used to route the traffic if that route is available.

- **Use this route to initiate demand-dial connections:** If you have configured at least one demand-dial interface for the router, this option is available. Select this option if you want the router to initiate a demand-dial connection when it receives traffic that matches the selected route.

Next, you create a static route to accommodate the 192.168.3.0 subnet. The data for this static route is the same as the one you just created, except the destination network address is 192.168.3.0. The Gateway is the same as in the previous route. The static routes you set up on Router C handle the traffic from that point, routing it to Router D.

Finally, you should create a default route on Router B that directs all other traffic not destined for subnets 1, 2, or 3 to Router A, with the assumption that the traffic is destined for a public address on the Internet. So, create another static route on Router B using the following values:

- **Interface:** LAN 0
- **Destination:** 0.0.0.0
- **Network mask:** 0.0.0.0
- **Gateway:** 192.168.0.1

- **Metric**: As desired
- **Use this route to initiate demand-dial connections**: As needed

It's not all that bad

You can see that setting up static routes takes a little work but can be an effective means of configuring routing for small networks. As the number of routers you manage grows, you'll likely turn to RIP and/or OSPF to provide dynamic routing. While RIP and OSPF are a little more complicated to set up, they are much easier to manage. In an upcoming article, we'll take a detailed look at both protocols, as well as demand-dial routing and multicast routing. ❖

Build an intranet for your business with Windows Small Business Server 2003 Remote Web Workspace

By Scott Lowe, MCSE

One compelling new feature in Windows Small Business Server 2003 (SBS 2003) is the remote access capability that this product brings to small businesses. With this capability, you can install a portal and read your mail, collaborate with other users via SharePoint, and manage your server all from the comfort of your home office or a hotel room.

Everything you need to enable these features—a database and a Web server—is standard fare in both the Standard and Premium editions of SBS 2003. Even better, at the client side, all you need in order to use these new features is a decent Web browser.

It all starts with the installation process, where you make sure the right components are selected. Next, there's a short configuration process to go through. Finally, your users can start using the Remote Web Workspace. By the end of this article, you'll have an SBS 2003-based Remote Web Workspace up and running with the default options.

What is the Remote Web Workspace?

The Remote Web Workspace is a sort of "meta intranet" for your SBS 2003 installation in that it encompasses all of the usual elements of an intranet—in this case, all of the features of SharePoint as well as additional functionality depending on the access level of the user connecting to the server. For example, in addition to being able to use the SharePoint intranet services, administrators are also provided the ability to connect to Windows XP workstations on the network using Remote Desktop and remotely manage the SBS 2003 server. Finally, Outlook Web Access is also included for environments that have opted to install the incorporated Exchange server.

Installing the Remote Web Workspace

Without installing it, your Remote Web Workspace won't go very far. Fortunately, Remote Web Workspace is a default component in the SBS 2003 setup.

After you reboot from the first part of the SBS 2003 installation (**http://techrepublic.preview.com.com:8001/5100-6345-5280235.html**), Setup continues and allows you to add more components such as Exchange and, for this article, the

Figure A

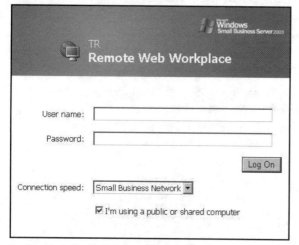

The Intranet component installs the remote Web services.

Figure B

Provide a login for the SBS 2003 Remote Web Workplace.

intranet services. On the first screen of the installation—the Component Selection screen shown in **Figure A**—just verify that the Intranet component is selected.

If you're running the Premium edition of SBS 2003, you'll also have the option of installing SQL Server as the backend data store for the intranet. However, Standard edition users aren't left out in the cold; the installer includes Microsoft's run-time edition of SQL Server: MSDE.

The next screen of the installation verifies installation paths for the various components. For this example, these are the SQL Server MSDE installation path, the shared folders, and the path to client applications. To change a path, select it and click the Change Folder button.

The last screen of the installation wizard verifies your choices. Click the Next button to proceed with the installation. This will take a few minutes, and you'll need to change CDs a couple of times. After the software installation completes, you'll be prompted to reboot your server.

Using the Remote Web Workspace

After the server reboots, you can immediately start using the newly minted SBS 2003 server to increase your productivity. At the server console, browse to **http://companyweb/ default.aspx**. The companyweb DNS entry is a pointer to the DNS entry for your server name and was created automatically as part of the server installation. If you want to call your intranet something other than companyweb, use the DNS configuration tool to create a different name.

Figure C

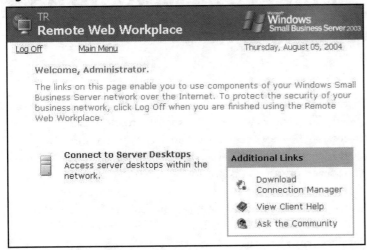

The Remote Web Workplace main menu

The first screen has four selections:

- **My Company's Internal Web Site:** This is a link to the standard SharePoint installation.

- **Network Configuration Wizard:** Provides an easy way to add a computer to the SBS 2003 domain.

- **Remote Web Workplace:** Launches the Remote Web Workplace. You have to provide a username and password for this section, as shown in **Figure B**.

- **Information and Answers:** Help and information for your SBS server.

The connection speed setting on the Remote Web Workplace screen lets you define how fast your connection is, which helps later on when you try to use Remote Desktop services to manage servers and workstations on your network. For example, if you're on a dial-up connection, you should use the appropriate option from the drop-down menu so that your RDP connection can be properly optimized. For this example, I'm on the same network as the SBS server, so I selected Small Business Network.

Once you log in, you'll see a screen similar to the one in **Figure C**. You may have more options depending on your version of SBS 2003 and the options you selected at installation.

The only useful item on the screen in Figure C is the ability to remotely connect to a server's desktop. This is particularly useful when you're on the road and need to add a user or fix a printer problem.

At this point, if you've been following along, you may have other options on your menu. It's safe to use them, but make sure any users that can log in and might be able to manipulate the server's desktop have strong passwords to protect you from the outside. ❖

Creating your SOHO Web site on Windows XP and IIS 5.1

By Michael Jackman

I f your small office or home office (SOHO) has access to high-speed cable or DSL Internet connections, you can take advantage of broadband and Windows XP Professional to host your own Web site. You can do so by installing the Internet Information Services (IIS) 5.1 that comes with the OS. IIS 5.1 is a client-side Web server. As such, it is not for hosting high-demand sites. In fact, 5.1 is limited to 10 simultaneous connections, though I have heard of an undocumented hack that will allow up to 40 simultaneous connections. Even if your business already contracts with a Web site host, you can still use IIS 5.1 to run a staging server or development platform.

Which version, which OS, again?

Windows XP Professional includes IIS 5.1 on the installation disk. The Web server is not available in XP Home Edition. Rumor has it that if you try to install IIS 5.1 from a Windows XP Professional disk onto an XP Home computer, it won't work reliably.

If you previously ran Microsoft's Web server under Windows 2000 Professional, you ran version 5.0. Though the flavors are similar, 5.1 is more secure and has some interface changes and more advanced features.

As with Win2K, XP's Web solution includes an SMTP mail server, FTP server, support for a site search engine, Active Server Pages (.asp), Front Page extensions, management interfaces, logging, and (less than ideal) documentation. In place of Telnet, however, remote management is accomplished via a remote desktop utility.

IIS 5.1, like 5.0, enables Web site authors to collaborate via Web folders using a scheme called Web Distributed Authoring and Versioning (WebDAV). While WebDAV can be valuable for collaborating on Web site design, it also adds some vulnerability to your system. 5.1's implementation is somewhat different here, as well, and won't be covered here.

Although you may prefer version 5.0, the catch is that Microsoft Web servers are platform-specific. Running 5.1 requires Windows XP, and running 5.0 requires Windows 2000. If you want version 6.0, you'll have to invest in Windows Server 2003.

Naturally, client-side Web hosts are less powerful than their server counterparts. For instance, the server editions of IIS can host many Web sites, while the clients can only run one site at a time. But for most do-it-yourself businesses one site is plenty.

Other SOHO Web site requirements

In addition to the minimum requirements of Windows XP and IIS 5.1, to run a full-time, secure SOHO Web site you will want to invest in:

- A computer that stays connected to the Internet 24/7 (therefore, your traveling laptop won't do).

- A static IP address. Most ISPs will provide one for an extra fee if it's not already included as part of your business account.

- Your own domain name, such as www.mybusiness.com. Purchase this name from a domain name registrar such as Network Solutions.

- A firewall to reduce your Web site and SOHO network's vulnerability to Internet mischief. A properly configured hardware or software firewall blocks all Internet activity except that which you authorize. For a quick software solution, consider using ZoneAlarm Pro ($50 per license).

- A router to enable you to share the cable or DSL broadband connection among your small office or home network computers. Often, routers include basic firewalls. You may want to configure it to isolate your Web site from the rest of your network.

Installing IIS

IIS does not install by default when you first set up Windows XP Pro. To add the client Web server later on, place your Windows XP Professional CD in the CD-ROM. Click Start | Control Panel | Add Or Remove Programs. Click the Add/Remove Windows Components icon on the left of the following dialog. Within the Windows Components Wizard, click the check box for Internet Information Services (IIS), as shown in **Figure A**.

Each IIS option adds a security risk to your network. Therefore, when configuring installation options, weigh necessity against vulnerability, and only install what you absolutely need. If you change your mind later, you can always add components then.

Note that the IIS checkbox is grey. This means there are further components that have not been selected. To view them, click the Details button.

FTP Server is unchecked by default. If you want to install this, check the File Transfer Protocol (FTP) Service box.

Consider unchecking the SMTP Service, which is checked by default. SMTP, or

Figure A

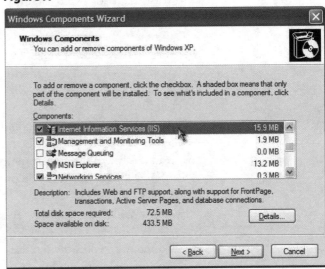

Check Internet Information Services (IIS) to add this component to Windows XP Professional.

Simple Mail Transport Protocol, allows your Web site to include its own mail server. But the advantage of sending and receiving e-mail with your domain name in the address (name@mybusiness.com) may not be worth the risk.

Some domain name registrars like Network Solutions offer the ability to forward mail with your domain name to your regular ISP account. If yours does so, use its mail forwarding service and let the registrar worry about SMTP security.

Note that within the Details window the World Wide Web Service option is also grayed out, which means you need to drill down another layer. Again, click Details. By default, both the Printers Virtual Directory and the World Wide Web Service are checked. You can also add Remote Desktop Web Connection if you need remote management (this is in place of Telnet), and a Scripts Virtual Directory, if you will be running scripts. I suggest leaving only the World Wide Web Service checked.

After customizing your installation, click OK to accept and dismiss both Details windows, then click Next to start the setup program. Installation will take a few minutes.

Configuring IIS 5.1

When installation is complete, you won't need to reboot. However, you *will* need to stop your new Web server, as Microsoft repeated the mistake it made with 5.0: when freshly installed, the server is up and running a default Web page. This is like leaving your front door unlocked when no one is minding the store.

Why didn't Microsoft leave the server off by default? Who knows? But until you have a chance to configure your system and update IIS with the latest patches, you don't want to be broadcasting to the Web.

At least Microsoft fixed one flaw. With 5.1, once you turn off a service, it stays off. In 5.0, when you rebooted, the Web site came right back on.

To turn off the server, open the Internet Information Services manager by choosing Start | Control Panel. In the Control Panel, double-click Performance And Maintenance. Highlight Internet Information Services and right-click. Select Pin To Start Menu so you won't have to drill down this far ever again. Then double-click the icon to open the Microsoft Management Console (MMC).

Expand the list of Web site components in the left pane's tree view until Default Web Site is visible. Right-click Default Web Site and select Stop. The left pane will now read (Stopped). Do the same for FTP, if you installed it. For SMTP, simply right-click Default SMTP Virtual Server on the tree and select stop. A red "x" will appear to show it's now disabled. The result should look like **Figure B**.

By the way, in Administrative Tools you'll find another new MMC, the Server Extensions Administrator, for configuring FrontPage Server Extensions if you installed them. If you were familiar with version 5.0, then you will note that two additional consoles are no longer present, the Personal Web Manager and Telnet Server Administration.

Updating, patching, securing

IIS 5.1 is no different from any other Web server in that when first installed it's a security risk. Now that you have disabled the Web server, you can prepare for publishing a more secure Web site.

First, apply or reapply Windows XP Service Pack 1 or 1a, whichever you installed. Previous IIS patches are combined in this Service Pack. Browse to Windows Update and download any new IIS patches. Among them, you will find Cumulative Patch 811114, released in May, 2003. This release affects IIS 4.0, 5.0, and 5.1 and its components, such as FrontPage Server Extensions.

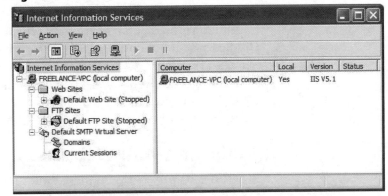

After installation, stop Web services so that your network isn't vulnerable to intrusion.

Next, download Microsoft's IIS Lockdown Tool version 2.1 from **www.microsoft.com/downloads/details.aspx?displaylang = en&FamilyID = DDE9EFC0-BB30-47EB-9A61-FD755D23CDEC**. This utility helps IIS by disabling features you don't plan to use. It does so by applying a template of options for specific Web site roles you select, such as Static Server or Dynamic Service with ASP enabled. You can run it as needed to reconfigure your site. According to Microsoft, the tool works with IIS versions 4, 5, and 5.1.

More IIS tweaks

An important step in the security process is to delete files and disable settings that can be compromised by hackers. For example, you should delete the directories c:\inetpub\isssamples and c:\windows\help\isshelp.

These directories of script samples and documentation present a security risk, as hackers have been known to use them to tunnel through IIS to the host OS.

In version 5.0, it was also considered proactive to disable unneeded file extensions (now called script mappings) that exposed dll calls, such as .printer and .idx (indexing service). But in 5.1, many of these extensions have been removed or their mappings moved to the Front Page Extensions folder.

The one remaining extension you might consider removing is called *.idc* (Internet database connector). To remove .idc, open the Internet Information Services Manager. In the left pane's tree listing of your as-yet unpublished Web site, right-click on the Web Sites folder, and select Properties.

In the Web Sites Properties sheet, click the Home Directory tab, and then the Configuration Button. This will configure all the properties of any Web site created from now on.

In the Application Configuration window, highlight .idc and any other file extensions you don't want, as shown in **Figure C**. Click Remove, then click OK.

As a further precaution, return to the Home Directory tab and uncheck Index This Resource to turn off file indexing for your Web site. Click OK to dismiss the menu.

An Inheritance Overrides dialog will inform you that the configuration of certain child nodes override the indexing property you just set. Select all the child nodes and click OK to turn off indexing.

Publishing your Web site

Now that you've made IIS 5.1 more secure, publish your Web site. Author Web pages using your favorite authoring tools and create images with a drawing program. Place them and any media files, such as sound and video files, in the directory c:\inetpub\wwwroot and the subdirectories you create, such as \images.

The wwwroot directory is mapped to the Default Web Site folder listed in the Internet Information Services MMC tree. You can verify this fact by highlighting Default Web Site, right-clicking, and selecting Properties. Then click the Home Directory tab. The local path text box contains the path to the default Web site (**Figure D**). If you wish you can change this path to another directory.

Note that via radio buttons you can also change the path of the default Web site to a share on another computer, and even redirect the site to another URL.

Figure C

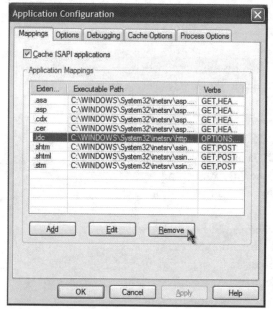

Remove unneeded extensions such as .idc that may be security risks.

Figure D

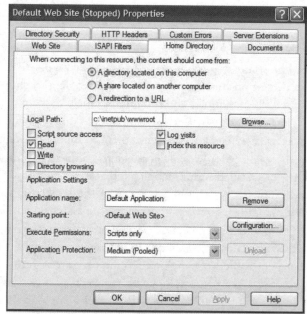

Use the Home Directory tab to change the location of your default Web site.

In the Web Site tab (**Figure E**), you can change your site's description displayed in the tree (Default Web Site isn't very interesting). This tab is also where you fill in your site's IP address. The currently assigned IP address will appear on the drop-down list, making it easy to enter this information. You can also make adjustments to ports, timeouts, and other advanced options here. These values should not need to be changed for basic Web sites.

Click OK. A message will inform you that IIS needs to be restarted for these changes to take effect. Click OK. Doing so will not publish the Web site to the Internet, it will only restart the IIS manager.

While the Web server is still stopped, test and edit your Web site. When you're ready, activate the IIS 5.1 Web service by right-clicking the Default Web Site in the Internet Information Services MMC tree and choosing Start. You're now broadcasting live.

Figure E

In the Web Site tab, enter a description for your Web site and an IP address from the drop-down list.

A new Web site will take a few days to propagate throughout the Internet. After waiting a reasonable amount of time, check that the Web site is really available to your customers. Do this from a remote computer connected to the Internet, not from your own computer on your SOHO network.

With a business site up and running, remember to periodically peruse Web access logs and firewall logs for visitor statistics, errors, and security problems.

Testing and troubleshooting

So you've purchased a domain name, installed IIS 5.1, built a Web site, and turned it on and it doesn't work. Here's a list of troubleshooting tips:

- Is IIS on, are your network cables connected, is your broadband modem connected, and is your service up and running? If you have a hardware firewall and router, check those as well.

- Are your Web files accessible? Verify that you've put your Web files in the correct folder and named them correctly—especially the default home page.

- Have you been hacked? If your Web site had been working, but pages now appear different or are no longer in your directory, immediately turn off your Web site, unplug from the network, and check your logs and files to see if a hacker has broken in. Run a virus scan.

- Is the problem outside your network? If you've received reports that your Web site cannot be reached, ask someone on a different network to try. It may be that one leg of the Internet is experiencing problems. You can help repair the broken leg by reporting problems to that visitor's ISP.

- Did your "static" IP address change? Go to Start | Run, type *cmd*, and press [Enter]. In the command line interface, type *ipconfig /all* and press [Enter]. Compare the IP address given in ipconfig with the address provided by your ISP. If they are different, perhaps your ISP didn't give you a static IP address after all. But before complaining, type *ipconfig/release* and *ipconfig/renew* and see if that fixes the disparity.

- Does your domain name or IP address work? If typing *www.mydomainname.com* doesn't work from your browser, try typing your IP address instead. Use the numbers given by ipconfig /all, as instructed above. If the address brings up your Web site, but the domain name doesn't, this suggests a DNS error. A call to your ISP is in order.

- Did you point your domain name to the correct IP address? Recheck your account with your domain name provider to see if your domain name is correct and is matched correctly with your IP address.

- Have you given Internet DNS servers enough time to update? If you just purchased a domain name or just changed an IP address, you should wait a few days for the Internet DNS servers to include your new information before calling for help.

- Are your routers and firewalls configured correctly?

- Is your cable or DSL modem configured correctly? For example, some DSL modems can function as network bridges or limited routers. You may need to switch to bridged mode for your Web site to work or further configure your modem.

- Is IIS getting through your firewall? Check your firewall configuration to see if it is allowing your Web site to pass through on port 80.

- Did you disable anonymous access in IIS 5.1, or did you configure permissions so that files can't be read by Web browsers? ❖

Create a SOHO Web site fast with Windows 2000 Professional and IIS

By Michael Jackman

I f you're based in a small office or home office, and you have access to high-speed cable or DSL Internet connections, you can take advantage of broadband Internet connections and Windows 2000 Professional to host your own Web site. You can do so by installing the IIS (Internet Information Services) 5.0 that comes with the operating system. IIS makes it possible for you to run a low-to-medium demand Web server (up to 100,000 hits per day). And even if you already have a hosted Web site, you can use IIS on your Windows 2000 Professional workstation as a staging server for revising and testing your business Web site.

IIS can run on Windows 2000 Professional?

The Windows 2000 Professional version of IIS 5.0 Web server is less powerful than the version that comes with Windows 2000 Server. For instance, it lets you host only one Web site at a time. But this is more than adequate for most small business needs. In addition to a Web server, IIS includes a mail server (SMTP), Telnet, and FTP server as well as support for a site search engine, Active Server Pages (.asp), Front Page extensions, management interfaces, logging, and documentation.

Comprehensive as IIS is, in addition to running it, you'll have a few other needs before you can host your own business Web site. You'll need:

- A computer to run Windows 2000 Professional and IIS, operating on and connected to the Internet as close to 24/7 as it can be. When your computer is down, i.e., for rebooting or maintenance, your Web site will be down. You can purchase a used computer just for running IIS or use your personal computer. But be aware that this increases the risk of losing data to hacking.

- A static IP address. This permanent Internet address provided by your ISP, in a four-part format such as 69.3.216.95, permits the vast network of Internet servers to find your Web site. Most ISPs use dynamic Web addressing as a security measure, meaning that each time you connect to the Internet, or after a certain number of days when your IP address "lease" expires, the address is rotated from an available address in the ISP's address pool. Most ISPs will provide a static IP address for a small monthly fee or include it as part of a business account.

- A domain name of your own, e.g., www.*yourbusiness*.com, to attach to your IP address. Purchase this domain name from one of the domain name registrars, such as Network Solutions. When you do so, you'll point the domain name to your static IP address. For example, my freelance writer's Web site points to 65.199.34.52. Your Web site will be inaccessible by name until you attach your domain name to your new IP address and for up to three days while Internet domain name servers (DNS) around the world update.

- A firewall to prevent Internet mischief, because a static IP address is an easier target for hackers in the same way a stationary target is easier to hit than a moving target. A properly configured firewall blocks all Internet activity except the activity you authorize, protecting you from attacks. There are hardware firewalls, such as the Linksys Broadband EtherFast Cable/DSL Firewall Router (**www.linksys.com/products/product.asp?grid=23&prid=433**), that you place between your cable or DSL modem and your network and software firewalls. Consider using ZoneAlarm, one of the top-rated software firewalls. It costs $40 per license for the Plus version, and $50 per license for the Pro version.

- A router to enable you to share the cable or DSL broadband connection among your small office or home network computers. Often, routers include basic firewalls.

Installing IIS

When you first installed Windows 2000 Professional, you most likely did not install IIS, since it's not part of the default setup. To install IIS on your workstation, place your Windows 2000 Professional CD in the CD drive. Click Start | Settings | Control Panel | Add/ Remove Programs. Click Add/Remove Windows Components from the icons on the left. In the Windows Components Wizard, click the check box for Internet Information Services (IIS), as shown in **Figure A**, and then click Next. Installation takes a few minutes.

After installation, several new services will be present on your system: FTP Publishing Service, IIS Admin Service, Simple Mail Transport Protocol (SMTP), Telnet Service, and the World Wide Web Publishing Service. You can view them by clicking the Services console in Control Panel | Administrative Tools.

Also in Administrative Tools, you'll find four new management consoles:

Figure A

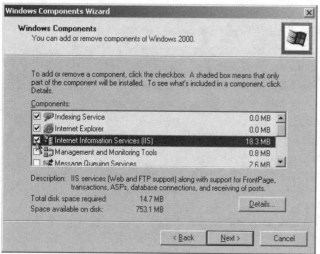

Check Internet Information Services (IIS) to add this component to Windows 2000 Professional.

- Internet Services Manager, a detailed management tool for IIS
- Personal Web Manager, a simple interface for rapidly configuring and controlling your Web site
- Server Extensions, a console for controlling additional Web capabilities
- Telnet Server Administration, a command line application for configuring Telnet

Updating, patching, and securing

Like most Web servers, IIS 5.0—when installed fresh off the CD—is vulnerable to various Internet exploits and suffers from a few program bugs. As a first step to patching and securing your new Web server, apply or reapply Windows 2000 Service Pack 3 (**www.microsoft.com/Windows2000/downloads/servicepacks/ sp3/download.asp**), which was released in August 2002 and contains quite a few fixes (**http://support.microsoft.com/default.aspx?scid=/support/ServicePacks/ Windows/2000/SP3FixList.asp**). Next, apply the Cumulative Patch for Internet Information Service (**www.microsoft.com/technet/treeview/default. asp?url=/ technet/security/bulletin/MS02-062.asp**), released on Oct. 30, 2002.

Now download and apply the March 17, 2003, patch for Windows 2000 (**www.microsoft.com/security/security_bulletins/ms03-007.asp**) to close a security hole that can allow hackers to take over your computer. Finally, run Windows Update (**http://v4.windowsupdate.microsoft.com/en/default.asp**) often to check for Microsoft's latest IIS and OS patches, and apply them as released.

Problems, problems

If IIS hangs upon starting after you apply an update, it's not because you did anything wrong. This difficulty occurs especially if you have firewall or other Internet security software installed that may not recognize modified IIS components and therefore prevents services from starting.

Your Event Viewer's System log may show an error such as, "The World Wide Web Publishing Service hung on starting." To check the log, go to Start | Settings | Control Panel | Administrative Tools | Component Services, and click Event Viewer, then System.

The solution is easy. First, change the startup option of the IIS Admin Service to Disabled. To do so, click Start | Settings | Control Panel | Administrative Tools. Click Services and then find and double-click the IIS Admin Service. In the Service Startup Option, choose Disabled from the drop-down list. Finally, reboot your workstation.

After security applications have loaded, change the Service Startup Option back to Automatic and start the IIS Admin Service. Apply any requested actions (such as ZoneAlarm requesting "Allow Internet Information Services to Access the Internet?"). The next time you reboot, IIS should start normally.

CREATE DESKTOP SHORTCUTS
To ease IIS administration, create a shortcut to the Administrative Tools folder on your desktop. This shortcut will put the management consoles for the following close at hand: Services, Task Manager, Component Services (including the Event Viewer), IIS Internet Services Manager, Personal Web Manager, and Server Extensions.

Configuring IIS

Since your goal is simply to serve up Web pages and not to invite trouble, as a final step in the security process, disable unneeded services, remote administration, sample scripts, and other files and settings installed by default that can be compromised by hackers. You can certainly peruse the samples while the Web server is off, but delete them before going live with your Web site.

To begin securing IIS, delete the following directories:

- c:\inetpub\isssamples
- c:\program files\common files\system\msadc
- c:\winnt\help\isshelp
- c:\winnt\system32\inetsrv\iisadmpwd

These directories of samples, DLLs, and documentation present a security risk, as a hacker could use them to tunnel through IIS to the computer. Another thing you can do to increase security is to disable unneeded file extensions. Most likely, your Web site will only use files with the extensions .htm or .html (Web pages); .stm, .shtm, or .shtml (for server side includes); and .asp (for Microsoft Active Server Pages). Remove any other extensions that could expose .dll calls, such as .printer (Internet printing capability); .htw, .ida, and .idq (Index Server); .htr (Web-based password reset); and .idc (Internet database connector).

To disable unneeded extensions, start the Internet Services Manager in your Control Panel's Administrative Tools app. In the left pane, you'll see a tree depiction of your as-yet unpublished Web site. Right-click on the Web site's root (here, Freelancer, the name of my computer), and select Properties from the menu, as shown in **Figure B**.

Click Edit for the Master Properties of the WWW service. This will configure all the properties of any Web site created from now on. Click on the Home Directory tab, then click the Configuration button. Highlight each file extension and click Remove, as shown in **Figure C**. Then click OK.

In the next window, highlight Default Web Site and click OK so it will inherit the new settings. Now return to the Home Directory tab and again click Configuration. Choose the APP Options tab and deselect Enable Parent Paths,

Figure B

Access Default Web Site's properties sheet to remove unneeded file extensions.

Figure C

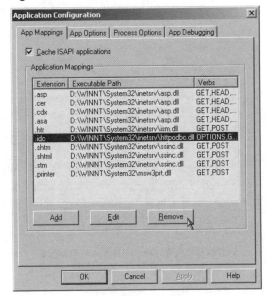

Remove extensions that can invite problems.

which is another potential threat if exploited. Again, set the Default Web Site to inherit the new setting.

Since you're running a small business, it's likely that you'll have limited experience in network security administration and limited time to spend on it. In such a setting, it's unwise to risk making FTP downloads available for visitors to your site, or to enable Telnet, SMTP, or the Indexing Service. Go to Administrative Tools | Services, double-click each of these services in turn, and set their Startup Type to Disabled from the drop-down list, as shown in **Figure D**.

Publishing your Web site

Now that you've made IIS relatively secure, you're ready to publish your Web site. Begin by authoring Web pages using your favorite authoring tool. You can create images with a drawing program. After you've created the pages and images, place them and any special files, such as sound files, in the directories and subdirectories you create.

Figure D

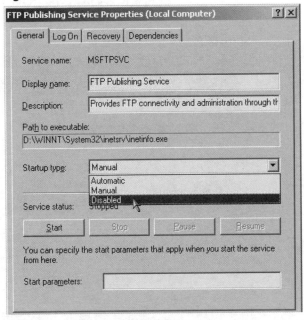

Disable the FTP, Indexing, SMTP, and Telnet services.

After you've set up the pages, test your Web page and edit it until it's ready. If everything looks good, turn on the IIS Web server and leave it on 24/7. You should periodically check Web access logs and firewall logs for visitor statistics, errors, and security problems.

Setting a default page

When visitors browse a Web site, the first page they see is the default home page. On UNIX-based Web servers, such as Apache, this file is named index.htm or index.html. In IIS, the home page is named default.htm (or default.asp, if you use Active Server Pages coding).

If you want, you can change the default page to index.htm (or any name you prefer). In the Internet Services Manager, right-click Default Web Site and choose Properties. Click the Documents tab and then click Add. Type *index.htm* in the box, then move it to the top of the list, as shown in **Figure E**.

Where to place your Web pages

Save your home page in the Web site's root directory; by default, this home directory is c:\inetpub\wwwroot. Save additional Web pages that are part of this site there as well, or in subdirectories you create. Keeping track of content is easier if you place images in the images subdirectory (already created), and organize related content in subdirectories. **Figure F** demonstrates the organization of my freelance writing Web site in IIS. (Note that my Web page is located in the D partition.)

Figure E

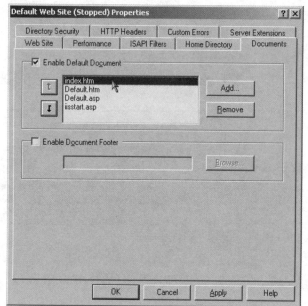

Add index.htm to the list of default home pages.

Figure F

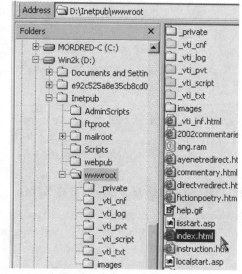

Place your Web site's content in c:\inetpub\wwwroot and subdirectories.

Figure G

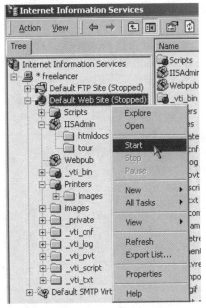

Start your Web site, and you're on the air.

Figure H

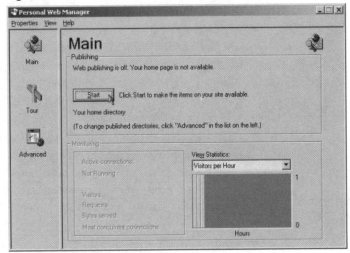

Using the Personal Web Manager is a simple way to start and stop your Web site.

You're on the air

When you're ready to publish "live," right-click Default Web Site in the Internet Services Manager tree and choose Start, as shown in **Figure G**.

Or, open the simpler Personal Web Manager and click the Start button, as shown in **Figure H**.

Testing and troubleshooting

You've bought your domain, installed IIS, built your Web site, and turned it on—and it doesn't work. Here's a list of basic testing and troubleshooting steps:

- Is IIS on, are your network cables connected, is your broadband modem connected, and is your service up and running? These first troubleshooting steps are the obvious but vital basics to complete before continuing. Don't forget to run your modem's diagnostics. If you have a router, check that as well.

- Have you been hacked or are your Web files accessible? Check to see if you've put your Web files in the correct folder and named them correctly—especially the default home page. If the Web site was working before, but pages are different or no longer there, immediately turn off your Web site, unplug from the network, and check your logs and files to see if a hacker has broken in. Run a virus scan.

- Is the problem outside your network? If you've had reports that your Web site cannot be reached, have someone else try. It may be that one leg of the

Internet is experiencing temporary problems. You could help by reporting problems to that visitor's ISP.

- Did your "static" IP address change? Go to Start | Run, type *cmd,* and press [Enter]. In the command line interface, type *ipconfig/all* and press [Enter]. Compare the IP address given in ipconfig with the address provided by your ISP. If they are different, perhaps your ISP didn't give you a static IP address after all. But before complaining, type *ipconfig/release* and *ipconfig/renew* and see if that fixes the disparity.

- Does your domain name or IP address work? If typing www.*mydomainname*.com doesn't work from your browser, try typing your IP address directly. Type *ipconfig/all* as instructed above, then enter the IP address given for your network connection. If the address brings up your Web site, but the domain name doesn't, this suggests a DNS error. A call to your ISP is in order.

- Did you point your domain name to the correct IP address? Recheck your account with your domain name provider to see if your domain name is correct and is matched correctly with your IP address.

- Have you given Internet DNS servers enough time to update? If you just purchased a domain name or just changed an IP address, you should wait a few days for the Internet DNS servers to include your new information before calling for help.

- If you use a router, it is configured correctly?

- Is your cable or DSL modem configured correctly? For example, some DSL modems can function as network bridges or limited routers. You may need to switch to bridged mode for your Web site to work or further configure your modem.

- Is IIS getting through your firewall? Check your firewall configuration to see if it is allowing your Web site to pass through on port 80. ❖

Small businesses can get big-business features with Windows Small Business Server 2003

By Scott Lowe, MCSE

Even with the occasional security issue, Microsoft's Windows Server 2003 line of products is a good choice for many companies. In particular, the Standard and Enterprise editions of this latest Windows incarnation are excellent choices for many companies, particularly when coupled with Microsoft's other products such as Exchange and SQL Server 2000. All together, Microsoft's suite of products built on Windows Server 2003 provides a powerful, integrated infrastructure.

However, a certain class of business—the small business—while it might want the features of this entire product suite, might not be able to justify the cost associated with separately acquiring the licenses and the hardware for everything that would be running. To that end, Microsoft makes available Windows Small Business Server 2003, a complete suite of products that provide up to 50 users with access to the most powerful applications Microsoft offers and at a reasonable price.

The components

Like its older brother, Windows Small Business Server 2003 is a complete suite of products handling a variety of computing needs for small organizations. Unlike older versions of the product, though, there are two separate editions of Windows Small Business Server 2003—Standard and Premium—each addressing different needs for different organizations. Not every company needs the advanced database offering, nor does every company need the powerful proxy/caching abilities in ISA Server. Microsoft offers these two versions of the software so that small businesses that don't need all of this software don't have to pay for it.

The Standard Edition of Server 2003 includes fax, firewall, and remote access services in addition to Exchange and server monitoring and administration tools. If you need additional functionality, consider the Premium edition, which includes everything in the Standard edition, but adds SQL Server 2000, ISA Server, and FrontPage 2003 to the mix. A pretty good offering for a small business!

Here are the main components available in the two editions of Small Business Server:

- **Windows built-in components -** Includes faxing services, firewall services for network protection, and remote access services to allow secure access to your resources from outside the office. Furthermore, standard Windows tools for server monitoring and administration are included in this category.

- **Exchange Server -** Provides powerful collaboration features to all users, including e-mail, calendaring, task tracking, and contact management.
- **SharePoint Services -** Provides a standards-based collaboration and portal environment.
- **SQL Server 2000 -** SQL Server 2000 is Microsoft's enterprise-caliber database platform, providing a solid foundation for your applications and data storage needs. (Premium Edition only)
- **ISA Server -** The Internet Security and Acceleration server goes a step beyond the included firewall services and lets you define and track all Internet activity. ISA Server also provides caching services to help keep your connection to the Internet at peak efficiency. (Premium Edition only)
- **FrontPage 2003 -** FrontPage 2003 can be used to help your small business meet its Web needs by providing a platform on which to develop your presence on the Internet. (Premium Edition only)

Pricing and licensing

Microsoft is betting that, as a small business product, the whole suite will be an enticing find over other products that are available, particularly on the open source front and from Novell, which is enjoying a resurgence in some markets.

Licensing

Unfortunately, in an effort to appear flexible, Microsoft has a tendency to confuse the buyer with somewhat complex terms. First off, you'll need to select between two types of client access licenses (CALs)—Device CALs and User CALs.

Device CALs allow a particular device to attach to the server, while User CALs provide access for a single user from any device used. Device CALs are useful in companies that require employees to share computers, such as shift-based workers. Rather than buying a separate license for three employees who use a single PC, just buy a device CAL for that PC. User CALs are just the opposite and are particularly useful when you have employees who wander from machine to machine or who might need to access the server resources from multiple locations.

Next, select from one of three licensing types: Retail, Open NL, or Open NL with software assurance. Software assurance provides you with two years of upgrades at no additional charge, but Microsoft hasn't been as successful as it had hoped with this new revenue effort.

A retail license is a little more expensive than an open NL license, but includes a full boxed product, whereas the NL license is just a license and media.

Pricing

Pricing for Small Business Server 2003 depends on the edition you buy, the program (retail or open NL), and the vendor. Microsoft's retail price for the boxed edition of Small Business Server 2003 Standard Edition is $599, while the Premium version runs $1,499. Each base product also includes five client access licenses that you can deploy either as user or device CALs. If you opt for the NL licensing program, these prices are $521 and $1,298, respectively, or $781 and $1,947 with software assurance.

These are just retail prices, though. I've seen street prices for the retail editions run around $440/$900 depending on the edition you choose.

To add CALs, you need to decide whether you'll add user or device CALs and choose the appropriate part number from Microsoft's site. CALs are available in packs of five and 20 users and run at a street price of around $440 for a pack of five licenses and just shy of $1,700 for a pack of 20 licenses.

Transition licenses

With this version of Small Business Server, Microsoft has realized that some customers will ultimately need the full line of standard products rather than the editions included in SBS. As a result, it has added "transition" licenses to the mix, providing an easy way to upgrade to Windows Server 2003, Exchange 2003, etc.

Transition licenses are useful if you need to scale your installation beyond 75 users or devices; if you need one of the enterprise editions of an SBS product; or if you need to separate the SBS components among different servers.

System requirements

For the Standard Edition, Microsoft recommends a server with at least a 550-MHz processor, 384 MB of RAM, and 4 GB of hard drive space. Furthermore, a fax board and two network adapters are required for the faxing and remote access/firewall functionality.

For the Premium Edition, Microsoft recommends the same speed processor, but at least 512 MB of RAM, 5 GB of available space, and the same additional hardware as above.

Personally, I think these are light recommendations and should be adjusted, particularly on RAM and disk space, both of which are cheap these days.

Big features for smaller organizations

Windows Small Business Server 2003 is a choice for small businesses that need a variety of software but don't want to plunk down huge hardware and software money. It includes the powerful applications that companies rely upon and provides an upgrade path as your business grows. ❖

Deploying Windows Server 2003 Small Business Edition

By Scott Lowe, MCSE

Microsoft created Windows Server 2003 Small Business Edition (WSBE) to make life easier for small businesses that need big business computing solutions. Rather than having to purchase and install multiple programs, Microsoft also streamlined the installation process. Here's what you need to know to deploy WSBE.

First things first

Before you start, make sure have you WSBE CDs in hand, are sitting at your server console, and are ready to do a full installation of this product including Windows Server with Active Directory and Exchange.

To get started, insert the first CD into your server and turn it on. If you've ever installed a Windows Server before, the first few screens will look mighty familiar as they're Microsoft's typical screens that tell you which drivers are being loaded for the installer (**Figure A**).

Once all of the drivers load, the Windows installer asks you to make a decision: Press [ENTER] to Install WSBE, [R] to launch the repair console to repair a damaged server installation, or [F3] to exit the installation. I'll assume that, for this article, you want to perform an installation. After you make this selection, you're asked to accept the terms of Microsoft's ever-so-generous license agreement.

Next, like a typical Windows Server install, you're asked to create a partition for the new server and can allocate as much space as you like, up to the maximum amount available on your disks (**Figure B**). For this installation, I'm installing WSBE onto a 4-GB partition on a system with a 1.6 GHz Pentium-M processor and 256 MB RAM.

After decided how much space to allocate to the server installation, you can choose either NTFS or FAT for a file system type. These days, anything less than NTFS isn't usually a good idea because of the security features inherent to NTFS and missing from FAT. Moreover, Active Directory requires an NTFS partition for its database. Subsequent to you making this selection,

Figure A

Driver information for the setup process

the text portion of the installation completes and you get a pretty, familiar GUI.

The GUI portion of the installer

Most of the questions asked at the beginning of the GUI portion of the WSBE installation are pretty standard, such as regional selections including language, currency, and keyboard language options.

The second screen in the GUI asks for your name and company name followed by a screen requesting the now-ubiquitous 25-character product key. Following the entry of the product key, choose a name for your server and assign an initial password for the administrator account as shown below in **Figure C**.

The next screen—the date and time—probably doesn't seem important, but it can be, particularly if you are running Exchange and/or your server is a domain controller. If the time or time zone on the server is not set correctly, Active Directory has synchronization problems, and your users might claim that e-mail date and time stamps are wrong. Lesson: Even for something seemingly innocuous like the date and time, be careful and make sure to check the time zone! After this set of screens, Windows completes the initial installation and the system automatically reboots.

Figure B

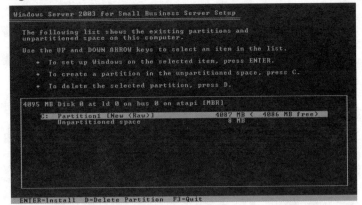

Decide how much space you want to allocate to WSBE.

Figure C

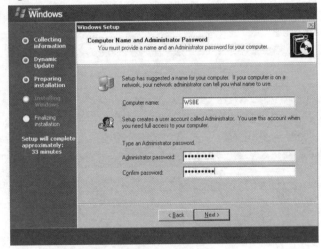

My sample server is named WSBE–original, eh?

After the reboot...

Once you log into the server after the reboot, the next part of the installer is launched, which is where the additional applications, including Exchange and SQL Server, are installed. This is also the utility that helps you configure Active Directory and other server components. See **Figure D** for a snapshot of this utility.

Before you get to the good stuff, WSBE wants to know some information about you such as your phone number, fax number, address, etc. This information—shown in **Figure E**—is used later on to help configure components.

Figure D

The installer tells you exactly what it plans to do

Figure E

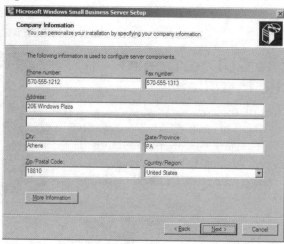

WSBE wants information about your company.

Figure F

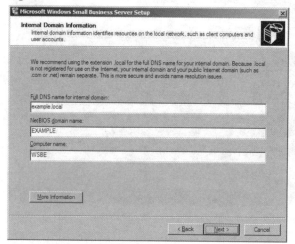

Internal domain naming information

Figure G

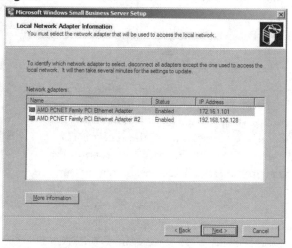

The first network adapter will connect to the local network.

Domain information

The next step in the installation starts the domain and Active Directory portion of the configuration. You are asked for three items:

● The full internal DNS domain you'd like to use

● The NetBIOS name you'd like to use

● The name of the server

The only one you have to fill in is the first one, as the NetBIOS name is generated from your internal DNS name, although you can override it if you want and use the machine name that was specified during the initial installation.

There's a reason that the default name specified in the internal DNS domain box ends with .local rather than .com, .edu, .org, or .whateverelseyoumayuse. In most cases, you probably don't want to use the same internal and external DNS name spaces. Since .local is not used anywhere in the Internet, you don't have to worry about overlap. Down the line, when you install Exchange, you'll probably be happy that your DNS namespaces don't overlap and your DNS mail-exchange records will work. If you overlap name spaces, mail routing becomes tricky sometimes.

For this example, I've named the internal domain example.local and accepted the default NetBIOS name of EXAMPLE as shown in **Figure F**.

Network adapter selection

Remember that WSBE 2003 includes powerful routing and remote access functionality meaning that you don't necessarily have to have a separate hardware router on your small network. You do need to have multiple network adapters to support this capability. The next screen in the installation asks you to select the network adapter that will access the local network. In **Figure G**, notice that I have selected the first Ethernet adapter—at 172.16.1.101—as the one that will be attached to the local network. Later, the second adapter will be configured to access the Internet. It's using a private address right now since my test machine is set up in my lab.

After network adapter selection, the Microsoft DHCP server is installed to provide dynamic IP addressing to your clients.

Next, to make sure your IP address is set up correctly and is static, which it must be, the installer asks you to set the server's LAN IP address, subnet mask, and default gateway. My selections are shown in **Figure H**.

Figure H

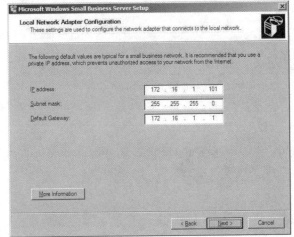

Local network adapter configuration

Figure I

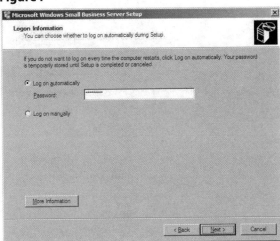

System logon information

Figure J

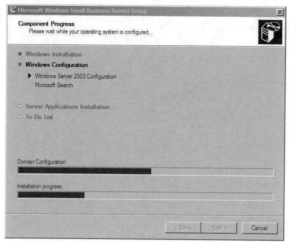

The server configuration progress screen

Figure K

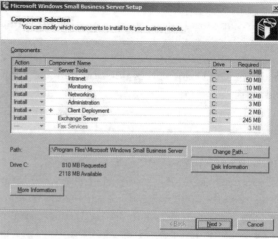

The component selection screen

Figure L

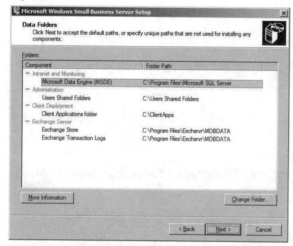

Use the Change Folder button to change the location of a component.

Figure M

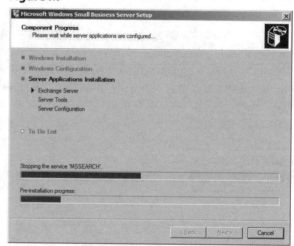

The server components installation dialog box

Security

Let's face it…Microsoft isn't the first company that comes to mind when you utter the word "security," unless your sentence starts with an expletive. The next step in the installation asks if you want to have the system automatically log in when you boot (**Figure I**). Ok, if you're in a small office with just trusted people, sure—this can make life easier. If you're not, though, don't do this as your log has full administrative rights to the system.

If you do want to allow the system to automatically log in, type the administrator password in the box. Otherwise, select Log On Manually. Click Next.

After this step, it takes up to 30 minutes for the server to run through your selections and configure the server (**Figure J**). During this time, the server will reboot, but the installation will continue on. Once this part is done, you'll move on to application installation.

Component installation

With the initial server installation and configuration under your belt, you're ready for the icing on the cake: the additional applications that give WSBE some guts. Note that I am using the Standard Edition of WSBE, so SQL Server is not available, but I will be installing the server tools and Microsoft Exchange server. **Figure K** shows you the initial installation screen.

Everything in WSBE is configurable, including the destination paths for each component and some dependencies. The next screen provides you with details on where each component or dependency will be installed and provides you with an opportunity—see **Figure L**—to adjust the location. For this example, I'll use the defaults.

The server component installation process takes a little time and also presents you with a pretty status screen like the one in **Figure M**.

When the process is complete, your server will restart.

The "to-do" list

Congratulations! At this point, you have a functional WSBE server running Exchange and Share Point portal services. After the obligatory Windows reboot, WSBE pops up a To Do list, just like the one in **Figure N**, detailing the next steps that you should take to complete this server's installation. The to-do items are explained below in greater detail.

View Security Best Practices

This to-do item features a detailed list of steps you should consider taking to secure your newly installed server. For example, components of this item include configuration of the included firewall, an analysis of user names and passwords, and other bits and pieces that make for a more secure server. This is mostly a list of documents outlining steps, rather than a wizard that walks you through the various steps.

Connect To The Internet

This starts a wizard that walks you through your networking configuration, including firewall and Web site settings. The wizard asks for your Internet connection type—dial-up or broadband, how you connect to your ISP (whether through a local router or via a direct connection), the networking configuration information from your ISP (including DNS server addresses and the IP address of the default gateway), and information on which connections belong to your ISP.

Figure N

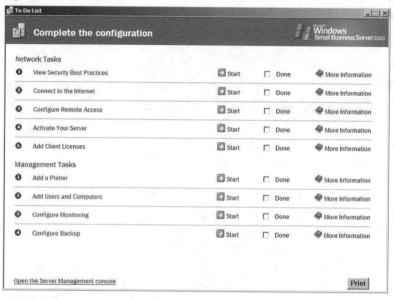

After installation, a number of tasks still remain.

Figure O

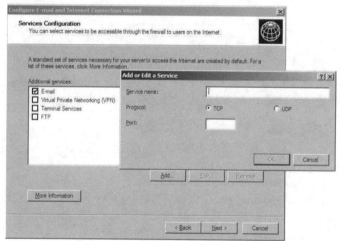

The firewall configuration step; here, e-mail is allowed into the server

Yeah, a lot of this seems redundant since you did some of it during the installation, but if you ever need to change things, this is a good place to do it. The part that is most important in this step is the firewall configuration. Via this step, you can enable or disable the firewall and then select what services you want to allow. If the service you need to add doesn't appear on the list, you can add it if you know its TCP and/or UDP port number. See **Figure O**. In **Figure P**, notice the ability to allow/disallow specific Web services to be accessible from the Internet.

The next step in this item is to create a server SSL certificate either locally or by making use of one from a trusted issuing authority.

Subsequently, you can either enable or disable mail to and from the Internet. If you want a local mail server only, disable Internet e-mail. If you enable Internet e-mail, you can either route all mail using separate DNS lookups for each recipient for each message or you can forward all mail to your ISP's SMTP server for delivery. See **Figure Q**. When possible, I highly recommend forwarding mail to your ISP's mail server. You'll use up much less of your Internet bandwidth, and your server won't be as busy processing mail.

Even more! Your WSBE-based mail server provides a number of different ways for your users to receive e-mail (**Figure R**). First, you can use an included connector that attaches Exchange mailboxes to external POP3 accounts. And second, you can just use Exchange directly, either with or without your ISP being in the middle.

The next e-mail configuration steps ask you to verify your external DNS name—in my case, I used example.com and set up a mail schedule, which you

Figure P

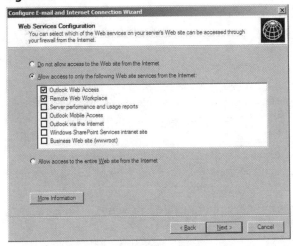

The Web services configuration window

Figure Q

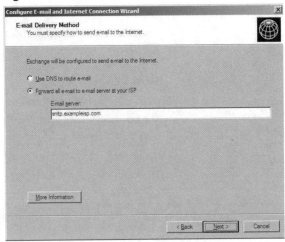

Decide how you want to send your Internet e-mail.

need to do if you use the POP3 connector option or decide to have your ISP hold mail until you pick it up. The default pick-up schedule is every hour.

You are also asked which attachment extensions you want to allow and disallow to your e-mail server. This step is important as it can directly affect how much time you spend managing your server. By default, Exchange severely limits what can be attached to incoming messages, so if you need to allow something, look for it on the list provided.

Once you're done, the configuration is updated and your new settings take effect.

Configure Remote Access

Your new WSBE server also acts as a Virtual Private Network [VPN] or dial-up remote access server, allowing you to securely access your files,

Figure R

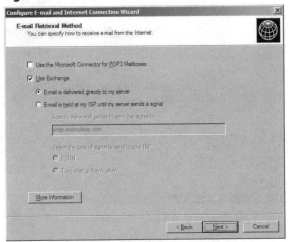

Configure your e-mail retrieval method.

folders, e-mail and other resources from anywhere. I don't have a modem in my server, so I only get an option to set up VPN services when I click this option in the To Do list.

The first step in the VPN configuration is to provide the full Internet name of your server. Be sure to provide the external DNS name for your server and not the local name. In my case, this would be WSBE.example.com, *not* WSBE.example.local.

That's it!

Activate Your Server

Microsoft requires that all new servers be activated within 14 days of installation or they'll stop working. Clicking the options starts the familiar "Let's Activate Windows" wizard.

Add Client Licenses

The title for this option is a little misleading as it also includes the ability to transfer client license from another WSBE server or to reactivate client licenses after you make a significant hardware change to the server.

To add licenses, you need to enter the 25-character product key that came with your license order. You can activate these licenses either over the phone or over the Internet.

To transfer licenses, you must use the telephone option presented in this item and call Microsoft for help.

Add A Printer

This is pretty self-explanatory and lets you add shared printers to your server to be used by multiple users.

Add Users And Computers

This wizard allows you to add new users and computers to your domain by using a simple wizard. With this wizard, you can create the user's login account, e-mail mailbox, and home folder, define his group memberships, configure his SharePoint access, and enforce disk quotas.

The wizard works on the basis of templates. Templates for normal users, remote users, power users, and administrators are supplied out of the box and you can also

Figure S

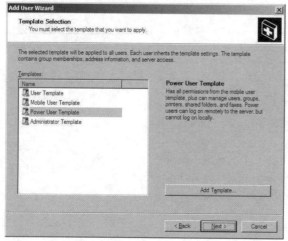

Create a new power user using a template.

Figure T

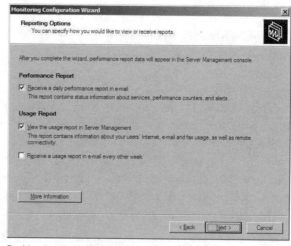

Decide what kinds of reports you'd like to receive.

create your own custom templates. For an example, I'll create a new Power User using a template, as in **Figure S**.

Once you select a template, you can either apply it to existing users or create a new user by following the simple instructions on the screen. I created a new user named ScottLowe and applied the Power User template.

That's all there is to creating a new user. The template idea makes this management task very simple.

Configure Monitoring

One of the new features in WSBE is the Configure Monitoring option that lets you set up alerts and provides you with server performance and usage reports.

The first screen in this wizard asks you to pick what kind of reports you'd like to receive via e-mail. You can choose performance and/or server usage reports which will also show up in the server management utility; see **Figure T**. On the next screen, type the e-mail address to which the reports should be sent.

The monitoring wizard also lets you send usage reports on business units to the appropriate manager, if you like.

Another very useful feature is the ability to more proactively manage server events such as low disk space, stopped services, and performance threshold violations. You can configure your server to send you an immediate alert when one of these events happens as shown below in **Figure U**.

Configure Backup

The final option on this server is the ability to back up your data, which is a critical task! Make sure your server has a tape drive big enough to hold all of your data, and follow the steps in this wizard to get it going.

That's all there is to it

Small Business Server 2003 is definitely a full-featured product, but Microsoft has made a serious attempt at usability by providing you with an easy To Do list that walks you through the important steps. The installation is easy and familiar and seamlessly sets up complex environments like Active Directory. ❖

Figure U

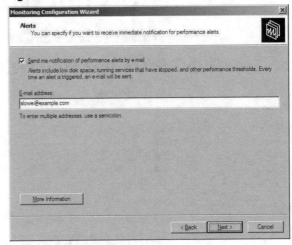

Configure your server to send an alert.

Working with Microsoft Windows Server 2003's Performance Monitor

By Eric Sheesley

Performance data can help you understand your workload and the effect it has on your system's resources. You can observe changes and trends over time, which will help you plan for future upgrades. Some counters in Performance Monitor will help you diagnose problems and target components or processes for optimization.

Using Performance Monitor

To start Performance Monitor, go to Start | Administrative Tools | Performance. Windows Server 2003 uses the Microsoft Management Console (MMC) to administer Performance Monitor, as shown in **Figure A**, so the screen has a different look than it does in Windows NT. You'll also notice a slight difference from the Performance Monitor in Windows 2000.

You should configure the performance logs and alerts to report data for the counters at regular intervals. The logs should be retained over an extended period of time. A database can use this data to perform queries.

Figure A

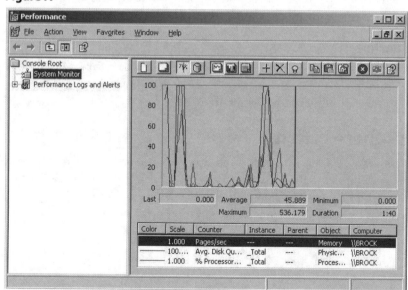

Windows Server 2003's Performance Monitor runs under the Microsoft Management Console.

To get a good snapshot of your server's performance, you should take the following actions:

- Disable any screensaver program that is running on the server.
- Stop any services that are not essential.
- Increase the size of the paging file to the total amount of RAM plus 100 MB.

Performance Monitor itself can create unnecessary overhead. You should not run Performance Monitor in Graph view all of the time. Monitoring too many counters at once or sampling at intervals less than three seconds apart can degrade system performance. It's also a good idea to log your information to a disk other than the one you're monitoring.

Performance objects and counters

Windows Server 2003 gathers performance data from components in your computer. A performance object is usually named for the component that generates the data. Some of the objects you will typically monitor are cache, memory, paging file, process, processor, server, and system. Some software applications, such as SQL Server, add additional objects that can be monitored.

Each object has multiple counters that represent data on specific aspects of a system. For information about a specific counter, click Explain in the Add Counters dialog box. While Performance Monitor has many different counters that you can monitor, you should monitor the activity of the following components first:

- Memory
- Processors
- Disk
- Network

While in the Performance Monitor application, click the plus (+) sign in the right-hand pane to add a performance counter. When you do, you'll see the screen shown in **Figure B**.

At a minimum, you should start monitoring the following objects:

Figure B

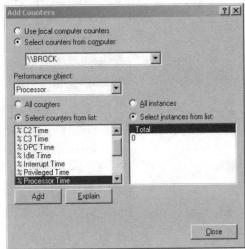

You can easily add performance counters.

Memory:
- Available Bytes
- Cache Bytes
- Pages/sec
- Page Reads/sec

Processor:
- % Processor Time (all instances)
- Interrupts/sec

Disk:

- Physical Disk\Avg. Disk Queue Length (all instances)
- Physical Disk\Disk Reads/sec
- Physical Disk\Disk Writes/sec

Network:

- Network Segment\% Net Utilization
- Network Interface\Bytes Total/sec
- Network Interface\Packets/sec
- Server\Bytes Total/sec

Other:

- Paging File\% Usage Object (all instances)
- Cache\Data Map Hits %
- Server\System\Processor Queue Length (all instances)

Some network counters require that you install the Network Monitor driver for Network Monitor in order to use them. Some of the counters listed here may not be available on your computer because a necessary service has not been installed or you have not activated the counters. For instance, in order to capture logical-disk counter data, you must type *diskperf –yv* at the command prompt, which allows the disk performance statistics driver to report data for logical drives. After you've selected your counters and start tracking events, you can watch Performance Monitor track the counters and draw a graph representing them.

Establishing a baseline

A baseline is a performance level that you determine to be acceptable. You should monitor your server over a period of time during normal work conditions to begin creating your baseline. Once you gather the data, you can analyze it to determine where there might be problems or bottlenecks. Microsoft has outlined some recommended baselines for different counters. The ones below will give you a good start for creating a baseline that meets your needs.

- Disk—Physical Disk\% Disk Time: 90%
- Disk—Physical Disk\Disk Reads/sec, Physical Disk\Disk Writes/sec: Depends on manufacturer's specifications (Check the specified transfer rate for your disks to verify that this rate doesn't exceed the specifications. In general, Ultra Wide SCSI disks can handle 50 I/O operations per second.)
- Disk—Physical Disk\Current Disk Queue Length: Number of spindles plus 2 (This is an instantaneous counter; observe its value over several intervals. For an average over time, use Physical Disk\Avg. Disk Queue Length.)
- Memory—Memory\Available Bytes: Less than 4 MB (Research memory usage and add memory if needed.)

- Memory—Memory\Pages/sec: 20 (Research the paging activity.)

- Network—Network Segment\% Net Utilization: Depends on the type of network (You must determine the threshold based on the type of network you are running. For Ethernet networks, 30% is the recommended threshold.)

- Paging File—Paging File\% Usage: 99% (Review this value in conjunction with Available Bytes and Pages/sec to understand paging activity on your computer.)

- Processor—Processor\% Processor Time: 85% (Find the process that is using a high percentage of processor time. Upgrade to a faster processor or install an additional processor.)

- Processor—Processor\Interrupts/sec: Depends on the processor (A dramatic increase in this counter value without a corresponding increase in system activity indicates a hardware problem. Identify the network adapter that's causing the interrupts.)

- Server—Server\Bytes Total/sec: If the sum of Bytes Total/sec for all servers is roughly equal to the maximum transfer rates of your network, you may need to segment the network.

- Server—Server\Pool Paged Peak: Amount of physical RAM (This value is an indicator of the maximum paging file size and the amount of physical memory.)

- Server—Server Work Queues\Queue Length: 4 (If the value reaches this threshold, there may be a processor bottleneck. This is an instantaneous counter; observe its value over several intervals.)

- Multiple Processors—System\Processor Queue Length: 2 (This is also an instantaneous counter; observe its value over several intervals.)

Addressing problems identified by Performance Monitor

Performance Monitor can help you identify performance problems and allow you to analyze the data. If your servers' resources are insufficient, you may need to upgrade components such as RAM, hard disks, paging files, etc. It may also be necessary to balance workloads among resources. Some programs monopolize a resource and won't allow other programs to use it. Those programs may need to be reconfigured or rewritten. The premier problem that your server will experience is a lack of memory.

It's important that you approach any performance problem systematically. Make only one change at a time. If you make too many changes at once, it may be impossible to accurately assess the impact of each change. Many performance problems generate errors that you can display using Event Viewer.

After you make a change, you should resume monitoring and compare the before and after data to determine if the change made an impact on the problem.

If you think that performance problems may be due to network components, you can compare the performance of applications run over the network with the performance of locally run applications.

The type of performance problems you are having determines the type of corrective action you should take. Let's look at some problems and common performance tweaks you can make.

- You can correct disk problems by installing additional drives or upgrading to faster drives.

- Use Windows Server 2003 Distributed File System (DFS) to balance the workload.

- Run disk defragmenters to optimize your disk space.

- Overcome memory problems by increasing physical memory, increasing the page file size, or creating multiple paging files.

- Add or upgrade processors to improve performance.

- Network problems can be the result of unneeded protocols. Remove protocols that are not used and be sure to place the protocol used most frequently at the top of the binding list.

- Use a 32-bit adapter instead of a 16-bit adapter for a significant increase in network performance.

Troubleshooting Performance Monitor

If you set up a counter but receive no data, you should check to see if the counter's associated DLL file has been deleted. Performance Monitor will not detect if the counter has been deleted once it is in use, but it will continue to report the counter data as zeros.

A counter may also report zeros if you do not have the appropriate permissions with which to monitor the computer. You'll get an error message when you attempt to set up the counter, but if you ignore the message, it will allow you to proceed.

You may notice gaps in your line graphs if the processing activity on a system becomes too heavy. The graphing will resume when adequate resources are available. The graph is also limited to 100 samples, so all values recorded in a log may not appear in the Graph view.

If Task Manager shows that a process is running but is still not reporting data, you can use the Exctrlst.exe utility included with the Windows Server 2003 Support Tools to verify that the counter DLL is enabled.

To monitor a 16-bit application, you must monitor the application via the NTVDM process. Only 32-bit processes appear in the Instances list. If you plan to use Microsoft Excel to analyze the log files, you will have to stop the performance logs and alerts because Excel requires exclusive access to the log files. ❖

Permissions and File Sharing 4

Create and control shared folders in Windows XP

By Dr. Thomas Shinder, MCSE

Creating file shares in Windows 2000 was easy: Right-click on the folder, click Properties, click the Sharing tab, and away you go. It just worked right out of the box. Not so with Windows XP. File sharing is more problematic in Windows XP because it's disabled by default. This is a more secure default configuration; users have to knowingly and actively enable file sharing for it to work.

As in previous versions of Windows, Windows XP offers three primary ways of sharing files:

- Create a share using Windows Explorer.
- Create a share using the Computer Management console.
- Create a share using the command line.

Create a share using Windows Explorer

The most common way to create shared files is via Windows Explorer. If you have a Windows XP computer that is a member of a Windows 2000 or Windows NT 4.0 domain, everything works pretty much as it used to. However, getting file sharing to work on a Windows XP computer that is a member of a workgroup can make for a wild ride. Let's look at the steps involved in creating a simple file share on a Windows XP Professional computer that is a workgroup member:

1. Create a new folder on the desktop and leave the name as New Folder. Right-click on the New Folder icon and click on the Sharing And Security command.

2. This will open the New Folder Properties dialog box with the Sharing tab exposed (**Figure A**). Notice that you can't immediately start sharing the folder. In the Network Sharing And Security frame, you have two choices: Network Setup Wizard or If You Understand The Security Risks But Want To Share Files Without Running The Wizard, Click Here. The former option opens a somewhat arcane wizard, which is aimed at home or SOHO users (who don't have system administrators on staff). The wizard helps set up home networking features, such as IP address configuration and workgroup name. As a system admin, you don't need to use the wizard. Just click on the latter option indicating that you understand the risks and want to start sharing files and folders.

Figure A

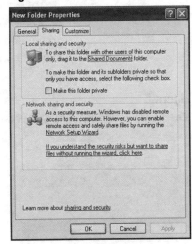

Figure B

Don't use the wizard.

3. You're not out of the woods yet. You'll next see the dialog box shown in **Figure B**. If you select Use The Wizard To Enable File Sharing (Recommended), you'll see the same wizard you tried to avoid earlier. Select Just Enable File Sharing and click OK.

4. After you enable file sharing, you'll see the screen shown in **Figure C**. This dialog box represents the *simple file sharing* method of sharing files. Notice the two frames: Local Sharing And Security and Network Sharing And Security. If you're used to the way things are done with Windows NT 4.0 or Windows 2000, you'll find this nomenclature somewhat odd. The Local Sharing And Security settings are related to NTFS access controls placed on the folder and its contents. When you use simple file sharing, other users won't have access to the folder or its contents unless you drag the folder into the Shared Documents folder. This is because NTFS ACLs prevent users from accessing the files. The ACLs on the Shared Documents folder allow everyone almost full control of what is contained in that folder. However, this isn't "sharing" as we're used to thinking about it, because file shares are accessible over the network. To share the folder, you must place a check mark in Share This Folder On The Network check box.

5. Next, the Allow Network Users To Change My Files option becomes available and is selected by default (**Figure D**). If you don't want to enable users to write or change the file, you must remove the check mark from this check box. Click Apply and then click OK.

When you share a folder using simple file sharing, the Everyone group is given permission to access the folder. If the Allow Network Users To Change My Files option is selected, then Everyone can write to and change the files. Someone must

Figure C

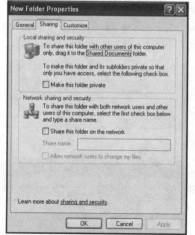

Here's the Sharing tab after you allow simple file sharing.

Figure D

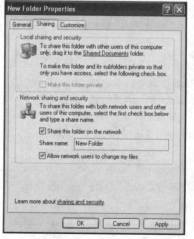

By default, everyone is allowed to change files in the share.

Figure E

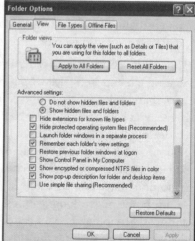

This last check box will enable or disable simple file sharing.

Figure F

Figure G

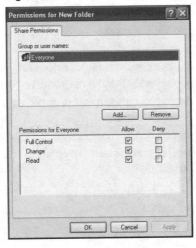

Figure H

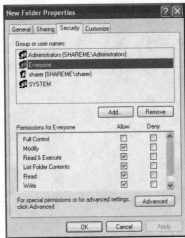

Create a share using traditional methods.

have thought this simple file sharing routine was easier than the traditional methods, but I find it very confusing. The problem with simple file sharing is that you have no idea what the exact share and NTFS permissions are on the folder. Simple file sharing completely hides NTFS permissions not only on folders but also on all files.

Let's fix this problem. Perform the following steps so that you can view the actual share and NTFS permissions on the folder:

1. Open the New Folder.

2. In the New Folder window, click the Tools menu and click the Folder Options command.

3. Click on the View tab and scroll down to the bottom of the list of options (**Figure E**). Remove the check mark from the Use Simple File Sharing (Recommended) option. Click Apply and then click OK.

4. Close the New Folder window. Right-click on the New Folder icon on the desktop and click the Sharing And Security command.

5. The Properties dialog box will have changed, as shown in **Figure F**. The Sharing tab shows a more traditional set of options, and the Security tab, on which you can view NTFS permissions, will now appear. To see the share permissions on this folder, click the Permissions button.

6. Now you can see that the actual share permission is Everyone Full Control (see **Figure G**). This is the share permission when you set simple file sharing to allow network users to change files. Click Cancel to close the Permissions dialog box.

7. Click on the Security tab. You'll see that the Everyone group has Modify, Read & Execute, List Folder Contents, Read, and Write NTFS permissions (see **Figure H**). Click Cancel to close the New Folder Properties dialog box.

NOTE
This method always works when the machine is a member of a Windows 2000 domain.

Create a share using the Computer Management console

You can sometimes use the Computer Management console to create new file shares on a machine in a workgroup environment. I say *sometimes* because it appears that, on some occasions, this option isn't available to Windows XP Professional computers that aren't members of a domain. But, if the machine was at one time a member of a domain and then was removed from the domain, *sometimes* the option to use the Computer Management console to create a new share is available. I suspect this is related to whether simple file sharing is available or not, but I haven't been able to identify consistent behavior in this area.

Perform the following steps to create a file share using the Computer Management console:

1. Click Start, then right-click on My Computer. Click the Manage command.
2. Expand the System Tools node and then expand the Shared Folders node.
3. Right-click on the Shares node and click the New File Share command.
4. In the Create Shared Folder dialog box (see **Figure I**), type the information for Folder To Share, Share Name, and Share Description. Click Next.
5. On the second page of the wizard (**Figure J**), select the option for the appropriate permissions. For maximum control, I suggest you select the Customize Share And Folder Permissions option. Click Finish after configuring the permissions. If you select the Customize option, you must click on the Custom button and configure the appropriate share and NTFS permissions or the Finish button won't be available.
6. You'll see a dialog box informing you that the share was created successfully. It will also ask if you want to create another share. Click No.

Create a share using the command line

Another popular way of creating file shares is to use the net share command line tool. Open a command prompt and type *net share /?*. You'll see the screen shown in **Figure K**.

Figure I

Make sure to type the full path to the folder, or use the Browse button.

Figure J

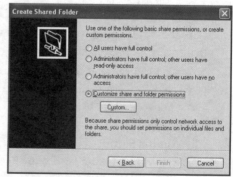

You can create or delete shares using the net share command. For example, if you have a folder on the C: drive named STUFF, you can share the folder by issuing the following command:

```
net share STUFF=c:\STUFF
```

Some switches allow you to limit the number of users that can connect to the share at the same time and set how file caching is performed for the share. Note that you cannot set share permissions using the net share command. If you don't specify these options, the defaults for your installation will be used. These defaults are different depending on whether or not your machine is a member of a Windows 2000 domain.

Managing file shares

You can do several things to manage and manipulate file shares on your machine. Many file share management tasks can be performed from the Computer Management console. To manage file shares from the Computer Management console, perform the following steps:

1. Click Start and right-click My Computer. Click the Manage command.

2. Expand the System Tools node and then expand the Shared Folders node.

3. Click on the Shares node (see **Figure L**). From here, you can view the current shares on the local computer and the number of current connections to a particular share. If you right-click on any of the shares, you can look at the share properties to view share and NTFS permissions. You can also un-share a folder by right-clicking on a share and selecting the Stop Sharing command. If you right-click the Shares node in the left pane, point to All Tasks, and click Send Console Message, you can send a net send message to the users connected to the share.

Figure K

The net share options are fairly straightforward.

Figure L

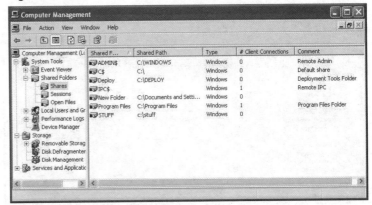

Figure M

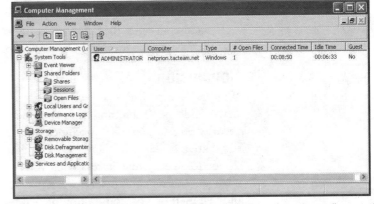

If you right-click the Sessions node in the left pane, you have the option to disconnect all users.

Figure N

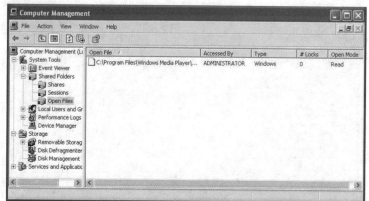

4. Click on the Sessions node and you'll see the screen shown in **Figure M**. In the right pane of the Sessions node, you can see which users are connected to the machine, how long they've been connected, and how many files the user has open. You can disconnect a particular user by right-clicking on the user entry in the right pane of the console.

5. Click the Open Files node in the left pane of the console (**Figure N**). Here, you can see which files or shares are open and which user has them open. You can right-click on the open file and close the file. If you want to close all open files, right-click on the Open Files node in the left pane and click the Disconnect All Open Files command.

Conclusion

Windows XP provides some new ways to configure file shares. The goal of the new Windows XP methods and approach to file sharing is to improve the level of security on Windows XP machines. If you use simple file sharing, you must explicitly share a folder with the knowledge that everyone has at least Read access. If you decide to give Change access, then you know that all users have permission to change a share's contents. However, Windows XP does allow you to use more traditional methods of configuring file shares, if you turn off simple file sharing. ❖

Establish the correct file-sharing permissions in Windows XP

By TechRepublic Staff

With the NT file system (NTFS) in Windows XP, you can set file permissions at the local PC level in addition to the file-sharing permissions of the network environment. Along with this additional functionality comes complexity and the potential for all kinds of admin headaches. One harried manager wants to know why he can't access data on a colleague's PC that he needs to assemble a presentation; another can't figure out why the mailroom intern was able to browse the files he thought he had secured. More options mean more chances for confusion and user error, and if you don't have a thorough understanding of the various permissions and their relationships, it can be nearly impossible to sort out a permission problem and find a solution.

We'll review the file and folder permissions in Windows XP. Once you understand Windows XP permissions and how they interact, you'll be able to troubleshoot permission issues that occur on your network more quickly.

Watch file-sharing and NTFS permission interactions

In any Windows network environment (peer-to-peer or server-based), you can set sharing permissions for drives and folders. By default, when you set up a PC on a network, no drives or folders on that PC are shared. The local user of that PC can then choose to share entire drives or individual folders on a drive. This type of security is not really that secure, however, because it affects only network access. Local access (that is, someone sitting down at the PC and logging on) is wide open.

For drives formatted with NTFS, you can also set NTFS permissions. These can affect drives and folders as well as individual files. NTFS permissions affect local users as well as network users and are based on the permission granted to individual user logons, regardless of where they're connecting. You also have a much wider variety of permissions to choose from with NTFS permissions, so you can more precisely control the rights being granted.

When file sharing permissions and NTFS permissions conflict, the most restrictive of the two wins. For example, if someone has full access to a certain file from NTFS permissions but has no sharing permissions to the folder in which it resides, he or she cannot access the file from the network. He or she can, however, physically sit down at the local PC containing the file, log in, and access it, because sharing permissions do not affect local access.

Working with shared folders

Shared folders provide remote access to the files on a PC. Folder sharing is available on drives using all types of partitions: FAT, FAT32, or NTFS. To share any folders (or any printers, for that matter) on a Windows XP PC, File And Printer Sharing For Microsoft Networks must be installed as a networking component. To check for it, right-click the Local Area Connection icon in the Windows XP taskbar and choose Status. From the Local Area Connection Status dialog box, select the Properties button to see the listing shown in **Figure A**. If File And Printer Sharing For Microsoft Networks doesn't appear on the list, add it by clicking the Install button and choosing it from the Services category.

After File And Printer Sharing For Microsoft Networks is in place, you can share individual drives and folders by right-clicking a drive or folder and choosing Sharing And Security. When you do, the Sharing tab of the Properties dialog box will open.

Sharing is slightly different for drives than for files. With a drive, you might see a default share already set up. These have a dollar sign ($) following the share name, as shown in **Figure B**. Such shares are for administrative use only; ordinary users won't be able to see or browse a drive shared in this way on the network. Consequently, if you want to share an entire drive like this on your network, you must create an additional share for it.

To create a new share for a drive, click the New Share button and then fill in the Share Name, any comment you want to make, and a user limit for concurrent usage (if desired). While you're in the New Share dialog box (see **Figure C**), you can click the Permissions button to specify who will have access to the shared drive, or you can save that for later.

For a folder, the process is more straightforward because there are no default administrative shares. By default, a folder is set to Do Not Share This Folder. To share it, right-click the folder and select Sharing And Security from the context menu. Choose the Share This Folder button and then enter a share name, comment, and user limit.

Regardless of whether you're sharing a folder or a drive, you can configure permissions the same way: Display the Sharing tab and click the Permissions button. A Permissions dialog box will appear, as shown in **Figure D**. By default, all permissions are granted to everyone.

If you plan to use NTFS permissions in conjunction with sharing permissions, you might want to leave the sharing permissions set at the default "free-for-all" settings and rely on the NTFS permissions to lock down certain sensitive items. However, if you aren't going to use NTFS permissions, or if you can't because the drive is FAT or FAT32, you can restrict access at the sharing level.

Note in Figure D the three types of sharing permissions:

- **Read:** Users can display the contents of the folder, open files, display attributes, and run programs.

TIP: DON'T DENY

The Deny option should be used sparingly because it overrides any more lenient permissions. For example, if you set Read access for a folder to Deny and the drive on which the folder resides allows Full Control, everything on that drive will have Full Control access except for that folder, which will have no access at all.

Figure A

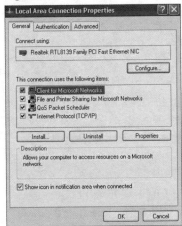

File And Printer Sharing For Microsoft Networks must be installed to share folders over a network.

Figure B

C$ is the default administrative share for this drive; it doesn't count as a user-to-user share.

Figure C

Create a new share to allow other users to access the drive.

Figure D

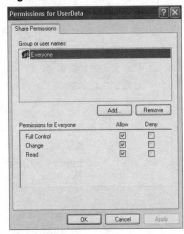

Limit permission to the folder or drive, if desired.

Figure E

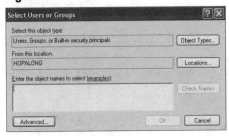

Specify other users or groups to receive permissions.

- **Change**: Users have all the rights of Read, plus the ability to create new folders and files within the shared folder or drive, open and change files, change file attributes, and delete folders and files.

- **Full Control**: Users have all of the rights of Change, plus the ability to take ownership of files and change file permissions.

Everything within a shared drive or folder inherits its sharing permissions. For example, if a shared drive has 10 folders, all of those folders have the same sharing permissions as the drive, unless they are set otherwise. Permissions are cumulative, which means that, in the event of a conflict between a specific folder's permissions and those it has inherited from the drive (or parent folder), the most lenient wins. For example, if you allow Read access on a folder and don't allow Change or Full Control on that folder, but the drive itself allows Full Control, that folder will also have Full Control access permitted.

For each setting (Read, Change, and Full Control), you can choose the option to Allow or Deny. The default is set to Allow. If you don't want to allow a particular permission, you simply deselect the Allow check box. "Disallowing" something (that is, turning off Allow permissions for it) takes away that right but enables the folder to inherit permissions from the parent folder or drive.

TIPS FOR USING SHARING PERMISSIONS EFFECTIVELY

- Grant only the permissions that a group or user needs; disallow all others. In most cases, Change permission is all a user needs for a drive or folder. Change enables users to run programs, edit files, and so on.

- Don't allow Full Control for a drive to the Everyone group. If certain users must have complete control of a drive, assign Full Control to a particular group or create a group for that purpose.

- Don't use the Deny option unless you have a specific reason to do so. It's easy to forget that you've used the Deny option and spend fruitless hours troubleshooting a file access issue because of it.

- Assign sharing permissions to groups, rather than individuals, to minimize administrative work.

- Use descriptive share names to help users locate the shared drives or folders they want.

- Group the folders that need to have the same sharing permissions assigned together in a single folder and then assign the permissions to the parent folder.

When you share a folder or drive, only one group has permissions assigned by default: the Everyone group. That means all users will have the same permission rights to the object, regardless of any group affiliation. You can delete the Everyone group from the list and/or add other groups or individuals to the permissions list. You might, for example, delete the Everyone group from the list entirely or leave it there and set it to allow Read permission only and then add the Administrators group to the list and grant that group Full Control.

To add a group or user to the permissions list for an object, start from the Permissions dialog box (Figure D), click the Add button, type the user or group you want in the Select Users Or Groups object name box (**Figure E**), and click the OK button. If you don't know the exact name of the group or user, click on the Advanced button and select Find Now to perform a search on the available choices. When you're finished, click OK to return to the Permissions dialog box. The users and groups you chose will appear on the Permissions list, ready to have their permission levels set.

Get file permissions right the first time

The proper sharing of files on a network is of extreme importance to you, the network administrator. Without a thorough understanding of how Microsoft configures file sharing, you'll find your users making daily demands of your time to fix file access problems. Upcoming articles will specifically address NTFS permissions in Windows XP and using the two types of permissions effectively. ❖

Effectively set and troubleshoot NTFS permissions in Windows XP

By TechRepublic Staff

Setting folder and file permissions gives you some network security, but it doesn't secure your PC desktop. When you use the NT file system (NTFS) in Windows XP, however, you can set file permissions at the local PC level. That means that a user sitting down at a PC—not just a user accessing the resource across a network—is bound by NTFS permissions.

NTFS permissions, which can be set only on drives partitioned with NTFS, can be assigned to drives and folders, just like sharing permissions, but they also can be assigned to individual files. Unlike sharing permissions, in which the default setting for a resource is Not Shared, NTFS permissions are set to allow access by default.

In this article, we'll cover the details of NTFS permissions in Windows XP. With an understanding of how NTFS permissions work, you'll be able to troubleshoot permission issues more quickly as they occur on your network and clients.

Folder and drive permissions

NTFS offers many more types of permission than the simple Read, Change, and Full Control of sharing permissions. For folders and drives, you can assign these permissions:

- **List Folder Contents:** View a folder's contents
- **Read**: View a folder's contents, open files, and view file and folder attributes
- **Read & Execute**: Same as Read, plus the ability to move through folders to reach other folders, even if no permission is granted for those folders
- **Write**: Same as Read, plus the ability to create and edit subfolders and change attributes
- **Modify**: Combination of Read & Execute and Write, plus permission to delete the folder
- **Full Control**: Same as Modify, plus the ability to change permissions, take ownership, and delete subfolders and files
- **Special Permissions**: Allows you to customize permissions on folders by selecting the individual components of the standard sets of permissions

File-level permissions

The list of permissions for individual files is the same, except for the List Folder Contents permission. For files, you can assign these permissions:

- **Read**: Open the file and view its attributes, ownership, and permissions
- **Read & Execute**: Same as Read, plus the ability to run applications

- **Write**: Same as Read, plus the ability to change file content and attributes
- **Modify**: Same as Write and Read & Execute combined, plus the ability to delete the file
- **Full Control**: Same as Modify, plus the ability to change permissions and take ownership
- **Special Permissions**: Allows you to customize permissions on files by selecting the individual components of the standard sets of permissions

Just like sharing permissions, NTFS permissions can be set to Allow with the Allow check box. Permissions are cumulative and can be inherited from parent folders or drives. NTFS permissions can also be set to Deny, but you should use Deny sparingly because it overrides more lenient permissions. For example, if you set Read access for a folder to Deny and the drive on which the folder resides allows Full Control, everything on that drive will have Full Control access except for that folder, which will have no access at all.

To set NTFS permissions, use the Security tab on the Properties page for a drive, folder, or file (see **Figure A**). The controls will seem familiar; they're almost the same as the ones for setting sharing permissions.

Special access permissions

In addition to the normal NTFS permissions, you can use 14 "special access" permissions. These let you fine-tune the permissions granted for a particular object. They're not actually separate permissions from the standard ones but refinements of them. For example, the standard Read permission actually involves

Figure A

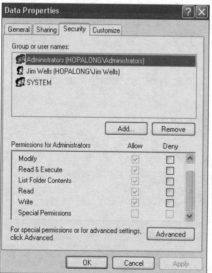

Set NTFS permissions on the Security tab on the Data folder's Properties box.

Figure B

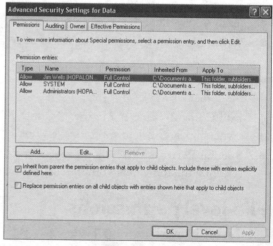

Control access for a resource more precisely from the Advanced Security Settings For Data dialog box.

four separate permissions rolled into one. The special permissions are the four separate settings: Read Data, Read Attributes, Read Permissions, and Read Extended Attributes. By default, the special access permissions are set according to the standard permission settings you have specified, but you can change them as desired.

To view the special permission settings, click the Advanced button on the Security tab to open the Advanced Security Settings For Data dialog box, as shown in **Figure B**.

From here, double-click one of the listed users or groups to display the settings for the 14 extra permissions. **Figure C** shows the Permission Entry For Data dialog box that will open.

Most of these special permissions are useful only in odd circumstances. For example, suppose you have granted a group Modify access to a particular folder, but you want to make it impossible for them to delete a certain file in that folder. You could set one of the special access permissions—Delete—to Deny for that file.

Figure C

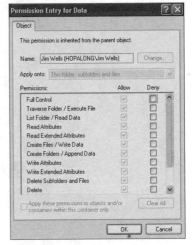

You can set more specific permissions here than are possible with the normal NTFS permissions.

Inheriting permissions

Notice the first check box at the bottom of Figure B. When this option is turned on, the folder or file will inherit the permissions of the parent object (that is, the drive or folder in which it resides). The grayed-out check boxes in Figure C indicate that those permissions are inherited rather than specific to this folder.

If you deselect the Inherit From Parent The Permission Entries check box, a dialog box will ask what you want to do about those inherited settings. (You won't see this on drives, because they have nothing to inherit from, being at the top level already.) You can choose to copy them or to remove them. If you remove them, all permissions and all users that were inherited are stripped out, leaving you a clean slate with which to create new NTFS permissions for the object. Any permissions that were specifically set for this resource beforehand remain. If you copy the settings, all the settings remain the same, but the check boxes become active, indicating that these settings are now independent settings for this folder or file only.

Ownership

You might use two special access permissions more frequently: Change Permissions and Take Ownership. You can find the Change Permissions feature on the Effective Permissions tab of the Advanced Security Settings dialog box. Change Permissions is a permission that normally comes only with Full Access, but you can specifically grant it for a resource here.

Located on the Owner tab of the Advanced Security Settings dialog box, Take Ownership allows a user to transfer the ownership of the file or folder to himself or herself. There can be only one "owner" for a file or folder at a time, and that user is the only member of the CREATOR OWNER group for that object. You can assign certain rights to that group, just as you can assign permissions to any other group. The Take Ownership permission enables someone to usurp the title of Owner from another for that resource.

Note that having *permission* to take ownership of a resource does not automatically *take* the ownership. If a user has the permission to take ownership, click the Owner tab and then choose yourself on the list of users. (You cannot choose anyone else; you must choose the user name with which you are logged on.) If you also want to take ownership of all subordinate folders and files, select the Replace Owner On Subcontainers And Objects check box.

What happens to permissions when you move or copy?

When you copy a folder that has specifically been shared (rather than just inheriting sharing from its parent), the original remains shared, but the copy is reset to Not Shared. However, if you copy the folder to a drive or folder that is shared, it will inherit the sharing setting of its new parent location. The same goes for moving a folder. Any specific sharing permissions it has are removed, but it's free to inherit sharing from the new location.

When you copy or move a file or folder from an NTFS drive to a FAT or FAT32 drive, all NTFS permission settings are removed, leaving it wide-open for anyone to access.

When you copy to another NTFS drive, or within the same drive, any old NTFS permissions assigned specifically to the original are stripped away, and it inherits NTFS permissions from the new location. To copy, you must have Write permission for the destination. The user doing the copying becomes the CREATOR OWNER of the copy.

When you move a file or folder to another NTFS drive, the permissions work just as they do when you copy them: Any old permissions are removed, and the

MORE TIPS FOR USING NTFS PERMISSIONS

- Try to assign NTFS permissions to folders rather than individual files and make sure that the files are set to inherit their permission from the folder. (That's the default setting, so you don't have to check every single file.)
- Create folders according to access requirements—for example, a folder for files that Marketing needs, another for files that Engineering needs, and so on—and assign NTFS permissions to those folders for the users who need them.
- To prevent users from accidentally deleting important applications or data, remove the Everyone permission and assign the Read & Execute permission to the Users group and the Administrators group for the folder.
- As with sharing permissions, give users only the access level that they require. In most cases, Full Control should reside only with the CREATOR OWNER group.
- Don't use Deny except when it is necessary, because it can create administrative headaches later.

file or folder inherits permissions from the new location. You must have Modify permission for the file or folder being moved and Write permission for the destination drive or folder. The user doing the moving becomes the CREATOR OWNER of the file.

When you move a file or folder to a different location on the same NTFS drive, however, permissions work a little differently. The moved file or folder does inherit permissions from the new location, but if any permissions were set specifically for that object, they're retained and they override the new inheritances. You must have Modify permission for the file or folder being moved and Write permission for the destination drive or folder. The CREATOR OWNER doesn't change.

NTFS means more permissions options

Windows XP NTFS permissions features allow greater control for you and more configuration schemes for your users. In this article, you learned to create folder and file permissions for groups and individuals using the NTFS file system. You also learned how NTFS permissions are inherited and what happens when you move or copy folders and files. ❖

Combining sharing and NTFS permissions in Windows XP

By TechRepublic Staff

In this article, we cover the tricky subject of what happens when you combine NTFS and file-sharing permissions in Windows XP. After reading this article, you'll be able to set up and troubleshoot permissions on your network and client more quickly.

Rules for combining permissions

Understanding how permissions interact isn't difficult if you stick with these rules:

- When working within a certain permission type (sharing or NTFS), permissions are cumulative. The most lenient setting wins for a particular user or group. Deny always overrides Allow and negates any permission with which it conflicts.
- When there's a difference between the sharing permission and the NTFS permission, the most restrictive setting wins.
- Permissions are not cumulative across groups; each group's permission is calculated separately. For example, if a user is a member of Group A, which has Full Control sharing permission but no NTFS permission for an object, and also of Group B, which has Full Control NTFS permission but no sharing permission for the object, that user has no permission for the object.

Examples

Let's look at some examples. Say that on Tim's PC is a folder, FOLDER-A, containing a file, PRIVATE.DOC. Tim has shared FOLDER-A with the Marketing group with Change permission and with the Everyone group with Read permission. In the NTFS permissions for the folder, he has allowed for the Marketing group to have only Read access. He has removed the default permissions to the folder for the Everyone group. If Sarah from Marketing accesses PRIVATE.DOC, will she be able to make changes to it? The Marketing group has Change (for sharing) and Read (for NTFS), with a net result of Read. The Everyone group has Read (for sharing) and None (for NTFS), with a net result of None. So Sarah's permissions are the least restrictive of Read and None—in other words, Read. So no, she cannot make changes (see **Table A**).

Now, suppose Tim adds another group to his list of NTFS permissions: Managers. He gives the Managers group Modify access to FOLDER-A. If Sarah is a member of the Managers group, will she now be able to make changes to PRIVATE.DOC? The answer is still no, because even though permissions are cumula-

Table A

	Sharing permission	NTFS permission	Net permission
Marketing group	Change	Read	Read
Everyone group	Read	None	None
Cumulative permission			**Read**

Table B

	Sharing permission	NTFS permission	Net permission
Marketing group	Change	Read	Read
Managers group	None	Modify	None
Everyone group	Read	None	None
Cumulative permission			**Read**

Table C

	Sharing permission	NTFS permission	Net permission
Marketing group	Change	Modify	Change/Modify
Managers group	None	Modify	None
Everyone group	Read	None	None
Cumulative permission			**Change/Modify**

Table D

	Sharing permission	NTFS permission	Net permission
Marketing group	Change	Modify	Change/Modify
Managers group	None	Deny Write	Deny Write
Everyone group	Read	None	None
Cumulative permission			**Deny Write**

tive within a type, they're calculated as a whole on each group. As you can see above, the new Managers group has no net permission to the folder because it has no sharing permission, so it doesn't enable Sarah to modify the file (see **Table B**).

If Tim wanted to make sure Sarah had the ability to modify the file, he could:

- Give the Marketing group Modify (or better) permission under NTFS permissions.

HINT
Permission changes don't take effect until the end user logs off and logs back on. After Tim changes the permissions, Sarah must log off and back on again or close the network connection to Tim's PC and reopen it in order for his permission changes to take effect on Sarah's end.

NOTE
Sharing and NTFS permissions use two different terms, Change and Modify, but both allow Sarah to make edits to the file.

- Give the Managers group Change permission under sharing permissions.

Let's say Tim takes the first option and changes the Marketing group's NTFS permission to Modify. Now the chart looks like **Table C**.

Now, suppose Tim uses the NTFS special permissions to deny the Managers group the Write permission. Will Sarah be able to edit the file? No, because the Deny option settings override any Allow settings. Even though the Marketing group still has the right to edit the file, Sarah is also a member of the Managers group, which is specifically denied access (see **Table D**).

If Tim wanted Sarah, but nobody else from the Managers group, to be able to change the file, he could either remove Sarah from that group or create a separate group containing everyone from Managers except Sarah and deny that group Write access instead of denying the Managers group.

Practice

The best way to get more confident in your understanding of permissions is to play around with them. Try re-creating the preceding scenario on two client PCs on your network and then experimenting with more "what if" scenarios. For example, what if:

- Tim turns off Deny Write for Managers and simply deselects the Allow check box for the Managers group? Can Sarah then edit the file?

- Sarah then tries to delete the file PRIVATE.DOC? Can she do it with her current permissions?

- Tim removes all permissions from the folder? Can he still read and modify the file himself?

- Sarah creates a subfolder within FOLDER-A on Tim's PC? Can Tim delete it?

You have our permission

You've now learned what the rules are when different sets of permissions interact. You also gained some practice in determining net permissions when NTFS and sharing permissions conflict for a user in multiple groups. You now have our permission to set up your network and client machines for the most robust security obtainable in a Windows environment. ❖

Lock down users with Special Permissions for printers in Windows XP

By Jim Wells, MBA

Accounting departments need to print documents in a secure environment, free from the prying eyes of other employees. R&D and Marketing departments use special printers with high costs per page. We IT pros are caught in the middle, with the responsibility to keep printing a painless process while protecting the company's resources. With Windows, you can control how users operate a certain printer based on their print permissions. The permission concept is not new, but later versions of Windows (such as XP) allow the administrator more choices when deciding who will have access to a certain printer. I'll cover the process for establishing print permissions for users or groups in Windows XP.

The printer Properties dialog box

To get to the printer Properties dialog box, from the XP Start menu, select Control Panel | Printers And Other Hardware. Choose the Printers And Faxes link to get a listing of the client's available printers. Right-click the printer you wish to assign

Figure A

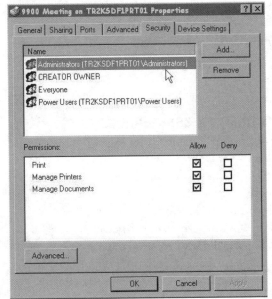

The Windows 2000 printer Properties dialog box

Figure B

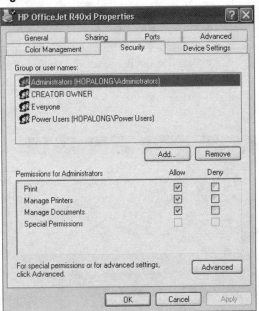

The Windows XP printer Properties dialog box

permissions to and choose Properties from the resulting context menu to bring up the printer's Properties dialog box. You'll notice that the Security tab in the Windows XP printer Properties dialog box is relatively unchanged from its NTFS cousin in Windows 2000 (**Figures A** and **B**), except for a few tweaks regarding placement of options and the addition of a Special Permissions category.

The layout should be familiar to you; it mirrors the permissions design used in the file permission dialog boxes. The area of most concern to IT support pros is the Permissions For Administrators section in the lower pane. In Windows XP, this area contains four unique permissions associated with printing. **Table A** explains what each print permission means.

Table A

Print permission	Description
Print	A user or group can connect to the printer in order to send a print job.
Manage Printers	A user or group can change the status of the printer.
Manage Documents	A user or group can change the status of a document in the print queue.
Special Permissions	Administrators can customize print options for the Print, Manage Printer, Manage Documents, Read, Change, and Take Ownership Permissions.

Create a user or group

Creating a user or group is a straightforward process. Just click the Add button on the Security tab to pull up the Select Users, Computers, Or Groups dialog box (**Figure C**). To find a user or group within the network, click on the Advanced button to display the Select Users Or Groups dialog box. Click the Find Now button and select the name of the account you want to add. Click the OK button to see the new user or group listed in the Group Or User Names pane of the Security tab.

Figure C

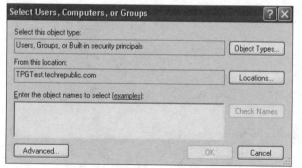

Permission assignment

Since IT departments differ in how they want users to control printer access, the best way to explain the permission assignment function is by example. Let's assume you have a new user of this printer in the Accounting department who requires Manage Document permissions. You don't want the user to have Manage Printer permissions on this particular printer within any group that the user might be associated with.

Figure D

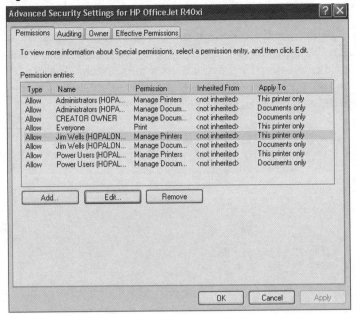

Notice that there are two permission entries for our new user, one for managing documents and the other for managing printers.

Figure E

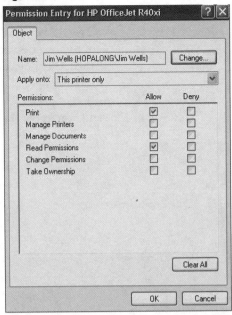

First, highlight the user in the Group Or User Names pane. In the Permissions pane below, check off the Manage Documents and the Manage Printers Allow check boxes. Next, click the Advanced button at the bottom of the Security tab and find the user in the Permission Entries pane of the Permissions tab on the Advanced Security Settings dialog box (**Figure D**).

Highlight the Manage Printers permission entry and click on the Edit button. You'll see the Permission Entry dialog box listing all the special permissions available (**Figure E**).

Select the Deny check box for the Manage Printers permissions and then click the Allow check box for the Print permission. Click OK and then click the Apply button on the Advanced Security Settings dialog box. Answer Yes to the warning message about the use of the Deny permissions setting. The Print Properties dialog box entry for your new user should look like the one shown in **Figure F**.

Now your user is free to pause, restart, resume, and delete documents in the print queue but is prohibited from controlling the status of the printer itself.

Figure F

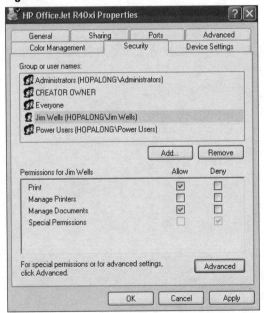

Notice that the Special Permissions Deny check box is grayed out. You can change Special Permissions only by clicking the Advanced button.

When in doubt, don't deny

Keep in mind that permissions are cumulative. If a user or group has been allowed Manage Printer access but has been denied Manage Printer access in another user or group listing, the Deny permission setting will always override all other Allow permissions. Companies that have employees working within several departments might not benefit from the Special Permissions option. However, use of Special Permissions can come in handy when restricted access is necessary and you know the employee will not move around much. ❖

Troubleshooting permissions problems in Windows Server 2003 and Windows XP

By Luke Swagger

S ave time. TechProGuild members can download the preformatted, ready-to-print version of this FastAnswer handout **http://techrepublic.com.com/ 5138-6346-5448793.html**. The next time this problem arises in your organization, simply print and distribute the file directly to end users or members of your IT staff.

The problem

Properly securing the file system on your workstation or on a network server may seem like an easy enough task. You merely set permissions on a file or folder, granting the rights you want users to have, and you're done. Unfortunately, it's not always that easy. You may go through the effort of setting up groups, creating shares, and granting rights, only to discover that users can access things you didn't intend.

The cause

The most common cause of permissions problems arises from conflicting permissions. As you get more groups and users on your network, and you set permissions on files and folders, you may find that permissions granted to one group or user conflict with those set by another group or user. The more groups you have, along with multiple shares to manage, the greater your chances of having conflicting rights. This can cause unexpected results.

The solution

To help sort out the confusion, Microsoft created a feature in Windows XP and Windows Server 2003 known as Effective Permissions. You can use this feature to quickly and easily determine what a user's or group's actual permissions are to a resource. This can help you sort out conflicts and determine why a user can or can't access a resource. Here's how you make it work:

1. In Windows Explorer, right-click the desired folder and select Properties.

2. When the Properties window appears, click the Security tab and then click Advanced.

3. On the Advanced Security Settings screen, click the Effective Permissions tab.

4. Use the Select button to choose the user or group for which you want to view effective permissions.

In the Effective Permissions box at the bottom of the Advanced Security Settings window, you'll see the effective permissions for the object. The results shown are based on the permissions granted to the user account as well as the permissions granted to any groups the user is a member of. It also takes into account the permissions received from the parent object.

Additional tips

The Effective Permissions box displays permissions only for the specific object. You can't make any changes to the permissions from this window. You must do that either on the Security tab in properties or on the Permissions tab in the Advanced Security Settings window. In order to troubleshoot a permission that doesn't seem to be working correctly, start by checking the effective permissions for the specific object itself. Then check all of the groups that the object belongs to. You may also want to check any parent folders to see what rights exist at that level; these rights can be inherited.

Administrators, have you encountered difficulties in troubleshooting permissions problems? Of course you have! Effective Permissions provides you with a quick and easy way to help troubleshoot resource access. ❖

Controlling access to shared resources in Windows 2003 Server

By Brien M. Posey, MCSE

One of the most fundamental tasks that any network administrator will face is controlling access to shared resources. Lately, it seems that there is a lot of emphasis placed on preventing outsiders from accessing your private network and on securing server and Web-based applications. However, it's just as important to secure your data internally. Here are some of the various aspects of controlling access to shared files on a Windows 2003 Server.

Share access vs. file access

In Windows Server 2003, there are basically two levels that you can give someone access to a file through. You may grant (or block) access at the share level or at the file level. The concepts behind both are very different, and both methods have their good and bad points.

Setting up share level access involves right-clicking on a folder and selecting the Sharing and Security command from the resulting shortcut menu. When you do, you will see the folder's properties sheet appear and the Sharing tab will be selected. Next, you must click the Share This Folder radio button and then enter a share name and a description for the share.

Now that you have created the share, you must click the Permissions button to control who has access to the share. By default, Everyone has Read access to the share. In Windows, *Everyone* refers to the group called *Everyone* which represents, as you can guess, every user object in Active Directory.

This is new for Windows Server 2003. As you may recall, Windows 2000 gave everyone full access to a newly created share by default. Generally speaking, share level security works well, but it does have its downside. Suppose for a moment that you created a directory named *Departments* and then created subfolders beneath it named *Finance*, *Marketing*, and *Sales*. Anyone that you gave access to the Departments share would automatically have access to the subfolders beneath it.

The problem comes into play if you wanted to create independent share points for the Finance, Marketing, and Sales folders. Suppose that you had a user that you wanted to have access to everything except for the sales folder. You could set the Sales folder's permissions to block the user at the share level. However, if the user had access to the Departments share, he would automatically have access to the Sales folder because it lies beneath it.

If you are wondering how this can be when you have explicitly denied the user access to the Sales folder, I have an explanation that might help. First, you haven't actually denied the user access to the sales folder. You've only denied the user access to the sales share. The user still has access to the Sales folder. The only restriction is that he can't pass through the Sales share to get to the Sales folder. Instead, he must find a different way into the folder. In this case, that alternate way in would be by passing through the Department share.

As you can see, you would only want to use share level security to secure folders that will use a single tier permission structure throughout the folder tree. For more complex security structures, you are much better off implementing permissions by using file level security.

Before you can implement file level security, the volume containing the folder or file that you want to secure must be formatted using the NTFS file system. If you have installed Windows Server 2003 from scratch, then this shouldn't be a problem. NTFS is the only file system that Windows Server 2003 is designed to use on newly created volumes or partitions.

However, if you have upgraded your server from Windows NT or Windows 2000, you might have a partition that is formatted as FAT or FAT-32. These partitions do not support file level security. If you have such partitions, you must convert them to NTFS prior to using file level security. You can do so with the CONVERT command. The syntax is *CONVERT drive_letter: /FS:NTFS* where drive_letter: is the drive that you want to convert. For example, if you wanted to convert the D: drive, you would enter *CONVERT D: /FS:NTFS*.

Once your partition is running the NTFS file system, you can apply permissions at either the file or at the folder level. To do so, right-click on the file or folder that you wish to secure and then select the Properties command from the resulting shortcut menu. When you do, you will see the file or folder's properties sheet. Next, select the Security tab and you will see who has access to the file or folder.

When you create a file or folder on an NTFS volume, there are some default permissions that are applied. Obviously, the Administrator is given full control. The Creator Owner is given special permissions which basically amount to having full control. The system is given Full Control and the Users group is given Read & Execute, List Folder Contents, and Read permissions. Again, this is a deviation from Windows 2000, which gives Everyone Full Control to a newly created folder.

Of course these default permissions apply only at the root level. At lower levels of the directory structure, permissions are inherited from higher level folders. Therefore, if the Users group was blocked at a higher level then the users would not have access to a subfolder of the blocked folder because the permissions would be inherited from the parent folder. Of course, you can always override inheritance, but I will talk more about that later on.

For now though, I want to address a more pressing question. Is it more appropriate to use file level security or share level security? The answer is that it depends on who you ask. There is a lot of contradictory information about the right way to secure files and folders. Even if you look at various Microsoft documents, you will find inconsistencies. Therefore, I tend to disregard the various TechNet articles and do security my way.

The way that I implement security is to secure files and folders at the file level. However, simply saying that I implement security at the file level isn't enough. There are several important ground rules that I follow to make things work correctly.

First, unless a user is accessing a file or folder directly from the server console, they will need a path through which to gain access to the file. In Windows, this path is usually a share point. Therefore, although I tend not to use share level security, I still use share points as a way of letting users access the protected files from across the network. The difference is that I set the security on my shares to allow everyone to have Full Control.

I want to clear up a common myth. In Windows 2000 Server, the Everyone group contained both authenticated and nonauthenticated (anonymous) users. This meant that in theory, someone who was just visiting your Web site and wasn't even logged into your network was a member of the Everyone group. In Windows Server 2003 though, anonymous users are not a part of the Everyone group.

With that said, I implement the real security permissions at the NTFS level. To avoid confusion though, I only grant permissions to security groups; never to individual users. I also grant permission only to folders; rarely to individual files. Using this technique eliminates the vast majority of the confusion that may occur when granting permissions and when trying to determine who has access to what.

Inheritance

Now that I have discussed the basic differences between share level and file level permissions, I want to address the issue of inheritance. Earlier I explained that a file inherits the permissions of its parent folder. However, there's quite a bit more to inheritance than that.

In previous versions of Windows, the only way to check a file or folder's permissions was to look at the permissions of the parent folder and any permissions that had been explicitly assigned to the file or folder. You would then have to combine the inherited permissions with the explicit permissions to determine the effective permissions for the file or folder. What made this tricky was that sometimes conflict would occur because contradictory permissions might be assigned to the parent folder and the current file or folder.

In such a situation, it was easy to resolve contradictions because explicit permissions always override inherited permissions. What wasn't so easy to figure out is the effective permissions for a particular user.

For example, what do you do if a user is a member of two different security groups with two different levels of access to a file or folder? Again, the rights are combined and an explicit deny overrides an explicit allow. It was possible to iron out such conflicts, but Windows 2000 file level security could be a nightmare if your file system, including inheritances, wasn't extremely well organized.

In Windows 2003, Microsoft took the initiative to make inheritances and effective permissions much easier to calculate. To see how the new mechanisms work, right-click on a file or folder and select the Properties command from the resulting shortcut menu. When you do, you will see the file or folder's properties sheet. Now, select the properties sheet's Security tab. The Security tab displays assigned rights, but not inherited rights.

If you want to view the inherited rights for the file or folder, you will have to click the Advanced button. When you do, Windows will display the Advanced Security Settings properties sheet for the file or folder.

This properties sheet contains a Permissions tab. The top portion of the Permissions tab displays all users and groups that have access to the file or folder. This list tells the user or group name, the type of permission (Allow or Deny), and the effective permission (Full Control, Read, etc.). The nice part about this list is that not only does it tell you the effective permission, it even tells you where the permission was inherited from. If a permission was directly assigned to the file or folder rather than being inherited, the Inherited From column will simply display the words <not inherited>. The table's last column even tells if the effective permission applies only to the current file or folder, or if it also applies to subfolders.

Another nice feature of the Permissions tab is that it contains its own set of Add, Edit, and Remove buttons. That way if you see a permission that you don't like, you can fix the problem directly from this screen.

The Permissions tab also contains two check boxes that are worth mentioning. The first check box, when enabled, is designed to allow inheritable permissions from the parent to propagate this object and to all child objects. Basically, this means that if you select this check box then the current file or folder will inherit permissions from the parent folder. It also means that if you happen to be working with a folder rather than a file, that any permissions used here, whether assigned or inherited, will apply to subfolders.

This check box is selected by default. Normally, you would want to leave this check box selected. From a Windows administration standpoint, it is considered to be bad management to deselect this check box. The reason is that if you disable inherited permissions, then it tends to become more difficult to figure out what permissions belong to which folder. There are certainly cases where you would want to deselect this check box, but don't deselect it unless you have no other choice.

The other check box is named Replace Permission Entries On Child Objects With Entries Shown Here That Apply To Child Objects. This is another check box that can get you into trouble. I strongly recommend never using this one.

Earlier I mentioned that the last column of the Permissions properties sheet tells whether the permission applies only to the current file or folder, or to subfolders as well. If you select this check box, then any permissions that show on the Permissions tab as being applicable to subfolders will be applied to subfolders. The catch is that these permissions will override any permissions that have been explicitly assigned to subfolders. You will almost never want to do this. The only time that I can see doing something like this is if you wanted to guarantee that a subfolder's permissions were never changed.

Effective Permissions

I have talked a lot about the effective permissions for a file or folder, but I have not yet answered every question. Earlier, I stated that it was possible for a user to belong to multiple security groups that have contradictory permissions to a resource. In Windows 2000, you had to calculate the effective permissions for the user yourself by examining which permissions belonged to each group. However, Windows Server 2003 makes this process much easier.

To find effective permissions, return to the Advanced Security Settings properties sheet for the file or folder that you are working with, and select the Effective Permissions tab. This tab allows you to enter a user name or a group name and will then display the effective permissions for that user or group. This takes all of the guesswork out of securing a file or folder.

Ownership

The last aspect of file security that I want to discuss is ownership. Every file on an NTFS partition has an owner. The owner is the user who created the file or folder. The owner is allowed to control who has what permissions to the file or folder.

The reason that I want to discuss this is because sometimes it's necessary to change ownership. For example, suppose that a user creates a folder and assigns some inappropriate permissions to the folder. The Administrator can't change the permissions without first taking ownership of the folder.

To take ownership, an Administrator would open the Advanced Security Settings properties sheet for the folder, select the ownership tab, and then use the Change Owner option. There is also an option to change the ownership on all subfolders.

Taking ownership of a file or folder is not purely an administrative function though. While it's true that an administrator always has the option of taking ownership of a file or folder, anyone can take ownership of a file or folder if she has been assigned the right, Take Ownership Of Files Or Other Objects. The Restore Files And Directories permission also allows someone to take ownership if necessary.

The file's current owner can also assign the Take Ownership permission to another user. When doing so, this only allows the recipient to take ownership of the current file or folder. It does not give the recipient global permissions to take ownership of any file or folder. Furthermore, simply conveying this right does not change the file or folder's ownership. The recipient actually has to take ownership to complete the process.

Easier than it seems

As you can see, file permissions are relatively complex. However, Windows Server 2003 makes it much easier to accurately assign permissions than previous versions of Windows did. You have plenty of flexibility when assigning permissions. Just be careful when assigning permissions so you don't create conflicts that can lead to troubleshooting headaches later. ❖

Troubleshooting 5

Troubleshooting TCP/IP

By Talainia Posey

The TCP/IP protocol is the backbone of the Internet. It's also heavily used in wide area networks. Unfortunately, due to the complexity of large networks, it can be especially difficult to obtain an accurate diagnosis when problems occur. In this article, I'll explain several techniques that you can use to troubleshoot TCP/IP when things go wrong.

Why troubleshoot TCP/IP?

So, why is troubleshooting TCP/IP such a big deal? TCP/IP isn't one of those components that you can say is either working or not working. Instead, TCP/IP may be partially functional, thus giving the illusion that it's working. This situation is possible because TCP/IP consists of many subcomponents.

Some background information

Before I go blazing gung-ho into the diagnostic procedure, it's important to understand some basics about the way that TCP/IP works. Unlike most other protocols, TCP/IP requires some configuration. This configuration may be automatic (through a DHCP server) or manual.

The most basic parts of the TCP/IP configuration are the IP address and the subnet mask. The IP address is a series of four numbers separated by periods. An IP address looks something like this: 147.100.100.62. A portion of the address contains the actual address that's assigned to the PC, while another portion defines a number assigned to the network. If this idea seems strange to you, imagine that you have a Web server. For users on the other side of the world to access that Web server, they must know the general location (the network number) before they can find the specific server within the network.

The portion of the address that makes up the network number is defined by the subnet mask. The subnet mask also consists of four numbers separated by periods, such as 255.255.0.0. A subnet mask like this one tells TCP/IP that two of the numbers make up the network number (147.100) and the other two numbers (100.62) are the computer's number. Keep in mind that this explanation is simplified. In real life, subnets may divide individual networks into smaller pieces. However, for the purposes of this article, you need only be familiar with the basic concept.

Another configurable parameter in TCP/IP is the WINS settings. As you may know, WINS is a service that provides NetBIOS name resolution on the local network. The WINS fields enable you to enter the IP addresses of a primary and a backup Windows NT Server that's running the WINS service on your network segment.

Figure A

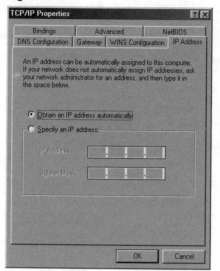

Determine whether your PC is using a static or dynamic IP address.

Figure B

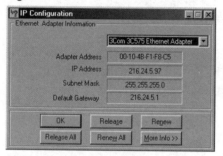

Take care to select the correct network adapter from the drop-down list.

Like the WINS field, the DNS fields allow you to enter the IP addresses of a primary and a backup Windows NT Server that's running the DNS service. DNS is responsible for resolving domain names. For example, the name TECHREPUBLIC.COM would be resolved through a DNS server.

Where do I begin?

Now that you have a basic understanding of some of the major portions of TCP/IP, you may be puzzled as to where to begin the troubleshooting process. When troubleshooting TCP/IP, I recommend starting close to home and working outward. Basically, that means making sure that your own machine is functional, testing your network in general, and then checking your Internet connection.

The local address

The first step in the troubleshooting process is to verify that your PC has a valid IP address with which to work. As I mentioned earlier, most of the PCs on a network can use either a static or dynamic IP address. To determine which category your PC falls into, open Control Panel and double-click the Network icon. When you see the Network properties sheet, select the copy of TCP/IP that's bound to your network card and click the Properties button. When you do, you'll see the TCP/IP properties sheet, as shown in **Figure A**.

If the Specify An IP Address radio button is selected, you should make sure that valid entries have been made in the IP Address and Subnet Mask boxes. If, on the other hand, the Obtain An IP Address Automatically radio button has been selected, you must verify that you're receiving an IP address from a DHCP server.

DHCP

DHCP stands for Dynamic Host Configuration Protocol, and it's a service that can run on one or more Windows NT Servers within your organization. When the Obtain An IP Address Automatically radio button is selected, Windows will scan your network automatically for a DHCP server and obtain an IP address. There are a couple of ways to find out if you're getting an address from the DHCP server. The easiest method involves opening an MS-DOS prompt window. If you're running Windows 9x, type *WINIPCFG* and press [Enter]. When you do, you'll see a summary of your TCP/IP configuration as Windows sees it. As you can see in **Figure B**, the IP Configuration dialog box contains a drop-down list of your system's various adapters. Make sure that you've selected the correct network adapter from the list before you jump to any conclusions. It's easy to select a nonexistent dial-up adapter by mistake.

If you're using Windows NT, the command is slightly different. Windows NT users should type *IPCONFIG*. Doing so will display a summary of the configuration information for all network devices, as shown in **Figure C**.

If you're trying to use a DHCP server to configure TCP/IP but aren't having any luck, there are some things that you should check. First, try reloading TCP/IP on your computer. It's possible that a file has become corrupted. If that doesn't solve the problem, verify that the DHCP server is running and that it's part of the same domain and subnet as your workstation. Next, check to see whether your co-workers' PCs are functional. If they are functional and rely on the DHCP server, it's a good bet that either the DHCP server has run out of addresses or that there's a physical problem with your machine, such as a bad network card or a disconnected network cable.

Go ping yourself

Once you've determined your IP address, you need to make sure that the basic TCP/IP components are functional. To do so, open an MS-DOS prompt window and try to ping yourself by typing *ping* and your IP address. For example, you might type *ping 147.100.100.62*

Under normal circumstances, pinging should generate four reply messages, as shown in **Figure D**. If you get an error message instead, such as *Destination Host Unreachable*, there's a good chance that Windows is messed up. If the ping is successful, it's time to move on to the next phase of the troubleshooting process.

IP address conflicts

As you probably know, each PC on your network must have a unique IP address. Duplicate addresses can cause all sorts of problems for your TCP/IP environment. Fortunately, IP address conflicts aren't quite as difficult to track down as most people think. If you suspect an IP address conflict, turn off your PC. If your network uses static IP addresses, when you turn the PC back on, you may receive a warning that the address is already in use. However, if you don't get the warning or if you use dynamic IP addresses, just leave

Figure C

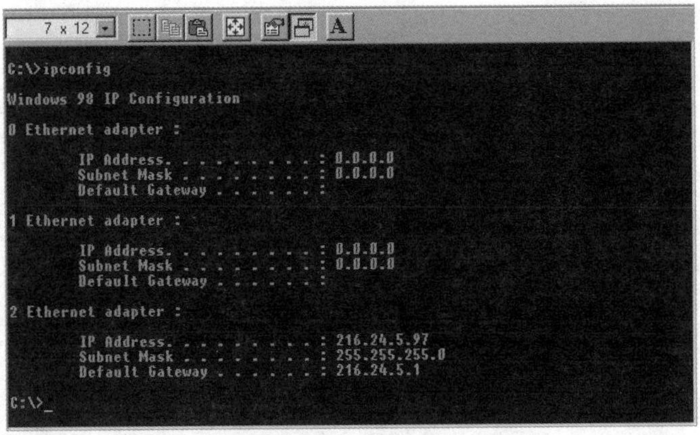

Windows NT displays all TCP/IP configuration information.

Figure D

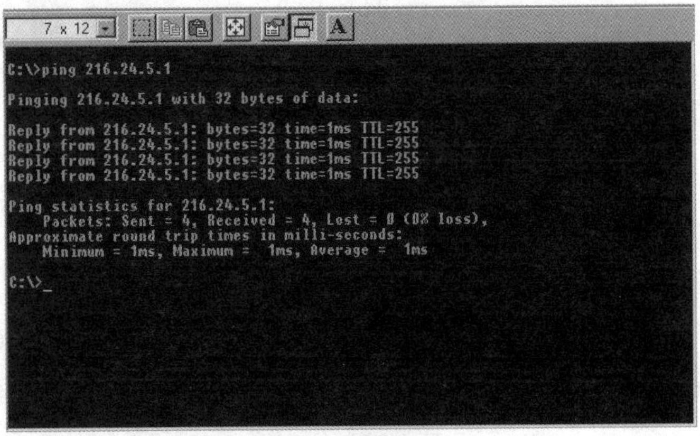

The ping should generate four reply messages.

your PC turned off for about an hour. Then, go to another PC and try to ping your IP address. If the ping comes back with a reply, there's a good chance that the address is in use by another PC. Double-check to make sure that your PC is still turned off (since many newer PCs come with a "Wake on LAN" feature). If your PC turns itself back on during the ping, try unplugging it and running the test again.

If you determine that an IP conflict exists, the ARP command can help you figure out which PC is the culprit. On some network configurations, the ARP command can resolve the IP address to the computer's host name. Often, the host name described the computer in some sort of detail. For example, a host name might be MARY, or Accounting2, or Basement.

To check for a host name, type the command *arp –a address* where *address* is the IP address that you want to test. If your network isn't configured to work with host names, this command will return the physical ethernet address of the machine.

The rest of the network

Once you've established with reasonable certainty that no IP address conflicts exist, that there isn't a problem with Windows, and that your network connection isn't unplugged, it's time to see if your computer can talk to the rest of the LAN. One of the easiest ways of doing so is to log on. If the computer logs on, that's a step in the right direction. Next, check Network Neighborhood to see if any other computers show up. If they do, you're probably okay on the local level. However, you should double-check to make sure that you don't have any other protocols loaded. That way, you can be certain that it's actually TCP/IP that's allowing you to see the other computers on your network.

WINS

If you can't see the other computers on your network, it may be due to a breakdown in WINS. Check to make sure that TCP/IP is configured to use a WINS server. Remember that you should check through WINIPCFG or IPCONFIG because they report the configuration as Windows sees it, rather than simply regurgitating the information that you've entered.

If your WINS entries look fine, check for more obvious problems like disconnected cables or bad network cards. If the physical hardware checks out, try pinging your WINS server, first by IP address and then by name. You don't have to be logged on to the domain for it to work. An example would be if you had a WINS server named Animal with an address of 147.100.100.28. First, try pinging 147.100.100.28. If the ping is successful, you've established that TCP/IP is definitely functional on your PC and that the physical link between your PC and the WINS server is good. Next, try pinging the WINS server by name, such as *ping Animal*. If this ping is successful, it means that the WINS server is functional and that your PC is using it correctly. Obviously, if you can ping the WINS server by number but not by name, there's a breakdown in the basic WINS service functionality.

The Internet

If everything so far has checked out, you're well on your way to solving the problem. The next step is to examine your Internet or wide area network (WAN) connectivity. Doing so uses the same basic principle as testing your local network. The main difference is that you'll be testing Domain Name Server (DNS) functionality rather than WINS functionality. The DNS is responsible for resolving domain names like www.techrepublic.com.

To test your DNS, open an MS-DOS prompt window and try to ping a favorite Internet site by name. For example, try typing *ping www.techrepublic.com*.

If the ping returns, then your DNS is working fine. If it doesn't return, try pinging another site, just to make sure that the first site you pinged wasn't down. If neither site generates a return, try pinging by the site's IP address. For example, to test your link to the TechRepublic Web site, type *ping 208.49.160.19*.

If that ping returns, then there's a breakdown in your DNS service. Try pinging your DNS server to make sure that it's available. If it's available but isn't functioning, try attaching to a different DNS server until you can fix your primary DNS server.

Is the host available?

If a numerical ping won't work, there are several possible causes. For example, your local router could be malfunctioning, the site that you're trying to access could be down, or a router somewhere on the Internet could be malfunctioning.

To find the culprit, try using Tracert (Trace Route). Running Tracert will tell you where the breakdown is. Open an MS-DOS prompt window and type *tracert*, followed by the IP address of the site that you're trying to access. Basically, Tracert will perform a ping on every router that it must use to get to that site. If a router is down somewhere, Tracert will fail, but it will tell you which router has the problem. You can see an example of Tracert in action in **Figure E**. ❖

Figure E

Tracert can help you to find problems on the Internet.

TCP/IP troubleshooting checklist

When a network connection fails, TCP/IP may be to blame. It's also possible, however, that the underlying hardware is the culprit. The troubleshooting road map is very similar whether you're running Windows, Linux, or NetWare. The sections that follow outline this road map and give instructions specific to the operating system where necessary.

What Changed Last?

We don't live in a perfect world. Equipment breaks or software changes are made, and it's up to us to resolve the ensuing problems. When we're faced with network troubles, our first step should be to answer one simple question: What has changed?

Many times, the answer will provide the solution to our problem. This guide offers some straightforward troubleshooting steps to help diagnose and resolve problems on misbehaving TCP/IP networks.

Determine the scope of the problem

When troubleshooting any problem, take a moment to absorb the big picture. Is one user or a single system affected, or does the problem have an impact on the entire department? First, call the help desk to see if it's receiving similar complaints. Determining the scope and nature of a problem will allow you to diagnose and resolve any issue correctly and efficiently.

Single-Client Problem

If a single client is having connectivity problems, you can follow these steps to restore network service to your users and systems.

❑ **Try to figure out what changed last.** A user will often be reluctant to tell you if anything has changed for fear of getting into trouble. If you suspect that the user has caused the problem by tinkering around with the machine, try to assure the user that he or she isn't in trouble and that knowing the cause of the problem will help you fix it more quickly. If the user still will not tell you anything useful, there may be clues in Windows' system log or audit log.

❑ **Duplicate IP addresses.** Obviously, each PC on your network must have a unique IP address. Duplicate addresses can cause all kinds of problems for your TCP/IP environment. Fortunately, IP address conflicts aren't quite as difficult to track down as most people think. If you suspect an IP address conflict, turn off your PC. If your network uses static IP addresses, you may receive a warning that the address is already in use when you turn the PC back on. If you don't get the warning or if you use dynamic IP addresses, just leave your PC turned off for about an hour. Go to another PC and try to ping your

IP address. If the ping comes back with a reply, there's a good chance that the address is in use by another PC. Just double-check to make sure that your PC is still turned off, since many newer PCs come with a "Wake on LAN" feature. If your PC does turn itself back on during the ping, try unplugging it and then running the test again.

If you determine that an IP conflict exists, the ARP command can help you figure out which PC is the culprit. On some network configurations, the ARP command can resolve the IP address to the computer's host name. The host name usually describes the computer in some sort of detail. For example, a host name might be MARY, or Accounting2, or Basement.

To check for a host name, use the command ARP –a address, where address is the IP address that you want to test. If your network isn't configured to work with host names, this command will return the physical Ethernet address of the machine.

❑ **Check physical connections.** Sometimes users move their computers and forget to plug in the network connection. Occasionally, the network connection is accidentally removed. Reconnect both ends of the network cable and check to see if the cable has been severed or crushed by a heavy piece of furniture. Even if the cable does not appear crushed, it may still be damaged. If a cable is firmly connected to the computer's NIC, and someone sits a cardboard box on the cable or rolls a chair over it, the resulting damage probably won't crush the cable or cause any obvious damage. However, such an action will often loosen the cable end just enough to prevent the network connection from working correctly. Try pushing the cable firmly into the RJ-45 connector.

❑ **Reboot the computer.** As simple as it may be, rebooting the workstation resolves many problems. Rebooting shouldn't make the problem worse, and it provides you with a good starting point for troubleshooting configuration issues.

❑ **Check the network signal.** Verify that the network card has a green light. This does not always mean that the signal is good, but it's a sign of connectivity. A card that shows a green light doesn't necessarily guarantee proper connectivity. But if no light is illuminated, it's a sure sign that connectivity does not exist or the card is damaged.

❑ **Use a line tester.** With the line tester, verify the physical cabling from the communications closet to the wall jack. This will allow you to confirm that the cable and the RJ-45 connectors are good.

❑ **Verify the line speed.** Using a line tester, verify the speed of the connection. Make sure that the switch port and the network card are not both configured to auto-sense the line speed. If they are, neither one will be able to determine the correct speed.

❑ **Check the communications closet.** If you aren't receiving a signal at the client, head for the communications closet. Reconnect both ends of the patch cable to ensure the connection is good. Next, check for a link light on the hub or switch port. If you don't have a link light, try another port because ports occasionally go bad. Finally, check for error lights on the network device and confirm that all cables are securely connected.

❑ **Try another computer on the problem connection.** If you have not yet been able to resolve the problem, try plugging the faulty machine's network cable into a laptop or into a nearby desktop. If the alternate machine can access the network, your cable and its connection to the hub or switch is good. If the alternate machine has a known good configuration and is unable to access the network when plugged into this connection, there's a physical problem with the cable, the RJ-45 connectors, or the hub or switch on the other end of the cable.

❑ **Use ping to test connectivity.** If all network hardware appears to be functional, the problem may be related to the TCP/IP protocol. Go back to the workstation and ping the local loopback address of 127.0.0.1. This will test the TCP/IP protocol stack and verify that it's working correctly.

Listing A

```
C:\WINDOWS>PING 127.0.0.1

PINGing 127.0.0.1 with 32 bytes of data:

Reply from 127.0.0.1: bytes=32 time<10ms TTL=32
Reply from 127.0.0.1: bytes=32 time<10ms TTL=32
Reply from 127.0.0.1: bytes=32 time<10ms TTL=32
Reply from 127.0.0.1: bytes=32 time=1ms TTL=32

PING statistics for 127.0.0.1:
        Packets: Sent = 4, Received = 4, Lost = 0 (0% loss),
Approximate round trip times in milli-seconds:
        Minimum = 0ms, Maximum =  1ms, Average =   0ms
```

Listing B

```
[root@gateway /root]# PING -c 4 127.0.0.1

PING 127.0.0.1 (127.0.0.1): 56 data bytes
64 bytes from 127.0.0.1: icmp_seq=0 ttl=255 time=1.2 ms
64 bytes from 127.0.0.1: icmp_seq=1 ttl=255 time=0.9 ms
64 bytes from 127.0.0.1: icmp_seq=2 ttl=255 time=0.9 ms
64 bytes from 127.0.0.1: icmp_seq=3 ttl=255 time=0.9 ms

--- 127.0.0.1 PING statistics ---
4 packets transmitted, 4 packets received, 0% packet loss
round-trip min/avg/max = 0.9/0.9/1.2 ms
```

The ping command works regardless of whether the workstation is running Windows or Linux. A successful ping in a Windows environment looks like **Listing A**, while a successful Linux ping looks like **Listing B**.

Note that in Linux, you must add "-c 4" to the command, which requests four pings. Otherwise, you must stop the test using [Ctrl]C.

❏ **Try to ping various locations on the network.** Start by pinging the IP address of a workstation on the same network segment as that of the non-working client. If you're able to ping this workstation, communications are working between the two machines. If the ping fails, the workstation isn't even able to communicate with a nearby machine.

❏ **Ping the default gateway.** If you're able to successfully ping the default gateway's IP address, communications across your current network segment are good.

In a Windows environment, you can determine the default gateway's IP address by entering the IPCONFIG command. In Linux, however, you must enter the NETSTAT-RN command.

❏ **Ping the IP address of a known good device on the other side of the default gateway.** This will allow you to confirm that the default gateway is forwarding your packets. If you're pinging a machine that's beyond your control (such as a Web server on the Internet), you must remember that many Web sites are configured so that they won't return a ping. Therefore, if the ping fails, the problem is not necessarily with your workstation. I recommend pinging a remote machine from a known good workstation first so that you can confirm the remote machine does indeed return pings.

❏ **Run TRACERT.** If you ping a known good remote machine and the ping fails, you need to run the TRACERT command against the address you tried to ping. TRACERT will show you all of the steps taken in trying to communicate with the remote machine. More importantly, though, it will show you the point at which communications are breaking down. A successful TRACERT looks something like this:

```
C:\Documents and Settings\Administrator>tracert www.techrepublic.com
Tracing route to c10-sha-redirect-rr.cnet.com [206.16.0.162] over a maximum of
  30 hops:
  1    1 ms    <1 ms    <1 ms     147.100.100.100
  2   18 ms    18 ms    18 ms     dsl6-1.rb.comporium.net [199.222.172.1]
  3   20 ms    20 ms    18 ms     ge0.1.rhcojm10.comporium.net [165.166.175.1]
  4   25 ms    24 ms    24 ms     165.166.125.193
  5   24 ms    24 ms    24 ms     dist-01.line-2.ncchrl.infoave.net [165.166.22.194]
  6    *       27 ms    25 ms     pos-1-2-1.c01.ncchrl.infoave.net [165.166.24.2]
  7   27 ms    25 ms    25 ms     ge-1-1-1.c01.scclma.infoave.net [165.166.25.18]
  8   34 ms    30 ms    30 ms     12.125.220.29
  9   39 ms    39 ms    39 ms     tbr2-p012301.attga.ip.att.net [12.123.149.5]
```

```
10    54 ms    53 ms    53 ms    tbr1-cl1.dlstx.ip.att.net [12.122.2.89]
11    92 ms    88 ms    88 ms    tbr1-cl2.la2ca.ip.att.net [12.122.10.50]
12   100 ms    96 ms    98 ms    tbr2-cl3.sffca.ip.att.net [12.122.10.25]
13    89 ms    89 ms    89 ms    gar4-p390.sffca.ip.att.net [12.123.13.178]
14   106 ms    89 ms    89 ms    idf22-gsr12-1-pos-7-0.rwc1.attens.net
                                   [12.122.255.218]
15    92 ms    89 ms    91 ms    mdf3-bi4k-1-eth-1-1.rwc1.attens.net
                                   [216.148.209.62]
16    95 ms    93 ms    93 ms    mdf3-bi4k-2-ve-57.rwc1.attens.net [63.241.72.146]
17    97 ms    94 ms    96 ms    c10-sha-redirect2.cnet.com [206.16.0.162]

Trace complete.
```

Typically, in a TRACERT, the first hop listed is to your default gateway. The second hop is typically from your default gateway to your ISP. Beyond that, remaining hops point to routers on the Internet used to get from your ISP to the destination server.

❑ **Substitute IP addresses for host names.** If the pings were successful, repeat your ping tests but substitute the IP addresses for the machine's host names. If you're able to ping a machine by IP address, but not by host name, the DNS resolution is failing. If so, you should check to make sure that the machine's TCP/IP configuration is set to use the correct DNS server and that you can ping the DNS server by IP address.

❑ **Release and renew the IP address.** If none of your pings were successful, the problem may lie in your local address configuration. This is especially common if the address is assigned by a DHCP server. You may be able to resolve the problem by releasing the current address and requesting a new one. To do so, open a Command Prompt window and enter the *IPCONFIG* command (this command is INIPCFG in Windows 98 and earlier operating systems). The current IP configuration will then be displayed. You can release the IP address by entering *IPCONFIG /RELEASE*. Once the address is released, you can get a new address by entering *IPCONFIG /RENEW*. In a Windows environment, the IPCONFIG command will look similar to this:

```
Microsoft Windows XP [Version 5.1.2600]
(C) Copyright 1985-2001 Microsoft Corp.

C:\Documents and Settings\Administrator>ipconfig

Windows IP Configuration

Ethernet adapter Local Area Connection:
     Connection-specific DNS Suffix  .     :
     IP Address. . . . . . . . . . . . : 147.100.100.98
```

```
Subnet Mask . . . . . . . . . .       : 255.255.0.0
Default Gateway . . . . . . . .       : 147.100.100.100
```
C:\Documents and Settings\Administrator>

In Linux, the command works similarly, but rather than using IPCONFIG, you'd use IFCONFIG. An IFCONFIG command output is shown below. Notice how it displays both the NIC's configuration and the configuration for the local loopback device.

```
[root@gateway /root]# ifconfig
eth0   Link encap:Ethernet  HWaddr 00:00:11:22:33:44
          inet addr:192.168.1.100  Bcast:192.168.1.255
            Mask:255.255.255.0
          UP BROADCAST RUNNING MULTICAST  MTU:1500  Metric:1
          RX packets:219876 errors:0 dropped:0 overruns:0
            frame:0
          TX packets:153838 errors:0 dropped:0 overruns:0
            carrier:0
          collisions:77 txqueuelen:100
          Interrupt:10 Base address:0x230


lo     Link encap:Local Loop back
          inet addr:127.0.0.1  Mask:255.0.0.0
          UP LOOPBACK RUNNING  MTU:3924  Metric:1
          RX packets:15 errors:0 dropped:0 overruns:0 frame:0
          TX packets:15 errors:0 dropped:0 overruns:0 carrier:0
          collisions:0 txqueuelen:0
```

❑ **Reinstall drivers.** If the previous steps don't fix your problem, try reinstalling the network card's drivers. Don't make the mistake of assuming that Windows has correctly identified the NIC. Windows is notorious for misidentifying network cards. It's best to open the case and confirm the make and model of the NIC. After doing so, use the Internet to download the latest available driver for the NIC.

In Windows XP, you can replace the current driver by opening the Control Panel and clicking the Performance And Maintenance link, followed by the System link. You'll see the System Properties sheet. Select the properties sheet's Hardware tab and click the Device Manager button. When the Device Manager appears, locate the malfunctioning NIC. Right-click the NIC and select the Update Driver command from the resulting shortcut menu. Now, simply follow the prompts.

The procedure for updating a device driver in Linux varies depending on the version of Linux that you're using. Updating a driver often means recompiling one or more modules.

❑ **Replace the NIC.** If updating the driver doesn't work, install a new NIC. Like any other device, NICs can and do go bad. Install a brand new card—not one that has been sitting on the shelf for the past six months—so that you don't introduce new problems into the already fuzzy equation.

Department or Area Connectivity Problem

When one or more segments of a TCP/IP network lose connectivity, the problem usually lies with the network equipment. Here are some troubleshooting tips that can help you isolate the problem and restore connectivity to your users and systems.

❑ **Reboot at least one workstation.** If the outage is brief, the workstations may regain connectivity after being rebooted.

❑ **Check the communications closet.** Collect a few data jack numbers of malfunctioning PCs and head to the communications closet. First, determine if all of the devices in the closet are powered on. A localized power outage is a common cause of network failures. Next, determine if all of the data jack numbers are connected to a single network device. If they are, move a couple to a different device and see if the problem goes away for the jacks that you have moved. Finally, look for error lights on the switch or hub and confirm that the network feeds are securely connected.

❑ **Ping the network equipment from the affected area.** Try to ping the switch from a workstation located in the affected area. If that's successful, ping the default gateway, followed by a device on the other side of the gateway. A failure on any of these devices should pinpoint the problem. For example, if you're able to ping the switch, but can't ping the default gateway, then the switch may be incorrectly configured, damaged, or disconnected from the default gateway.

❑ **Use TRACERT to test connectivity.** As described in the previous section, use TRACERT to quickly test the network devices from the affected area to the Internet. If you use TRACERT from a working area and then from the nonworking area, are both routes the same? If they aren't, the differences may help you pinpoint the problem.

❑ **Verify any router or network changes.** Because an entire area has been affected, it's possible that someone has made changes to a router or network device. Ask someone from the WAN team to confirm that the device is configured correctly. If the connection is made through a leased line, contact the provider's support desk to verify that the device is working correctly.

File Server TCP/IP Problem

If the problem appears to be widespread and you've confirmed that the workstations, switches, and hubs are all working correctly, the source of trouble may be on one of your servers. The procedure for troubleshooting a server is very similar to the procedure for troubleshooting a workstation. The main difference is that while a workstation will typically have a single NIC, a server may have multiple NICs. In this section, I'll provide a brief description of the steps you can use to troubleshoot a server, giving NetWare- or Windows-specific instructions where appropriate. Consider the following before you begin:

- Was any software recently installed on the file server?
- Has the server gone down lately? Why was it down?
- If you're running a Windows server, try checking the system, application, and audit logs for anything that might give clues as to recent changes.
- If your server is running NetWare, press the up arrow key to scroll back through many of the recent commands that have been executed and look for something to be loaded, unloaded, set, or changed.

❑ **Check the physical connections.** While it's normally rare to find your server unplugged from the network, you should never overlook the obvious. An operator or cleaning person could have accidentally disconnected the network connection without realizing it.

❑ **Check the network signal.** Verify that the network card has a green light to indicate that a network signal is present. Using a line tester, verify the physical cabling from the communications closet to the wall jack.

❑ **Verify the line speed.** If your network contains segments with differing speeds, use the line tester to verify the speed of the connection. Switch ports can accidentally be forced to a slower speed, and network cards can be configured incorrectly.

❑ **Check the communications closet.** Since most servers are in a secured area, many of the communications closets are also well secured. However, if you're not receiving a signal at the server, head for the closet. Check the patch cable and reconnect both ends to ensure the connection is good. Next, check for a link light on the hub or switch port. If you don't have a link light, try another port. Look for error lights on other ports and verify that the network feed is securely connected. You might also try a different port on the network device, or even try a different network device altogether. Before doing so, verify that the new device is working correctly.

❑ **Are both network cards having problems?** If the file server has two network cards, determine whether one of them is having a problem or if they both have similar problems. It's rare for both network cards to physically fail at the same time. If one is working and the other one is not, check the configuration of the failing card. If both cards have failed, inspect the server for other damage. It may have been hit by lightning.

❑ **Check CONFIG.NCF and AUTOEXEC.NCF.** If your server is running NetWare, check CONFIG.NCF and AUTOEXEC.NCF for changes. Verify that all the settings in these two boot files are correct. Someone may have recently changed something that is causing the problem.

❑ **Verify bindings and network card configuration.** Make sure that the network card bindings and configuration are correct. Try uninstalling the card and reinstalling it. Sometimes reseating a card will fix the problem. While you're at it, verify that the server's TCP/IP configuration is set correctly and update the NIC driver.

❑ **Use ping to test connectivity.** Use the ping command to search for the server's local loopback address to verify that the TCP/IP stack is working correctly. If this test is successful, ping a device that's on the same segment as the server, followed by the default gateway and a device on the other side of the gateway. A failure on any of these devices should pinpoint the problem.

❑ **Use TRACERT.** This command can test connectivity between the server and a remote host. If you're using a NetWare server, you'll use the IPTRACE utility instead. IPTRACE is very similar to TRACERT. Choose an IP address from a distant router or the Internet; at the server console, type *IPTRACE <IP address>*. You'll be taken to a new screen that shows the route that the ICMP packet took to reach the destination.

NetWare-specific solutions

❑ **No dropped packets.** If your server is running NetWare, you can verify that the server is not discarding TCP/IP packets. From the server's system console screen, enter *SET TCP IP DEBUG = 1*. The console screen should immediately start scrolling TCP/IP information. To stop the log, enter *SET TCP IP DEBUG = 0*, and you shouldn't see any packets being discarded. In a Windows environment, you can accomplish the same type of diagnostics by using a protocol analyzer.

❑ **Use TCPCON.** In a NetWare environment, you can use TCPCON to gather TCP/IP statistics. You should be able to see the values in the middle of the screen changing as network traffic flows to and from the server. Verify that IP routing is enabled by selecting Protocol Information -> IP > IP Packet Forwarding. The IP Packet Forwarding field should be set to Router. TCPCON can also be used to verify the IP Routing Table.

If All Else Fails

❑ **Install a new NIC.** If you determine that the network card is bad, install a new one. Keep in mind that doing so will require you to take your server offline, and any users who are able to connect to the server will be disconnected.

❑ **Reboot the server.** Note that rebooting will interrupt any active sessions or processes that may be running. ❖

New to networking? Introducing the ping command

Greg Shultz

As more and more people are creating small or home offices, there's greater need than ever to go over some basic networking tools you can run from Windows client machines. In this chapter, I'll explain the venerable ping command.

History of ping

It's been said that the command ping is an acronym for Packet Internet Groper, which more or less accurately describes what the command does. However, the author of the original ping program for UNIX, Mike Muuss, says that the name was inspired by the fact that the ping program uses the same echo-location technique that submarine sonar uses, so he named his program after that sound—ping. Mike designed ping in 1983, and it has since been ported to just about every operating system. For more information on the origins of the ping command, check out Mike Muuss's Web page (**http://ftp.arl.mil/~mike/ping.html**).

How it works

Ping has one simple job to perform, which is to find out whether a specific IP address is working. In order to do so, the ping command sends a special packet of information to a specific IP address and then listens for a reply. This special packet is called the Internet Control Message Protocol (ICMP) echo request packet. ICMP packets are IP control messages that two systems on a TCP/IP network use to communicate various needs. When a system receives an echo request, it answers back with an echo reply, which includes the original echo request packet in the data field of the echo reply.

To use ping in Windows, open an MS-DOS prompt (Windows 9x/Me) or command prompt (Windows 2000/NT). Type *ping* followed by the name or IP address of the computer whose network connectivity you are testing. For example, if a computer on your network has the IP address 63.24.3.105, at the command prompt, type:

```
Ping 63.24.3.105
```

If that computer were assigned the name Bart, you would simply type:

```
Ping Bart
```

The Windows version of ping sends the specified computer four packets, each one containing 32 bytes of data, and compiles statistics for each one as the packets return. When the ping command receives an echo reply, it displays the results on the screen in the format:

```
Pinging bart.techrepublic.com [63.24.3.105] with 32 bytes of data
Reply from 63.24.3.105: bytes=32 time=761ms TTL=127
Reply from 63.24.3.105: bytes=32 time=761ms TTL=127
Reply from 63.24.3.105: bytes=32 time=761ms TTL=127
Reply from 63.24.3.105: bytes=32 time=761ms TTL=127
```

The first piece of information in this display is the IP address of the responding system, the second is the number of bytes in the reply, the third is the number of milliseconds it took to get a reply, and the last piece of information is the Time To Live (TTL) field.

The first two pieces of information are very simple. The responding system sends back its address as a confirmation, and the number of bytes sent back is the same as the number of bytes sent.

The time field tells you how long, in milliseconds, it took the packet to get to the remote system and back. The rule of thumb here is that for optimal network performance, this round-trip time should be under 200 milliseconds.

The TTL field provides important information in a roundabout way. When the ping command sends out an ICMP echo request packet, the packet has a limited lifetime. This lifetime value is used so that if the packet doesn't find its target, it won't bounce around the network forever—it will eventually cease to exist. More specifically, the ping command initially gives the packet a TTL value of 255. As the packet zooms out across the network, one is subtracted from the TTL value each time the packet passes, or hops, through a router. Thus, when the packet returns, you can look at the TTL value and determine how many router hops the packet went through on its trip—just subtract the returned value from 255.

Following the main reply, the ping command will display some statistics about the operation. The statistics include the number of packets sent and lost, as well as a rundown of the round trip times. It appears in the following format:

```
Ping statistics for 63.24.3.105:
    Packets: Sent = 4, Received = 4, Lost = 0 (0% loss),

Approximate round trip times in milli-seconds:|
    Minimum = 0ms, Maximum = 1ms, Average = 0ms
```

As you can see, the ping command is useful for testing the condition of your network. You can ping an address that exists within your LAN or over the Internet. Sometimes, when your Internet or LAN connection seems to be down, pinging can tell you whether or not the problem concerns the name resolution or whether or not that computer can be reached at all. For example, if pinging Bart returned this message:

```
Unknown host Bart
```

but pinging Bart's IP address 63.24.3.105 returned results, you know that the computer is on the network, but for some reason the name Bart is not being recognized.

Command-line switches

Ping has a few useful command-line switches. For example, if you know a computer's IP address but want to find out its name, you can type:

```
Ping -a 63.24.3.105
```

Ping will resolve the IP address into a name and include the name in its report. The table below lists some of ping's more helpful command-line switches. The switches are the same for Windows 9x, Me, 2000, and NT. As with many other commands, you can combine command-line switches. You can always get ping to list these for you by typing (at the command prompt):

```
Ping -?
```

Ping command-line switches

Switch	Description
-a	Resolves IP addresses to hostnames
-i	Lets you set Time To Live (TTL)
-l	Lets you set the packet size
-n	Lets you set the number of echo requests (the default is 4)
-t	Pings the computer you specified until you type *Control-C* (While ping is running, typing *Control-Break* inserts statistics.)
-w	Lets you set the number of milliseconds to wait before each reply times out

Conclusion

Ping is one of the most important basic commands to learn if you're maintaining a network of any size. Once you're familiar with this tool, you'll find it easier to diagnose network and Internet problems. ❖

Using Windows' IP Configuration utility to troubleshoot TCP/IP

By Greg Shultz

Troubleshooting and diagnosing TCP/IP problems on a Windows network can be difficult. However, the task is easier if you understand how to use the native tools. One such tool is the IP Configuration utility, designed to provide detailed information on a Windows system's TCP/IP network configuration. This information can be used to help verify network connections and settings. Along with other TCP/IP tools, IP Configuration can help you solve Windows TCP/IP problems.

In this article, I will show you how to use the IP Configuration utility, and I'll point out some new features that have been added to this utility in Windows 2000.

Graphical vs. command line

Windows 95 and Windows 98 come with a version of the IP Configuration utility that has a graphical interface, while the Windows NT and Windows 2000 versions use the command line. Note also that Windows 98 contains both the graphical and command-line versions.

To launch the graphical version in Windows 95 and Windows 98, choose Start | Run, type *Winipcfg.exe*, and click OK. To launch the command-line version in Windows 98, Windows NT, and Windows 2000, open an MS-DOS or command prompt, type *Ipconfig.exe*, and press [Enter]. To see a list of the parameters that you can use with this command, type *Ipconfig.exe /?*.

Figure A

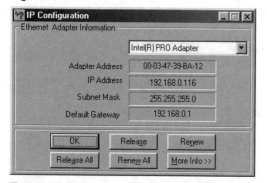

The initial IP Configuration dialog box displays basic information about the system's TCP/IP network configuration.

Looking at the basic display

The main function of the IP Configuration utility is to provide you with a Windows system's TCP/IP configuration. When you run the graphical interface in Windows 95 or Windows 98, you'll see a dialog box like the one shown in **Figure A**.

The top of the IP Configuration dialog box shows the name of the network card to which all the rest of the information in the dialog box applies. If you have more than one network card or a have a modem installed on the system, you can use the drop-down arrow to select the other device and view its information.

Just below the name of the network card, you'll see the Media Access Control (MAC) or physical address of the network card. The MAC address is a unique hexadecimal code that's stored in a read-only memory (ROM) chip on the network card and is used to identify a computer on the network.

The next three boxes show typical IP address configuration information: the IP address assigned to the system, the subnet mask, and the default gateway. When you type *Ipconfig* at a command prompt in Windows NT or Windows 2000, you'll see a listing like the one shown in **Figure B**. As you can see, Windows 2000's basic listing displays the Connection-Specific Domain Name System (DNS) Suffix, as well as the typical IP address configuration information. Windows NT's basic listing only displays the typical IP address configuration information.

The Connection-Specific DNS Suffix is a special feature Windows 2000 brings to the table. This feature allows a Windows 2000 Dynamic Host Configuration Protocol (DHCP) server to assign a DNS suffix to the network card to specifically identify the system on the network. For more detailed information on the Connection-Specific DNS Suffix feature, see the Naming Hosts And Domains section of the Windows 2000 DNS chapter in the Windows 2000 Resource Kit. This chapter is available on the sample online version of the Windows 2000 Resource Kit at **www. microsoft. com/windows2000/techinfo/reskit/ samplechapters/ cncf/cncf_imp_vsin.as**.

Looking at the detailed display

Click the More Info button on the graphic version of IP Configuration in Windows 95 or Windows 98 to expand the display. Doing so reveals even more useful information on the TCP/IP configuration and the network card, as shown in **Figure C**.

The Host Information section of the IP Configuration dialog box displays the system's host name and DNS server address. If the system leases an IP address from a DHCP server, you'll see the node type and NetBIOS scope ID. You can

Figure B

Windows 2000's basic IP Configuration display presents essentially the same information as Windows 98's basic IP Configuration dialog box.

Figure C

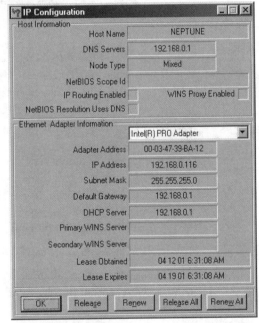

When you click the More Info button, the IP Configuration dialog box displays detailed information about the system's TCP/IP network configuration.

Figure D

```
Command Prompt                                               _ □ ✕
C:\>ipconfig /all

Windows NT IP Configuration

        Host Name . . . . . . . . . : neptune
        DNS Servers . . . . . . . . : 192.168.0.1
        Node Type . . . . . . . . . : Mixed
        NetBIOS Scope ID. . . . . . :
        IP Routing Enabled. . . . . : No
        WINS Proxy Enabled. . . . . : No
        NetBIOS Resolution Uses DNS : No

Ethernet adapter E100B1:

        Description . . . . . . . . : Intel(R) PRO Adapter
        Physical Address. . . . . . : 00-03-47-39-BA-12
        DHCP Enabled. . . . . . . . : Yes
        IP Address. . . . . . . . . : 192.168.0.146
        Subnet Mask . . . . . . . . : 255.255.255.0
        Default Gateway . . . . . . : 192.168.0.1
        DHCP Server . . . . . . . . : 192.168.0.1
        Lease Obtained. . . . . . . : Thursday, April 12, 2001 5:55:41 PM
        Lease Expires . . . . . . . : Thursday, April 19, 2001 5:55:41 PM

C:\>
```

Using the Ipconfig /all command displays the IP address configuration information for a Windows NT or Windows 2000 system.

also find out whether IP Routing is enabled, whether WINS Proxy is enabled, and whether the NetBIOS Resolution is using DNS.

In the Ethernet Adapter Information section, you'll see the address of the DHCP server, as well as the addresses of the primary and secondary WINS servers. You can also determine when the DHCP lease was obtained and when it expires.

In Windows NT and 2000, the command Ipconfig /all shows the same information that is displayed in Windows 98's expanded IP Configuration dialog box, as shown in **Figure D**.

Releasing and renewing IP addresses from a DHCP server

If a system obtains its IP address from a DHCP server, you can troubleshoot IP configuration problems by releasing and renewing a system's dynamic IP address. When you do, the system will release its current IP address and then be assigned a new one from the DHCP server.

To release and renew a system's dynamic IP address in Windows 95 and Windows 98, click the Release and Renew buttons to refresh the system's IP address for the network card shown in the dialog box. If the system contains more than one network card, you can use the Release All and Renew All buttons to refresh the IP addresses for all the network cards.

In Windows NT and Windows 2000, type the command *Ipconfig / release [adapter name]* and then type *Ipconfig / renew [adapter name]* to refresh the system's IP address for a specific network card. If the system has more than one network card and you want to refresh all of the IP addresses, leave off the network card's name.

DNS resolver cache

Windows 2000's new TCP/IP features are designed to simplify and optimize the use of TCP/IP in high-bandwidth network environments. One of these features is DNS resolver caching, in which Windows 2000 caches DNS names as queries are made. This allows the system to respond more quickly to subsequent queries. In order to provide information on and troubleshoot the new DNS resolver caching feature, Windows 2000's Ipconfig command comes with two options. The command Ipconfig /displaydns displays the contents of the DNS resolver cache. When you use this command, you may also see local host and loopback addresses, as well as unresolved or invalid DNS names. While the former is a normal occurrence and has no negative effects, you may want to clean out the unresolved or invalid DNS names when troubleshooting DNS problems. To do so, you use the command Ipconfig /flushdns, which purges the DNS resolver cache.

DHCP class IDs

Windows 2000 Server supports the use of class IDs for grouping DHCP clients according to their needs, which results in more-efficient management of DHCP resources. For example, mobile clients can be assigned shorter leases than desktop clients. In order to troubleshoot the new DHCP class IDs feature, Windows 2000's Ipconfig command comes with two new options. The command Ipconfig /showclassid displays all of the class IDs allowed for a particular system. The command Ipconfig /setclassid allows you to modify the DHCP class ID for a particular system.

More DNS and DHCP help

Windows 2000's Ipconfig command includes an additional troubleshooting feature that you can use to completely refresh your TCP/IP configuration when you're using DHCP. To do so, type the command *Ipconfig /registerdns*.

This command will refresh all of the DHCP leases and reregister all of the DNS names. Using this command can assist you when troubleshooting a failed DNS name registration or in resolving a dynamic update problem without having to reboot the system.

Conclusion

The ability to troubleshoot TCP/IP on the client side will help you with your IT responsibilities. Ipconfig.exe is a useful command for exploring and fixing TCP/IP problems. You'll want to know both the graphic and command-line versions, as well as the new switches supported by Windows 2000. ❖

PAGING THE OUTPUT
When you open a command prompt window in Windows 2000 and type *Ipconfig /displaydns*, the DNS resolver cache may be so large that the results scroll out of view before you can read them. Fortunately, you can pipe the results through the More command by adding | More to the command string. When you do, you'll see the contents of the DNS resolver cache, one screen at a time.

Using performance-monitoring tools to troubleshoot network problems

By Talainia Posey

When some people think of performance monitoring, they tend to think about how fast a computer is running. In fact, Microsoft's philosophy about performance monitoring is that you should first establish a performance baseline and then watch a machine's performance from time to time to determine how much the machine slows down when you add a heavier load.

There's more to performance monitoring than just seeing how fast your machine is running, however. You can use the various performance-monitoring tools to diagnose problems you're currently experiencing, whether or not you've established a performance baseline. In this article, I'll explain how to use performance-monitoring tools to troubleshoot network problems.

Understanding the process

Before I get started, I want to explain a little about the process and why it works. The primary performance-monitoring tool you'll be using is the Windows 2000 Performance Monitor. Performance Monitor doesn't simply gauge the system's overall performance the way some performance-monitoring tools do.

For example, Norton's System Works simply provides a benchmark that measures the performance of your system as a whole. This type of performance monitoring is great for determining system speed, but it's lousy for troubleshooting a system.

Rather than measuring the system as a whole, the Windows 2000 Performance Monitor measures extremely specific attributes of your system's performance. The devices used to measure these attributes are called counters. Because Performance Monitor counters measure such specific information, it's difficult to get an overall picture of your system's performance through Performance Monitor, but Performance Monitor is great for tracking down problems.

The basic technique I'll be using involves measuring the values that are associated with certain counters and looking for values that are out of whack. Even if you don't know what values are normal for your server or your network, some values always signal a problem. The trick is knowing where to look for these problematic values, and that's what I'll show you how to do.

Keep in mind, however, that there are a million different types of network problems. Obviously, it's impossible for me to walk you through the process of solving every possible network problem. Therefore, I'll simply show you some counters to check and explain what values to look for on each counter. I'll also explain what values indicate a potential problem and what the problem may be, based on the values you've measured.

Working with Performance Monitor

You access the Performance Monitor by clicking Start | Programs | Administrative Tools | Performance. When Performance Monitor loads, you'll see System Monitor selected by default. The right side of the screen will contain a graph. You'll use this graph to see the values of the various counters. Above the graph, you'll see several icons. Click the Plus icon to add a counter to the graph.

When you've clicked the Plus icon, you'll see the Add Counters dialog box. This dialog box is pretty simple to interact with. First, select the machine you want to measure. If you're having network problems, I strongly recommend making the measurements locally. For example, if a specific server is having trouble communicating with the rest of the network, then you should run Performance Monitor on that server.

Next, you need to specify the performance object, which is simply a way of dividing the counters into categories. Using the performance object, you can choose to work with counters related to the processor, memory, hard disk, network, and so forth. All you have to do is select a counter, click the Add button, and then click the Close button.

It's possible to select more than one counter by clicking the Add button after each counter and waiting until you've selected all the desired counters to click the Close button. I recommend looking at one counter at a time; however, looking at more than one at a time can be confusing. In addition, you may get inaccurate results because some of the system's power is consumed by the monitoring process. The only time you should look at multiple counters simultaneously is when you need to compare two or more values to each other in real time.

Troubleshooting network problems

Now that I've introduced you to Performance Monitor and explained a bit about the process I'll be using, let's get started. There are actually quite a few counters you can use under a variety of performance objects. One of the most important counters is the Redirector object. Let's take a quick look at it and the counters you can use to monitor network performance.

Redirector

The Redirector performance object contains a series of counters that correspond to the way Windows 2000's network redirector is functioning. The Redirector performance object is a great place to begin troubleshooting because it's located toward the top of the network food chain. This is because the redirector can do its job only if the protocols and the network adapter are also doing their job. Some of the key counters you'll use with the Redirector object are:

- Bytes Total/Sec
- Bytes Transmitted/Sec
- Bytes Received/Sec
- Network Errors/Sec

Bytes Total/Sec

The first counter I recommend testing under the Redirector performance object is Bytes Total/Sec. Add this counter to the chart and then try performing some tasks that would normally generate network traffic. Now, go back and check the counter. You're looking for a non-zero value.

If the counter never rises above zero, you have a fairly serious problem. A zero value on this counter means that traffic isn't getting in or out of the machine. Many times, such a problem is related to the way the redirector itself is configured. For example, there may be a binding problem in which the redirector isn't properly linked to the underlying protocols.

Sometimes, you can solve this problem by simply reinstalling the latest service pack for Windows 2000, currently Service Pack 1. However, if this doesn't work, you may have to resort to uninstalling the various networking components and reinstalling them. In an extreme case, you may have to resort to reinstalling Windows.

Bytes Transmitted/Sec

Once you've confirmed that some traffic is at least flowing through the redirector, you'll need to determine whether the traffic is inbound, outbound, or both. You can check outbound traffic through the Bytes Transmitted/Sec counter. Again, add the counter to the chart and perform a few tasks that should generate some network traffic. Since we're checking for the number of bytes transmitted per second, you should generate some outbound traffic by browsing Network Neighborhood or by trying to access a document from another server.

Once you've done this, go back and check the chart and look for a non-zero value. A non-zero value means that data is leaving the PC and reaching at least as far as the network card's communications port. Remember, though, that a non-zero value means only that the redirector is doing its job. It's possible to disconnect the network cable from the machine and still get a non-zero value on this counter.

Therefore, to determine whether the outbound communications are working, it's helpful to set up another PC with a share point that you can attempt to access from the PC that's having the problem. You can then monitor the share point using a technique to determine whether the packets are actually making it out of the PC and to their destination.

Bytes Received/Sec

When you're testing redirector communications, you'll also need to test inbound packets. Testing inbound packets is actually a better test than testing outbound packets. This is because packets coming into your PC were generated from another PC. Therefore, if your PC is able to detect the inbound packets, you can rest assured that the packets have successfully flowed from the PC that generated them—across the LAN, into your NIC, through your protocols, and to your redirector.

Unlike with testing outbound packets, there's really no guesswork involved in testing inbound packets. Either the packets have arrived or they haven't—there's no false positives generated by packets that made it "halfway," as can happen with outbound packets. To test for inbound packets, simply add the Bytes Received/Sec counter to the chart and perform some task that would normally cause a server to respond by sending data to your PC, such as opening a document. Once you've done so, check the chart for a non-zero value. If the chart remains at zero, then communications are breaking down somewhere along the line, and more testing is necessary.

When I was discussing the Bytes Transmitted/Sec counter, I mentioned the technique of setting up a share point on another PC and testing the malfunctioning PC's ability to connect to that share point. Simply using the Bytes Received/Sec counter to measure inbound data on the test machine is an inaccurate way of testing the malfunctioning PC's ability to connect. The reason is that the Bytes Received/Sec counter measures all traffic coming into the redirector, regardless of where the traffic came from. To test the malfunctioning PC's ability to transmit data, you'll have to use a method that can single out the data coming specifically from that PC.

Network Errors/Sec

Sometimes, you look at the number of bytes transmitted and received per second and it appears that communications are functioning properly, but you know there is still a problem. If this is the case, some of the packets might be corrupted somewhere along the way. One way of testing for this is to check the number of network errors per second.

To do so, add the Network Errors/Sec counter to the chart and then try to generate some network traffic. Obviously, you want the Network Errors/Sec counter to remain at zero. However, if you do detect some network errors, it usually points to a serious problem, especially if you're receiving more than just a couple of errors. If you detect network errors, the best thing to do is check the event logs because the errors will show up in the logs.

A number of things can cause these errors. In my personal experience, most of the time when I've seen a PC generating network errors, it's been due to a defective NIC or a network cable that has a short. ❖

Using the Windows 2000 Network Diagnostics tool

By Brien M. Posey, MCSE

Anyone who's ever managed a large network knows that sometimes solving a network problem can be a little tricky, to say the least. In the past, Windows NT network administrators had to rely primarily on third-party tools for troubleshooting. However, Windows 2000 contains several brand-new networking tools. In article, I'll discuss the Network Diagnostics tool. I'll explain what this tool does and show you how to use it.

Network Diagnostics

The Network Diagnostics tool is a command-line utility designed to test the functionality of your network client. One of the best things about this tool is that although it's powerful, it's very easy to use. Therefore, when problems occur, you can get right down to business without having to waste time learning how to use a new tool. There are a few command-line switches that go along with the Network Diagnostics tool, but not nearly as many as you'd expect from such a powerful tool.

The Network Diagnostics program examines all aspects of a client's network configuration. For example, it can analyze a client's TCP/IP configuration. If you happen to be running NetWare, you can test the NetWare client along with the IPX/SPX protocol.

Installation

To install the Network Diagnostics tool, log on as Administrator and run the 2000RKST command from the \Support\Tools directory of your Windows 2000 CD. Doing so will launch the Windows 2000 Support Tools Setup Wizard. There's also a Setup program in this directory, but it doesn't appear to actually do anything. When the wizard completes, it will have installed a plethora of new tools under the Start | Programs | Windows 2000 Support Tools | Tools menu. For our purposes, we'll stick to the Network Diagnostics tool that is only available via the command prompt.

Using the Network Diagnostics tool

As I mentioned, the Network Diagnostics tool must be run from the command line. The executable program is called NetDiag.exe. The command syntax is:

```
NETDIAG [[/Q | /V | /DEBUG] [/L] [/D:DOMAIN NAME] [/FIX]
    [/DCACCOUNTENUM] [/TEST:TEST NAME | /SKIP:TEST NAME]]
```

The switches that go along with the executable include:

- **/Q**—Lists only tests that return errors.
- **/V**—Displays detailed information as tests are performed.
- **/DEBUG**—Displays a very high level of detail.
- **/L**—Stores errors in NetDiag.log in the current directory. (I recommend you always use the /L switch since the program's output is almost always more than a screenful.)
- **/D:domain name**—Finds the domain controller.
- **/fix**—Fixes DNS errors on the domain controller.
- **/DCAccountEnum**—Enumerates computer accounts on the domain controller.
- **/TEST**—Performs a single test.
- **/SKIP**—Skips a test.
- **Test Name**—Provides the name of the test to perform or skip.
- **/?**—Provides help.

Now that I've examined the Network Diagnostics tool's syntax, it's time to explain a little bit about each test. In the sections that follow, the name of the test is listed in the heading, followed by a description of the test and a sample test output. You specify these test names if you want to skip a test or run a single test. In most cases, I've abbreviated the sample output because it was often scattered throughout the log file and because many of the test results were long.

NDIS

The NDIS test is the first test that's performed by default. The NDIS test checks the status of your network adapter. If the test fails, then all other tests are aborted. The NDIS test checks such things as your network adapter's name, configuration, GUID, media type, and statistics. Below is a sample of the output you can expect to see from this test:

```
Netcard queries test . . . . . . . : Passed
 Information of Netcard drivers:
 _____

 Description: Realtek RTL8139(A) PCI Fast Ethernet Adapter
 Device: \DEVICE\{73EABE7A-930F-4312-BEB6-824C21596E69}

 Media State:       Connected
 Device State:      Connected
 Connect Time:      00:12:05
 Media Speed:       100 Mbps

 Packets Sent:      474
 Bytes Sent (Optional):   0
```

```
           Packets Received:     1292
           Directed Pkts Recd (Optional): 414
           Bytes Received (Optional):  0
           Directed Bytes Recd (Optional): 0
           ─────────────────────────────────────

           [PASS] - At least one netcard is in the 'Connected' state.

       Per interface results:

           Adapter : Local Area Connection
               Adapter ID . . . . . . . . . : {73EABE7A-930F-4312-BEB6-
                                               824C21596E69}

               Netcard queries test . . . : Passed

               Adapter type . . . . . . . : Ethernet
               Host Name. . . . . . . . . : CARTMAN
               Description. . . . . . . . : NDIS 5.0 driver
               Physical Address . . . . . : 00-E0-7D-75-78-9F
               DHCP Enabled . . . . . . . : No
               DHCP ClassID . . . . . . . :
               Autoconfiguration Enabled. : Yes
               IP Address . . . . . . . . : 147.100.100.34
               Subnet Mask. . . . . . . . : 255.255.0.0
               Default Gateway. . . . . . :
               Dns Servers. . . . . . . . :
               IpConfig results . . . . . : Passed

               AutoConfiguration results. . . . . . : Passed
                AutoConfiguration is not in use.

               Default gateway test . . . : Skipped
                [WARNING] No gateways defined for this adapter.

               NetBT name test. . . . . . : Passed
                NetBT_Tcpip_{73EABE7A-930F-4312-BEB6-824C21596E69}
                CARTMAN   <00> UNIQUE  REGISTERED
                CARTMAN   <03> UNIQUE  REGISTERED
                CARTMAN   <20> UNIQUE  REGISTERED
                BUD    <1E> GROUP  REGISTERED
                INet~Services <1C> GROUP  REGISTERED
                IS~CARTMAN.....<00> UNIQUE  REGISTERED
```

```
NetBios Resolution : Enabled

        Netbios Remote Cache Table
 Name    Type       HostAddress    Life [sec]
 _____

 TALAINIA   <20> UNIQUE   147.100.100.25   510
 SCOOBY     <20> UNIQUE   147.100.100.31   587
 BUD     <1B> UNIQUE   147.100.100.31   580
 BUD     <1C> GROUP   147.100.100.31   567
 TITANIUM   <20> UNIQUE   147.100.100.30   510


 WINS service test. . . . . : Skipped
   There is no primary WINS server defined for this adapter.
   There is no secondary WINS server defined for this adapter.
   There are no WINS servers configured for this interface.
 IPX test : IPX is not installed on this machine.
```

IPConfig

The IPConfig test is nothing short of fantastic. It combines several manual TCP/IP diagnostic techniques into one easy test. The IPConfig test displays most of the information you'd normally expect to see if you ran the IPConfig/All command-line utility. In addition, it pings DHCP and WINS servers and tests for the correct location of the default gateway. Below is a sample of the output you can expect to see from this test. Although you can't see the results of the pings in this particular segment of code, the tests were conducted earlier.

```
IP General configuration
 LMHOSTS Enabled. . . . . . . . : Yes
 DNS for WINS resolution. . . . : Enabled
 Node Type. . . . . . . . . . . : Broadcast
 NBT Scope ID . . . . . . . . . :
 Routing Enabled. . . . . . . . : No
 WINS Proxy Enabled . . . . . . : No
 DNS resolution for NETBIOS . . : No
```

Member

The Member test outlines the terms of your domain membership. For example, it tells your server's role in the domain, as well as the domain's GUID and SID. You can also see which domain you're currently logged in to, along with the user account you're using. Here's a sample of the output you can expect to see from this test:

```
Domain membership test . . . . . . : Passed
 Machine is a . . . . . . . . . : Member Server
 Netbios Domain name. . . . . . : BUD
 Dns domain name is not specified.
 Dns forest name is not specified.
 Domain Guid. . . . . . . . . : {00000000-0000-0000-0000-
                                      000000000000}
 Logon User . . . . . . . . . . : Administrator
 Logon Domain . . . . . . . . . : CARTMAN
```

NetBTTransports

The NetBTTransports test lists NetBT transports that are managed by the redirector. If your computer isn't set up to use NetBT transports, it's normal for this test to generate an error. Here's a sample of the output you can expect to see from this test:

```
NetBT transports test. . . . . . . : Passed
 List of NetBt transports currently configured:
  NetBT_Tcpip_{73EABE7A-930F-4312-BEB6-824C21596E69}
 1 NetBt transport currently configured.
```

Autonet

The Autonet test checks to see whether any adapter in your machine is using automatic IP addressing. Here's a sample of the output you can expect to see from this test:

```
Autonet address test . . . . . . . : Passed
 PASS - you have at least one non-autoconfigured IP address
```

IPLoopBk

The IPLoopBk test is useful for testing to see whether the various TCP/IP components are functional. This test pings the address 127.0.0.1. If this ping fails, there's a problem with the way TCP/IP is installed. Your best bet in such a situation is to uninstall TCP/IP from the computer, reboot, and reinstall it from scratch. Below is a sample of the output you can expect to see from this test:

```
IP loopback ping test. . . . . . . : Passed
 PASS - pinging IP loopback address was successful.
 Your IP stack is most probably OK.
```

DefGw

The DefGw test pings each network card's default gateway. As you can see from the sample output below, this test failed on my test server. Normally, a failure in this area would indicate that the computer would be unable to communicate with

other subnets. However, because of the way my Proxy Server is configured, this
server doesn't have a default gateway. Thus, the test results are normal and don't
actually point to a critical failure.

```
Default gateway test . . . . . . . : Failed
 [FATAL] NO GATEWAYS ARE REACHABLE.
 You have no connectivity to other network segments.
 If you configured the IP protocol manually then
 you need to add at least one valid gateway.
```

NbtNm

This test checks the NBT names to make sure they aren't in conflict. It compares
the workstation service name to the computer name to make sure they're the same.
It also compares the messenger service name and the server service name to
ensure they don't conflict. Here's a sample of the output you can expect to see
from this test:

```
NetBT name test. . . . . . . . . . : Passed
 No NetBT scope defined

 PASS - The NetBT is properly configured.
  There is at least one interface where the <00>
       'WorkStation Service',
  <03> 'Messenger Service', <20> 'WINS' names are defined and
       they are not in conflict.
```

WINS

The WINS test takes the NBT names determined earlier and sends NBT name
queries to the WINS server, to make sure that the WINS server is functional.
Because a WINS server isn't used on my test network, I don't have any sample output for this test.

Winsock

The Winsock test looks at Windows Sockets to determine which transport protocols are available. This test is useful when trying to diagnose TCP/IP problems in
which some TCP/IP ports work and others don't. For example, you might use this
test if you can connect to the Web but can't connect to your mail server. Below is
an abbreviated sample of the output you can expect to see from this test:

```
Winsock test . . . . . . . . . . . : Passed
 The number of protocols which have been reported : 10
  Description: MSAFD Tcpip [TCP/IP]
   Provider Version :2
   Max message size : Stream Oriented
```

```
Description: MSAFD Tcpip [UDP/IP]
 Provider Version :2
Description: RSVP UDP Service Provider
 Provider Version :4
Description: RSVP TCP Service Provider
 Provider Version :4
 Max message size : Stream Oriented
Description: MSAFD NetBIOS [\Device\NetBT_Tcpip_{73EABE7A-930F-
     4312-BEB6-824C21596E69}] SEQPACKET 0
 Provider Version :2
Description: MSAFD NetBIOS [\Device\NetBT_Tcpip_{73EABE7A-930F-
     4312-BEB6-824C21596E69}] DATAGRAM 0
 Provider Version :2
Description: MSAFD NetBIOS [\Device\NetBT_Tcpip_{67EFB851-D60A-
     4DC6-BEFE-6846B81647EC}] SEQPACKET 1
 Provider Version :2
Description: MSAFD NetBIOS [\Device\NetBT_Tcpip_{67EFB851-D60A-
     4DC6-BEFE-6846B81647EC}] DATAGRAM 1
 Provider Version :2
Description: MSAFD NetBIOS [\Device\NetBT_Tcpip_{5077D5BE-A8E7-
     4918-8642-7EBFFBA04477}] SEQPACKET 2
 Provider Version :2
Description: MSAFD NetBIOS [\Device\NetBT_Tcpip_{5077D5BE-A8E7-
     4918-8642-7EBFFBA04477}] DATAGRAM 2
 Provider Version :2

 Max UDP size : 65527 bytes
```

DNS

This test looks to see whether the DNS server is running and whether the computer in question is correctly registered within the DNS. If the computer you're testing is a domain controller, the test checks to make sure all computers listed in the NetLogin.dns file are actually registered within the DNS database. If the entries appear to be incorrect, you can use the /FIX switch that I discussed earlier to correct the problem. As you can see by the sample output, the computer that I tested wasn't attached to a DNS server.

```
DNS test . . . . . . . . . . . . . . : Failed
[FATAL] Cannot get the DNS Adapter Information from the registry,
error 0x267c DNS_ERROR_NO_DNS_SERVERS
```

Browser

The Browser test actually tests the redirector and the browser. As you can see from the sample test below, the Browser test checks to ensure that the browser is bound to all NetBT transports and that the computer can send Mailslot messages.

```
Redir and Browser test . . . . . . : Passed
 List of transports currently bound to the Redir
  NetbiosSmb
  NetBT_Tcpip_{73EABE7A-930F-4312-BEB6-824C21596E69}
 The redir is bound to 1 NetBt transport.
 List of transports currently bound to the browser
  NetBT_Tcpip_{73EABE7A-930F-4312-BEB6-824C21596E69}
 The browser is bound to 1 NetBt transport.
 Mailslot test for BUD* passed.
```

DSGetDC

The DSGetDC test checks for a generic domain controller, a primary domain controller, and a Windows 2000 domain controller. This test can compare the GUID located in the LSA (Local Security Authority) to the GUID actually stored on the domain controller. If the numbers don't match, you can correct the problem by using the /FIX option. Here's a sample of the output you can expect to see from this test:

```
DC discovery test. . . . . . . . . : Passed


Find DC in domain 'BUD':
Found this DC in domain 'BUD':
 DC. . . . . . . . . . . . : \\TITANIUM
 Address . . . . . . . . . : \\TITANIUM
 Domain Name . . . . . . : BUD


Find PDC emulator in domain 'BUD':
Found this PDC emulator in domain 'BUD':
 DC. . . . . . . . . . . . : \\SCOOBY
 Address . . . . . . . . . : \\SCOOBY
 Domain Name . . . . . . : BUD
 Flags . . . . . . . . . : PDC WRITABLE


Find Windows 2000 DC in domain 'BUD':
 [WARNING] Cannot find Windows 2000 DC in domain 'BUD'.
    [ERROR_NO_SUCH_DOMAIN]
```

> This isn't a problem if domain 'BUD' does not have any Windows 2000 DCs.

DcList

This test is designed to compile a list of domain controllers within a given domain. The test begins by examining the directory service on an active domain controller. If this information is unavailable, another type of query is run against the directory service. If necessary, this test will also use the browser to get a list of domain controllers. Once the list has been compiled, the Network Diagnostics tool will add the controllers to the list to be tested. Below is a sample of the output you can expect to see from this test:

```
DC list test . . . . . . . . . . . : Passed
 List of DCs in Domain 'BUD':
  TITANIUM
  SCOOBY
  TALAINIA
```

Trust

The name of the Trust test is a bit deceptive since the test doesn't look at trust relationships between domains. Rather, it looks at inner domain trusts, such as the relationship between workstations or member servers and domain controllers. This test checks the SID that it uses to access the domain controller for accuracy. It then tests for a secure channel between itself and the domain controllers. Here's a sample of the output you can expect to see from this test:

```
Trust relationship test. . . . . . : Passed
 Test to ensure DomainSid of domain 'BUD' is correct.
 Secure channel for domain 'BUD' is to '\\TALAINIA'.
 Secure channel for domain 'BUD' was successfully set to DC
'\\TITANIUM'.
 Secure channel for domain 'BUD' was successfully set to DC
'\\SCOOBY'.
 Secure channel for domain 'BUD' was successfully set to DC
'\\TALAINIA'.
```

Kerberos

The Kerberos test runs only if the computer is a member computer or a domain controller in a Windows 2000 domain. The test logs into the LSA and checks the Kerberos package. It then gets the ticket cache of the Kerberos package and verifies whether Kerberos has a ticket for the local computer and for the primary domain controller. Notice in my sample test that I was unable to run this test because I wasn't logged into a Windows 2000 domain.

```
Kerberos test. . . . . . . . . . . . : Skipped
  This machine's membership domain is not a Windows 2000 domain.
  Kerberos cannot be tested.
```

LDAP

The LDAP test is effective only if the computer is a member of a domain that's
running directory services. When active, LDAP connects to the domain controllers
and searches the LDAP directory, testing all three types of authentication (unau-
thenticated, NTLM, and negotiate). In my sample test below, you can see that I
wasn't running Active Directory.

```
LDAP test. . . . . . . . . . . . . . : Passed
  DC '\\TITANIUM' isn't running the DS. Cannot test LDAP.
  Cannot test LDAP to 'TITANIUM' since it isn't running the DS.
[Test skipped.]
  Cannot test LDAP to 'SCOOBY' since it isn't running the DS.
[Test skipped.]
  Cannot test LDAP to 'TALAINIA' since it isn't running the DS.
[Test skipped.]
```

Route

Anyone who's ever done extensive TCP/IP work over a large network is familiar
with the Route command. The Route test prints much of the same information
normally associated with the TCP/IP Route command. As you can see in the
abbreviated sample below, the Route test checks static and persistent routes. It also
displays the subnet mask, gateway, interface, and metric for each route.

```
Routing table test . . . . . . . . : Passed
Active Routes :
Network Destination  Netmask      Gateway     Interface Metric
  127.0.0.0     255.0.0.0    127.0.0.1     127.0.0.1  1
  147.100.0.0   255.255.0.0 147.100.100.34 147.100.100.34  1
 147.100.100.34 255.255.255.255   127.0.0.1     127.0.0.1  1
147.100.255.255 255.255.255.255 147.100.100.34 147.100.100.34  1
  224.0.0.0     224.0.0.0 147.100.100.34 147.100.100.34  1
255.255.255.255 255.255.255.255 147.100.100.34 147.100.100.34  1
No persistent route entries.
```

NetStat

The NetStat tool is very valuable. I haven't included a sample output from the
NetStat test because the NetStat test generates so much information. It includes such
information as protocol statistics and the current TCP/IP network connections.

This is one of the best tests for troubleshooting a really tricky problem because you get such detailed information on your network connections.

Bindings

As you're probably aware, the Windows 2000 network infrastructure depends on various layers of the operating system working together. The way that some of these layers attach to each other is called bindings. For example, a protocol might be bound to a network card. If you're having a network problem, you can use the Bindings test to view an exhaustive list of all of the bindings within your computer. Here's an abbreviated sample of the output that you can expect to see from this test:

```
Bindings test. . . . . . . . . . . : Passed
 Component Name : Point to Point Tunneling Protocol
 Bind Name: mspptp
 Binding Paths:


 Component Name : Layer 2 Tunneling Protocol
 Bind Name: msl2tp
 Binding Paths:


 Component Name : Remote Access NDIS WAN Driver
 Bind Name: NdisWan
 Binding Paths:
  Owner of the binding path : Remote Access NDIS WAN Driver
  Binding Enabled: Yes
 Interfaces of the binding path:
  -Interface Name: ndiswanasync
   Upper Component: Remote Access NDIS WAN Driver
   Lower Component: RAS Async Adapter


  Owner of the binding path : Remote Access NDIS WAN Driver
  Binding Enabled: Yes
 Interfaces of the binding path:
  -Interface Name: ndiscowan
   Upper Component: Remote Access NDIS WAN Driver
   Lower Component: WAN Miniport (L2TP)
```

WAN

The WAN test displays the settings and information related to current remote access connections. As you can see from the sample test, no one was dialed in to my RAS server at the time of the test. However, it struck me as interesting that

Microsoft chose to include a test for RAS connections in the mix of traditionally LAN/WAN-oriented connections.

```
WAN configuration test . . . . . . : Skipped
 No active remote access connections.
```

Modems

Under normal circumstances, the Modems test queries all of the modems within your system. It then displays any available information about each modem's configuration. My test machine doesn't contain a modem, so I didn't include a sample output from this test.

NetWare

The NetWare test examines your connection to a NetWare network. It begins by determining if you're connecting to a NetWare server through a bindery connection or a directory service connection. It then determines your default context or default server. I haven't included sample output because NetWare isn't present on my test network.

IPX

Like all of the TCP/IP tests, the IPX test provides you with a wealth of information. If IPX is installed on your network, this test will tell you the internal network number, the frame type, and the router MTU. The IPX test will also tell you whether packet burst and source routing are enabled. I haven't included a sample output of the IPX test because IPX isn't present on my test network.

IPSec

One of the new features in Windows 2000 is the ability to create and enforce an IP security policy. The IPSec test checks to make sure that the IP Security Policy Agent is functional. If it is, then the test goes on to see which policy, if any, is currently active. Here's a sample of the output you can expect to see from this test:

```
IP Security test . . . . . . . . . : Passed
 IPSec policy service is active, but no policy is assigned.

 There are 0 filters
```

Conclusion

Diagnosing network problems can be a real pain in the neck. In this article, I've shown you several tests that are built into the Windows 2000 Network Diagnostics program. I've also explained how each of these tests works, and I've shown you what type of results you can expect. ❖

Use Windows XP Pro's Network Diagnostics tool for comprehensive troubleshooting

By Greg Shultz

One of the biggest pains when troubleshooting network problems is gathering all the information you need just to get started. Doing so usually involves running a series of operations, such as checking configuration settings in various dialog boxes or running DOS-based commands, such as ping, from the command line. Now, however, you can use the Network Diagnostics tool in Windows XP Professional to save time in the information-gathering phase of your search. In this article, I'll show you how to configure and use this tool to make quick work of your next network troubleshooting expedition.

A little background information

The Network Diagnostics tool is unique because it is actually based on the Windows Management Instrumentation (WMI) framework and implemented via an ActiveX object run from an HTML page in the Help and Support Center rather than from an executable file. When run, the ActiveX object polls the computer and its network connections, performs a series of network connectivity tests, collects all the results, and then delivers the data back to the page in an XML format.

Launching Network Diagnostics

The main place to launch Network Diagnostics is from the Help and Support Center. To begin, click the Start button and select Help And Support. On the Help And Support Center page, select the Tools button under the Pick A Task category. When the Tools page appears, select Network Diagnostics from the scrolling list in the Tools panel.

You can also launch the Network Diagnostics tool from the Control Panel. To begin, click the Start button and select Control Panel. If you're using Category View, select the Network And Internet Connections category. Then, select Network Diagnostics from the Troubleshooters panel. If you're using Classic View, select the Network Connections icon. Then, select Network Troubleshooter from the See Also panel.

Figure A

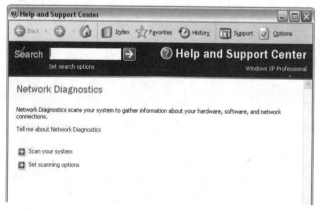

The Network Diagnostics tool runs from an HTML page in the Help and Support Center.

You'll then select the Diagnose Network Configuration And Run Automated Networking Tests link.

When you launch the Network Diagnostics tool, it displays the page shown in **Figure A**. The Network Diagnostics page provides you with two options: You can immediately launch the scan operation with its default settings, or you can customize the scan operation such that it runs only those tests that you choose. Since customizing the scan operation can help you quickly drill down on the problem you're attempting to solve, let's take a closer look at the settings revealed by selecting the Set Scanning Options button.

Configuring Network Diagnostics scanning options

When you select the Set Scanning Options button, the page will expand to show you a list of check boxes that you can use to configure the Network Diagnostics tool, as shown in **Figure B**. The check boxes are broken down into two sections: Actions and Categories. There are five Actions that work in conjunction with the 14 Categories.

By providing you with the ability to pick and choose from Actions and Categories, the Network Diagnostics tool allows you to fine-tune your search to track down very specific problems. For example, if you suspect that there's a TCP/IP connectivity problem somewhere on the network, you can quickly confirm your suspicion by selecting only Ping under Actions and only Network Adapters under Categories. Network Diagnostics will then ping the gateway, DHCP, and DNS servers, as well as the IP address assigned to the network card, and display the results in an easy-to-read HTML format.

Figure B

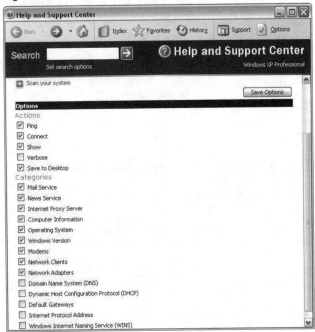

There are a number of options you can use to configure how and what the Network Diagnostics tool tests during its scanning operation.

If you hover your mouse over any of the Actions or Categories, Network Diagnostics will display a tool tip containing a description. For your convenience, **Tables A** and **B** contain a list of all the Actions and Categories along with the descriptions. The tables also specify whether the settings are enabled by default.

If you select a custom set of scanning options, you may want to repeat that same set of tests at a later date. If so, you can click the Save Options button.

Running a test

Once you've configured Network Diagnostics to perform the tests in which you're interested, you can then initiate the scan operation by clicking the Scan Your System button. When you do, you'll see a progress bar as well as a percentage that indicates the status of the operation. You'll also see a brief message indicating which test is occurring at any one time, as shown in **Figure C**.

Analyzing the results

Once Network Diagnostics completes the scanning operation, it displays the results of the test in the same window in an easy-to-use HTML format, as shown in **Figure D**. The results are categorized under the following three headings:

▶ **Internet Service:** Displays information related to Internet Explorer Web Proxy and Microsoft Outlook Express mail and news configuration.

▶ **Computer Information:** Displays information about the local computer, including the computer name, hardware state and capabilities, operating system, and version information.

▶ **Modems And Network Adapters:** Displays network hardware and software information, such as domain name, MAC address, IP address, and subnet information.

Table A: *Network Diagnostics' Actions: In its default configuration, Network Diagnostics will track down basic information about the computer, enumerate network adapters, attempt resource connections, and attempt to ping configured network services.*

Default	Option	Description
Yes	Ping	Tries to contact a remote computer on the network. Successfully contacting the computer does not imply that the required network service is running.
Yes	Connect	Checks whether a remote computer appears to be supporting a networking service.
Yes	Show	Gathers basic computer information for certain categories.
No	Verbose	Gathers advanced computer information for certain categories.
Yes	Save To Desktop	Saves report file to the desktop for easy access.

Table B: *Network Diagnostics' Categories: You'll notice that the last five categories aren't selected by default. However, these tests are already included in the Network Adapter test. They're listed separately to allow you more latitude in your testing and to help you narrow down the cause of the problem.*

Default	Option	Actions	Description
Yes	Mail Service	Ping, Connect	Displays inbound and outbound mail server host name, port number, and mail type.
Yes	News Service	Ping, Connect	Displays the default Outlook Express news server name and port number.
Yes	Internet Proxy Server	Ping, Connect	Displays Internet Explorer's server name, port number, and whether the proxy is enabled.
Yes	Computer Information	Show, Verbose	Displays information about your local computer.
Yes	Operating System	Show, Verbose	Displays information about your operating system.
Yes	Windows Versions	Show, Verbose	Displays all your Windows version information.
Yes	Modems	Show, Verbose	Displays all modems.
Yes	Network Clients	Show, Verbose	Displays all your network clients.
Yes	Network Adapters	Ping, Show, Verbose	Displays all active and inactive adapters on your network.
No	Domain Name System (DNS)	Ping	Displays the Domain Name Servers for each network adapter.
No	Dynamic Host Configuration Protocol (DHCP)	Ping	Displays the DHCP servers for each network adapter.
No	Default Gateways	Ping	Displays the default gateway server for each network adapter.
No	Internet Protocol Address	Ping	Displays the Internet Protocol Address for each network adapter.
No	Windows Internet Naming Service (WINS)	Ping	Displays primary and secondary WINS servers for each network adapter.

Figure C

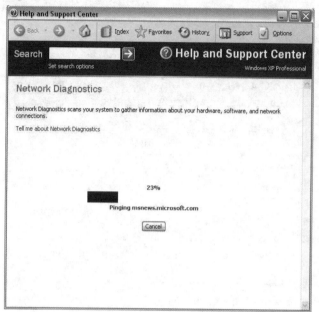

While Network Diagnostics is scanning your system, it keeps you apprised of its progress.

Figure D

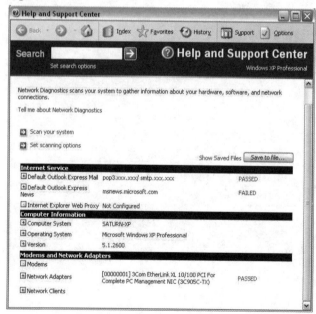

Network Diagnostics displays the results of the test in the same window in an easy-to-use HTML format.

As you can see in my example test, Network Diagnostics scores each completed test as either Passed or Failed. Of course, if the feature isn't in use, Network Diagnostics lists the result as Not Configured. You can get more details on each test by clicking the (+) button to drill down on the result listing.

By clicking the (+) button on the Default Outlook Express News result, we can determine that the test failed because the ping operation was unsuccessful, as shown in **Figure E**.

If you plan on retesting the system after tinkering with the problem, you will want to save the results of your first test so that you can compare them with subsequent test results. To do so, click the Save To File button. Two copies of the file are saved on the hard disk. One copy is saved on your desktop for easy access (unless you deselected that option), and the other copy is saved for archival purposes in the C:\Windows\ PCHealth\Helpctr\System\Netdiag folder.

You can then view the results at any time from within your Internet browser.

Working from the command line

In order to provide a comprehensive solution, Microsoft also included a command-line version of the Network Diagnostics tool. This serves two purposes: First, it gives the IT professional who prefers working from the command line a way to use this great tool, and second, it provides a way to build a custom set of diagnostics using scripting techniques.

The Network Diagnostics tool is provided to the command line via what Microsoft calls a "helper" to the Netsh utility. To access the Network Diagnostics tool from the command line, you'll open a Command Prompt window and type the command:

```
Netsh -c diag
```

Figure E

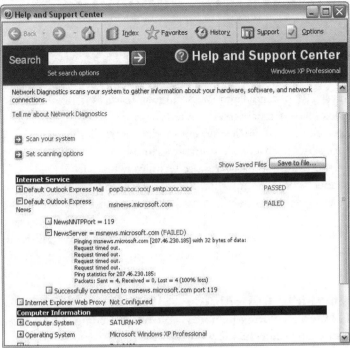

NOTE
The workings of the Netsh utility, which is a command-line scripting utility that you can use to display or modify the network configuration of a local or remote computer, are beyond the scope of this article.

By clicking the (+) button, you can drill down on any of the results and get more details.

Once you do, you can learn more about using Network Diagnostics commands by typing any one of the following:

"*?*" or "*help*"

"*c*" or "*connect*"

"*p*" or "*ping*"

"*s*" or "*show*"

Conclusion

Windows XP provides you with an automated network-troubleshooting tool called Network Diagnostics that can instantly perform a wide variety of common troubleshooting tests and display the results in an easy-to-read format. You should now feel comfortable enough with Network Diagnostics to configure and use this tool to get the most out of your next troubleshooting mission. ❖

REMOTE ASSISTANCE: WHAT IT IS AND WHAT IT ISN'T

The Remote Assistance feature is new to XP, but it's based on a technology that has been around for quite a while.

TIP

If you're on a LAN, the firewall configuration might prevent you from using Remote Assistance. Remote Assistance uses the same port as Terminal Services (3398); you may need to have an administrator open that port for you.

Virtual support with XP's Remote Assistance

By Debra Littlejohn Shinder, MCSE

One of Windows XP's potentially most useful new features is Remote Assistance. This feature is particularly suited for help desk personnel on a corporate network because it allows them to view users' desktops and take control remotely to perform troubleshooting tasks and resolve problems. Home users can utilize the feature to allow a more technically knowledgeable friend to provide assistance across the Internet. Remote Assistance works over a LAN or WAN and is supported by both Windows XP Home and Professional Editions.

In this article, you'll learn how to deploy, configure, and use this new XP feature to make the whole process easier for both those who provide technical support and those who need assistance.

Planning for deployment of Remote Assistance

Consider several issues before deploying Remote Assistance, including system and configuration requirements and understanding the available modes and options.

System and configuration requirements

The following requirements must be met to use Remote Assistance:

- Both computers must be running XP Home or Pro, or .NET Server.
- If the user is using XP Home Edition, he or she must be logged on with an Owner account.
- To request assistance, the user must have Outlook, Outlook Express, or Windows Messenger installed or have another way, such as IM, to transfer a file to the helper.

Remote Assistance options

Remote Assistance options can be configured on the user's computer via the Control Panel | System Properties | Remote tab, shown in **Figure A**. Clicking the Advanced button gives you a few more options, as shown in **Figure B**.

By default, Remote Assistance is configured to allow helpers to view the desktop but not control it. To allow the helper to take control, select the Allow This Computer To Be Controlled Remotely check box in the Advanced settings. You can also specify a maximum number of minutes, hours, or days that your invitations to assist will remain open. The default setting is 30 days; the maximum is 99 days.

Remote Assistance modes

A helper can assist a user in one of two modes:

- **View Only**: The helper can connect to the user's desktop and see everything being done in a terminal window but can't do anything (open or close programs, move items, perform actions on the computer, etc.).

- **Remote Control**: The helper can perform tasks on the user's computer as if he or she were sitting at it locally.

See the previous section for instructions on allowing Remote Control. If you attempt to take control of an XP computer that is set to the defaults (Remote Control disabled), you'll see a message box advising that Remote Control is not allowed. If Remote Control is enabled, you'll see the message shown in **Figure C**.

Security issues

Remote Assistance, like any other service that opens a computer to access across a network, can present a security risk if improperly configured.

Microsoft has built-in security safeguards; for example, when a helper offers to assist a user, the user will be required to give permission before the helper can connect to his or her computer. When a user sends a request for assistance, it's encrypted using public key technology and sent using XML. Users can configure settings for more security, such as using passwords to protect assistance invitations.

If you're in a high-security environment in which very sensitive data is stored on your computer or on the network, your organization's policies may require that Remote Assistance be disabled.

Setting invitations to expire

When users send invitations to helpers to assist them, they can increase security by

Figure A

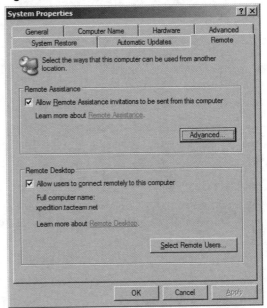

On the user's computer, make sure that Allow Remote Assistance Invitations To Be Sent From This Computer is selected.

Figure B

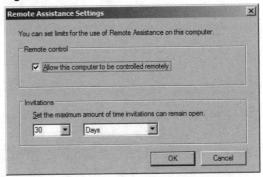

Figure C

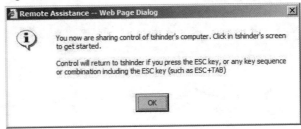

You can take control of a user's computer if it's configured to allow Remote Control.

A little background

The technology behind Remote Assistance was originally developed by Citrix and then licensed by Microsoft and first implemented as a special version of Windows NT Server, called Terminal Server Edition.

Windows Terminal Services technology

Those familiar with NT and Windows 2000 Terminal Services will recognize the terminal session connection window when they connect to a computer to provide Remote Assistance. As with Terminal Services, the remote client, in this case the helper's computer, accesses the other computer's desktop. The helper (or Expert User) is able to troubleshoot problems that the user (the Novice) is having as if the helper were at the user's computer.

Remote Assistance vs. Remote Desktop

With Windows NT and 2000, only computers running Server operating systems (and only the special Terminal Services edition of Server in

NT) could be remotely connected to via Terminal Services. A limited implementation of this functionality, Remote Desktop, has been added to Windows XP Professional.

Although it uses the same technology as Remote Assistance, Remote Desktop is a separate feature. Both are available—and configured separately—on XP Pro.

Remote Desktop is not available on Windows XP Home Edition. However, all versions of Windows can act as Terminal Services clients. The Terminal Services client software must be installed on versions other than XP Pro; the remote desktop software built into XP can be used to connect to Windows NT, 2000, or .NET terminal servers, as well as other XP Pro computers. Unlike Remote Desktop, Remote Assistance allows simultaneous sharing of control of the computer between the user and helper as well as communication between the user and helper via text chat or voice. (The latter requires the proper hardware.)

Selecting secure passwords

Security based on passwords is only as strong as the passwords you select. When choosing a password to protect your Remote Assistance invitation, follow these guidelines:

1. Don't use your Windows or domain logon password.
2. Choose a long password. A minimum of seven characters is recommended.
3. Use a mixture of alpha, numeric, and symbol characters.
4. Don't use words or numbers associated with you as the password, such as your spouse's name or your Social Security number.
5. Don't use common words or phrases found in a dictionary.
6. Do make the password easy for you to remember so you won't have to write it down.

Following these guidelines will make it more difficult for an unauthorized person to guess the password or crack it using a brute-force attack.

configuring the invitations to expire in a specified time period. The default setting is one hour.

Using password protection

When users send invitations, they can require that the helper enter a password before being allowed to connect to their computers. This should always be a secure password. I'll illustrate the process of setting a password in the section titled Requesting Remote Assistance.

Taking back control and disconnecting a Remote Assistant

If a user has granted the helper permission to remotely control the computer, the user can end the Remote Control by either clicking Stop in the chat window or pressing [Esc]. This stops the helper from controlling the computer, but he or she will still be able to view the user's desktop and chat or talk with the user.

The user can also disconnect the remote helper entirely by clicking the Disconnect button in the Remote Assistance window, shown in **Figure D**.

Requesting Remote Assistance

A Remote Assistance session can be initiated in two ways. Either the user can send a request, or the helper can send an offer. The first is the more common method. When a user needs help, he or she can request Remote Assistance by sending an invitation to a helper/administrator.

Figure D

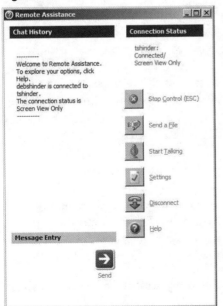

The user disconnects the remote helper by clicking the Disconnect button.

Figure E

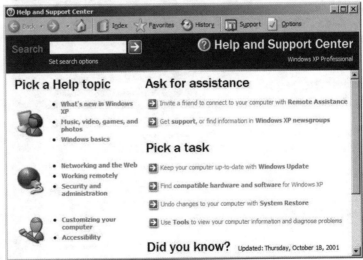

A user can ask for assistance using the XP Help And Support Center.

Figure F

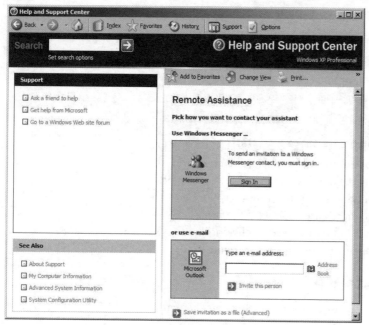

To request assistance, the user opens the Help And Support Center from the Start menu and, under the Ask For Assistance section, clicks Invite A Friend To Connect To Your Computer With Remote Assistance, as shown in **Figure E**.

The user sends the request in one of three ways:

- Windows Messenger
- E-mail
- By saving the invitation as a file and transferring it to the helper (see **Figure F**).

Sending invitations via Windows Messenger

If the user chooses to send the invitation via Windows Messenger, both the user and helper must be using Windows Messenger Service. Both will be prompted to log on to the service using .NET passport accounts.

Sending invitations via e-mail

If one or both parties don't use Windows Messenger, the easiest way to request assistance is via an e-mail invitation. When the user selects this method, he or she will need to type in the helper's e-mail address. Then the E-mail An Invitation wizard will appear, as shown in **Figure G**.

The e-mailed invitation will include an attachment. When opened, the attachment will contain a button the helper can click to connect to the user's computer. An example of an e-mail invitation appears in **Figure H**.

Sending invitations as saved files

In addition to using Windows Messenger or e-mailing the Remote

Figure G

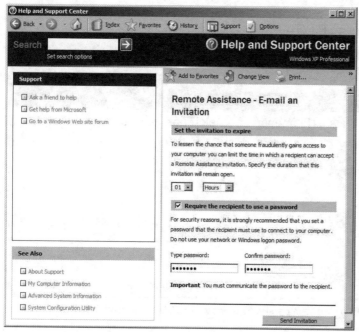

You can set expiration and password protections on an e-mailed request.

Assistance request, users can save the request as a file and transfer it across the network to the helper by placing it in a shared folder to which the helper has access, or by manually attaching it to an e-mail message, for example.

When users select this option, the file is saved by default in their My Documents folder, with the .msrcincident extension. The helper can open the file by double-clicking it (and entering the password, if the user has set one). When the helper opens the file, a dialog box similar to the one shown in **Figure I** will be displayed.

Offering Remote Assistance

In a corporate environment, it may be desirable for the tech support personnel to initiate Remote Assistance sessions. Several additional requirements exist for offering assistance that don't apply to user-initiated requests:

- Both computers must be in the same Windows domain.
- The helper must have administrative privileges.
- The helper must know the computer name or IP address of the machine for which assistance is being offered.
- The user's computer must be configured to receive Remote Assistance offers.

Configuring the user's computer to receive offers

By default, XP computers aren't configured to receive Remote Assistance offers. You must edit the local group policy to enable receipt of offers. To do so, follow these steps:

1. Open the Group Policy console by selecting Start | Run and typing *gpedit.msc*.
2. In the Group Policy MMC's left console pane, expand the Computer Configuration node, expand the Administrative Templates subnode, double-click System, and then double-click Remote Assistance.

Figure H

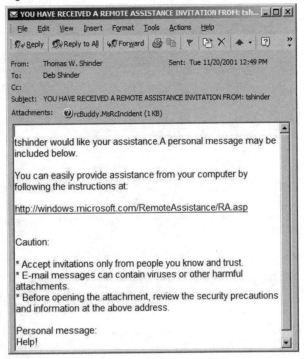

The helper will receive the e-mailed invitation with an attachment.

Figure I

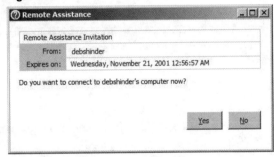

The .msrcincident file contains a dialog box that allows the helper to connect to the user's computer.

Figure J

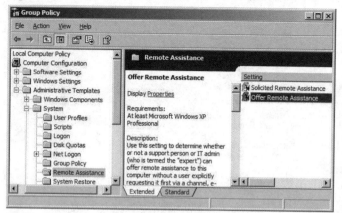

You must edit the local group policy to enable receipt of Remote Assistance offers.

Figure L

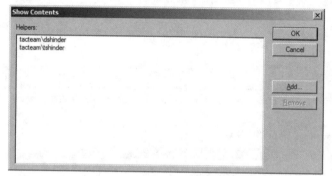

You must specify which users are allowed to initiate Remote Assistance offers.

Figure K

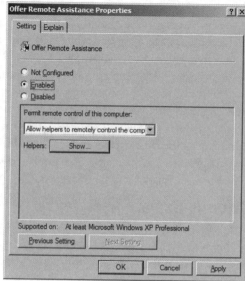

You must enable the policy before you can receive assistance offers.

Figure M

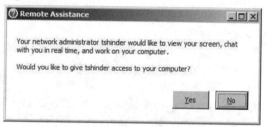

The user can choose whether to allow the helper to connect to the computer.

3. In the right details pane, double-click Offer Remote Assistance, as shown in **Figure J**.

4. In the Offer Remote Assistance Properties box, select the Enabled radio button. Select whether to allow helpers to remotely control the computer or only view the desktop, by using options in the drop-down box. Then click the Show button, as illustrated in **Figure K**.

5. You can add users who are allowed to initiate Remote Assistance sessions in the Show Contents box, shown in **Figure L**.

Sending the offer

Once the user's computer is configured to allow Remote Assistance offers, the helper can send an offer by clicking on Offer Remote Assistance in the Help And

Figure N

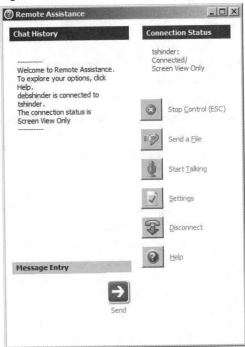

Type a message in the Message Entry field and click Send to chat.

Figure O

You can use a voice connection to talk over the Internet.

Support Center. You are then asked to specify the IP address of the machine you want to connect to. Click Start Remote Assistance and follow the same procedure you would if a user had invited you to assist. The user will see a dialog box like the one shown in **Figure M**.

It's important to note that the administrator cannot connect unless the user gives permission.

Connecting to and controlling the remote computer

Whether initiated by the user or the helper, once connected to the remote desktop, the session will begin in View Only mode.

View Only mode

In View Only mode, the helper can see the user's desktop and any actions the user performs. The helper and user can chat by typing text messages in the Message Entry field and clicking Send, as shown in **Figure N**.

To use voice communications, click the Start Talking button. The dialog box shown in **Figure O** will appear. Click Yes to talk. You may be prompted to configure your hardware at this time.

Taking control

If the user's computer was configured in the Control Panel | System applet to allow Remote Control, the helper can take control by clicking Take Control at the top of the terminal window.

The user will see a dialog box asking him or her to give permission for the helper to take control. If the user clicks Yes, a message will announce that control will now be shared, and both the user and helper can move the cursor and perform tasks on the user's computer. Remember, though, that the user can revoke Remote Control or disconnect the helper at any time.

Conclusion

We've all been there. The user has a machine that keeps locking up and can't really explain the problem over the phone. When you can't be there to shoulder-surf someone having difficulty, Remote Assistance gives you a unique way to connect to and assist users. Remote Assistance is rich with features, including chat and voice communications, and allows View Only or Remote Control sessions. Sessions can be initiated either by users (using three different methods) or by helpers who have administrative privileges, if both computers are in the same domain and group policy on the user's computer is properly configured. ❖

Solutions to problems with Windows XP's Remote Assistance feature

By Debra Littlejohn Shinder, MCSE

Windows XP's Remote Assistance feature allows users to request help across the network from tech support personnel or other experienced users. The helper can view the requesting user's desktop "live" and, with the user's permission, can remotely take control and perform tasks on the user's computer to troubleshoot and fix problems.

But what if there are problems with the Remote Assistance feature itself? Here are some tips on how to identify the most common problems that can occur with Remote Assistance and how to rectify them so users can take full advantage of this new feature.

Configuration problems

Most problems with Remote Assistance are due to faulty configuration, on either the requesting user's or helper's computer.

- If a user is unable to send a request for assistance, make sure the computer is configured with the proper settings. Go to Start | Control Panel | System. On the Remote tab, verify that the check box to allow Remote Assistance invitations to be sent is selected, as shown in **Figure A**.

- If a user is unable to send a remote assistance request and is using Windows XP Home Edition, ensure that he or she is logged on with the Owner account.

- If a user can send a request for remote assistance but the helper is unable to take control of the desktop after he or she connects, click the Advanced button found on the Remote tab in Figure A, and ensure that the check box to Allow This Computer To Be Controlled Remotely is selected, as shown in **Figure B**.

This option is disabled by default, and if a helper attempts to take control when it has not been enabled, he or she will receive this message: Remote Control Of This Computer Is Not Allowed.

Problems sending assistance requests

Outside of configuration issues, there are a number of factors that can affect a user's ability to send assistance requests via the various supported methods. In the sections below, I will explain how to correct such problems when using Windows Messenger, Outlook or another Simple MAPI mail client, or saved files.

Figure A

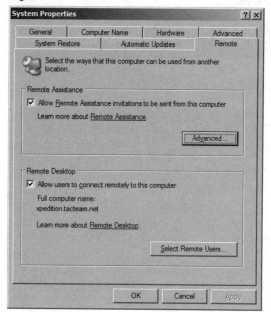

Figure B

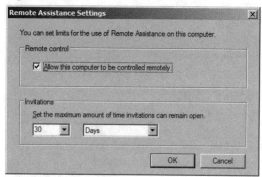

Figure C

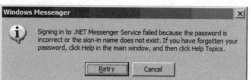

You must have a valid .NET account and password to send a request via Windows Messenger.

Problems sending requests via Windows Messenger

To send a request using Windows Messenger, a user must have Windows Messenger service installed and must have a .NET passport account and password. Both the requester's computer and the helper's computer must be connected to the Internet to access the .NET passport service.

If a user receives the error message shown in **Figure C** when attempting to send a request, check his or her .NET account and password information. If the user doesn't have a .NET passport, use the .NET Passport Wizard to obtain one.

The steps for setting up a .NET password depend on the type of network the computer is on:

- If the computer belongs to a domain, click Start | Control Panel | User Accounts, select the Advanced tab, and then click the .NET Passport Wizard button.

- If the computer belongs to a workgroup (a peer-to-peer network with no Windows domain controller), click Start | Control Panel | User Accounts. If you have Administrator rights to the PC, click your account name. Then click Set Up My Account To Use A .NET Passport to start the wizard.

The wizard will walk you through the steps for getting a .NET passport. You will need a valid e-mail address. If you don't have one, you can use the wizard to obtain a free MSN e-mail account. Also, any MoneyCentral, MSN, or Hotmail accounts are already .NET passports. Many people have such accounts and don't know they are already .NET capable.

If you have a valid .NET passport and you are connected to the Internet but are still unable to send a request via Messenger, this may be because the .NET service is temporarily busy or down. Wait a while and try again, or send your Remote Assistance request via another method.

Problems sending requests via e-mail

If a user is unable to send an assistance request via e-mail, ensure that he or she is using Outlook, Outlook

Express, or another e-mail client that supports Simple MAPI as his or her e-mail client. Also, make sure the helper's e-mail address has been entered correctly.

If a user attempts to use an e-mail client that does not support SMAPI, he or she will not be able to send the request directly via e-mail using the Ask A Friend For Help function in the Help And Support center. However, a user can select the Save Invitation As A File option instead of the e-mail option, save the remote assistance invitation as a file, and send the file as an e-mail attachment or put the file in a shared folder that the helper can access across the network.

Problems sending requests via a saved file

If the port used by Remote Desktop has been changed, it's possible for an invitation file created with a Windows XP Professional machine using the Remote Assistance request wizard to contain an incorrect port number. In such a case, the helper will not be able to establish a remote assistance session.

However, it's possible to edit the invitation file to correct this problem by following these steps:

1. Open the invitation file in Notepad or another text-editing program.
2. Under the section that begins RCTICKET=, you will see a number following a colon, such as :3389. Change this number to the correct port number for the Remote Desktop.
3. Save the file.
4. Send the file to the helper as an e-mail attachment or make it available for the helper to access in a shared network folder.

Problems sending and receiving offers to assist

Generally, the user who needs help initiates a remote assistance session by sending an invitation. However, it is possible for the helper to initiate the session by sending an offer to assist. But the helper can only do this if the user's computer is set up to receive such offers; Windows XP Professional computers don't have this feature enabled by default, so you need to enable it before the computer can receive offers.

If a helper is unable to send an offer of assistance, check the remote user's local Group Policy settings. See "Virtual support with XP's Remote Assistance" for detailed instructions on how to configure the user's local group policy.

Note that the group policy setting for accepting offers of remote assistance is available only in Windows XP Professional, not in Windows XP Home Edition. Also, offers can be sent and received only between computers that are members of the same domain. If the computers do not belong to the same domain, the assistance session must be initiated by a request from the user.

Other communication and connection problems

Other things that can prevent you from being able to connect and communicate over a Remote Assistance session could be related to firewall problems, licensing

TIP
When you create an invitation file, it is automatically saved to your disk with the .msrcincident extension so you can locate it easier on the hard drive.

issues, or terminal services settings. In the next few sections, I will explain such problems and their solutions.

Firewall-related problems

Remote Assistance uses the Remote Desktop Protocol (RDP), which is part of Windows terminal services technology that uses TCP port 3389 to communicate. If this port has been blocked on the network's firewall, users will not be able to use Remote Assistance across the firewall. An administrator must open port 3389 to allow Remote Assistance communications to pass through.

If a user has set up the built-in Personal Firewall feature on a Windows XP computer that is multihomed—one that has more than one network interface—the helper may not be able to establish a remote assistance session in response to a request to assist. This connection problem also applies when one of the network interfaces is a modem. This happens because the firewall port will be opened only on the network interface that is first in the binding order. Microsoft has released a fix for this problem, which is available from the Download Center at **http://v4.windowsupdate.microsoft.com/en/default.asp**. For more information about using the Personal Firewall with a multihomed computer, see Q308210 in the Microsoft Knowledge Base at **http://support.microsoft.com/ default.aspx?scid = kb;en-us;Q308210**.

Network Address Translation (NAT)

If the user is on a network that uses Network Address Translation (NAT) or Microsoft's Internet Connection Sharing (ICS), which is a "light" version of NAT, he or she will not be able to initiate a Remote Assistance session via e-mail. In this case, try using Windows Messenger Service to send the assistance request.

Licensing issues

Windows XP's licensing protections may cause problems if the user's computer and the helper's computer had Windows XP installed by the same OEM or if the OSs were installed using volume licensing. When this occurs, a user cannot establish a Remote Assistance session; instead he or she will get a message that says You Have Been Disconnected From <*computername*>, where *computername* indicates the name of the computer from which he or she was disconnected. This can be corrected by installing a free fix available from Microsoft's Download Center at **www.microsoft.com/downloads/release.asp?releaseid = 33873**.

Terminal Services settings

The XP Remote Assistance feature uses Windows Terminal Services technology, as does the Remote Desktop feature, which is available on Windows XP Professional and Home but not supported in Windows XP Home.

Some Terminal Services settings can affect a user's ability to use the Remote Assistance feature, as in the following situations:

- If the number of allowed terminal connections is set to zero, a user will not be able to establish a remote assistance connection.

- If a maximum time limit for terminal sessions has been set and terminal services is configured to terminate the session when that time limit is reached, a Remote Assistance session will be abruptly disconnected when a user reaches that time limit.

Problems with voice communications

The novice user and helper can also communicate during the Remote Assistance session using live voice communication. If the voice communication doesn't work, check the following:

- Ensure that both computers have full-duplex sound cards.

- If Remote Assistance is used across the Internet or another WAN connection, make sure the connection speed is at least 28.8 Kbps. Note that even if you have a 28.8 Kbps or better modem, your connection speed could be lower due to "dirty" phone lines or other factors.

- If sound quality is poor and you have a 64 Kbps or faster connection, click Settings in the Chat window and select the High Quality Sound option.

- Assistance works best with a reasonably high-speed network connection. This probably will not be an issue over a LAN, but if you are using Remote Assistance over the Internet and the connection is too slow, the computer may hang up during the session.

Conclusion

The Windows XP Remote Assistance feature makes it much easier for administrators, tech support personnel, and experienced users to provide help to other Windows XP users across a LAN or WAN. But for this feature to work efficiently and effectively, you must make sure the proper settings are enabled. If problems persist, look for causes in some of the areas I've identified. ❖

Troubleshoot USB problems in Windows XP

By Brien M. Posey, MCSE

While I think it's fair to say that USB devices are generally easier to configure and less prone to problems than their serial- and parallel-based ancestors, problems can still occur. When USB devices fail to function properly in Windows XP, you should tailor your troubleshooting efforts to the type of problem and when it occurs. Here are some examples of the more common USB configuration problems, and their corresponding solutions.

USB problems after Windows XP upgrade

As with other peripherals, it's not uncommon for USB devices to cause problems after upgrading a computer from Windows 98, Me, or 2000 to XP. If you encounter a problem after upgrading, you'll first want to determine whether the device is compatible with XP. Check the Windows XP hardware compatibility list (HCL) and manufacturer's site for information regarding XP compatibility. You should also download and install the latest device drivers.

Unfortunately, neither action is guaranteed to solve the problem. I've seen devices listed on the XP HCL not function properly and devices not listed on the HCL function perfectly, depending on the particular driver used. Sometimes it just comes down to a process of trial and error. For more information on ensuring your hardware plays nice with Windows, check out the TechRepublic article from John Sheesley at **www.techrepublic.com/article.jhtml?id=r00320030616joh01.htm**.

Windows XP's failure to recognize any USB devices

When Windows XP won't recognize any USB device, regardless of which port it's connected to, there is likely a BIOS or Windows configuration problem. On some computers there is a configuration option in the BIOS that asks whether an IRQ should be assigned to USB. Although the option's actual wording varies among BIOS manufacturers, you must enable this option by setting it to either On or Yes (depending on your BIOS manufacturer and BIOS version). Otherwise no USB devices will work on XP.

A problem with Windows XP's USB Controller configuration can also prevent any USB devices from working. To determine whether the USB controllers are working properly, open Device Manager and expand the Universal Serial Bus Controllers node. Beneath this node, you should see a USB Universal Host Controller and a USB Root Hub. Depending on your PC, there will either be a USB Universal Host Controller and a USB Root Hub listed for each of your computer's USB ports or a USB Universal Host Controller and USB Root Hub for multiple ports.

All of my test machines, for example, have a separate USB Universal Host Controller and USB Root Hub entry for each USB port, as shown in **Figure A**, while my editor's HP Kayak has a single USB Universal Host Controller and USB Root Hub for both of his machine's ports. I'm not entirely sure why this is, but I assume it depends on the PC's motherboard. Some motherboard manufacturers may place multiple ports on a single USB controller while others place each port on a separate controller.

Regardless of how many USB Universal Host Controller and USB Root Hub entries your PC has, if any of the icons have a red X over them, they've been disabled. If a device is disabled, you can enable it by right-clicking the device and selecting Enable from the resulting shortcut menu.

While you have Device Manager open, I also recommend you check the driver that is being used for your USB ports. To do so, right-click on a USB component and click Properties and select the Driver tab. Unless you are running some abnormal hardware, the Driver tab should list the Driver provider as Microsoft, as shown in **Figure B**. The Digital Signer should be Microsoft Windows XP Publisher. If you have anything else, then you have a couple of options available to you.

You could supply a new device driver by clicking the Update Driver button. If, on the other hand, you had recently updated the driver and then started having problems, you could click the Roll Back Driver button to revert to the previous version.

If the driver appears to be OK, but you can't seem to make any USB device function, then use the Uninstall button. This will allow you to remove the driver completely and make Windows think that the USB ports don't even exist. After doing so, you can return to the System Properties sheet and click the Add Hardware Wizard button. This will allow Windows to redetect your computer's USB ports. Normally, during the redetection process, Windows will try to enable the ports using the standard Microsoft drivers. Assuming that there is nothing physically wrong with your computer's USB ports, this should fix the problem.

Figure A

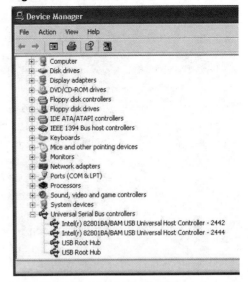

Expand the Universal Serial Bus Controllers node to look for problems.

Figure B

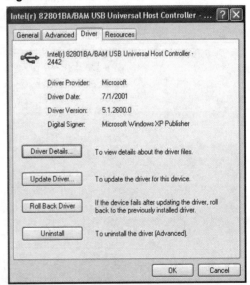

The Driver tab should list Microsoft as the Driver Provider and should list Microsoft Windows XP Publisher as the Digital Signer.

Bandwidth and power problems

Another common problem with USB devices is that you can only use so many USB devices simultaneously. This is because each USB 1.1 port is limited to 12 Mbps (megabits per second) of bandwidth (USB 2.0 allows for 480 Mbps) and 500 mA. If you exceed either of these limitations, then the USB devices will cease to function.

Let's take a look at bandwidth limitations first. Unfortunately, I can't tell you the exact number of USB devices that will exceed your bandwidth limitations and there is no Performance Monitor option to examine USB bandwidth. The type of USB device and how the device is used both affect the amount of bandwidth the device consumes. For example, scanners and digital cameras tend to consume a lot of bandwidth because they transfer large chunks of data to the computer. At the same time, though, a scanner will consume almost no bandwidth unless you are actively in the process of transferring data.

The best way to tell if you might be exceeding your USB bandwidth limitation is to take a look at the number of devices connected to a particular USB port, how those devices are being used, and then apply some common sense. If you have many USB devices connected or your devices tend to transmit and receive a lot of data, then you could be pushing the limits of a port's available bandwidth.

Power consumption is a lot easier to figure out than bandwidth consumption. To figure out how much power you are consuming, there are a few things to keep in mind. First, each USB port on your computer supplies 500 mA. This 500 mA has to be shared among all devices connected to it. If you connect a single device to a USB port, power consumption isn't a consideration, because most USB devices only consume around 100 mA.

Things start getting interesting when you start connecting USB hubs. If you connect a USB hub to a USB port, then the port's 500 mA must be shared between the USB hub and all of the devices connected to the hub. You can also daisy chain USB hubs. If you daisy chain USB hubs together, you can have up to five hubs connected in a series. Remember, though, that 500 mA must be sufficient to power all connected hubs and devices. A USB hub does consume power, even if no other devices are connected to it.

To get around this problem, many manufacturers have started making USB hubs that have an external power supply. If you have a USB hub with an external power supply, the power supply will supply a total of 500 mA to the hub. This means that if you have multiple powered hubs daisy chained together, then each hub will be self sufficient and will consume almost no power from the computer's USB port or from other hubs in the chain.

Even if all of your hubs are powered, though, there are still limitations that you must be aware of. First, the five-hub limit still applies whether the hubs are powered or not. The other limit is that you must still avoid overburdening any one hub with USB devices with excessive power consumption. Finally, external power sources do nothing to provide extra bandwidth. If you were to interconnect five hubs with four devices each, you could connect 20 USB devices to a single USB port, as long as none of the devices had excessive power consumption. At the same time, though, these 20 devices would have to share the 12 Mbps of available bandwidth.

When I first started talking about power consumption, I said that it is easier to determine whether you are using too much power than it is to determine if you are using too much bandwidth. Windows will actually tell you how much power your USB devices are using. Before I show you how to figure this out, though, there is one thing that you need to understand. The number that I am about to show you doesn't actually measure power consumption, but rather how much of the USB port's power is being used. Remember that you can have powered USB hubs connected to the computer. If a powered hub is connected, then the devices will be feeding off of the hub's power, not off of the computer's power. Therefore, the computer will show you that there is very little or no power being drawn from the USB port.

To view USB power consumption, return to the Device Manager, right-click the USB Root Hub entry, and click Properties to display the USB Root Hub Properties sheet. Select the Power tab and you will see how much power is being drawn from the USB ports, as shown in **Figure C**.

If a device (or a combination of devices) draws too much power, then the hub will usually turn off the port. To get the port to function again, you must disconnect the device and reattach it to the port. Depending on the type of hub that you are using, there may also be a dialog box that prompts you to reset the port.

Troubleshooting a specific USB device

If you are having trouble with one particular USB device rather than with all of your USB ports, there are some relatively easy steps that you can take to get the device working. I recommend unplugging all USB devices from the system, including USB hubs. Next, take a known good USB device and attach it to the system. If the known good device works, then you can be sure that there is nothing wrong with the port itself.

Now take the device that was malfunctioning and plug it directly into one of the computer's USB ports while no other USB devices are connected to the system. If the device starts working, there are a couple of possible reasons for the earlier problem. More than likely, the device was conflicting with another USB device. One way that USB devices can conflict with each other is if they share a common

Figure C

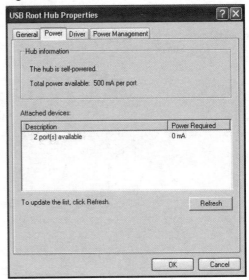

The Power tab shows how much power your USB devices are drawing.

serial number. Each USB device in a system must have a unique serial number. Having two devices with a common serial number is very rare, but there are documented cases of it happening.

If the device now works and it isn't sharing a serial number with another device, it more than likely was malfunctioning due to an overloaded USB hub or a conflicting device driver. The only real way to sort out the problem is to use trial-and-error by plugging in various combinations of USB devices until you find the device or devices that the malfunctioning device is conflicting with. Once you track down the offending device, you can often solve the problem by moving the devices to different physical USB ports or by updating the drivers for both devices.

If plugging in the malfunctioning device without any other USB devices being plugged in doesn't cure the problem, you aren't completely without options. I recommend checking the computer's Event Logs for clues to the malfunction. If the event log doesn't give any clues, try plugging the malfunctioning device into another computer. If the device works on the other computer, then you can be sure that the device is good.

If the alternate computer is using an operating system other than Windows XP, it could be that the device or its driver isn't Windows XP-compatible. If this is the case, you might call the device's manufacturer to see if there are any known issues with using the device with Windows XP. I have run into a couple of cases in which a USB device simply required a new driver and a firmware upgrade to work with Windows XP.

If the alternate computer is running Windows XP and the device is working, then I recommend checking out what version of the device driver is being used on each machine and using the one that works, even if it isn't the most recent. ❖

Troubleshoot server ports in Windows with Portqry.exe

By Jeremy Smith, MCSE, CNE, Network+

Many IT pros are quite proficient with Telnet and use it adroitly in testing and troubleshooting ports and connectivity. However, Telnet has its limitations for port testing. For instance, it can't determine whether the port is being filtered, and it's unable to test UPD traffic like LDAP or RPC. That's where Portqry.exe (**http://support.microsoft.com/?kbid=310099**) comes into the picture. Microsoft has developed this utility to aid in troubleshooting connectivity issues by allowing for better scanning of ports. Here's how to unleash the power behind this utility.

A direct approach

Portqry.exe is actually a pretty straightforward tool. Once you learn the syntax and see a few basic usage examples, you will be ready to use it. When you run the Portqry command, this tool will report the status of the port on a particular host in one of three forms:

- **Listening:** When you receive this status back, it means that there is a process listening on the port you specified on your target host.
- **Not Listening:** A node reporting this status type indicates that there is no process listening on that port on the target computer.
- **Filtered:** Portqry.exe has a leg up on other similar utilities with its ability to report whether a target computer is filtering out a specific port. Most utilities simply report Not Listening if filtering is occurring, but not Portqry.exe. It will query a port up to three times to determine the correct status.

How to use the utility

As with any command line utility, syntax is paramount. Here are the various switches you can pass this utility from the command line:

- -n [*server*]—IP address or name of server to query
- -p [*protocol*]—TCP or UDP or BOTH (default is TCP)
- -e [*endpoint*]—single port to query (valid range: 1-65535)
- -r [*endpoint range*]—range of ports to query (start:end)
- -o [*endpoint order*]—range of ports to query in an order (x,y,z)
- -l [*logfile*]—name of log file to create
- -s—"slow link delay" waits longer for UDP replies from remote systems

- -I—bypasses default IP address-to-name lookup; ignored unless an IP address is specified after -n
- -q—"quiet" operation runs with no output

Next, we'll look at some examples of how you might put the above variables together in a command that can execute various options.

Determine whether SMTP is available on a node

If you want to verify that the SMTP protocol is running on an Exchange Server, you could issue the following iteration of Portqry.exe to ascertain its status:

```
portqry -n YourNode -p tcp -e 25
```

In the above command sequence, you are telling the program to verify that *YourNode* (-n parameter) is listening on TCP (-p parameter followed by tcp) port 25 (specified by the –e parameter and then the port number). If you were to issue this command against a node actually running SMTP, the following response would be returned to you:

```
TCP port 25 (SMTP service): LISTENING
```

In addition, the port would return data similar to the following:

```
220 YourNode domain.com Microsoft ESMTP MAIL Service, Version:
5.0.2195.2966 ready at date and time -0900
```

If SMTP is not listening, it would return this data:

```
TCP port 25 (SMTP service): NOT LISTENING
```

Determine whether LDAP is available on a node

Because Telnet cannot easily test for UDP-based ports, Portqry.exe becomes a viable asset if, for instance, you want to test for LDAP availability on a node. For example, if you wanted to verify connectivity from a client to an Active Directory domain controller, you could issue the following command from the client:

```
portqry -n yourserver.domain.com -p udp -e 389
```

In this case, the –n identifies your server, the –p identifies your protocol (in this case, UDP), and the –e signifies an endpoint or the port you specifically want to query (LDAP, in this example, over port 389). The response you could receive back might look like **Listing A**.

A useful trick

As with any tool, it's always nice to know what unique things you can do with it, outside the standard usage. One the cool things I found was that Portqry.exe uses a Services file located in the %systemroot%\system32\drivers\etc directory. (Every Windows 2000 and Windows XP system has one of these.) Portqry.exe uses this file to resolve the port numbers entered by the user to their corresponding service names; hence, the contents of this file control which ports Portqry.exe sends its

Listing A

```
Querying target system called:
            Yourserver.domain.com
             Attempting to resolve name to IP address...
             Name resolved to 192.168.1.25
             UDP port 389 (unknown service): LISTENING or FILTERED
             Sending LDAP query to UDP port 389...


            LDAP query response:


            currentdate: 4/4/2003 16:09:51 (unadjusted GMT)
            subschemaSubentry:
CN=Aggregate,CN=Schema,CN=Configuration,DC=domain,DC=com
dsServiceName: CN=NTDS
Settings,CN=yourserver,CN=Servers,CN=Sites,CN
=Configuration,DC=domain,DC=com
namingContexts: DC=domain,DC=com
defaultNamingContext: DC=domain,DC=com
schemaNamingContext:
CN=Schema,CN=Configuration,DC=domain,DC=com
configurationNamingContext:
CN=Configuration,DC=domain,DC=com
rootDomainNamingContext: DC=domain,DC=com
supportedControl: 1.2.840.113556.1.4.319
supportedLDAPVersion: 3
supportedLDAPPolicies: MaxPoolThreads
highestCommittedUSN: 815431405
supportedSASLMechanisms: GSSAPI
dnsHostName: MYDC.domain.com
ldapServiceName: domain.com:yourserver$@DOMAIN.COM
serverName:
CN=YOURSERVER,CN=Servers,CN=Sites,CN=Configuration,DC=domain,DC=com
supportedCapabilities: 1.2.840.113556.1.4.800
isSynchronized: TRUE
isGlobalCatalogReady: TRUE


======== End of LDAP query response ========
UDP port 389 is LISTENING
```

messages to. Now, if you happen to have a protocol that is not using its conventional port, you can simply edit this file and provide the port you need by adding or changing the port number resident in the file.

What it cannot do

Just like any utility, Portqry.exe has its limitations. Although it is uniquely designed for port verification, it is a little slow. Microsoft makes it clear that this tool is not a "security verification tool," but rather it is a troubleshooting tool, much like Ping, Traceroute, and other built-in Windows network utilities.

A handy tool for verifying port status

All in all, this little utility is a nice tool for a network admin to have available. You probably will not need to use it to the extent that you might use Ping or Ipconfig, but nevertheless it's a great tool to have in your repertoire when you need to verify whether a port is open, closed, or being filtered. ❖

Troubleshooting hardware installation problems in Windows Server 2003

By Brien M. Posey, MCSE

Whether you're upgrading an existing server or setting up a new server, having Windows fail to recognize your hardware is always a frustrating experience. Unfortunately, there are a number of reasons why a piece of hardware might not work correctly with Windows Server 2003. Here are some of the hardware problems you may face and how to resolve hardware compatibility problems.

The hardware compatibility list

Before I get into the actual troubleshooting process, I want to take a moment and discuss the hardware compatibility list (HCL). When Windows NT was first released so long ago, Microsoft worked hard to give people the impression that their hardware absolutely would not work unless it appeared on the HCL.

Since that time, the HCL has perhaps become one of the most ignored aspects of Windows. After all, just about every hardware manufacturer provides Windows drivers for their hardware, whether the device is actually on the HCL or not.

Although most hardware components may come with a Windows driver, it doesn't necessarily mean that you should use them. In fact, the last time that I called Microsoft's technical support about a potential hardware problem, they wouldn't even talk to me until I replaced the failing device with a device that was listed on the HCL. Although that happened a while ago, I suspect that Microsoft's policy hasn't changed.

When Windows Server 2003 was released, Microsoft emphasized the importance of the HCL by removing several well-known network cards from the HCL. It isn't that these network cards won't work with Windows, but rather that Microsoft finds them to be inadequate for a server environment. The list consists of ISA plug-and-play adapters for reliability reasons, PCMCIA adapters (because you shouldn't be using a laptop as a server), and USB adapters (because of bandwidth limitations). You can find the complete list in the Microsoft Knowledgebase **http://support. microsoft.com/default.aspx?scid=kb;en-us;317594**.

In case you're wondering, Microsoft doesn't ship a copy of the HCL with Windows because the list is constantly changing as new products are released. Instead, you can find the HCL on Microsoft's Web site **www.microsoft.com/whdc/ hcl/default.mspx**.

Troubleshooting an unknown device

The first step in troubleshooting a hardware problem is to make sure that Windows recognizes the malfunctioning device. After all, if Windows doesn't even know that the device exists, you can't expect the device to work. You can see exactly what components Windows recognizes by using the Device Manager.

To access the Device Manager, right click on My Computer and select the Properties command from the resulting shortcut menu. When you do, you'll see the System Properties sheet. Now, select the Hardware tab and click the Device Manager button.

When the Device Manager appears, you'll first want to look under Other Devices. Usually if a device is listed under Other Devices, the device appears next to a yellow circle containing an exclamation point. This means that the device is unrecognized because it does not have a device driver.

Most of the time, this tends to occur with USB or Firewire devices. The reason is that most USB and Firewire devices are designed to be automatically detected and to use drivers that are built into Windows. However, this does not apply to all such devices. For example, I have a USB modem that, when plugged in, produces the unknown device error. Unfortunately, Windows does not automatically recognize the modem, so a third-party driver is required.

As strange as it may sound, there are also circumstances in which you can provide Windows with a perfectly good device driver for an unknown device and Windows will still fail to recognize the device. Most of the time this happens when you supply a VXD-based driver. As you may know, VXD drivers are virtual device drivers. VXD files were originally intended for use in Windows 9x. Even so, VXD files were also supported in Windows 2000. Windows Server 2003, however, is specifically designed not to use VXD files. If you try to install a VXD file, though, Windows will usually place the device on the Other Devices list rather than giving you a message stating that you are using an incompatible driver. In such cases, the only way to make the device work is to get your hands on a driver that's supported by Windows Server 2003.

Another reason that a device may appear in the Other Devices portion of Device Manager is that it may have an invalid device ID number. Every plug-and-play device has an ID number assigned to it. The device ID number might be made up of a variety of components, such as the manufacturer's ID number, the system vendor ID, or even the revision level. Since the device ID number is required for plug-and-play devices, any device without a device ID number or using an invalid device ID number may be listed in the Other Devices section of Device Manager.

Typically, you won't run into this problem unless you're using a poorly written device driver on a really cheap device. However, there are circumstances in which good hardware with a good device driver can produce such a condition. For example, Compaq produces a software application called Compaq Insight Manager. This software is designed to monitor the hardware for potential problems. To do this, the software creates virtual device drivers that it uses for linking to the hardware. Keep in mind that Windows Server 2003 doesn't support virtual device drivers. Therefore, it is very possible that you could have been running Compaq Insight Manager under Windows 2000 Server with no problems. If you then upgraded the server to Windows 2003, the virtual device drivers would be unrecognized and would therefore appear in the Other Devices column.

There are other types of device drivers that can use perfectly valid drivers but cause a device to appear in the Other Devices column. Typically, this occurs with drivers designed to make a device emulate a different device. For example, drivers that are designed to make a parallel port emulate a SCSI port are notorious for having this problem.

Software-based virtual device drivers

Another common problem is that some device drivers are entirely software based. For example, I have a program that allows you to turn any printable document into a PDF file. This software installs itself as a print driver, even though there is really no hardware associated with the driver. Although there are exceptions, software-based devices are incompatible with Windows Server 2003.

If you have a malfunctioning device and you suspect that the device might be software based, there is an easy test that you can use to find out. Simply boot the machine into Safe Mode and then pull up Device Manager. If the device isn't listed while the machine is running in Safe Mode, then you can be sure that the device is software based. However, if the device remains while in Safe Mode, it is not an absolute guarantee that the device is hardware based. There are conditions in which a software-based driver may still load in Safe Mode.

Once you determine that a device driver is or may be related to a software device, it's time to figure out where the device is being loaded from. If the device driver appears in the Device Manager when the system is running in normal mode, but not when the system is running in Safe Mode, then one of the programs being launched during Startup is loading the Device Driver. You can check the system's Startup folder and the system tray for clues as to the program that may be loading the driver. However, on most systems there are way more background programs running than the ones that appear on the Startup menu or in the system tray.

The easiest way to find out exactly what is running at Startup is to look at the system registry. Once you know what is running at Startup, you can use the process of elimination to narrow down the software component that is loading the invalid device driver. To do so, you might disable one registry key at a time or rename one file at a time that's being called by the registry.

I should point out that editing the registry is dangerous. Making an incorrect change to the registry can destroy Windows and/or your applications. Therefore, you should make a full system backup before messing with the registry. With that said, you can open the Registry Editor by entering the REGEDIT command at the Run prompt. Once the Registry Editor opens, you can find the programs that are set to run at Startup by going to

`HKEY_LOCAL_MACHINE\Software\Microsoft\Windows\CurrentVersion\Run`

If you are uncomfortable with using the Registry Editor or if the list of programs that load at Startup is just too long, there is another way that you can track down the program that's calling the device driver. Try looking at your event logs. Often, the event logs will contain clues as to which program might be causing the problem.

The system information console

Another tool that can really help you to track down a hardware problem is the system information console. You can access this console by entering the MSINFO32.EXE command at the Windows Run prompt. When the console loads, navigate through the console tree to the Components section. The Components section lists all of the add-on components in your system. For example, the components section will document things like network cards, modems, and sound cards. Unlike the Device Manager, though, it does not document your system board or disk controllers. For the components that are addressed, the System Information console tends to provide a bit more information than the Device Manager does.

While the information given for each device is helpful, you should focus on a container within the Components section called Problem Devices. The Problem Devices container gives you the name of any device that the system sees as malfunctioning. It then goes on to give you a little bit more information that you can use to help to identify the device and/or the problem.

For example, on my test computer, the Device Manager was displaying a PCI Simple Communications Controller in the Other Devices section. When I looked in the Problem Devices section of the System Information console, I found a listing for the PCI Simple Communications Controller. The console also told me that the device's PNP ID number was

`PCI\VEN_14F1&DEV_2F1&SUBSYS_201616EC&REV_01\4&351887D&0&58F0`

The console also gave me this error message:

`The Drivers For This Device Are Not Installed`

By using this information, I was able to tell that the error was related to a PCI card for which the system had no drivers. To give you a little history behind this error, this was a brand new computer that had shipped with the Home Edition of Windows XP. When I brought the system home, I formatted the hard drive and loaded a default installation of Windows Server 2003. Since I didn't use the system's drivers CD, there was simply one hardware device within the system for which Windows Server 2003 didn't have a driver. A quick check of the back of the computer revealed a modem that was not listed within Device Manager.

To fix the problem, I went back into the Device Manager and right-clicked on the PCI Simple Communications Controller listing found in the Other Devices section. I then selected the Properties command from the resulting shortcut menu to reveal the device's properties sheet. I clicked the Reinstall Driver button found on the properties sheet's General tab. This launched the Hardware Update Wizard. The wizard asked if I wanted to automatically install the driver or if I wanted to install a driver from a specific location. I used the option to install a driver from a specific location, inserted my drivers CD, pointed the wizard to the CD, and soon had a functional modem. The problem was solved.

Physical hardware failures

This was an easy problem to fix because I had a brand new computer with a device that I assumed to be good, which was simply missing a device driver. But what do you do if a device driver is loaded and Device Manager recognizes the device, but the device is still malfunctioning?

The first thing that you should do in such a situation is to ask yourself if the device has ever worked. If the device has worked in the past, ask yourself what has changed since the device last worked? Was a service pack applied to the computer? Was a new driver installed?

If the device previously worked, this might be a good time to try out Windows 2003's driver rollback feature. To do so, open the Device Manager, right-click on the malfunctioning device, and select the Properties command from the resulting context menu. When you do, you'll see the device's properties sheet. Now, select the properties sheet's Driver tab and click the Roll Back Driver button. This will revert the system back to using the previous driver for the component.

Hopefully, this will get the job done. If not though, you probably either have a bad component or an incorrect device driver. It is also possible that the device is conflicting with some other device in the system, but conflicts are much more rare than they used to be.

The next step that I recommend is to go to the Internet and download the latest device drivers for each device in your system. You can then install these device drivers by right-clicking on the appropriate device, selecting the Properties command from the resulting shortcut menu, and then going to the Driver tab of the device's properties sheet and clicking the Update Driver button.

Driver signing

While I'm on the subject of updated drivers, I want to take a moment and discuss signed drivers. For workstations, I usually don't worry too much if a driver isn't signed. However, in the case of a production server, you should always use signed device drivers. If a manufacturer doesn't provide signed device drivers, then I would seriously think about switching to a different hardware manufacturer.

If you want to see which, if any, of your current device drivers are unsigned, enter the SIGVERIF command at the Start menu. This launches the Signature Verification utility. Normally, this utility will scan all Windows system files. However, you can use the Advanced button to tell the tool to only scan the \%SYSTEMROOT%\System32\Drivers folder. The program will create a log file named SIGVERIF.TXT. You can view the log file by clicking the utility's Advanced button, selecting the Logging tab and clicking the View Log button.

If you want to ensure that only digitally signed files are installed onto the server in the future, you can do so by opening the Control Panel, clicking the System icon, and selecting the Hardware tab from the System Properties sheet. This time though, instead of going into the Device Manager, click the Driver Signing button. By default, the system is configured to warn you before installing unsigned drivers. However, the Driver Signing Options dialog box also contains an option to block the installation of unsigned drivers.

Bad hardware

If the new device drivers don't fix the problem, then you either have a bad hardware component or you have a device conflict. To find out which is the case, try replacing the malfunctioning device with a known good one. If the new component works, then you know that you had a bad component. If the known good component fails, then you have a conflict somewhere.

Troubleshooting conflicts is difficult, and I could easily write an entire article on the subject. However, what I can tell you in this limited amount of space is that the easiest way to troubleshoot a conflict is to remove all add-on components from your system except for the known good version of the malfunctioning component. When you boot the system, the component should work because anything that it might be conflicting with is gone.

Now, start putting the other components back into the system one at a time, testing the system between each one. You should be able to use this technique to find the conflict. ❖

Troubleshooting DNS problems in Windows Server 2003

By Scott Lowe, MCSE

Windows Server 2003's DNS service is integral to the proper functioning of Active Directory and the proper functioning of the network. Even though it's a well-known and well-understood service, Windows Server 2003's DNS implementation can still create headaches for the administrator that needs to maintain it. Here are some problems that you might encounter with the Windows 2003 DNS service and the steps that you need to take to correct them.

Firewalls and EDNS

New in Windows Server 2003 is support for Extension Mechanisms for DNS (EDNS) as defined in RFC 2671. These extensions allow for the transfer of DNS packets in excess of 512 bytes, which was the restriction imposed by RFC 1035. When Windows Server 2003 contacts a remote DNS server, this capability is negotiated and enabled if both ends support it, resulting in DNS record sets of a size greater than 512 bytes.

Unfortunately, some firewalls have trouble with this enhancement as they are configured to drop DNS packets in excess of 512 bytes. As you can imagine, this will result in significant problems with DNS servers on opposite sides of the firewall!

EDNS can be turned off in Windows Server 2003. Disabling EDNS results in your server never advertising that it has the capability to handle DNS packets in excess of 512 bytes. It will drop back to using the RFC 1035 defined limits.

To disable this capability, type *dnscmd /Config /EnableEDnsProbes 0* at the command prompt. Dnscmd.exe is a part of the Windows Server 2003 Support Tools. These tools are located in the Support Tools folder on the Windows Server 2003 CD and can be installed by running the suptools.msi installation program located there. You should restart the DNS service after you make this change.

Hosting internal sites

A common problem faced by many organizations is the need to host sites behind the firewall or in the DMZ that are also behind NAT IP addresses. Web interfaces to e-mail servers are an instance of this need. As an example, consider an Outlook Web Access front end sitting behind a company's firewall. Assume that the Web Access server is assigned 192.168.1.10 as an IP address, which is NAT-resolved to a "real" IP address so that it's accessible from the outside of the network. The local machines need to address the machine using the private IP address while external clients need to use the real IP address.

Windows 2003 can be used to service the needs of the local clients and can be configured to forward external requests to your ISP's DNS servers. In this example, your internal clients will resolve internal addresses using the local DNS servers. In turn, this server will use your ISP's DNS servers for requests that it can't handle. External clients will use your ISP's DNS servers to get the real IP address of the Web server.

To configure forwarding on your Windows Server 2003 DNS server, start the DNS manager at Start | Administrative Tools | DNS. Right-click the name of your DNS server and select Properties from the shortcut menu. On the Forwarders tab, add the IP addresses for your ISP's DNS servers or the addresses to which this DNS server should resolve requests. **Figure A** below shows a sample of this window.

The case of the missing SRV records

If you implement DNS on a Windows 2003 system and the server is using DHCP to get its address, DNS is configured without dynamic updates being enabled, and your DNS zone name is different than your Active Directory domain name, you may run into a problem. When you run the DNS manager again, you'll notice that the service resource records (SRV records) for the domain are missing. These records are critical to the proper functioning of Active Directory as a pointer to the location of directory services.

Figure A

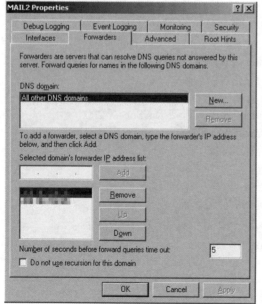

DNS forwarders are configured to handle requests that this server can't.

Figure B

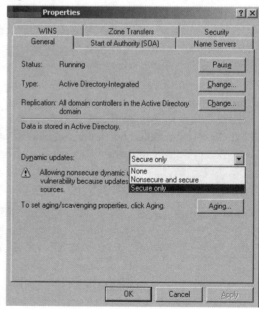

To correct the problem, make sure that the zone name has the same name as the Active Directory domain and that it is configured to allow dynamic updates. Also make sure that the server has a static IP address. To make sure that the domain allows dynamic updates, start the DNS manager and right-click the zone name you want to verify. From the shortcut menu, select Properties. On the General tab's Dynamic Updates selection, make sure that either Nonsecure And Secure or Secure Only is selected, as shown in **Figure B**.

Restart DNS services to make the changes take effect. If this doesn't work, stop and restart the netlogon service to force the records to be reregistered.

Incorrect name resolution is taking place

Incorrect name resolution can wreck your whole day as it can be a bear to track down. When it happens, you can't get to where you need to go, services break, and your users are generally not pleased.

With Windows Server 2003's DNS service, there are some common causes of this problem. The first thing to check is that a mistake wasn't made in a manual entry for a DNS record. It's easy to transpose the numbers in an IP address! This information can be verified by performing an nslookup on the name in question and verifying the address, or by checking it using the DNS manager.

Second, there could be a stale entry in the DNS server cache that is causing your problem. The DNS server cache can be cleared in a couple of ways: (1) using the DNS console or (2) using the command line. To clear the DNS server cache using the DNS server console, open up the DNS manager and right-click the DNS server. From the shortcut menu, select Clear Cache, as shown in **Figure C**.

Alternatively, you can use the command line to perform the same action. To do this, type *dnscmd ServerName /clearcache* at the command line replacing 'ServerName' with the name of the server whose DNS cache you need to clear.

Figure C

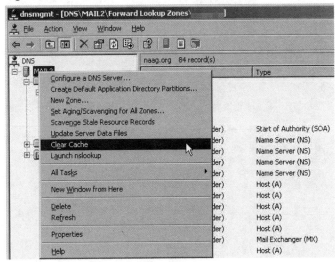

Clearing the DNS server cache from the GUI

Is the problem limited to resources outside your network?

If you're having problems resolving resources outside your network, make sure that the DNS forwarders on the local DNS server are properly configured, as discussed earlier in this article.

DNS server is not responding

Probably the easiest type of problem to diagnose is a situation in which the DNS

Figure D

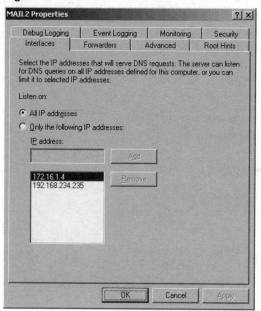

The DNS server listening interface configuration

server isn't responding to clients at all. A consistent problem is always easier to solve than an intermittent problem or a problem where the cause is difficult to determine.

The most obvious potential problem lies with the DNS server service itself. Make sure it's running! If it's not running, it's going to have a really hard time serving clients!

Second, make sure that the DNS server service is bound to an IP address on which the client's request can be answered. If you've configured your DNS server to only listen on an interface that is different from the interface that your clients use, they will be unable to use the service.

This parameter is configured by right-clicking the name of your server in the DNS manager and selecting the Properties option. On the Interfaces tab, you can either select All IP Addresses or specify exactly which addresses the server should listen on, as shown in **Figure D**. Verify that the server is listening on the right address.

That's it!

Windows Server 2003's DNS service is robust and easy to administer but there may come a day when you'll run into a problem with it. These few tips will get you started on your troubleshooting endeavor and will hopefully cut down the time it takes to resolve a problem! ❖

Troubleshooting access to shared resources

By Scott Lowe, MCSE

Like previous versions of Windows server, Windows Server 2003 allows access to resources at a very granular level. This means that you can determine specifically who should be allowed access to a particular resource and be confident that only those intended to have access will in fact have access. One caveat: You'll need a thorough understanding of share permissions, NTFS permissions, and permissions inheritance. The following are problems you may run into that are related to accessing shared resources and some suggestions on how you might fix them.

The basics

When you run across a client that is unable to access a share point or a printer on your Windows Server 2003 system, the problem is generally in one of three areas: network connectivity, share permissions, and NTFS permissions.

Network connectivity

Network connectivity problems resulting in difficulty accessing shared resources could be located at either the client or the server. A symptom of a problem with network connectivity at the server level includes the inability for multiple clients to access a particular resource. In these instances, make sure that the network cable is properly attached to the server and to the network equipment and that the cable is good.

However, don't automatically assume there's a problem with the resource server if multiple clients can't access a resource, as the problem may be related to a problem with another network service such as DHCP. If the problem is only affecting a single client, also check the network cabling and hardware.

Networking services

If the physical network is good, there could be a problem with an IP address or another service such as DNS. First, if the server gets its IP address via DHCP, make sure that service is functioning properly. Likewise, make sure that DHCP related to clients is also working. Of course, if it's not, you'll usually know fairly quickly, since DHCP problems tend to result in complete outages rather than spots here and there.

Additionally, make sure that the server and client IP addresses and subnet masks are properly configured. If you've mistakenly assigned an IP address or subnet mask to a client or server that doesn't match the rest of the network, you'll never be able to access the shared resources until you correct the problem.

Finally, as Windows has matured as a product, it has grown ever more reliant on DNS. If client DNS settings are not configured correctly or the DNS service is not available, clients might have problems accessing services for shared resources that are dependent on the inaccessible DNS.

Share permissions

With potential physical problems and client configuration problems out of the way, you can start to focus on the resource itself to determine the cause of the problem. The first place to check is the share information, including shared permissions. If your users are having trouble writing to a shared folder, for example, make sure that the share permissions are configured to allow them to write files to the shared location.

When you create a new share on a new Windows Server 2003 installation, by default, the assigned permissions grant Read access to Everyone. To modify the default permissions, right-click the shared folder and choose Properties. On the properties page, click the Permissions button. You'll then see the screen shown in **Figure A**.

To assign (or deny) a specific permission for a user or group, select the user or group from Active Directory by clicking the Add button. To allow both Change and Read access, use Full Control. Otherwise, select the appropriate rights and click Apply.

A second potential problem related to share permissions is if you limit the number of concurrent users on a particular share. This is done on the Sharing tab on the properties page for the share. If you have some users that can access the share and others that can't, make sure the user count isn't set too low. In **Figure B**, the allowed user count is set to 10 concurrent users.

Figure A

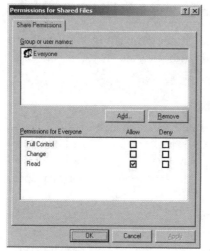

This share allows Everyone to read the files.

Figure B

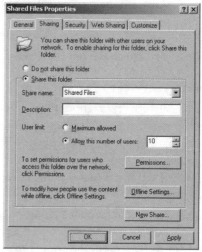

Concurrent user count for the share

To change the count, either select the Maximum Allowed setting or provide the number of users that should be able to access the share.

In many environments, administrators simply assign Full Control permission to all shares and then use NTFS permissions to lock down the files and folders. For these administrators, it's easier to keep track of one set of permissions than two.

NTFS

If users are either unable to access a resource or are allowed to do too much, NTFS permissions and inheritance settings are a good place to look. For this demonstration, I'm using a subfolder under a shared folder in the examples I'll go over with you. The parent folder is named Shared Folder while the subfolder inside this folder is named Subfolder.

Inheritance

If you've done any Active Directory or Novell Directory Services administration, the concept of inheritance should be familiar to you. NTFS also uses inheritance, as permissions from a parent folder flow down through the subfolder hierarchy. This means that a folder three levels down in the hierarchy will have the same permissions as the top-level folder unless explicit permissions have been assigned to subfolders or you've blocked permissions at some point.

Figure C shows the advanced security settings for subfolder. It also shows where the permissions came from. In many cases, in this example, the permissions were inherited from C:\.

If you want to disable these permissions from flowing down through the folder hierarchy, deselect the box Allow Inheritable Permissions From The Parent To Propagate To This Object And All Child Objects. Include These With The Entries Specified Here.

When you do this, you'll see a message box like the one in **Figure D** indicating that parent permissions will no longer be applied to this folder. You'll get two options. First, you can choose to copy the permissions and explicitly apply them to this folder, or you can choose to remove the inherited permissions and use only the explicitly assigned permissions.

Figure C

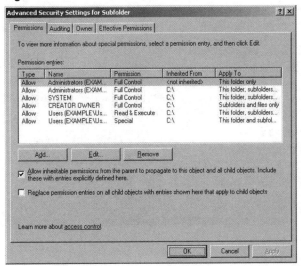

Permissions for subfolder

Figure D

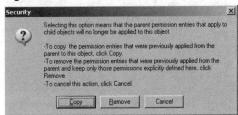

You can choose to either copy or remove the inherited permissions.

In **Figure E** below, I've opted to remove the inherited permissions.

The second option you have related to inheritance is to apply the permissions from the current folder to all subfolders. This is accomplished by selecting the box marked Replace Permission Entries On All Child Objects With Entries Shown Here That Apply To Child Objects. This is useful in cases where you've been working on permissions on a child object and totally screwed them up. It, at least, gives you a baseline with which to start.

Figure E

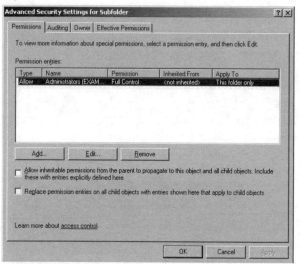

The inherited permissions have been removed from subfolder.

Permissions

NTFS permissions are pretty easy to troubleshoot. Either a user has rights or he doesn't. A very quick way to determine if a user is allowed access to a resource is to determine that user's effective permissions for the resource, including how inheritance affects the user's permissions. In Windows Server 2003, this is a quick task with the help of the Effective Permissions tool available on the advanced security settings screen for a resource.

To see the effective permissions tab, right-click a resource and select Properties. From the Security tab on the window, click the Advanced button and select the Effective Permissions tab. You'll then see the screen shown in **Figure F**.

Figure F

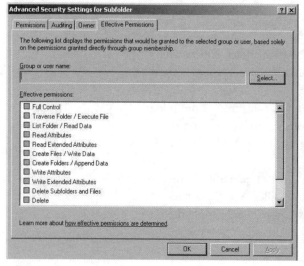

The Effective Permissions tab

Figure G

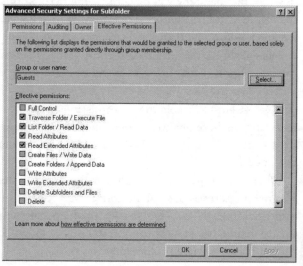

Effective permissions for Guests

Once you're on this tab, to see the effective permissions for a particular user, click the Select button and choose the user or group for which you would like to see the effective permissions. In **Figure G**, I have shown the effective permissions for the Guests group.

A method before your madness

In a few places—and particularly with the help of the Effective Permissions tool—you can quickly isolate the cause of an access problem on a shared resource. First, track down the scope of the problem and figure out if anything was recently changed. After that, look at the network and share permissions for wide scope problems and the NTFS permissions and inheritance for smaller scopes. ❖

NOTES:

Wireless Networking

How to select the right wireless hardware for your home network

If you're thinking about setting up a wireless connection on your home network, you have some homework to do before you'll be ready to make the leap. For starters, you have two choices, depending on whether you already have an existing broadband home network or whether you're starting from scratch. If you already have an existing home network and want to add a wireless connection to it, you'll just need a Wireless Access Point (WAP). If you're building a broadband home network from scratch and want to add wireless connections, you'll want to look at getting a wireless broadband router.

In this chapter, we'll examine each of these wireless options in detail. As we do, we'll help you decipher the technical terminology associated with wireless networking, and we'll discuss examples of some available products.

How wireless networking works

If you're new to wireless networking, you probably have a lot of questions, with the biggest one being how does it work. Well, wireless networking is simpler than you might think.

The easiest way to grasp the technology is to compare it to the little walkie-talkie sets that you played with as a kid. Each person has a portable handset unit with an antenna that allows each of them to wirelessly send and receive voice messages. You speak into a walkie-talkie, which converts your voice into radio waves and broadcasts them out over a small area. The antenna on the other walkie-talkie receives those broadcast radio waves and converts them back into voice waves that are then played on the walkie-talkie's speaker. The devices have a set range that allows users to communicate while they roam a relatively small area.

The principle is the same in wireless networking, except you're sending and receiving data instead of voice signals. Data travels to a wireless network device, where it is converted into radio waves and broadcast to a relatively small area. Another wireless device receives those radio waves and converts them back into data.

On one end of the communication you have a base station, or WAP, that is physically attached to the network via a standard network cable. On the other end you have a wireless network card that will be connected to a desktop computer via a standard PCI slot, just like any other card. In the case of a laptop computer, the wireless network card could be in the form of a PCMCIA card with an attached antenna. Or the wireless network card could be built in to the laptop, with the antenna embedded into the lid on either side of the screen. Alternatively, you can also get wireless network adapters that attach to your computer's USB port.

Understanding wireless terminology

When you begin investigating wireless networking, you'll want to be familiar with wireless terminology, mainly in regard to wireless specifications or standards. These standards are designated by the number 802.11, along with a letter appended to it. The 802.11 designation is simply a number that was assigned to the wireless technology when the Institute of Electrical and Electronic Engineers (IEEE) began working on the project in the late '90s. Since the initial standard was finalized in June of 1997, several revisions have been made to the 802.11 standard, and that's where the letters come from. The revisions you'll run into when investigating wireless technology are *a* and *b*.

The 802.11b standard is the most common specification for consumer-oriented wireless products. It's also taken on a user-friendlier name, *WiFi*, which is short for Wireless Fidelity. In addition to the user-friendly name, the WiFi moniker specifies products that are completely compatible with each other; a wireless product from one manufacturer that carries the WiFi logo will work with any other manufacturer's products that also carry the WiFi logo. Furthermore, WiFi products are priced within the reach of the average consumer (more on pricing in a moment).

Wireless networking products marked as 802.11b, or WiFi, work in the 2.4GHz band, have a maximum transmission speed of 11Mbps, and operate in a range of around 100 feet indoors. If the WAP has a direct line of sight to the outdoors, the operating range at 11Mbps jumps to 500 feet. Of course, you can still get a connection beyond 100/500 feet, but transmission speeds drop off.

The 802.11a standard is the most common specification for business-oriented wireless products. Wireless devices that use the 802.11a specification work in the 5GHz band and have a maximum transmission speed of 54Mbps. They also have an indoor operating range of around 300 feet and an outdoor range of a little over 1,100 feet. As you can imagine, the cost of 802.11a equipment is typically more than the average consumer wants to spend.

The stand-alone WAP

As we mentioned earlier, if you already have an existing home network and want to add wireless networking, you'll just need to add a WAP to your network. A WAP physically connects to your home network's hub or switch via a standard network cable. The WAP then allows a computer equipped with a wireless network card to communicate with the network. You can get a basic WAP for anywhere from $100 to $200 from companies such as LinkSys, U.S. Robotics, 3COM, Belkin, D-Link, and Netgear.

The broadband router/WAP combination

If you're just starting out and are building a broadband home network from scratch, your best bet is to get a broadband router/WAP combination. As you can imagine, these devices provide all the same features as a broadband router and also function as a WAP. (For more information on the function of a broadband router, see our discussion of that topic earlier in this book.) You can get a broadband router WAP combination for anywhere from $100 to $300 from leading vendors, including those we mentioned above.

The wireless network card

If you'll be connecting desktop PCs to your wireless network, you'll need to get wireless PCI network cards for each system. These range in price from $10 to $50. If you'll be connecting a laptop to your wireless network, you'll need to get a wireless PCMCIA network card. You can spend anywhere from $25 to $90 for this upgrade.

If you don't want to mess around with opening up your desktop PC or with PCMCIA cards for your laptop, you can get a USB wireless network adapter for around $50.

If you're purchasing a new laptop to connect to your wireless network, you should ask the manufacturer about getting a built-in wireless adapter. Not only will this save you from having to insert and remove your wireless network device all the time, but you'll also find that the built-in antenna is more powerful than those used in the typical wireless networking PCMCIA card.

Depending on where you shop for your wireless networking devices, you may be able to track down a bundle deal that provides both the WAP and a set of wireless network cards. ❖

Windows XP offers groundbreaking WLAN functionality

By Jason Hiner, MCSE, CCNA

Imagine that you're working on an important new project. You took your laptop home last night so that you could surf for some cool pictures to download and add to the PowerPoint presentation you created for today's meeting. This morning, you bring your laptop into work, pop it into its docking station, and make a few last-minute additions and corrections to the presentation. At 8:55, you pop your laptop out and head down to the meeting, where you hook it to the projector, make your PowerPoint presentation, and then surf through a few competitors' Web sites to give your peers a better idea of what you're talking about.

After the meeting, you and your laptop take the half-mile walk over to the building where your CTO has her office. You meet with the CTO and give her the abridged version of the presentation, surfing a couple of competitors' Web sites to give her some examples.

Finally, at the end of the day, you take two of your company's developers out for a cup of coffee at Starbucks, where the three of you sit down—with your laptops, of course—and discuss some of the technical details of your proposal. Unfortunately, one of the developers forgot to print out an important document that the three of you were going to discuss. No problem. You simply make a VPN connection to the office and grab the document off the file server and then you e-mail it to the other two developers, who receive the file in less than a minute.

In this scenario, you roamed across four networks in five physical locations. If your laptop had been configured with Windows XP and a wireless network card, you would have had network connectivity at each stop and, better yet, you would not have had to do any reconfiguration as you roamed to each place. Of course, this assumes that each location had connectivity to a wireless access point, but with the rapidly declining prices of wireless hardware and the adoption of WLANs in corporations and public spots such as Starbucks, this is definitely a plausible scenario.

Wireless LANs in Windows XP

The kind of network roaming depicted in this example would have been much more difficult (impossible in most cases) in Windows 2000 and other versions of Windows. That's because in Win2K, wireless networking configuration is handled primarily by third-party utilities that are installed along with WLAN network card drivers that come from WLAN vendors. The best part of Windows XP's enhanced WLAN support is that driver and WLAN configuration are absorbed directly into

XP's NIC configuration, and WLAN network roaming is handled with precision and simplicity.

Here are the three major improvements that make WLANs work so well in Windows XP:

- **Zero configuration**—The third-party drivers and WLAN configuration utilities used with previous versions of Windows can be described as inelegant, at best. Windows XP makes the process much simpler by automatically recognizing almost all WLAN network cards (eliminating the need for third-party drivers). To configure the WLAN, you simply go into the Properties for the network card, where you will automatically find an extra tab named Wireless Networks. There you can choose from among available networks or manually configure preferred networks. This network configuration is smart, too. For example, it automatically detects when a wireless access point changes its channel ID, and if the system plugs into a 100Base-TX landline connection, it tells the system to use that connection rather than the slower (11-Mbs) WLAN connection.

- **WLAN roaming**—Our scenario showed an example of the kind of roaming that's possible with the combination of WLANs and Windows XP. Multiple preferred networks can be configured in the XP Wireless Networks tab. This can even include options in which some of these networks use static IP addresses, while others rely on DHCP. Of course, the real coup is the fact that you do not have to reboot your machine, select any menu options, or perform any configuration activities. Once you have WLANs specified in your preferred networks, you can leave your laptop running and simply move from one WLAN network to the next. Your laptop will automatically change network configuration.

- **Better and easier security**—Of course, no conversation about WLANs is complete without giving some attention to security. Fortunately, Windows XP also builds in measures that can make WLANs more secure and that greatly simplify security configuration for administrators. XP implements support for Wireless Encryption Privacy (WEP) and IEEE 802.1x, which provides port-based, authenticated network access for wireless networks (although it can also be used for standard wired networks). Basically, the latter is built into network card configuration, and it makes it easy to configure RADIUS authentication, smart card authentication, certification management, and other standard security protocols that handle identity management and keep intruders from being able to infringe on corporate WLANs.

Bottom line

Windows XP takes WLANs to the next level of functionality in a way that no single WLAN vendor ever has. Better yet, XP does not care what brand of WLAN network card you are using. It recognizes virtually every WLAN card available and simplifies their configuration into standard operating system menus. ❖

XP UPGRADE CAUTION
One word of warning about zero configuration: If you have a pre-Windows XP system on which you have installed a WLAN driver and utility, you need to uninstall that software before you upgrade that system to XP. Otherwise, there can be some conflicts, and you will probably encounter some errors and problems when attempting to use your WLAN card in XP.

Configuring a wireless LAN connection in Windows XP

By Jason Hiner, MCSE, CCNA

I love it when things work like they're supposed to!" That has long been my favorite little catch phrase when setting up and configuring new IT solutions. Sadly enough, that phrase has become even more special to me because it's so rarely that I actually get to say it when working with today's technologies.

However, I was able to enthusiastically utter this phrase when configuring a wireless LAN connection using Windows XP. As I wrote in "Windows XP offers groundbreaking WLAN functionality," the most valuable new feature of Windows XP is the way that it seamlessly handles WLAN configuration and roaming. Now it's time to walk you through the process of setting up a WLAN network card in XP to prove just how intuitive it is.

Install the WLAN network card

Of course, the first thing to do is pop a WLAN network adapter into your system—and it's still best to do this while the system is shut down. In most cases, you'll probably be putting a PC Card adapter into a laptop system. However, there are also PCI and USB adapters for desktop systems.

For this example, I am installing an ORiNOCO Gold PC Card into a Dell laptop. I chose the ORiNOCO card because it had good reviews from industry experts and buyers, and I was happy with the choice; the card proved to have excellent range while holding a strong signal. I highly recommend the card for corporate installs.

In my case, Windows XP was already installed on the system before I added the WLAN network adapter, but for the purposes of this tutorial, you will achieve the same effect by installing the WLAN card before loading Windows XP. If you had already installed a WLAN card (and its drivers and utilities) in a previous version of Windows, and you are now upgrading to XP, you need to watch out for a gotcha: Before upgrading to XP, uninstall the drivers and utilities that came with the WLAN card. If you don't, you could run into some errors and conflicts with your WLAN configuration when you upgrade to XP.

Verify that XP recognizes the WLAN card

Once you power on your system, Windows XP should automatically recognize your WLAN card. (It has a vast database of WLAN adapter drivers built in.) After the card is recognized, Windows will automatically add it to the list of available interfaces in Network Connections. To verify this:

Figure A

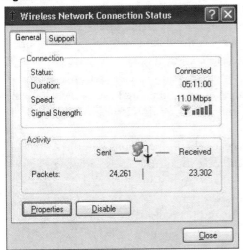

The WLAN status box shows the signal strength of the wireless connection.

1. Click Start | Control Panel.

2. Click Network And Internet Connections.

3. Click Network Connections.

You should then see an icon that says Wireless Network Connection. Double-click that icon to bring up the Wireless Network Connection Status dialog box (**Figure A**). This should look familiar. It's basically the same as the Local Area Connection Status dialog box you see when you double-click on a standard Ethernet NIC, but there's one distinction. The wireless version has a nice little graphic with green bars to show the signal strength of your radio wave connection.

Configuring wireless networks

When you're ready to configure your WLAN settings, click the Properties button. This will bring up the network settings properties (**Figure B**) that you're probably familiar with. They're the same as the network properties for a standard Ethernet NIC, but with one important addition: When you are configuring a WLAN network card, you will see a tab called Wireless Networks.

Figure B

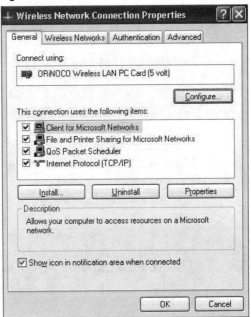

WLAN adapters have an additional configuration tab, Wireless Networks.

Figure C

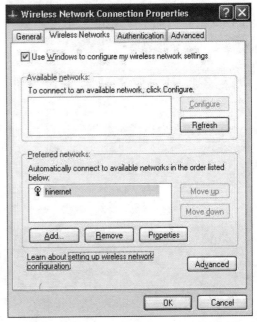

The Wireless Networks tab is where you handle WLAN setup.

Click on this tab, as we've done in **Figure C**. Now you can configure your WLAN adapter to connect to various wireless access points (WAPs).

First, you'll need to make sure the Use Windows To Configure My Wireless Network Settings check box is selected. (This is the default setting.) You'll notice that there are two sections to this tab: Available Networks and Preferred Networks. In the Preferred Networks section, you can manually set up a connection to a WAP by clicking the Add button. You can then enter the Network Name (SSID) for the access point and set up Wireless Encryption Privacy (WEP), as shown in **Figure D**.

Another way to connect to a WAP is to click the Refresh button in the Available Networks section. Windows will go out and look for nearby access points and give you a list of them. Just click on the one you want to use and then click Configure. This will pull up the same Wireless Network Properties screen that you saw in Figure D, only the network name will automatically be displayed. After you tinker with the settings and click OK, the WAP will be placed on your list of Preferred Networks.

Now when you roam to new locations (especially ones that you'll probably be returning to later), you can simply let Available Networks find the access points, and you can add them to your preferred networks with a few clicks. When you return to that location, your laptop should then automatically connect you to the WAP, and you'll have network access without having to do any special reconfiguration.

If you have multiple access points in a single location, you can add them all to your Preferred Networks list and simply use the Move Up and Move Down buttons to prioritize them.

Figure D

The Wireless Network Properties screen enables you to set up a connection to an access point.

There's one more setting you should be aware of on this screen, which you can access by clicking the Advanced button. Here, you set your preference in terms of connecting to WLANs powered by access points or connecting to peer-to-peer WLANs (basically just connecting to other client machines that have WLAN network adapters installed). You also have a third option of connecting to Any Available Network, which will show you both of these categories. Obviously, in a corporate environment, you'll probably want to rely on access points. You'll also probably want to leave the Automatically Connect To Non-Preferred Networks check box deselected.

WLAN authentication and security

Another nice feature of the Windows XP implementation of WLANs is that it has built-in support for IEEE 802.1x security. This makes it easy to require identity verification for WLAN adapters via a variety of standard authentication mechanisms, including RADIUS, smart cards, and certificates. This can be configured on the Authentication tab (**Figure E**) of the network adapter's properties page.

It's important to note that 802.1x security is not limited to WLANs. It can be used for standard 10/100 Ethernet connections as well.

Basic monitoring and troubleshooting

Once you make your WLAN connection, you can easily monitor the reception and bandwidth of your connection. First, go into the properties of your WLAN network adapter (which appears in Figure B). Then, select the Show Icon In Notification Area When Connected check box. This will put a small icon with two computers in the system tray (in the lower-right corner of your screen). The icon will change colors when data is being sent over this network interface. (The little computer screens change from navy blue to sky blue when data is moving.) When you hover your mouse over this icon, you'll see a screen tip displaying connection information. This includes the name of the wireless network that you are connected to (usually the WAP), the connection speed (in Mbps), and the signal strength of your radio wave connection (from Very Low to Excellent).

Summary

All in all, Windows XP greatly streamlines the configuration and implementation of WLANs. In addition, it improves functionality (especially roaming) and makes it easier to implement security features such as WEP and RADIUS. To my surprise, I even found that the WLAN client software that's built into XP is superior to the third-party drivers and utilities that come with WLAN cards for use in older versions of Windows. I found that in XP, the WLAN cards have an easier time locating and holding wireless connections, and they don't suffer from as many inconsistencies and hiccups.

I have not been a huge fan of XP. However, its WLAN implementation is the one area where XP is head-and-shoulders above all previous versions of Windows client operating systems. If you want to configure laptops for extensive use of WLANs, you should definitely consider upgrading them to XP, especially if they are going to be roaming among different access points and/or different physical locations. ❖

Figure E

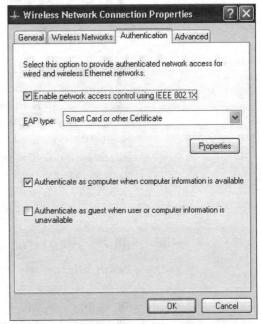

The Authentication tab makes it easy to configure 802.1x security.

The pitfalls of MAC filtering

By William C. Schmied

If you're familiar with 802.11b wireless networking, you've no doubt heard the horror stories about how weak Wired Equivalent Privacy (WEP) is. In the rush to move away from WEP and its supposed weakness, many organizations have implemented Media Access Control (MAC) filtering as their sole wireless access point (WAP) security measure. What they may not know is that MAC filtering is extremely ineffective as a sole security measure. In reality, relying on MAC filtering to protect your wireless network is pretty much the same as leaving the front door open and asking an intruder to come on in and stay a while. In this chapter, I'll show you how MAC filtering works and describe some of its pitfalls.

MAC filtering basics

Before I discuss why MAC filters aren't the perfect security solution, let's examine what MAC filters are and how they work. MAC filtering is the process of configuring an access point with a list of MAC addresses that will either be allowed or not allowed to gain access to the rest of the network via that WAP. The most common configuration has a list of allowed MAC addresses—the trusted and known MAC addresses that are supposed to be on the wireless LAN.

Exactly where you enter the allowed MAC addresses varies, depending on the WAP you use. Normally you'll enter this information into the WAP's configuration utility, usually from a Web-based interface, although you can also do it from a console session or some other form of remote control. No matter how it's done, the end result is a list of MAC addresses that you use to allow or disallow access.

In **Figure A**, which was generated from a Cisco 1200 AP, you can see quite a few clients making connections to the WAP. Some are merely authenticated, while others are completely associated. In wireless-speak, "to authenticate to a WAP" simply means to announce your identity to the other station—in this case, the AP.

Figure A

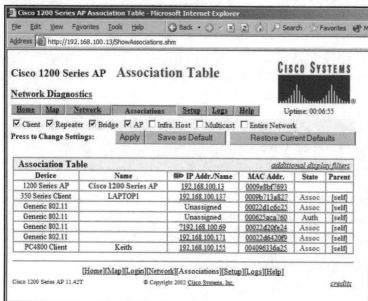

Clients can be either authenticated or associated.

Authentication can take place using either open system or shared key (WEP) methods. To be associated with a WAP implies that the client is fully connected to the WAP and is now allowed to pass traffic through the AP. In short, the client now has complete access to the rest of the network, both wireless and wired. MAC filters act to keep unauthorized clients from becoming associated with the WAP.

An open door to intruders

The problem comes when an intruder wants to gain access to your network and has decided to sniff your wireless network traffic. Sitting in your parking lot or some other easily accessible location, an intruder armed with the right hardware and software can easily sniff your wireless network and capture all packets sent to and from your access points. The captured data packets contain all the information the intruder needs to make a connection to your wireless LAN. This information includes the following:

- Authorized MAC addresses
- IP addresses
- IP subnets
- Wireless LAN SSIDs

The intruder can easily configure a wireless device with a captured IP address and subnet in the device's TCP/IP Properties window. Configuring captured SSIDs varies from one type of NIC to another, but it's done from within the configuration software provided with the NIC—again, a very easy configuration to make.

The tricky part comes in spoofing the MAC address itself. However, even an unskilled attacker can spoof a MAC address by making one quick registry edit. Using the Registry Editor, all the attacker has to do is check the value of the NetworkAddress key, as shown in **Figure B**.

If the NetworkAddress string value doesn't already exist for the NIC, or if it's blank, Windows reads the MAC address from the NIC's firmware. Entering a captured MAC address into the NetworkAddress string value for the rogue NIC tells Windows to use this MAC address for all communications emanating from the NIC. This registry setting only works if the NIC in the attacker's wireless device uses a PCI bus. This rules out most Flash Card-based NICs, but all PCMCIA cards, which appear on most laptops, use this bus.

Figure B

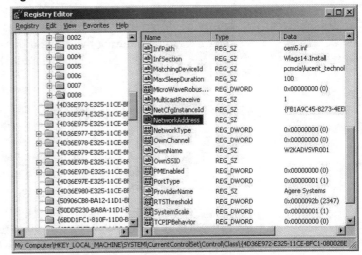

A place to reconfigure the MAC address of the rogue NIC

After reconfiguring the rogue NIC with the stolen MAC address of an authorized client, the intruder will be able to seamlessly associate with the WAP, which knows no different and is doing its job as it was configured to. If an attacker steals the MAC address during the day and doesn't use it until later—after the authorized user has left for the day—then the odds that the intruder will ever be caught are small.

Defense in depth

Just about all 802.11b access points support MAC filtering in addition to WEP. When used together, they form a pretty good security solution that will stop all but the most experienced and determined intruders. But MAC filtering alone won't cut it—even a relatively inexperienced attacker can get by it in 10 minutes or so.

So what do you do if you're responsible for a SOHO wireless network? You basically have two choices: 1) upgrade to wireless hardware that supports the Temporal Key Integrity Protocol (TKIP), which provides strengthening corrections for WEP, or 2) implement security by using both WEP and MAC filtering. For large, enterprise-level solutions, you should talk to your hardware vendor for a supported solution that increases your security. No matter what you do, don't go another day relying on only MAC filtering to keep intruders out of your network. ❖

Six quick wireless security tips

By Scott Lowe, MCSE

Implementing a wireless networking system can result in serious security problems if the system is not properly secured. This is true of a wireless network deployed at home or one deployed in the office. In fact, some residential Internet service providers have clauses in their agreements that indicate that service is not to be shared with people outside of those covered by the agreement. If you deploy an insecure wireless network, it could result in a loss of service, or in the use of your network as a launching pad for attacks against other networks. To help you close these security holes, here are six quick wireless networking tips.

Why do I want to close the loop?

The point of properly securing a wireless access point is to close off the network from outsiders who do not have authorization to use your services. A properly secured access point is said to be "closed" to outsiders. A wireless network is more difficult to secure than a typical wired network due to its nature. A wired network has a limited number of fixed physical points of access while a wireless network can be used at any point within the range of the antennas.

Plan antenna placement

The first step in implementing a closed wireless access point is to place the access point's antenna in such a way that it limits how much the signal can reach areas outside the coverage area. Don't place the antenna near a window, as the glass does not block the signal. Ideally, your antenna will be placed in the center of the area you want covered with as little signal leaking outside the walls as possible. Of course, it's next to impossible to completely control this, so other measures need to be taken as well.

Use WEP

Wireless encryption protocol (WEP) is a standard method to encrypt traffic over a wireless network. While it has major weaknesses, it *is* useful in deterring casual hackers. Many wireless access point vendors ship their units with WEP disabled in order to make the product installation easier. This practice gives hackers immediate access to the traffic on a wireless network as soon as it goes into production since the data is directly readable with a wireless sniffer.

Change the SSID and disable its broadcast

The Service Set Identifier (SSID) is the identification string used by the wireless access point by which clients are able to initiate connections. This identifier is set by the manufacturer and each one uses a default phrase, such as "101" for 3Com devices. Hackers that know these pass phrases can easily make unauthorized use of your wireless services. For each wireless access point you deploy, choose a unique and difficult-to-guess SSID, and, if possible, suppress the broadcast of this identifier out over the antenna so that your network is not broadcast for use. It will still be usable, but it won't show up in a list of available networks.

Disable DHCP

At first, this may sound like a strange security tactic, but for wireless networks, it makes sense. With this step, hackers would be forced to decipher your IP address, subnet mask, and other required TCP/IP parameters. If a hacker is able to make use of your access point for whatever reason, he or she will still need to figure out your IP addressing as well.

Disable or modify SNMP settings

If your access point supports SNMP, either disable it or change both the public and private community strings. If you don't take this step, hackers can use SNMP to gain important information about your network.

Use access lists

To further lock down your wireless network, implement an access list, if possible. Not all wireless access points support this feature, but if yours does, it will allow you to specify exactly what machines are allowed to connect to your access point. The access points that support this feature can sometimes use Trivial File Transfer Protocol (TFTP) to periodically download updated lists in order to prevent the administrative nightmare of having to sync these lists on every unit. ❖

XP client configuration for enhanced security on a Linksys wireless network

By Lauri Elliott

Chances are that some of your clients will be migrating from Windows 98 or 2000 to Windows XP this year. If your clients have a wireless network, you'll obviously want to take advantage of the security features offered in both the OS and the wireless network equipment. If, for example, you've configured a Linksys wireless network, the next step is to configure the Windows XP client—a topic I'll cover in this article.

(**Note:** This article assumes that you have successfully installed the device driver for the Linksys network adapter and connected to the wireless network before applying the security enhancements.)

Configure wireless network adapter in Windows XP

Because of wired equivalent protocol (WEP), Windows XP's wireless zero configuration utility (WZC) (**www.win2000mag.net/Articles/Index.cfm?ArticleID=23294**) will not be able to automatically connect the wireless network. Therefore, you will need to set some additional options in Windows XP. To make these changes, you'll need to:

- Double-click the network connection icon for the wireless network in your system tray on the desktop.
- Click the Advanced button at the bottom-left corner of the Wireless Network Connection dialog box (see **Figure A**).
- To add the wireless network as a preferred network, click the Add button in the Preferred Network section. You'll then see the screen shown in **Figure B**.
- Type the service set identifier (SSID) for the wireless network in the Network Name field.
- Check the Data Encryption (WEP Enabled) check box.
- Check the Network Authentication (Shared Mode) check box.

Figure A

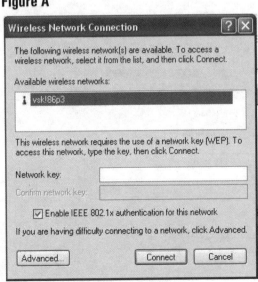

Figure B

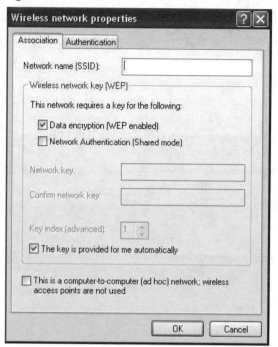

Figure C

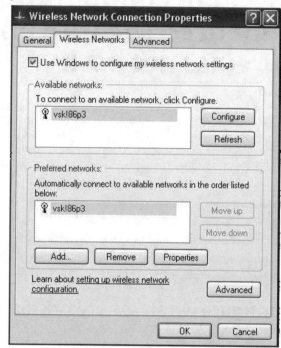

Figure D

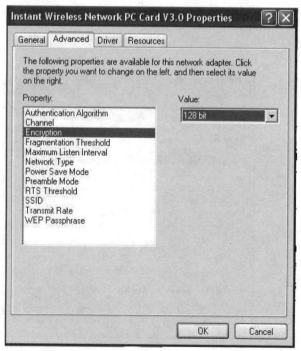

- Check The Key Is Provided For Me Automatically check box. (If you still have problems connecting to the wireless network, uncheck this option, then type in the first key generated by the WEP passphrase. You can get this information from the WEP Settings page in the Web-based administration utility for the access point.)

Problem locating the wireless network

Once you turn off the SSID broadcasting, clients might not be able to locate or connect to the wireless network. I discovered this problem with Linksys PCMCIA network adapters (WPC11 version 3). Linksys says this happens because WZC does not support disabling SSID broadcasting. Therefore, this is a problem you might find with any Linksys network adapter that supports WZC.

Both Microsoft and Linksys indicate this is a problem, but they offer few workarounds. Linksys recommends that you use earlier versions of Linksys network adapters, e.g., WPC version 2.5, that do not support WZC.

Disable the WZC utility

The WZC service is not a requirement for a successful wireless network connection in XP. You can disable the service and get a slight improvement in system performance. To turn off the Windows XP WZC, do the following:

1. Right-click the My Network Places icon on your Windows desktop.
2. Choose the Properties option.
3. Right-click the network connection for the wireless network adapter.
4. Choose the Properties option.
5. Click the Wireless Networks tab.
6. Uncheck the Use Windows To Configure My Wireless Network Settings option (see **Figure C**).

You can turn off this feature entirely by disabling the WZC service in the Services Manager.

Device settings

When you disable WZC, you need to configure the wireless network connection options on the device profile. To access the device settings to be changed, as shown in **Figure D**, you need to:

1. Right-click the My Computer icon on your Windows desktop.
2. Choose the Properties option.
3. Click the Hardware tab.
4. Click the Device Manager button in the Device Manager section.
5. Under the network adapters branch, right-click the Linksys wireless network adapter profile.
6. Choose the Properties option.
7. Click the Advanced tab.
8. Change the values for specific properties defined for the network adapter. The values to change are Encryption, SSID, and WEP Passphrase. Each should match the settings you defined on the access point.

Cutting down on the administrative headaches

In conjunction with these tips, there are a few techniques you can employ to reduce your share of administrative overhead:

1. Create a suborganizational unit just for Windows XP systems. (Windows XP has additional registry settings and policies that Windows 2000 does not.)

2. To make management cleaner, you can apply a group policy on an organizational unit that affects all computers for settings that would apply to all client computers in your environment. Then, create the suborganizational unit for Windows XP clients to manage only the XP-related settings. One of these settings can be for the WZC in the registry.

3. Customize an administrative template just for Windows XP systems. This administrative template will be attached to group policy on the suborganizational unit for just XP systems. To learn how to do this, check out the Microsoft TechNet article "Implementing Registry-Based Group Policy for Applications" (**www.microsoft.com/technet/treeview/default.asp? url=/TechNet/prodtechnol/windows2000serv/deploy/regappgp.asp**) and the Microsoft Knowledge Base Article "HOW TO: Create Custom Administrative Templates in Windows 2000" (**http://support.microsoft.com/default.aspx? scid=kb;en-us;323639**).

4. Add the WZC service as an option in the customized administrative template. This will then be applied to all XP systems in the organizational unit.

5. Use AutoIt (**www.hiddensoft.com**) to automate configuring device settings. This free application records keystrokes in Windows. You could record the keystrokes on the first system configured, then create a script to use with other systems. ❖

Fix hardware and configuration issues common to wireless LANs

By Brien M. Posey, MCSE

With decreasing prices of wireless hardware, wireless networks are fast becoming more popular in small office networks. Both the money savings and the ease-of-use of wireless LANs are beneficial to the small office—until something goes wrong. Then it becomes all too apparent that, while wireless networks are growing, troubleshooting resources for wireless LANs are not.

When a wireless network fails, there are a few key areas to look to first. In this article, I'll discuss some of the more common hardware problems that can cause a wireless network to fail. As well, I'll cover the configuration issues that can also plague a wireless LAN. With this information, you can troubleshoot your wireless network with confidence. (This article assumes that you're troubleshooting an infrastructure network, and not an Ad Hoc network.)

Hardware troubleshooting

When you have only one access point and only one wireless client that are having connection issues, then you've already determined the scope of the problem. It's your one client that is having trouble attaching to the network. However, if you've got a larger network, then the process of determining the scope of the problem becomes a little more involved.

If lots of users are having trouble connecting, but there are still some users who are able to work, the problem is most likely that your network has multiple access points and that one of the access points is malfunctioning. Often, you can take an educated guess as to which access point is malfunctioning by looking at the physical locations of the users who are having the problem, and then figuring out which access point serves that portion of the building.

If no one can connect to the wireless network, then there are several things that could be going on. If your network uses a single wireless access point, one possibility is that the access point could be malfunctioning or could contain a configuration error. The problem could also be related to radio interference or to a break in the physical link between the wireless access point and the wired network.

Check connectivity to the access point

First, you should perform a communications test to see if the access point is responding. To do so, open a Command Prompt window on a PC on your wired network and ping your wireless access point's IP address. The wireless access point should respond to the ping. If it doesn't, there's either a break in the communications link or the access point is completely malfunctioning.

To figure out which is the case, try pinging the access point's IP address from a wireless client. If the wireless client is able to ping the access point successfully, then the problem is almost certainly a broken communications link, such as a damaged cable.

If the wireless client is unable to ping the access point, then the access point could be malfunctioning. Try unplugging the access point to reset it and then plug it in again. Wait for about five minutes and then try pinging the access point from both the wireless and the wired clients again.

If both pings still fail, then it is likely that the access point is damaged or has an invalid configuration. At this point, I recommend focusing your initial efforts on getting the access point to communicate with the wired network. Plug the access point into a known-good network jack using a known-working patch cable. You should also verify the access point's TCP/IP configuration. After doing so, try pinging the device from a wired client again. If the ping still fails, then the unit has probably been damaged and should be replaced.

Configuration issues

I've found that wireless networking equipment is fairly reliable, and the vast majority of problems are related to the network's configuration rather than to a hardware malfunction. With this in mind, I'll discuss several common hardware configuration problems that lead to a disruption of wireless services.

Test the signal strength

If you can ping the wireless access point from a wired client, but not from a wireless client, then the access point is probably just experiencing a temporary problem. If the access point continues to have problems, I recommend checking the signal strength. Unfortunately, there's no standard method for doing this. Most wireless NIC manufacturers, however, include some mechanism with the NIC for measuring signal strength.

Try changing channels

If you determine that you're getting a weak signal, but nothing has physically changed in your office, then I recommend attempting to change channels on the access point and on one wireless client to see if a different channel improves the signal strength. I run a wireless network in my home office, and I've found that one of my cordless phones interferes with my wireless network when the phone is in use. The 802.11b wireless networks function on the 2.4-GHz frequency, just like many higher-end cordless phones. Changing channels on all of your wireless clients can be a big undertaking. Therefore, I recommend testing the new channel with one client first. Remember that your problem could go away as soon as someone hangs up a phone or turns off a microwave oven.

Verify the SSID

Awhile back, I took my laptop to a friend's house to work. Because my friend had a wireless network in place, I decided to connect to his network for the duration of my visit. Upon returning home, I didn't use my laptop for a couple of weeks. The next time that I went to use my laptop, it wouldn't connect to my network. The problem was that I had forgotten to reset the SSID (Service Set Identifier) back to my own network identifier. Remember, if the SSID doesn't specify the correct network, then you won't be able to ping the access point. Instead, your laptop will ignore the access point's existence and search for an access point with the specified SSID.

Verify the WEP key

I recommend checking out the wired equivalent privacy (WEP) encryption configuration next. If WEP is configured incorrectly, you will not be able to ping the access point from a wireless client. Different brands of NICs and access points require you to specify the WEP encryption key differently. For example, one brand requires you to enter the encryption key in hex format, while another brand requires the key to be entered in decimal format. Likewise, some brands support 40-bit and 64-bit encryption, while other brands support only 128-bit encryption.

In order for WEP to function, all settings must match exactly between the client and the access point. I have run into several situations in which clients that seemed to be configured perfectly simply could not communicate with an access point that was using WEP. During these situations, I usually had to reset the access point to the factory defaults and reenter the WEP configuration information. Only then did WEP begin to function.

Tricky WEP configuration issues

By far the most common configuration-related problems involve the use of the WEP protocol, so WEP deserves some more discussion. Troubleshooting a WEP problem can be especially tricky, because a WEP mismatch has symptoms that are similar to a more serious failure. For example, if WEP is configured incorrectly, a wireless client won't be able to get an IP address from a DHCP server (even if the access point has a built-in DHCP server). If the wireless client is configured to use static IP addresses, the wireless client won't even be able to ping the access point's IP address, thus giving the illusion that no connection exists.

The trick to figuring out whether a problem is related to a WEP configuration error rather than a hardware malfunction is to be aware of the diagnostic capabilities built in to the NIC driver and in to the operating system. For example, one of my laptops is running Windows XP and has a Linksys wireless NIC. Notice in **Figure A** that if I move my mouse pointer over the top of the wireless icon in the taskbar, I see a summary of my connection information. In the figure, the connection strength is Excellent. As long as the channel and SSID are configured correctly, you can connect to the access point, even with a WEP configuration error. Had

Figure A

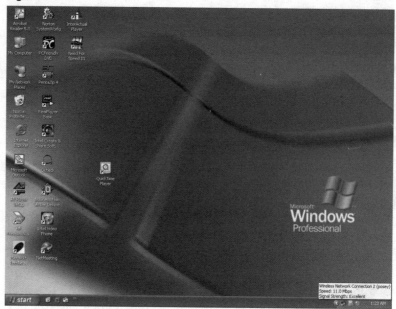

The signal strength is a big clue as to the nature of your problem.

there been a physical connection problem, the connection strength would be None, not Excellent. Linksys cards will show you the connection strength whether WEP is configured correctly or not. Therefore, you can validate that a connection exists, even if you can't ping the access point.

If you right-click on the wireless networking icon in the taskbar and select the View Available Wireless Networks command from the resulting menu, you'll see the Connect To Wireless Network dialog box. This dialog box displays the SSID of any wireless network on your present channel to which you are not currently connected. If the name of your wireless network shows up on this list but you can't seem to connect, then you can rest assured that your connection is good and that you've got a configuration problem.

DHCP configuration issues

Another tricky problem that can prevent you from successfully interacting with a wireless network is a DHCP configuration error. The DHCP server that you connect to can play a major role in whether you are able to use a wireless network.

Many of the newer access points have an integrated DHCP server. Typically, these access points assign the 192.168.0.x address range to clients. Often, DHCP access points will not accept connections from clients to which they have not issued an IP address. This means that clients with static IP addresses or clients that might have somehow acquired an IP address from another DHCP server could be unable to connect to the access point.

The first time that I installed an integrated DHCP server access point onto my network, I decided to allow the access point to assign IP addresses to my wireless clients. However, my network uses the 147.100.X.Y address range. This meant that although wireless clients were able to communicate with the access point and were able to acquire an IP address, they were unable to interact with the rest of my network because of the IP address range mismatch.

There are two solutions to this problem:

- Disable the access point's DHCP services and allow the wireless client to lease an IP address from a normal DHCP server.
- Override the IP address range by configuring the DHCP address scope with your own block of IP addresses.

Either solution will work, but you'll have to work within the limitations imposed by your access point's firmware. Many access points will allow you to use only one solution or the other, but not both.

Multiple access point problems

Suppose for a moment that two access points are in use, both with the default settings. If this is the case, then both access points are assigning clients IP addresses in the 192.168.0.X address range. The problem is that the two access points are completely unaware of which IP addresses the other access point has leased. Therefore, it's only a matter of time before there are duplicate addresses on your network.

The solution to this problem is to define a unique scope of addresses for each access point. By doing so, you'll prevent IP address overlaps.

Watch out for client lists

Some access points contain an allowed client list, which can be the root of wireless configuration problems. The allowed client list is a list of MAC addresses of permitted wireless clients. This is a security feature that's designed to prevent unauthorized users from connecting to your network. Normally, the allowed address feature is disabled by default. However, if a user has accidentally clicked the Enable button, then the allowed address list will be enabled but won't contain any MAC addresses. This means that no wireless clients will be able to connect to the access point, regardless of any other configuration settings.

I've also seen the allowed address list become a problem when multiple access points are in use. Many administrators incorrectly assume that just because they enter the allowed addresses into the list, the addresses are then globally permitted to access the network. However, in most cases, this simply grants the users permission to access the network through the designated access point. If you want users to be able to go through other access points, you'll usually have to configure those access points separately. ❖

NOTES:

Security and Business Continuity 7

Implement port security to maintain security behind the wall

By Mike Mullins

Controlling the devices that are plugged into your internal network is one of the most fundamental aspects of network security. While most security administrators do a good job of erecting a fortress wall to keep the Internet at bay, we don't tend to maintain security behind that wall quite as well.

To improve security behind the wall, document every device that's plugged into the network, and secure it for both least privilege and least traffic before it's physically connected. That will mean developing a technical implementation guide for each device, turning off unneeded services, and securing the OS.

All devices that haven't been secured and any equipment that power users bring in and connect without your knowledge is unauthorized. For example, this includes printers running unnecessary protocols, as well as a hub in a user's cube that has a wireless access point attached. Depending on the device, the security consequences of unauthorized devices can be catastrophic.

Using port security on your switches is one of the primary methods for controlling access to the "wire." But then again, there's always an argument for both sides.

Port security: Pro

Enabling port security on your switches gives you total control over every device connected to the switch. Anyone who tries to connect unauthorized equipment to a switch port won't be able to communicate with any internal or external devices. It's that simple. You have total control over what will be connected to your internal network.

Port security: Con

Chief among the arguments against enabling port security is that you have to enable or change switch configuration each time a device is added, or whenever a NIC fails. You'll also have to document every Media Access Control (MAC) address on your internal network. Depending on the size of your network, this might involve considerable work.

Enabling port security could lead to more people being involved in after-hours troubleshooting. Also, it tends to invoke a blame the switch mentality, such as, "The switch is the reason I can't get my e-mail."

Implementation methods

If you have Cisco switches and decide you'd like to implement port security, there are two preferred methods: MAC Access Groups and Port Security. Both methods are applied to the inbound, or wire side, of the switch port.

MAC Access Groups

MAC Access Groups are generally used for small networks of 20 devices or less. You create the MAC Access Group in the global configuration mode. An example would be:

```
mac access-list extended name

permit {any | host source MAC address} {any | host destination
  MAC address}
```

Add a permit statement for all of your workstations, servers, printers, and router interface MAC addresses and apply the access list to each interface. This will limit inbound traffic to that interface to only those MAC addresses on your list.

Port Security

Port Security is the more secure method of the two. To use it, map a switch port to the specific MAC address of the connected device (e.g., workstation or server). Execute the following command in the global configuration mode for each interface:

```
switchport port-security mac-address mac-address
```

Final thoughts

I highly recommend enabling some type of port security for your organization's network. The additional entries of MAC addresses will either come from your network documentation or force you to properly document your network. Properly documenting your network is always a step toward a more secure network.

Port security has become necessary for total network security. It is another tool in your Defense in Depth security layer. Without port security, you don't really have control over what is connected to your network—unless, of course, you can physically see every device connected to it. ❖

Secure Windows Server 2003 Active Directory

By Brien M. Posey, MCSE

I f I were to tell you that Windows NT Server 4.0 was a lot more secure than Windows 2000 Server, you would probably think that I had lost my mind. Sometimes, though, truth is stranger than fiction. In some ways, Windows NT Server was more secure than Windows 2000 Server. However, Microsoft learned from their mistakes and implemented a Windows NT-like security structure into Windows Server 2003's Active Directory. Let's discuss these security issues and learn some tips you can use to build a secure Active Directory (AD) environment.

Physical security is job 1

When attempting to secure AD, it's critical that you implement physical security first. If anyone you wouldn't trust with the Administrative password has physical access to a domain controller or to your DNS servers, you don't have a secure AD. Many administrative and disaster recovery tools exist that can easily double as hacker tools.

Given physical access to the server, it is easily possible for someone with minimal computer knowledge to hack the server in a matter of minutes. So don't even bother trying to secure AD until you've made sure that all of your servers are placed in a secure location.

Windows NT vs. Windows 2000

Don't get me wrong. In many areas, Windows 2000's security is far superior to that offered by Windows NT. However, there is a basic law of computing that states that the more complex a piece of software is, the greater the chance that it will contain a security hole or a major bug that can be exploited. As we all know, Windows 2000 is a lot more complex than Windows NT.

Perhaps the best example of simplicity and security going hand-in-hand involves the domain model implemented by each server operating system. In Windows NT, the domain was pretty much the only organizational structure that existed. A domain often contained all of the users, groups, and computers for an entire organization. If an organization was really big, they could create multiple domains and have the domains trust each other; but, each domain was an independent structure.

When Microsoft created Windows 2000, they realized that the Windows NT domain model just didn't scale well into larger organizations. So, they based the AD on a structure called a forest. A forest is basically a collection of domain trees. Within a forest, you can have many different domains and can even use parent and child domain trees. Just as was the case with Windows NT, each domain has its own Administrator. This is where the similarities end, though.

In Windows 2000, Microsoft decided they needed to make the domains more manageable. They created different levels of domain administration. For example, a member of the Domain Admins group could typically administer the current domain and any child domains beneath it. A member of the Enterprise Admins group had the ability to administer any domain within the entire forest. Herein lies the problem.

The fatal flaw in the Windows 2000 AD model is that every domain completely trusts every other domain within the forest. This causes a couple of problems. First, if security has not been applied properly, administrators can just add their accounts to the Enterprise Admins group to gain control over the entire forest. If the domain is a bit more secure, rogue administrators need only to tamper with the SID history and launch an elevation of privileges attack against the forest. By manipulating the SID history, administrators could give themselves Enterprise Admin status.

There are other inherent weaknesses in the Windows 2000 AD security model as well. As you probably know, each domain requires at least one domain controller. Likewise, each domain controller contains information relating not only to the domain, but also to the forest. Such information includes AD's schema and some basic configuration.

Now, imagine you had an administrator who wasn't being intentionally malicious, but who installed a malicious application or incorrectly modified an AD. If the change that the administrator made was to a forest-level AD component, the change would eventually be propagated to every domain controller in the entire forest, thus corrupting every single copy of AD and potentially crashing the entire network.

Let's compare this situation to Windows NT. Even if one domain trusts another domain, both domains include a copy of the Security Accounts Manager pertaining to their own domain only. In this way, rogue administrators can't make a change to the SAM in their domain and then use that change to corrupt other domains. Likewise, there is no all-powerful group within Windows NT that a rogue administrator could use to gain control over every domain in the entire organization.

Another nice thing about the way that Windows NT's trust relationships worked was that trust relationships could either be one-way or two-way, and they were never transitive in nature. This meant that if you had a Users domain and an Admin domain, you could either allow both domains to trust each other or you could configure the network so that the Users domain trusted the Admin domain, but not vice versa. It also meant that if Domain A trusted domain B and domain B trusted domain C, then domain A didn't trust domain C unless you told it to.

Windows Server 2003 security

You're probably wondering what all of this has to do with Windows Server 2003. I went into the long comparison between Windows NT and Windows 2000 because in Windows Server 2003, Microsoft incorporated the best of both worlds. And so, to properly secure your Windows Server 2003 network, you need to understand the strengths and weaknesses of both security models.

The biggest AD security weakness in Windows 2000 is that all domains within a forest are linked together by a common administrative structure, the forest itself. In Windows Server 2003, the forest structure still exists and works almost identically to the way it did in Windows 2000.

What is different about the forest structure in Windows Server 2003 than that of Windows 2000 Server is that Windows Server 2003 makes it relatively easy to establish trust relationships between forests. Inter-forest trusts were possible in Windows 2000; but, in Windows Server 2003, inter-forest trusts are actually useful. When a trust relationship exists between forests, an administrator can grant access to a resource in a user from a foreign forest in the same manner that they would if the user existed within the local forest.

Single forest vs. multiple forests

A single forest environment is ideal for most small to medium-sized companies. Single forest environments are easy to manage. But larger companies often need each office or each department to be able to have full administrative capabilities over its own users and computers. In such environments, there is often a high degree of distrust between these various groups. In a situation like this, interconnected forests are ideal because they give each group total autonomy.

At the same time, even though the administrative burden is distributed, such a model usually has a much higher administrative burden than a single forest environment, which results in higher administrative costs to the company as a whole. My point is that, in a Windows Server 2003 AD environment, there is a trade-off between cost and security.

Inter-forest trusts

Let's discuss the specifics behind using multiple forests as a mechanism for securing your organization's AD. First, each forest has its own AD; there is no common thread of any kind tying the forests together. So, it's possible to configure each forest to use a common DNS server. Assuming that the DNS server and backup DNS server are managed by someone trustworthy, DNS server consolidation is a great way to reduce cost and lessen the administrative burden. On the flip side, sharing a common DNS server can also be a single point of failure for the network if no backup DNS server is used.

There are some prerequisites you must meet before you can establish a trust relationship between forests in Windows Server 2003. Perhaps the most difficult of these is that any forest involved in the trust must be running at Windows Server 2003 forest functional level. Windows 2000 allowed you to run AD in either mixed mode or in native mode. The functional level in Windows Server 2003 is very similar to this. Setting a forest to Windows Server 2003 forest functional level requires every domain controller within the forest to be running Windows Server 2003.

Also, to create an inter-forest trust, you must be a member of the Enterprise Admins group. You must also have your DNS server configured so that it can resolve the names of domains and servers within the forest with which you're establishing the trust relationship.

Finally, you may recall from Windows 2000, every forest has a root domain and all other domains fall beneath the root. Windows Server 2003 can create an inter-forest trust only from the root domain, because inter-forest trusts are transitive at the domain level. This means that if you were to establish a trust between Forest A and Forest B, then every domain in Forest A will trust every domain in Forest B, and vice versa. Forest trusts are not transitive at the forest level, though.

For example, if Forest A trusts Forest B and Forest B trusts Forest C, Forest A will not trust Forest C unless you tell it to do so. As you can see, the transitive nature of inter-forest trusts makes them fairly powerful. If your forest has multiple domains, you don't want an administrator of some lower-level domain creating an inter-forest trust without your knowledge or consent. That would cause huge security problems. This is why you can only create an inter-forest trust at the forest root level.

Another interesting thing about creating trusts with Windows Server 2003 is that you don't necessarily have to create a full inter-forest trust. Suppose your business needs to establish a trust relationship with a supplier. You probably need only to establish a trust relationship with one of the supplier's domains. You probably aren't interested in the supplier's human resources or marketing domains. In such a case, you can create what's called an external trust.

An external trust is a trust relationship between domains, similar to the trust relationships that existed in Windows NT. An external trust can be established from any domain within your forest and links to a domain in a foreign forest. Aside from being able to establish the external trust at any domain level, there are other critical differences between an external trust and an inter-forest trust.

Unlike an inter-forest trust, an external trust is completely nontransitive, which means the trust applies only to the domains that the trust is assigned to. Other domains within the two forests don't acknowledge the trust relationship.

Whether you are forming an inter-forest trust or an external trust, you have the option of creating a two-way trust, a one-way incoming trust, or a one-way outgoing trust. A two-way trust simply means that both domains trust each other. A one-way incoming trust means that users in the current domain or forest can be authenticated by the foreign domain or forest. Likewise, a one-way outgoing trust means that users in the foreign forest or domain can be authenticated by the local domain or forest.

Cross forest authentication

Windows Server 2003 inter-forest trusts support cross forest authentications. Suppose a user who normally logged into Forest A made a business trip to the company hosting Forest B. With forest authentication, users from Forest A could log into Forest B just as though they were logging into Forest A.

This might seem strange at first since neither the domain controllers nor the global catalog in Forest B would have any knowledge of a user from Forest B. When the user tries to log in, the computer checks the domain controller and then the global catalog for the user's account. Because the account is not found, the system implements a cross forest, name-matching function. This function compares the user's credentials with those found within all recognized namespaces (forests). The comparison is made via Kerberos and NTLM, so the process is secure.

Cross forest authorization

Another feature that's great about Windows Server 2003 is cross forest authorization. This allows you to assign permissions to users within both the local forest and trusted forests directly through an Access Control List (ACL). This comes in handy for both granting and denying permissions.

Suppose you were an administrator for your company's research and development department and that your job was to keep all of the files on your server confidential. The forest-level administrator for your company didn't know what he was doing, and he created an inter-forest trust with a competitor. If you wanted to keep users at the competitor's firm from being able to access your data, you could give those users an explicit deny at the root level of each of the servers in your domain.

As nice as this capability sounds, though, there is a catch. You must completely type in the names of users or groups from trusted forests. Enumeration and wild cards aren't supported. This means that you can't just implement a blanket policy that says don't let anyone from that other forest access any of my data. You could, however, get the names of each of the domains belonging to the other forest and deny access to the Everyone group belonging to each of those domains.

The best of both worlds

Even though Windows 2000 is newer than Windows NT, some of the improvements actually decreased security in your organization. Windows Server 2003 gives you added flexibility to restore that security. One way to achieve effective security within an organization is to implement multiple forests and create trust relationships between them. However, this isn't a process to be taken lightly, because there are many prerequisites and the process tends to increase costs and the administrative burden. ❖

Choose a network management tool that can also help secure your systems

By Mike Mullins

In small to midsize companies, the administrator in charge of managing the network is also usually the person responsible for securing the network. As such, the individual disciplines of security management and network management have begun to converge into the broader field of network operations.

Network management tools are abundant and expensive, but more administrators are beginning to realize the value of using these tools to also ramp up security. However, using network management tools for security is a new concept to most vendors.

Most management tools do an excellent job of keeping track of your network interfaces, server processes, and network statistics. But you can get the maximum benefit from network management tools by selecting the right tool and using it to keep your network secure.

Know what you're looking for

When researching network management tools, keep in mind that the best tools have three key features.

- **One simple interface:** All of the information you need should be on one interface; you shouldn't have to switch between different screens. The interface should be Web-based and customizable for each administrator who needs to see the information. By giving system administrators, managers, and department heads a customized view that they can work with, they can become another set of eyes for your network operations.

- **Ability to recognize normal operations:** Most security-related events occur outside of the normal operating parameters of your network. Your tool must be able to tell the difference between normal traffic and abnormal traffic, and it should be able to report that information accurately.

- **Actionable information:** If you're going to use the tool to manage the security of your network, you must be able to act on that information from the same screen that delivered it. In other words, you should be able to detect a security-related event and then use the same tool to deal with the problem.

Find the right tool

At one point or another, I've used several of the most well-known tools, including HP OpenView, SolarWinds Network Management Toolset, and Cisco Network

Management Toolkit. While these are all viable choices, I recommend using Aprisma's SPECTRUM suite of solutions.

SPECTRUM offers a simple OneClick interface that's Web-based and customizable for a variety of users. With SPECTRUM, you can build a normal traffic pattern for your network, deliver a variety of reports on that traffic, and receive notification when something out of the ordinary occurs.

In addition, the information that the SPECTRUM interface delivers is meaningful. It allows you to drill down to the problem and find a quick solution.

For example, a company recently called me in to troubleshoot a performance problem on a network. Using SPECTRUM, I was able to quickly discover that virus activity was consuming most of the bandwidth.

This was a large network, but SPECTRUM was able to identify the MAC address of the infected machine and shut off the switch port. Once SPECTRUM recognized that the traffic pattern wasn't normal, I was able to use the built-in event correlation tool to stop a virus from infecting the entire enterprise and beyond.

Final thoughts

In today's corporate environments, budgets and personnel remain highly constrained. If your network management tool doesn't recognize what's normal for your network, it's time to find another tool.

Whatever network management tool you choose for your organization, it must also be able to deliver security management. Select the right dual-use network management tool, and you'll have more time to devote to securing your network. ❖

Learn how to set up an IPCop firewall

By Jason Hiner, MCSE, CCNA

Firewalls are everywhere. They are standard issue, par-for-the-course, ticket-to-ride technology that every network, system, and device that is connected to the Internet now requires. Firewalls also take on a lot of different forms, from software solutions to small devices you can pick up at an electronics store to high-end boxes from vendors such as Cisco.

All of the different firewall choices can get a little overwhelming for IT professionals, especially when you only need to set up a simple firewall to protect a small or remote office network. In that case, one of the best solutions for combining low-cost, ease-of-use, and beefy functionality is IPCop.

What is IPCop?

Essentially, IPCop is a Linux-based firewall that turns an x86 system into a firewall appliance. You could call IPCop a Linux firewall distribution, because it has a self-contained kernel and operating system. In other words, you do not have to install IPCop on top of a standard Linux distribution such as Red Hat. You install IPCop like you would an operating system, and once it is installed it completely monopolizes the machine for use as a firewall appliance.

After installation, IPCop is controlled by a Web-based GUI and does not require any knowledge of Linux. It leverages the strengths of open source—it's free and continually updated and patched—and it takes advantage of the power of Linux firewall and security software such as IPTables, Snort IDS, and FreeS/WAN VPN and simplifies their usage and configuration into its Web-based interface.

The following are some of the features that IPCop includes:

- Network Address Translation (NAT)
- DHCP server
- VPN server
- Transparent Web proxy
- Secure Shell (SSH) access
- Port forwarding
- DMZ setup
- Detailed, well-organized logs
- Intrusion Detection System (IDS)
- Traffic statistics and graphics

For more details on the features and development of IPCop, take a look at my TechRepublic article on the subject (**http://techrepublic.com.com/5100-6264-5035202.html**).

What does it require?

IPCop is software that turns an x86 machine into a hardware appliance—a firewall/gateway/router in this case. You can run an IPCop firewall on minimal hardware. However, for a business deployment I would recommend the following minimum requirements:

- 300-MHz CPU
- 256 MB of RAM
- 5-GB hard disk
- Two 3Com NICs

These minimum requirements assume that we're dealing with a small or remote office with a DSL Internet connection (or equivalent) and up to about 30 client machines. You can get by with less than the hardware I've recommended, but this is a solid starting point. If you are supporting more than 50 client machines, you should probably go with at least a 500-MHz CPU, 512 MB of RAM, and a 10-GB hard disk (the extra disk space is needed for IPCop's Web proxy).

As you can see above, I also recommend using 3Com NIC cards. That's for two reasons. First, they tend to fail less than other NICs (Intel cards are pretty sturdy, too). Second, IPCop usually has an easy time recognizing these cards, and that makes installation a lot easier. You can use up to three NICs with IPCop—one for the internal network, one for the Internet, and one for a DMZ.

Pre-installation preparations

In this tutorial, I'm going to be walking through the most common configuration for IPCop, which is to set it up as a firewall/gateway running two interfaces and no DMZ. During the IPCop installation, this setup is called a GREEN + RED configuration, in which the green interface is the NIC connected to the local network (usually a hub or a switch) and the red interface is the NIC connected to the Internet (such as a DSL/Cable/T1 router).

Before you start the installation, you need to make sure you have the following information ready:

1. What static IP address will be used for the green interface (this will eventually become the default gateway address for the client systems on your network)

2. How you need to obtain the IP address for the Internet (RED) interface—this could be static, DHCP, PPTP, or PPPoE (if the address is obtained via DHCP, check to see if you need to provide a hostname)

OTHER FIREWALL DISTRIBUTIONS
IPCop is not the only Linux firewall distribution. Most notably, IPCop is a derivative of the free version of SmoothWall, which is now a subset of a commercial firewall product called CorporateServer 3.0. Other firewall distributions include Devil-Linux and the Coyote Linux Floppy Firewall.

3. Whether you will be running a DHCP server from the firewall/gateway, and if so, what range of addresses will be handed out by the DHCP server

Once you have this information hammered out, you are ready to install. You will need to download the IPCop software (**www.ipcop.org/cgi-bin/twiki/view/IPCop/IPCopDownload**). This comes in the form of an ISO image that can be turned into a bootable installation CD using a CD burner. For example, you can download the ISO and burn it in Windows using Easy CD Creator (**www.roxio.com**) or similar programs (you can look in the help files of your CD-burning software for information on how to burn ISOs).

Perform the installation

Once you have your IPCop installation CD made, pop it in the CD drive of the target system and restart. The system should automatically boot into the CD (if it doesn't, then you probably need to change the boot order in the system's BIOS so that the CD is the first device that the system tries to boot from). If you have successfully booted from the IPCop CD, you'll see the welcome screen in **Figure A**.

Figure A

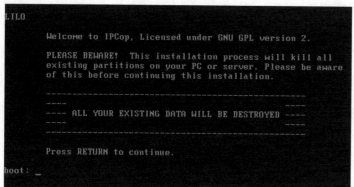

At the welcome screen, press [Enter] to start the installation. After the installer loads, the first thing you will be prompted to do will be to select a language.

The next selection you will have to make involves the installation media. Choose CDROM. You may get a message that tells you to insert the CD into the computer. It should already be there, but if not then insert it and click OK.

Figure B

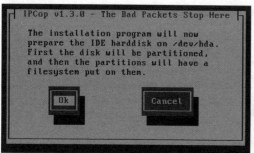

Figure C

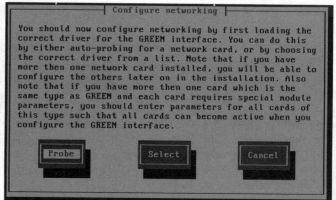

The next message you get on the screen will tell you that IPCop is about to repartition the target hard drive and will tell you which drive it is going to format (e.g. /dev/hda1), as shown in **Figure B**. Once this operation is completed, all the data on the selected disk will be wiped out, so make sure you have the correct hard disk installed in your system and that IPCop has selected it correctly.

Once the partitioning is complete, you'll get a message asking if you would like to restore an IPCop system configuration (from a past installation). I assume you don't have a backup from a previous IPCop installation, but if you do, put the floppy disk in the system and select Restore. Otherwise, select Skip.

Next, it's time to start the preliminary network configuration. You will be prompted to configure the GREEN (internal network) interface (**Figure C**). Click Probe.

IPCop shouldn't have any trouble identifying your network adapters (especially if you're using 3Com NICs, as I recommended). You'll get a message telling you the vendor name of the NIC that IPCop identified as the GREEN interface, and then you will be prompted to enter a static IP address.

After you set the IP address and subnet mask of IPCop's GREEN interface, the installation will spit out the IPCop CD and you will get a message telling you that the installation was successful, but that there are a few more steps to complete. Remove the CD and select OK.

Figure D

You'll then be prompted to select the keyboard type that you are using and select your time zone. Then you select a hostname for the IPCop machine (**Figure D**). The default is "ipcop" (which I would recommend changing so that you don't simply give away its identity to potential attackers).

The ISDN Configuration Menu pops up next. This is only needed if you have an internal ISDN card. If you do want to use ISDN, I would recommend using a separate ISDN router and then connecting its network interface to the RED interface of IPCop. On this menu, simply select Disable ISDN.

You are now prompted with the Network Configuration Menu. Highlight Network Configuration Type, then press [Tab] to select OK and press [Enter].

In the Network Configuration Type Menu (**Figure E**), select GREEN+RED to set up a standard firewall in which one network adapter goes to the internal network (GREEN) and the other adapter connects to the Internet (RED).

Figure E

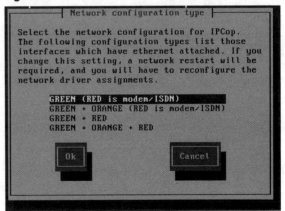

Figure F

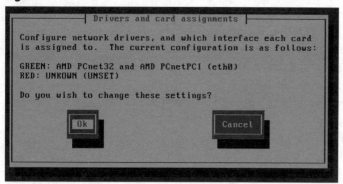

Figure G

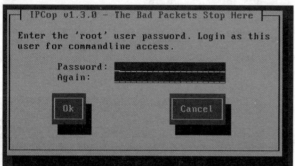

After you select GREEN+RED, you'll go back to the Network Configuration Menu. This time you should select Drivers And Card Assignments, then tab over to OK and press [Enter]. You'll receive a screen that shows the current card assignments and asks if you want to make changes (**Figure F**). Click OK and IPCop will probe for your NICs and attempt to allocate the second NIC to the RED interface.

Once that's complete, you'll return to the Network Configuration Menu again. This time you should select Address Settings, and then you'll be prompted to select the appropriate interface. You should select RED.

This will lead you to the RED interface configuration screen. It looks similar to the GREEN interface configuration screen, except that you have four selections at the top: Static, DHCP, PPPOE, and PPTP. In most cases, this basically comes down to a choice between Static and DHCP, and it simply depends on whether your ISP has assigned you a static IP address or if the address is assigned automatically via DHCP. If the answer is DHCP, highlight that option and press the spacebar to select it. If it is Static, you'll also need to enter the IP address and subnet mask.

When you're finished and you select OK, you'll return to the Network Configuration Menu. If you are using DHCP on the RED interface, you can select Done. However, if you have a static IP address, you need to select DNS And Gateway Settings, which will provide a screen for you to enter two DNS servers and a default gateway.

Select Done, and you will then be prompted with the DHCP Server Configuration dialog box. IPCop can act as a DHCP server for the internal network (via the GREEN interface). If you would like to use IPCop as a DHCP server, simply press the spacebar to select Enabled, then enter the range of addresses you would like to allocate and fill in other DHCP settings.

After you're done with the DHCP server configuration, you will be prompted to enter passwords for three users: root, setup, and admin. The root account is for console access, the setup account is for getting back into the installation menus, and the admin account is for logging into the Web administration interface.

Once you have entered the passwords, you will receive a message that says *Setup is complete*. Click OK to reboot the IPCop server.

Confirm that it works

After the IPCop firewall restarts and is ready to go, you'll hear a unique series of three beeps that tells you IPCop is now live. The first test you should run is to open up a command prompt from a machine on the same internal network as the GREEN interface of IPCop and try to ping the IP address of IPCop's GREEN interface.

If that works, then you can open up a Web browser and connect to IPCop's Web administration module. You can connect via HTTP or HTTPS and you can use either the IP address or the hostname of the GREEN interface, but you have to append specific port numbers (81 for HTTP and 445 for HTTPS). For example, these four URLs demonstrate the format:

- http://ipcop:81
- https://ipcop:445
- http://192.168.1.1:81
- https://192.168.1.1:445

Obviously, you should replace *ipcop* and *192.168.1.1* with the hostname or IP address that you assigned for your firewall. When you successfully connect to the Web interface and click the menu items on the left navigation bar (e.g. Information, Logs, System), you'll be prompted for a username and password, as shown in **Figure G**. You should use the "admin" username along with the password you assigned to it. ❖

Manage local security with WinXP's Security Configuration And Analysis Snap-in

By Brien M. Posey, MCSE

Whether your organization uses site, domain, or organizational unit (OU) group policies, you can use the Windows XP's Security Configuration And Analysis Snap-in to configure and enforce local group policies to make your XP workstations more secure. Let's discuss how it works.

A crash course in Windows XP group policies

Before I can show you how to use the Security Configuration And Analysis Snap-in, you need to understand a few things about the way that group policies work. Group policies are hierarchical in nature. They are applied at various levels and are combined to form what's known as the resultant set of policy.

The hierarchy comes into play when a workstation connects to a network that utilizes Active Directory. When a user logs on, the local Windows XP group policy is applied. After that, additional group policies are applied at various levels of Active Directory (assuming that the policies exist). Group policies can be applied at the site, domain, and organizational unit level.

What makes things interesting is that each group policy contains identical group policy elements (settings). Most of the time, a group policy won't even come close to using every available policy element. Even so, the potential exists for setting contradictions to occur. Windows resolves conflicts by using a "most recent policy wins" algorithm. For example, the final group policy to be applied in the hierarchy is the OU level policy. So if a policy element in the OU level group policy contradicts a policy element implemented at a lower level, the previous policy element will be overwritten by the policy element in the higher level group policy.

The local group policy is the first one applied at login. So elements within the local group policy are very likely to get overwritten by higher level group policy elements. Even so, it's important to make sure your local group policies are strong, because there are situations in which higher level group policies may not be available. In these situations, the local group policy becomes the machine's only line of defense. This situation would occur if a user logged in using a local user account rather than a domain account. It might also occur if a user attempted to log into a domain, but the domain controller could not be contacted. In either case, any group policies contained within Active Directory are unavailable and the local security policy forms the machine's entire resultant set of policy.

Creating an effective local security policy

Although Windows XP's local security policy doesn't have a single policy element set by default, Windows XP includes a number of templates that you can use to configure precisely the policy elements needed to secure Windows XP within your particular environment. These templates have two different purposes. First, they can be used to activate the necessary group policy elements within the local security policy. Second, they can be used to audit the local security policy. Remember that security isn't a "set it and forget it" operation. You need to make sure that the security policy elements that you set are still properly set. The templates can assist with this by comparing the existing security settings with the desired security settings to make sure that everything still matches.

Now that I have explained how group policies work and what the templates do, let's take a look at how to use the templates. You must begin by opening an empty Microsoft Management Console (MMC) session. To do so, enter the *MMC* command at the Run prompt. Next, select the Add/Remove Snap-Ins command from the console's File menu. You'll see the Add/Remove Snap-In properties sheet. Click the Add button on the properties sheet's Standalone tab and you'll see a dialog box containing all of the available snap ins. Scroll toward the bottom of the list and select the Security Configuration And Analysis option from the list and click the Add button. Then click Close and OK.

If this is the first time you've used the Security Configuration And Analysis tool on this machine, you'll need to create a new database. Right-click on the console's Security Configuration And Analysis container and select the Open Database command from the shortcut menu. Windows will launch the Open Database dialog box. Since no databases presently exist, just type a name that you would like to call your database and then click Open.

Windows will display the Import Template dialog box. This dialog box allows you to select which template to use to secure or to audit the workstation. Technically, you aren't limited to using a single template. You can import multiple templates into the database. If you do import multiple templates, the group policy elements within those templates will be combined. In the event of contradictory group policy elements within the templates, the template that was the most recently imported takes precedence. In most cases, though, I don't recommend importing multiple templates because things can get too confusing. If you really need a policy that is made up of elements from various templates, you're usually better off creating a custom template of your own than to try to combine the various templates.

In case you are wondering, a template is really nothing more than an .INF file that's located in the \WINDOWS\SECURITY\TEMPLATES folder. The template basically tells Windows which registry keys to modify or check. You can see a small portion of a template file's contents in **Figure A**.

Windows XP gives you seven templates to choose from (or you can create your own). Each of these templates gives you a different level of security. But not all of

Figure A

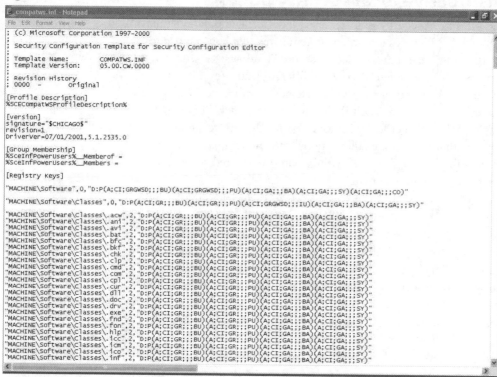

This is what a template file looks like in text form.

Figure B

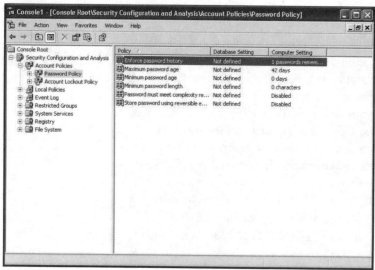

Auditing the PC allows you to compare the computer's current settings against those defined in the template.

these templates are appropriate for Windows XP. Microsoft actually ported the Security Configuration And Analysis Snap-in and all of the templates directly from Windows 2000. So some of the templates are intended to be used on servers and are inappropriate for a Windows XP workstation.

You can get a feel for which template was designed for what purpose by looking at the template's file names. For example, COMPATWS is a basic workstation template, HISECWS is a high security workstation template, and SECUREWS is a medium security workstation template. You probably want to avoid some of the other templates though. For example, the HISECDC template was originally intended for a high security domain controller.

After selecting the appropriate template, click Open to import the template into the Security Configuration And Analysis Snap-in. Even though the template has been imported into the database you created, the console will still appear to be blank, because you've told Windows which template that you would like to use, but you haven't done anything else. To perform any additional actions, you must right-click on the Security Configuration And Analysis container and select the appropriate action. The two primary choices are Analyze Computer Now and Configure Computer Now, but you can also use this menu to import additional templates if necessary.

Auditing the computer

While it might be tempting to jump right in and apply the security template, I recommend auditing the system first, because an audit will compare the computer's current settings against the settings within the template and notify you of any differences. This provides you with a great opportunity to study the group policy element settings within the template and to check for any undesirable settings. If you do find undesirable settings, you can change them or make a custom template.

To perform an audit of the current security settings, select the Analyze Computer Now option. Windows will prompt you to enter the error log file path. The default location is the \My Documents\Security\Logs folder. Make your selection and click OK to begin the audit.

When the audit completes, Windows will display the group policy tree within the console window. As you navigate through the tree, select any branch that you would like to examine. When you do, the pane on the right will display all of the group policy elements within that branch. Alongside of these elements, you'll see the database setting for that group policy element and the computer's current setting. This allows you to look for discrepancies (see **Figure B**).

Just look to see which group policy settings differ and if anything needs to be changed. Then after you have applied your desired policy, if you were to run this audit again, nothing should differ unless a database setting is not defined. If a database setting hasn't been defined and the policy element has been defined within the computer, the computer setting will remain.

Building a custom template

Basically, you want to create a custom template any time none of the built-in templates meet your needs. I also recommend creating a custom template if you've had to import multiple templates into the database. Even if you haven't changed anything after importing multiple templates, creating a custom template will save you work in the long run, because when you next audit the system, you don't have to import a bunch of templates. Instead you can use a single template that contains

Figure C

This is a properties sheet for a group policy element.

Figure D

Applying the security templates takes a few minutes.

the resultant set of policy from the multiple templates that you originally assembled.

For now, though, let's assume that you have only imported a single template and need to make some changes to it. Making the change is easy. Simply right-click on the group policy element you want to modify, and then select the Properties command from the shortcut menu. You'll see a properties sheet for the policy element, similar to the one shown in **Figure C**.

The value displayed within this screen is the computer's current value, not the template's value. If you want to modify the template, select the Define This Policy In The Database check box. You may also modify the policy element's value if necessary. For example, in Figure C, the computer is configured to keep a single password in the password history. When modifying the database, I could keep this value or I could change it to remember 24 passwords. Just remember that if you change the value, it doesn't have any direct effect on the computer. It only modifies the database. Click OK to make the modification within the database.

Once you've made the necessary modifications to the database, you must build your custom template. Keep in mind that creating a custom template simply involves exporting the settings from the database into an .INF file. The procedure that you'll use is the same whether you have imported a single template or multiple templates into the database.

To create the custom template, right-click on the Security Configuration And Analysis container and select the Export Template from the shortcut menu. You'll be asked what name you would like to give to the new template. Enter a name and Windows will create an .INF file in the Templates folder that you can use as your own custom template.

Applying the template

When you're ready to apply the policy elements within the database to the computer, right-click on the Security Configuration And Analysis container and select the Configure Computer Now command. When you do, Windows will prompt you for the path to the error log file. Make your selection, and then click OK to apply the template. You'll see a screen similar to the one shown in **Figure D**.

After a few minutes, all of the policy elements within the template should be applied. You can verify this by running another audit of your system. ❖

Examine common RAID levels for small businesses

By Mike Talon

I've heard from many TechRepublic members who have asked me to address disaster recovery options for small businesses. In an effort to meet this request, I'll address RAID systems, which have been around for many years now—offering protection for disk systems and the data they contain.

Depending on whom you ask, RAID stands for either Redundant Array of Inexpensive Disks or Redundant Array of Independent Disks. Both definitions are generally valid, especially when applied to smaller businesses that use self-contained RAID arrays.

While RAID arrays can't prevent software or site failure, they can protect your organization from physical hardware failures at the disk level, which is a very common occurrence. RAID systems are a series of physical disks that act in concert to increase performance and/or protect the system and its data against the failure of any one disk (and in some cases, against the failure of multiple disks).

We can define RAID systems by the type of array in use. Let's look at some of the most common RAID systems.

RAID 0

This involves "striping" the disks, which distributes data across multiple disks but appears to the operating system as a single drive. This level offers no protection, but it does speed up disk operations in most cases. Most hardware- and software-based RAID systems support this type of array.

RAID 1

Also known as disk mirroring, this RAID system duplicates any disk operations to multiple disks. When you write data to what appears to be a single drive, you actually write it to two or more disks.

This level offers data recoverability, but it comes at the cost of performance, since every disk action occurs multiple times. Once again, both hardware and software systems usually support this type of array.

RAID 5

Offering distributed data with parity, this RAID system provides data redundancy and increases speed. RAID 5 stripes data across multiple disks (like RAID 0) while maintaining a system of parity blocks that allow the array to know what data is on each physical disk, even if a disk is lost due to malfunction.

This level requires at least three physical disks. In addition, you lose a portion of your space in order for the system to save the parity data and recover lost data in case of failure.

For RAID 5, you generally need hardware-based RAID controllers. However, most servers come with a RAID controller option, so even smaller shops can take advantage of this RAID level.

RAID 10 and RAID 0+1

These levels are two of the most popular. RAID 10 involves mirroring a striped disk set to another striped disk set. RAID 0+1 stripes and mirrors to an identical set of disks, as opposed to only one disk.

Once again, you'll most likely want to use hardware-based controllers rather than software RAID systems. While these systems offer the best speed and protection, they are also among the most expensive due to the number of disks you'll need to set it up.

Of course, this is just a sampling of the types of RAID systems available to smaller organizations. There are a large number of vendor-specific and intermediate types of RAID arrays, and you should talk with your storage vendor to determine what it can offer.

In addition, keep in mind that Windows OSs can often handle different types of RAID without hardware controllers, so you may be able to create a RAID array without swapping out hardware.

Except for RAID 0, any form of RAID offers same-server data protection against hardware failure. You should supplement all RAID systems with some other form of protection against larger and/or software-based failures, such as tape backup or replication.

However, RAID is a great first step toward disaster recovery planning. RAID arrays offer a lot of flexibility and a great way to protect against hardware failure. ❖

Explore tape backup options for small businesses

By Mike Talon

Many smaller shops can't afford replication and other advanced DR solution sets, and they sometimes resort to hoping that the disk mirroring they've set up on the single server in the office will be sufficient.

While disk-based backups aren't a bad thing to have, they won't protect your organization from an office flood or the next huge virus taking out the entire server. For that eventuality, you need to have a point-in-time copy of your data stored away from the server itself.

Choose a backup device

First, decide what kind of backup device to use. If you only have a few megabytes of vital data, you can probably get away with a removable device such as a ZIP drive. The only drawback is that these devices have limitations on the amount of data they can hold, which is usually around 750 MB per cartridge.

If you have more data to protect, you'll need a larger removable device. Tape backup systems generally allow for the storage of 40 to 120 GB per cartridge, providing enough room to back up most of your data to one tape in many circumstances.

Midsize companies may need to purchase a small jukebox device. These devices can usually hold up to five tapes at once, allowing you to back up even larger data sets and multiple server systems. While they're more expensive than single-tape systems, they generally fall within the budgets of most companies that require them.

Select backup software

Next, find some form of backup software to transfer the data to the tape itself—and to recover it when necessary. If you're using Windows NT, 2000, or 2003, you can use the built-in backup tools.

While these tools can do the job, you might want to check out some of the more advanced tools on the market. They allow you to take advantage of more types of tape systems, back up to both disk and tape with more options, and perform a host of other advanced operations.

Most backup tools also employ agents to back up locked and/or open files, and they back up the system state in such a way as to be able to restore the entire server if you lose everything. These "bare-metal" or "emergency recovery" systems take up more tape space, but they help you quickly get back in action should something such as a virus attack destroy all of your data and the operating system.

Find alternative storage space

Finally, find a place to store the tapes besides the office. Companies that store backup tapes on a shelf next to the servers have found out the hard way that disasters that strike the server can very often take out that shelf as well.

For smaller businesses, the best bet is for someone to take the tapes home each night, storing the monthly backups in a safe or a safe deposit box. Somewhat larger companies can contract with a firm that will pick up and store tapes and that will return them when needed.

Tape backups and removable media offer a low-cost methodology to keep point-in-time copies of your data away from your server systems. The up-front investment in tapes and a tape device (or removable media and a drive) will provide a return on investment many times over the first time you have to use the system to restore vital data. ❖

Develop a solid disaster recovery strategy for a small business

By Mike Talon

Large businesses aren't the only organizations that need disaster recovery plans; small businesses must also prepare for any number of catastrophes. For small companies, large-scale disaster recovery tools may not be fiscally feasible, but they may also not be very necessary.

While small businesses do indeed need DR systems in place, they generally don't need to protect systems at the same level as large organizations. This isn't because the data isn't as important—there probably just isn't as much data as you would find in large companies. Real-time replication and other higher-end technology is definitely an option, but it's usually not mandatory.

Tape is always a good starting place for small firms. You can purchase many tape systems for a reasonable price, and they can back up your entire infrastructure at once in many cases.

While some small organizations may need to find a slightly larger tape system, the basic systems will work just fine in the majority of cases. This typically entails a daily copy of all changed data and a weekly full copy of all data.

After making the tapes, be sure to remove the copies from the office, leaving only the most recent tapes in the facility. If there's a flood, fire, or some other physical mishap that destroys the on-site tapes, you'll still have backup copies.

Small organizations that have more than one office can find many host-based replication systems that don't require higher-end disk arrays to transmit data. These tools use the operating system on the individual servers to send copies of data between locations.

While this solution requires a server at both sites, it typically doesn't require much else. Of course, you don't want to eliminate tape from your environment, so use this solution in addition to using a tape backup system.

Host-based replication systems cost more than tape backup alone. However, if you have data that you must protect in real-time or near-real-time, this is a cost-effective method of gaining the protection your organization needs.

In addition, remember that a lot of data in small companies resides on laptops and desktops. Therefore, you must take steps to prevent data loss at this level.

Beginning with Windows 2000, you can use offline folders to keep the My Documents folder automatically updated both on the local machine and on a file server. For other operating systems, you can find tools or use corporate mandates to ensure that users back up or otherwise protect important data.

Recent advances in technology offer even more options that can help protect small businesses against data loss. For example, the new Windows Storage Server

2003 provides the ability to take point-in-time snapshots called volume shadow copies. Other network-attached storage (NAS) devices offer similar capabilities—if your budget allows for their purchase.

No matter how you protect your data, there's no reason to ignore DR just because you work for a small business. With the right combination of technology and insight, even small firms can provide their end users with high-end DR plans. ❖

NOTES:

NOTES: